Categories

Categories
A Study of a Concept in Western Philosophy and Political Thought

Luke O'Sullivan

EDINBURGH
University Press

Edinburgh University Press is one of the leading university presses in the UK. We publish academic books and journals in our selected subject areas across the humanities and social sciences, combining cutting-edge scholarship with high editorial and production values to produce academic works of lasting importance. For more information visit our website: edinburghuniversitypress.com

© Luke O'Sullivan, 2024, 2025

Edinburgh University Press Ltd
13 Infirmary Street
Edinburgh EH1 1LT

First published in hardback by Edinburgh University Press 2024

Typeset in 11/13 Goudy Old Style by
IDSUK (DataConnection) Ltd

A CIP record for this book is available from the British Library

ISBN 978 1 3995 2415 5 (hardback)
ISBN 978 1 3995 2416 2 (paperback)
ISBN 978 1 3995 2417 9 (webready PDF)
ISBN 978 1 3995 2418 6 (epub)

The right of Luke O'Sullivan to be identified as the author of this work has been asserted in accordance with the Copyright, Designs and Patents Act 1988, and the Copyright and Related Rights Regulations 2003 (SI No. 2498).

Contents

Preface	vi
A Note on the Texts	viii
Introduction: Why Categories Matter	1

Part 1: Categories in Platonic and Aristotelian Thought

1. Plato: Forms as Categories of Ideal Being	33
2. Aristotle: Categories as not-Forms, or Substances	67

Part 2: Categories in Modernity: Kant and Hegel

3. Kant: The Categorial A *Priori*	107
4. Hegel: The Dialectical Dynamics of Categories	148

Part 3: Contemporary Theories of Categories

5. Fragmentarians: The Categorial Kaleidoscope	193
6. Subordinationists: The Quest for a Master Category	232
7. Pluralists: The Search for Categorial Limits	270
Conclusion: The Inescapability of Categoriality	305
Index of Subjects	323
Index of Proper Names	331

Preface

The following is a report from the farther shore of a journey that began long ago in search of the origins of the notion of a mode of experience. That point of departure gradually vanished over the horizon along the way, and as is typical of forays into the unknown, the eventual destination had an unexpected aspect. The original impetus for the trip might nevertheless still be detectable, appropriately enough for a book entirely about things unseen, in the form of an invisible point on the compass used in navigation.

During the ensuing lengthy and largely solitary pursuit of some highly abstruse abstractions, the temptation to test the patience of various colleagues and friends, some former students among them, still sometimes proved irresistible. In particular, I must thank William Bain, Antony Black, Brian Charles, Peter Finn, Bjorn Gomes, Knud Haakonssen, Chandran Kukathas, Linh Mac, Haig Patapan, Terry Nardin, Lisa Raphals and Benjamin Schupmann for the forbearance they have shown at various times. I am deeply grateful to Vasileios Syros for the initial suggestion that Edinburgh University Press might publish it, though it did not land quite where he wanted. Christopher Adair-Toteff, David Boucher, Athina Karatzogianni, Catherine Marshall, Paul Roth and Martyn P. Thompson all supported the subsequent proposal. None of them have the slightest responsibility for the evident shortcomings of the finished work.

At Edinburgh University Press, Ersev Ersoy and Beatriz Lopez likewise displayed great patience while bringing the final version into the world, especially given my egregious violation of the contractual word limit (the penalty for which was the mournful sacrifice of a bibliography, though all the works cited are listed in the notes). The reader should nonetheless hopefully find that there is very little repetition; despite the length of the volume, there has only been space to say most things once. I am also indebted to Grace Balfour-Harle for overseeing the production and to Stephanie Pickering for assistance with the laborious task of copy-editing.

Though conceived earlier, the following pages were mostly written while I was at the National University of Singapore, which generously provided a grant to help Edinburgh University Press with the increased costs of production inflicted by my hubristic insistence that sacrificing any of them would mean doing violence to the argument. Without the continuing love and support of my family, the whole would never have been finished. Readers may judge for themselves whether it was worth finishing – a book once completed no longer belongs to the author.

LOS

Singapore 2023

A Note on the Texts

In the late twentieth and early twenty-first century there was a fortunate upsurge in efforts to retranslate, and provide new critical editions, of works by many of the major thinkers discussed here, including Plato, Aristotle, Kant, Hegel and Nietzsche. These latest versions have been used wherever possible. But in citing these authors, whose work is available in multiple editions, references have been given to conventional line or section numbers rather than (or as well as) pages, in acknowledgement of the fact that other versions remain widely in use.

Where quotations are used, the specific translator is always noted in the first reference. While relatively little hopefully turns on questions of translation for the argument as a whole, on a few occasions discussion of specific terms has required reference to works in the original language. Lengthy quotations in languages other than English have generally been avoided, however. Words from ancient Greek have been transliterated without accents where they are not parts of titles, as recommended by the *Chicago Manual of Style*.

The quotations are intended to establish that the interpretations being advanced have textual support in the works of the thinkers discussed; the footnotes augment them with supporting references to the scholarly literature, sometimes offering further brief discussion of particularly important or notable points. Where there is a debt to other scholars for the arguments put forward, as is frequently the case in a work of this kind, every effort has been made to ensure it has been duly acknowledged.

To compensate for the lack of a bibliography, a full citation has been given in the footnotes the first time a work is mentioned in each chapter. The footnotes should also provide a useful resource to any reader interested in the subject of categories. The literature is often diverse and dispersed, and so, regardless of their opinion of the present work, readers may find value in having some of it drawn together. After all, the one thing agreed upon on more or less all sides is the fundamental nature of the topic.

Introduction: Why Categories Matter

We could begin by saying that this is a book all about things that don't exist. But this would prejudge a question about the nature of categories that we will be less interested in answering than in historising. Or perhaps we could commence instead by saying that what is particular and what is universal is the great question of our age. Yet that opening would only return us at once to the problem of categories, since particulars and universals are themselves categories of a kind. So let us start simply with the observation that whether categories exist or not, and whatever we consider to be particular or universal, or whatever we consider particulars and universals to be, the best authorities insist that categories structure our world.[1]

Supposedly, there is 'inherent with humans . . . "a kind of categorizing behaviour" that translates a myriad of sensory data into manageable meaning clusters'.[2] In learning to inhabit a meaningful world, the first problem that all new human beings face is one of categorisation. We must commence life by distinguishing ourselves from everything else, including other people – a process which inaugurates the drama of individuality.[3] As adults, we are said to 'live by' categories; they are integral to our personal identities.[4] Our beliefs, to the effect that someone or something has this

---

[1] Daniel Kahneman, *Thinking, Fast and Slow* (London: Penguin Books, 2012), 357, states that 'our world is broken into categories for which we have norms'.
[2] Sharon Bracci Blinn and Mary Garrett, 'Aristotelian "Topoi" as a Cross-Cultural Analytical Tool', *Philosophy & Rhetoric*, 26:2 (1993), 93–112, 94.
[3] Jacques Lacan, 'The Mirror Stage as Formative of the I Function as Revealed in Psychoanalytic Experience', in *Écrits*, translated by Bruce Fink in collaboration with Heloise Fink and Russell Grigg (New York: W. W. Norton, 2006 [1966]), 76–81, 76, refers to this as 'the transformation that takes place in the subject when he assumes an image'.
[4] Ásta, *Categories We Live By: The Construction of Sex, Gender, Race, and Other Social Categories* (Oxford: Oxford University Press, 2018).

or that property, or should be classified under this or that heading, are categories in action.⁵ Categories are also said to be social as well as individual: they are treated as a fundamental condition of community.⁶

If anything is 'natural' to us, therefore, it is the use of categories; *homo distinguens* is at least as good a label for the species as *homo sapiens*.⁷ Human beings are not the only animals to use categories, but they are the only ones to talk about it.⁸ But our use of categories also arouses deep suspicion. The injustice of judging people simply for belonging to a particular ethnicity, gender, or sexuality has become a tenet of contemporary progressive morality.⁹ We are cautioned to beware of implicit biases that might cause us to commit such injustices unawares.¹⁰ Critics of progressive claims regarding the sovereignty of self-identification, meanwhile, are effectively disputing the nature of the relation between classification and reality.

As a result, there is widespread contemporary recognition that categories are both important and problematic. A non-exhaustive list of academic fields and disciplines in which issues to do with categories arise

---

⁵ Martin Fishbein and Icek Ajzen, *Belief, Attitude, Intention, and Behaviour: An Introduction to Theory and Research* (Massachusetts: Addison Wesley, 1975), 131, define beliefs as 'judgments concerning . . . a relation between the object of the belief and some other object, value, concept, or attribute', where the objects can also be persons.

⁶ Étienne Balibar, *On Universals: Constructing and Deconstructing Community* (New York: Fordham University Press, 2020 [2018]), 81, argues that 'the pragmatic categories . . . of *incomprehension* and *differend*' are the 'paradoxical condition of possibility' of community, because people necessarily learn to live together by working out their differences with one another. Emphasis in original.

⁷ Paul Rakita Goldin, *Rituals of the Way: The Philosophy of Xunzi* (Illinois: Open Court, 1999), 81, asserts that in ancient Chinese thought it was the rituals marking the boundary between humans and the rest of the world which constituted 'The human being [as] *homo distinguens* or *homo civilis*'. Emphasis in original.

⁸ Christopher Peterson, *Monkey Trouble: The Scandal of Posthumanism* (New York: Fordham University Press, 2018), 42, writes: 'The unlikelihood of an ape presenting a scholarly paper to his or her peers on the question of human language does not demonstrate that apes lack symbolic language, but it does underscore a fundamental asymmetry between human and nonhuman animals'.

⁹ See Cristian Tileagă, Martha Augoustinos, and Kevin Durrheim, eds, *The Routledge International Handbook of Discrimination, Prejudice and Stereotyping* (Abingdon and New York: Routledge, 2022).

¹⁰ Natalia Washington and Daniel Kelly, 'Who's Responsible for This? Moral Responsibility, Externalism, and Knowledge about Implicit Bias', in *Implicit Bias and Philosophy*, vol. 2: *Moral Responsibility, Structural Injustice, and Ethics*, ed. Michael Brownstein and Jennifer Saul (Oxford: Oxford University Press, 2016), 10–36, 11, argue that in at least some cases 'an individual should be held responsible for actions that are influenced by her implicit biases'.

includes anthropology, critical theory, cultural studies, feminist studies, history, linguistics, philosophy, political science, political theory, post-colonial studies, post-modernism, post-humanism, psychoanalysis, psychology, rhetoric and sociology. It is clear, moreover, that this recognition reflects the situation in society at large. Popular authors articulate a pervasive feeling that 'Things are in the wrong place. Religion is in the box where science used to be. Politics is on the shelf where you thought you left science the previous afternoon.' Categorial worries have penetrated public as well as academic discourse.[11]

Making sense of contemporary category discourse thus clearly requires knowing what we mean by the term. Unfortunately, the word 'category' has many uses. It may denote the particular properties of persons and things; persons and things as members of classes or species; things and classes as divisible into parts and wholes; universal terms; those universal terms or general concepts allegedly specifically implied by our knowledge of persons and things (such as quantity, quality, modality and relation, or space, time and causation); general concepts that make a particular form of knowledge distinctive, particularly its presuppositions; the ideas that distinguish a particular school of thought within a given form of knowledge; and finally, social and political classifications.[12] These, moreover, are only the informal uses; there are also formal, logical and mathematical, senses which we shall largely have to pass over.[13] The initial difficulty raised by categories then, is that the meanings of the term are so various.

As we have already observed, the question of what, if anything, the word 'category' refers to is a vexed one. Categories fit uneasily with any naïve empirical account of knowledge because they are neither visible nor tangible. A category is something undetectable by any instrumentation, presumably because there is nothing there for any of our five senses to detect. Yet categories have nonetheless been said to have being in an ideal fashion. Philosophers have argued that there is a conceptual realm in which categories, perhaps conceived as purely logical entities, subsist. Those denying the being of such a realm may still treat categories as instantiated in some other manner, for example as somehow inhering in the phenomena.

---

[11] Charles P. Pierce, *Idiot America: How Stupidity Became a Virtue In the Land of the Free* (New York: Anchor Books, 2010), 30.

[12] This list is adapted from D. Goldstick, 'Against "Categories"', *Philosophical Studies*, 26:5–6 (1974), 337–56, 337.

[13] Eugenia Cheng, *Cakes, Custard, and Category Theory Easy Recipes for Understanding Complex Mathematics* (London: Profile Books, 2015) provides an introduction to mathematical category theory.

A classic debate on this topic in Western philosophy that continues to inform current discussion involved Plato and Aristotle. Plato projected a world of Ideas or Forms that supplied the templates, so to speak, for the world as we experience it; Aristotle, who introduced the word 'category' as a technical term into philosophy, explicitly rejected the being of Plato's Forms and treated categories as substances or essences that were immanent in existent persons and things instead. Both thinkers regarded categories as real, but disagreed on what that meant. When modern writers argue that categories are purely linguistic and have no existence beyond their status as meanings, they are, in effect, rejecting both these realist views of categories as Forms or substances.

Categories therefore have significant implications for knowledge. Defenders of science against religion, for example, regularly accuse their opponents' arguments of making category mistakes that confuse authentic knowledge with unjustified belief.[14] Believers reply that science is not the only valid form of knowledge, and that religious claims are also entitled to that status.[15] Relations between Western and non-Western knowledge are likewise fraught. The West is alleged to have used categories in imperialistic ways to suppress local knowledge.[16] There is said to be a general contradiction in Western thought 'between what is essentially *local*, and thus "particular" about its methods and styles of thought, or more profoundly its *categories*, and what is global about its ambitions'.[17]

As these examples indicate, theories of categories typically also have political ramifications extending all the way to the civilisational level. Categories have political significance because one of their functions is differentiating between persons in ways that have far-reaching implications for how society will develop. For instance, requiring all boys and girls to study science in school will create a very different future to prioritising the maintenance of a tradition of religious instruction restricted to boys. As a corollary, those on either side of this question will necessarily hold different views concerning the past. For monotheists, the past represents an earlier phase of a divine plan (a view which still tends to covertly inform much secular progressivism) while for their scientific critics,

---

[14] Dr Peter Capon, a member of the General Synod of the Church of England, declared that 'we make a category mistake if we try to read [the Bible] as a modern scientific textbook'. *The Guardian*, 12 February 2010.

[15] See, for example, Daniel Dennett and Alvin Plantinga, *Science and Religion: Are They Compatible?* (Oxford: Oxford University Press, 2011).

[16] Susanne Hoeber Rudolph, 'The Imperialism of Categories: Situating Knowledge in a Globalizing World', *Perspectives on Politics*, 3:1 (2005), 5–14, 5.

[17] Balibar, *On Universals*, 62. Emphasis in original.

it can only be understood in terms of chains of causation composed of unintended consequences.[18]

Categories thus turn out to be inseparable from questions to do with time and history as well as knowledge and politics. It is worth pointing out in this regard that the term itself carries a history. The word 'category' is a dead metaphor. It was originally created via a familiar process of metaphor formation according to which a concrete and literal usage is replaced with a more abstract and general one perceived as similar in some respect.[19] Etymologically, in ancient Greek, a *kategoria* or category was a statement or an accusation made in a formal legal context by a prosecutor or litigant.[20] The exact steps in the transition to the more abstract usage are obscure, but appear to have involved fixing on the act of predication involved in making an accusation.

To accuse someone of something, to claim that they are guilty of a certain offence, is to assert that they possess a certain quality; the attribute of being a thief, for example. In virtue of this particular quality, the accused also belongs to a certain group, in modern parlance the set of all thieves, which functions as a universal category. Aristotle's philosophical usage thus stood at the end of a process that abstracted the logical features of predication and speciation from the original meaning of an accusation.[21] But his philosophical coinage equally marked the beginning of a process of transformative transmission that has stretched into modernity. In the later eighteenth century, Immanuel Kant could still think of his theory of categories as a more or less direct response to Aristotle, even though Kant's understanding of categories was, even on his own account, vastly different.

Given the fundamental importance of categories and the far-reaching nature of the issues their interpretation raises, then, an inquiry focused on

---

[18] For the origins of the modern secular idea of progress in Christian beliefs about history as a movement towards salvation see J. B. Bury, *The Idea of Progress: An Inquiry Into Its Origin and Growth* (London: Macmillan, 1920).

[19] See George Lakoff and Mark Johnson, *Metaphors We Live By* (Chicago: Chicago University Press, 1980), especially ch. 22, 'The Creation of Similarity'.

[20] See 'κατηγορία', Henry George Liddell and Robert Scott, *A Greek-English Lexicon*, 8th edn (USA: American Book Company, 1897), 785.

[21] The traditional meaning of an accusation remained current in Aristotle together with the philosophical sense. See, for example, Aristotle, *Ars Rhetorica*, trans. W. D. Ross (Oxford: Clarendon Press, 1959), 1358b, where *kategoria* was used in its original accusatory meaning in the statement that 'The forensic kind [of rhetoric] is either accusatory or defensive'. Indeed, *kategoria* still needed disambiguating centuries later: Porphyry, *On Aristotle Categories*, trans. Steven K. Strange (London and New York: Bloomsbury Academic, 2014 [1992]), 30, remarked that *kategoria* is 'applied in ordinary usage to the speech of the prosecution which presents evidence against a defendant'.

the changing philosophical meanings of the term has value. As George Lakoff has remarked, philosophy matters far more than is often realised. Metaphysical distinctions 'induce' epistemological ones.[22] But as we have just observed, they also induce political and historical ones. It enhances our understanding of the past to appreciate that ideas about categories that inform current conversations typically emerged first in a philosophical context before permeating wider society.

Describing several of these textual contexts is not equivalent to a comprehensive history of the concept of a category. Such a history does not currently exist, and would require many volumes. But too specialised a history would also risk missing much of what has made categories so important in contemporary debates. We must also appreciate that it is the ways in which the concept of a category has been related to knowledge, politics, and history that make categories so central to the issues facing contemporary modernity.

This study prefaces an investigation of these relations in contemporary thought with studies of several of their most important ancient and modern exemplars, Plato, Aristotle, Kant and Hegel. These four thinkers have been chosen because they are the generally acknowledged sources for the great majority of the theories of categories developed in Western thought.[23] Yet Plato, Aristotle, Kant and Hegel all differed significantly from one another in their detailed understanding of what categories were.[24]

As we have already noted, it was Aristotle who first made the word 'category' a technical term. Plato, therefore, cannot strictly be said to have had a philosophical doctrine of categories. But our argument is that Aristotle's categories must be understood as 'not-Forms'. Aristotle understood Plato as holding that reality as we experience it is structured by

---

[22] George Lakoff, *Women, Fire, and Dangerous Things: What Categories Reveal about the Mind* (Chicago: University of Chicago Press, 1990 [1987]), 157, 172.

[23] Kenneth R. Westphal, 'Kant's Critique of Pure Reason and Analytic Philosophy', in *The Cambridge Companion to Kant's Critique of Pure Reason*, ed. Paul Guyer (Cambridge: Cambridge University Press, 2010), 401–30, 429, argues that 'There are five truly great theories of particulars and universals . . . Four are those of Plato, Aristotle, Kant, Hegel', with the nominalism of Ockham and Sellars constituting the fifth and final such theory.

[24] It can be objected that Plato did not have a theory of categories at all, and terminologically at least this is correct. Francis Macdonald Cornford, *Plato's Theory of Knowledge: The* Theatetus *and the* Sophist *of Plato translated with a running commentary* (London: Kegan Paul, Trench, Trubner; New York: Harcourt, Brace, 1935), 106, n. 3, held Plotinus responsible for the allegedly 'entirely gratuitous confusion' of Plato's Forms with Aristotle's categories. But we shall see in the next chapter that some modern scholars have made the case for Plato as a theorist of categories *avant la lettre*.

ideal Forms subsisting outside space and time and independently of ourselves.[25] As a philosophical explanation of how we understand the world without resorting to the concept of Forms, Aristotle's theory of categories was an explicit critique, if not a rejection, of Plato's arguments.

Aristotle's theory thus illustrates the general principle that to understand a theory fully, one must also understand the theory to which it is an objection and a reply. Likewise, we shall argue that contemporary theories of categories must generally be interpreted as reactions, both positive and negative, to Hegel; but Hegel must be seen as responding to Kant, who in turn believed he was improving on Aristotle. A review of Plato, Aristotle, Kant and Hegel thus turns out to be the bare minimum needed to set contemporary theories of categories in context.[26]

Let us begin with a pattern of association found in Plato's writings. We call it a pattern of association to indicate that we are concerned with a kind of intellectual order that defines a philosophy or even an era without necessarily hanging together in a strictly logical way.[27] Our primary focus is less on the soundness and validity of the arguments we are addressing, therefore, than on the way in which they tended to solidify into habits of mind, which have been at least as powerful

---

[25] See Aristotle, *Metaphysics Books Z and H*, trans. David Bostock (Oxford: Clarendon Press, 2004 [1993]), 1208b: 'others think that there are more substances that are not perceptible, and that they are substances to a higher degree, because eternal. Thus Plato held that the forms and the objects of mathematics were two kinds of substance, perceptible bodies being the third kind.'

[26] Bernard Williams, 'Descartes and the Historiography of Philosophy', in *The Sense of the Past: Essays in the History of Philosophy*, ed. Miles Burnyeat (Princeton: Princeton University Press, 2006), 257–64, 257, suggested that there are two different approaches to the history of philosophy, one internal to philosophy itself, and the other belonging to historiography. The former aims at 'more systematic regimentation of the thought under discussion', while the latter 'looks sideways to the context'. But Michael Beaney, *Frege: Making Sense* (London: Gerald Duckworth & Co., 1996), 3, observes that 'any useful historical reconstruction requires skill in contemporary rational argument, and any convincing rational reconstruction requires sensitivity to the historical context'. What is required from this point of view is 'a *synthesis* (Beaney's emphasis) of rational and historical reconstruction' that might be called 'dialectical reconstruction'. The approach (or 'method') we shall employ is similar to the one Beaney recommends, resting on the fault line, as it were, between the history of philosophy considered as a branch of intellectual history, and as a department of philosophy itself.

[27] Michael Walzer, 'On the Role of Symbolism in Political Thought', *Political Science Quarterly*, 82:2 (1967), 191–204, 192, observes that the early modern world rested on a cosmology in which the 'various parts hung together in a way which implied no necessary logical connection'. The idea of a pattern of association suggests that the same is true of the thinkers studied here.

as logical entailment in the history of ideas. So, in Plato the understanding of the Forms was connected with a conception of individual identity. It was the rational element of the soul of the individual that apprehended the Forms. Plato in turn connected the Forms with the divisions of knowledge; with the basis of claims to authority; and finally, with knowledge of the historical process. We may briefly summarise the content of this pattern.

The Forms first became accessible via mathematical and dialectical knowledge, genres that the philosopher must master in order to enjoy a vision of the Form of the Good which was both immediate and self-authenticating.[28] One could not have it and not know it, and when one had it, one could not be mistaken about it. Ultimately, this knowledge of the Forms established a legitimate title to govern based on superior wisdom. Those who govern on this basis had the advantage of understanding what drove the repetitive cycles visible in history. But they had no need to engage (as Plato's older contemporary Thucydides did) with actual historiography.

The effect of these views on the subsequent course of Western thought can scarcely be overstated. Isaiah Berlin traced what he described as the positively anti-historical tendency of modernity to the influence of Descartes.[29] But in fact this tendency goes much further back than Berlin suggested. In medieval philosophy, the view that 'De singularibus non est scientia', which is to say 'there is no science of singulars', was already present.[30] What changed in Descartes' era was the meaning of 'science',

---

[28] Plato, *Republic*, ed. G. R. F. Ferrari, trans. T. Griffith (Cambridge: Cambridge University Press, 2000), 508d, made an analogy between eyes looking at the sun which cannot help but see, and the soul that 'focuses where truth and that which is shine forth'. All references to Plato use the Stephanus numbers rather than pagination.

[29] Isaiah Berlin, 'The Concept of Scientific History', in *Concepts and Categories: Philosophical Essays*, ed. Henry Hardy (Princeton: Princeton University Press, 1999), 103–42, 103, argued that for Descartes historiography was 'beneath the dignity of serious men seeking ... the discovery of the truth in accordance with principles and rules which alone guarantee scientific validity'.

[30] T. K. Scott, Jr., 'John Buridan on the Objects of Demonstrative Science', *Speculum*, 40:4 (1965), 654–73, 656, observes that for a medieval scholastic thinker like Gregory of Rimini (1300–58), Aristotle's remark that the objects of knowledge are eternal and necessary entailed that God was the only object of true science and that 'no contingent particulars can be objects of knowledge' in the strict sense. As the meaning of 'science' shifted, the study of contingent particulars acquired a place under the heading of 'natural history', but it remained the poor relation of 'natural philosophy'. 'Civil history' remained excluded from the early modern sciences, as it was in Hobbes, *Leviathan*, ed. Richard Tuck (Cambridge: Cambridge University Press, 2003 [1991]), 61, which retained the old demonstrative conception of 'science'.

not the prejudice against historicity, which the medieval era had itself inherited from classical sources. In modernity we could say, no doubt very roughly, that 'science' shifted from being a demonstrative to an empirical form of knowledge; but the conviction that true knowledge is of what does not change persisted, often unstated. Hence the consternation caused by the repeated demonstrations in the twentieth century that even the categories of scientific knowledge were subject to historicity.[31]

The fact that categories display historicity does not necessarily require looking at what Plato and the other thinkers we are concerned with had to say about history in order to understand their ideas on categories. But the fact (if it is a fact, which remains to be shown) that all of them, from Plato onwards, clearly had a sense of historicity in the sense that they were keenly aware of the difference between past and present, and were also familiar with the existence of a dedicated type of knowledge devoted to the understanding of the past, and yet consistently marginalised historical knowledge, does require some explanation. The answer, we are suggesting, lies precisely in the fact that they entertained theories of categories that gave priority to allegedly universal and atemporal aspects of reality.

While the content of this pattern of association visible in Plato subsequently changed radically, the pattern itself, we shall argue, has remained present, not only in Aristotle, Kant and Hegel, but in modern thought. Because its content has changed so significantly, the pattern is sometimes hard to see. But we shall argue it is there, nonetheless. The vital question is therefore whether the claim that there is such a pattern is genuinely derived from, or is merely being imposed on, the texts? In dealing with problems of interpretation, 'Seek, and ye shall find' is a terrible warning to the questing hermeneut.[32] Seeing patterns where only randomness obtains is a characteristically human failing (albeit the defect of a virtue).[33] Some

---

[31] Still probably the best-known example in the anglophone world is Thomas S. Kuhn, *The Structure of Scientific Revolutions*, 3rd edn (Chicago: University of Chicago Press, 1996 [1962]), but in the francophone world, writers including Georges Canguilhem and George Sarton were already arguing for the historicity of science before the start of the 1939–45 war.

[32] Matthew, 7:7 (King James version).

[33] Kahneman, *Thinking*, 115, notes that there may be 'evolutionary advantages' to our tendency to always look for patterns: 'We are automatically on the lookout for the possibility that the environment has changed', which enhances our survival prospects. But this identity as 'pattern seekers' and 'believers in a coherent world' may also mislead us into seeing regularities that 'appear not by accident but as a result of mechanical causality or of someone's intention', even when no such forces are at work. Nicholas Taleb, *The Black Swan: The Impact of the Highly Improbable* (London: Penguin Books, 2010 [2007]) makes a similar point regarding financial markets.

delusions can be terribly persistent; but in this case no amount of rubbing of the eyes has turned the giants back into windmills. The reader must decide for themselves at the end whether we have been in pursuit of an illusion all along.

We shall label the three main contemporary schools of thought on categories since Hegel fragmentarians, subordinationists, and pluralists, respectively. These labels need some initial elucidation. Fragmentarians held that there was no possibility of a comprehensive categorial scheme of the sort attempted by Kant and Hegel. They self-consciously employed the idea of the fragment (a familiar Romantic trope) to convey this situation, and as a metaphor for the contemporary situation more generally. Subordinationists aimed to restore a single privileged form of knowledge of some kind, whether in the form of one particular categorial arrangement, or by transcending categories altogether. They often shared the fragmentarian diagnosis, but entertained a different solution. Finally, pluralists sought a middle ground. They rejected the idea of one kind of knowledge as privileged above all others, thus rejecting subordinationism, but still believed that the possible major viewpoints were delimitable, thus also repudiating fragmentarianism. This, however, was a minority view; the most influential modern thinkers have been either fragmentarians or subordinationists.

Our fragmentarians are Friedrich Nietzsche, Theodore Adorno and Michel Foucault. The subordinationists are mainly represented by logical empiricists like Otto von Neurath and W. V. O. Quine, on the one hand, and Martin Heidegger, on the other. The pluralists are the Englishman R. G. Collingwood; the German Ernst Cassirer; and the Frenchman Paul Ricoeur. Collectively, they cover the period from the second half of the nineteenth century to the early twenty-first. They were chosen because they were all sufficiently wide-ranging for it to be possible to examine whether the pattern in which we are interested really was present in their writings; and because they are all well-known. Many contemporary philosophers are unsuitable simply because of the specialisation that has accompanied professionalisation. For better or for worse, the demand for ever-more-detailed analyses of specific problems has been inimical to the kind of broad outlook found in Plato, Aristotle, Kant and Hegel.

Admittedly, covering even these ancient, modern and contemporary thinkers in a single volume is fraught with intellectual peril. In particular, the risk is of being at once too comprehensive and not comprehensive enough. Every thinker discussed here has a literature, often very considerable in size, devoted to their works. Aristotle's *Categories* alone has accrued a veritable library of commentary since ancient times. Scholars who have devoted themselves to mastering the works of a single thinker will rightly be wary of such an attempt. It requires a first-hand familiarity with the works of many acknowledgedly great writers which, if it stops short of mastery, must go well beyond superficiality.

No doubt, also, the history of philosophy is best told in detail, globally, and 'without any gaps', not by jumping between a handful of major names in the classical, modern and contemporary canons.[34] Yet precisely because, in a truly comprehensive history of philosophy, all aspects of every thinker's work must be considered, it becomes harder to single out any particular subject as a guiding thread. There thus remains, or so we must hope, a middle ground from which one can make a study of a long-term theme that goes beyond the work of any individual thinker and yet does not claim to deal with everything. The specialist in one or another of the authors discussed may still find some interest in an account that relates their specialty to a broader theme in a novel way, and in reading about authors with whom they may be less familiar.

Several specific omissions nevertheless deserve notice. One is the lack of a separate consideration of medieval ideas. This would be essential in a complete intellectual history of categories. But in this context the justification is that the medieval Christian world was indebted from first to last for its philosophical foundations to Graeco-Roman thought. Platonism was infused into Christianity early on, in the gospel of Saint John.[35] The later theological constructions of Catholic Christianity rested heavily on Neoplatonism. Saint Augustine's theory of the Trinity depended on prior Neoplatonic speculation about the inherent disjunctive qualities of the One, for example.[36] The considerable ingenuity and innovation that medieval authors displayed was always predicated on a shifting blend of Platonisms and Aristotelianisms, even when they criticised Plato and Aristotle themselves.[37] The Western world became

---

[34] Peter Adamson's project of *A History of Philosophy Without any Gaps* is exemplary in this regard.

[35] John 1:1: 'In the beginning was the word.'

[36] See Augustine, *Confessions*, bk VII, ch. 9, on the 'books of the Platonists' in Augustine, *Confessions and Enchiridion*, trans. Albert Cook Outler (Kentucky: Westminster John Knox Press, 1955 [2006]), 144: 'therein I found, not indeed in the same words, but to the selfsame effect . . . that "in the beginning was the Word"'. Plotinus, *Enneads*, trans. A. H. Armstrong, 7 vols (Cambridge: Harvard University Press, 1989), v.41, previously attributed to Plato the so-called 'doctrine of the Three Hypostases', saying that 'Plato knew that Intellect comes from the Good and Soul from Intellect'.

[37] Peter Adamson, *Medieval Philosophy: A History of Philosophy without Any Gaps*, vol. 4 (Oxford: Oxford University Press, 2019), 11, argues that scholars typically 'tend to underestimate' the degree of continuity between ancient and medieval culture, even allowing for the rise of Christianity and the loss of knowledge of the Greek language along with most of Latin literature.

modern precisely to the degree that this ceased to be true (which is consistent with thinking that we still remain medieval to some degree even now).

Certainly, in many ways the medieval Christian world constituted a radical break with paganism. The Hebraic idea of a God who made the world by fiat, and whose actions and motivations as the ultimate source of human trials and torments were fundamentally inscrutable, was genuinely different from increasingly rationalistic ancient Greek conceptions of divinity. Aristotle had described the unmoved mover as thought thinking itself (a conception that Hegel strove to re-interpret).[38] Saint Augustine's achievement was to synthesise this Greek idea of God as reason with the Hebraic idea of God as a supreme creative will. He reconciled Greek omniscience with Hebraic omnipotence via the Christian idea of love.[39]

Yet Augustine still followed Platonic precedent in making a grasp of the most fundamental concepts (the persons of the Trinity) an urgent task for the believer.[40] This enterprise was associated in turn with a privileged form of knowledge (the interpretation of the Bible); a claim to authority (the godly should be in charge); and a theory of history (as a movement towards salvation).[41] In other words, Augustine likewise

---

[38] See Aristotle, *Metaphysics Bk Λ*, trans. Lindsay Judson (Oxford: Clarendon Press, 2019), 1074b: '*Itself*, therefore, is what it thinks, seeing that it is the greatest thing, and its thinking is a thinking of thinking.' Compare Hegel, *Philosophy of Mind*, trans. W. Wallace and A. V. Miller, rev. Michael Inwood (Oxford: Clarendon Press, 2010 [2007]), §577: 'The eternal Idea, the Idea that is in and for itself, eternally remains active, engenders and enjoys itself as absolute mind.'

[39] See Augustine, *On the Trinity* Books 8–15, ed. Gareth B. Matthews, trans. Stephen McKenna (Cambridge: Cambridge University Press, 2003 [2002]), 31: 'the knowledge of the mind that knows and loves itself is in the mind and in its love; because it loves itself as knowing and knows itself as loving'.

[40] See Augustine, *On the Trinity*, 171: 'we inquired, how [the God who begot the Son and ... the Holy Spirit] may be called one essence, three persons, or by some Greek authors, one essence, three substances ... we are compelled by necessity to speak in this manner, that so we might be able to answer in one word when anyone asks, what the three are whom we truly confess to be three'.

[41] Augustine, *Confessions*, bk 4, ch. 15, concluded that the question he had posed ('What, therefore, is my God?'), was not answerable in the same way as for the earthly, temporal objects discussed in Aristotle's *Categories* (although Aristotle would in fact have agreed that God was very unlike any earthly thing). For Augustine, God could not be understood as 'subjected to thy own magnitude or beauty, as if they existed in thee as their Subject – as they do in corporeal bodies' because 'thou art thyself thy own magnitude and beauty'. Nor was Platonism sufficient; revelation was required. *Confessions*, bk 6, ch. 7, affirmed the proposition that 'those Scriptures were imparted to mankind by the Spirit of the one and most true God as 'the point that

follows our pattern. The same can easily be shown in respect of Thomas Aquinas.[42]

The later medieval world also prepared the momentous change from thinking about the composition of the world in terms of substance to the modern understanding of it in terms of matter. For Aristotle and his medieval scholastic followers, the world was composed of different kinds of substances or stuffs arranged in a continuous hierarchy that connected the visible to the invisible order.[43] A person is the highest kind of earthly substance, an individual combination of form and various kinds of matter.

---

was most of all to be believed'. Augustine, *De Doctrina Christiana*, ed. and trans. R. P. H. Green (Clarendon Press, Oxford, 1995), bk 2, ch. 24, also argued that Scripture should ideally be interpreted only by those who have completed a seven-stage process of spiritual purification, a 'holy person' with 'a heart so single-minded and purified that he will not be deflected from the truth'. Augustine conceived this knowledge as the foundation of Christian authority. Augustine, *Political Writings* (Cambridge: Cambridge University Press, 2001), ed. E. M. Atkins and R. J. Dodaro, letter 133, 63, writes to Marcellinus that 'as I am addressing a Christian, it would not be very presumptuous of me in such a situation to say, "You should listen to me as to a bishop giving you orders"'. Also included in this knowledge was a special insight into the future, in which salvation could be expected, thus rendering it of greater interest than the past. Saint Augustine, *The City of God Books VIII–XVI*, trans. Gerald G. Walsh and Daniel J. Honan (Washington DC: Catholic University of America Press, 2008 [1954]), 18, declared that 'it will be found, provided the Holy Spirit teaches us to read the Scriptures rightly, that they seem even more – assuredly not less – concerned with prophecy than with history'.

[42] Thomas Aquinas, *On Being and Essence: A Translation and Interpretation*, trans. Joseph Bobik (Notre Dame: University of Notre Dame Press, 2007 [1965]), §13, 49, was more sympathetic to Aristotle's *Categories* than Augustine, arguing that the earthly substances it described were continuous in nature with God's essence as a simple substance. Aquinas, *Summa Theologiae*, 61 vols, trans. Thomas Gilby et al. (Cambridge: Cambridge University Press, 2006 [1964]), i.7, nevertheless made clear that philosophy alone was inadequate, saying that 'human well-being called for schooling in what God has revealed, in addition to the philosophical researches pursued by human reasoning'. Aquinas declared (i.11) that he was explicitly following Augustine in making theology a sacred science uniquely capable of 'begetting, nourishing, protecting, and making robust the healthiest faith'. The final arbiter of theological doctrine and indeed of the value of human knowledge in general was the 'sovereign Pontiff', the head of the universal Church, which 'cannot err, since she is governed by the Holy Ghost'. Although Aquinas also followed Augustine in declaring it impossible to put an exact date on the apocalypse, he accepted the scriptural assertion that history was moving towards the final cleansing of the world by fire. Both thinkers saw the human past as interesting primarily in terms of its significance for sacred history.

[43] See C. S. Lewis, *The Discarded Image: An Introduction to Medieval and Renaissance Literature* (Cambridge: Cambridge University Press, 1964).

Descartes in contrast treated persons as combinations of two different types of homogeneous substance, material and mental.⁴⁴ These two substances were fundamentally unlike one another, so that the question of how they were mutually related was problematic. But Descartes's assertion that substance was a simple duality was preceded by nominalist arguments in medieval theological and philosophical thought that had already begun to reject ancient rationalism and realism about categories.⁴⁵

The change was due not least to the problems raised by studying the heavens, which stubbornly defied mathematical representations matching classical accounts of their perfect circular motions. The deep irony of the slow breakdown of the medieval geocentric cosmology of substance was that these nominalist arguments and astronomical observations were intended to shore up ancient tradition by making it more conceptually and mathematically satisfactory. Yet they gradually worked its destruction from within, by undermining its assumptions.⁴⁶

Another omission, from a global standpoint, is the lack of consideration of any non-Western philosophers. One can certainly find categorial

---

[44] René Descartes, *Meditations on First Philosophy*, in *The Philosophical Writings of Descartes*, trans. John Cottingham, Robert Stoothoff and Dugald Murdoch, 3 vols (Cambridge: Cambridge University Press, 1995 [1984]), ii.1–62, 30, wrote 'I think that a stone is a substance, or is a thing capable of existing independently, and I also think that I am a substance. Admittedly I conceive of myself as a thing that thinks and is not extended, whereas I conceive of the stone as a thing that is extended and does not think, so that the two conceptions differ enormously; but they seem to agree with respect to the classification "substance".' P. M. S. Hacker, 'Substance: Things and Stuffs', *Proceedings of the Aristotelian Society, Supplementary Volumes*, 78 (2004), 41–63, 49, argues that 'It was a confusion of Descartes's to suggest that matter is a kind of substance, and a worse confusion to suggest that mind is another.' There is warrant for Hacker's view in Aquinas, *Being and Essence*, §15, which asserts very clearly that 'matter is not essence'. Hacker is arguing in effect that the history of modern philosophy, and even of science, was based on a fertile mistake, insofar as materialism took itself to be refuting a picture of reality that medieval scholasticism did not actually hold.

[45] See, for example, John Duns Scotus, 'Six Questions on Individuation', Q. 1, in Paul Vincent Space, *Five Texts on the Medieval Problem of Universals: Porphyry, Boethius, Abelard, Duns Scotus, Ockham* (Indianapolis: Hackett Publishing Company, 1994), 64: 'a nature, according to its being, is not of itself universal but rather universality is accidental to the nature according to its primary aspect according to which it is an object'.

[46] Katharine Park and Lorraine Daston, 'Introduction: The Age of the New', in *The Cambridge History of Science*, vol. 3, *Early Modern Science*, ed. Katharine Park and Lorraine Daston (Cambridge: Cambridge University Press, 2006), 8, argue that 'the process of change was gradual and sporadic, shaped well into the first half of the seventeenth century by serious, widespread, and accepted efforts to accommodate ancient texts to newer methods and discoveries'.

conceptions in at least two other great ancient philosophical traditions, the Indian and the Chinese. As is often pointed out, Chinese thought is an especially important source of comparison, since it developed altogether outside the Indo-European setting that constituted the common root of both Indian and Western thought.

In fact, although surviving classical Chinese texts do not seem to contain any explicit lists of categories of the kind found in Aristotle, there is still reason to believe that classical Chinese thought employed categorial distinctions.[47] Indian philosophy had an explicitly categorial dimension. The *Nyāya-sūtra* in Indian philosophy has been said to be comparable to Aristotle's *Categories* insofar as it too treats universals as instantiated concepts that make the world intelligible.[48]

Nevertheless, while the existence of non-Western traditions of categorial thought is indisputable, the questions to do with categories faced by contemporary modernity originated in Western thought. Insofar as the West was the first mover in the creation of a global world, it also exported its categorial terms and conditions, and no doubt also its confusions. But the lack of a detailed examination of whether the pattern of association between categories, knowledge, politics and history that we are claiming can be found in the West was also previously present elsewhere only reflects the space available (and the competence of the author), not the interest and importance of the question.

There are prima facie reasons to think that such a pattern can indeed be found in non-Western contexts. In particular, the study of comparative mythology has led some notable thinkers to the conclusion that there are significant formal or so to say structural similarities between the classical texts of the various major traditions.[49] All three ancient civilisations, Graeco-Roman, Chinese and Indian, invoked a normative cosmological hierarchy, knowledge of which was thought to legitimate

---

[47] A. C. Graham, *Studies in Chinese Philosophy and Philosophical Literature* (New York: SUNY Press, 1990), especially 'Relating Categories to Question Forms in Pre-Han Chinese Thought', 360–411.

[48] See *The Nyāya-sūtra: Selections with Early Commentaries*, trans. and intro. Matthew Dasti and Stephen Phillips (Indianapolis: Hackett Publishing, 2017), 139: 'A universal is manifest in individual instances that are located in time and space. For example, cowhood, what it is to be a cow, is manifest in innumerable individual cows in various places and times. A similar theory is present not so much in Plato as in Aristotle.'

[49] See, for example, Claude Lévi-Strauss, '"Primitive" Thinking and the "Civilized" Mind', in *Myth and Meaning* (London and New York: Routledge, 2005 [1978]), 7: 'notwithstanding the cultural differences between the several parts of mankind, the human mind is everywhere one and the same and . . . has the same capacities'.

authority over the government of earthly matters. The concepts featuring in this cosmology certainly varied greatly and were not necessarily compatible or consistent with one another. Nor do profound concepts such as the Chinese idea of *chi* or the Indian idea of *prana* have readily obvious Western counterparts. No doubt other examples can easily be produced. Yet significant substantive similarities between the various traditions have also been pointed out.

Scholars have long argued for important resemblances between the figure of the Confucian sage or *jun zi* and the Platonic philosopher-ruler, for instance.[50] Confucius and his followers considered themselves qualified to rule, or at least to advise rulers, in virtue of their superior knowledge of the Way. The Chinese tradition typically favoured a more literary kind of knowledge than the geometrical orientation prioritised by the Platonic academy under the influence of Pythagoras (though mathematics was not absent from traditional Chinese thought). Mastery of the canon of the Chinese classics both legitimated authority and made sense of Chinese history.[51] Likewise, in an Indian context, the position of the Brahmins at the head of the hierarchical caste system was sustained by their command of the texts of Hinduism, which also served, amongst many other things, to make sense of their being in time.[52] This knowledge in turn entitled the Brahmins, if not to wield power, then at least to direct its use.

If ancient Western thought should indeed turn out to be just one instance of a tendency to associate categories, knowledge, politics, and

---

[50] See Carsun Chang, 'A Comparison of Confucian and Platonic Ethical Views', *Philosophy East and West*, 13:4 (1964), 295–309, 295: 'Both the Greeks and the Chinese proclaimed the power of the human intellect and the autonomy of reason.' Similarities have likewise been found between Confucius and Aristotle. For instance, both argued that the acquisition of the virtues requires 'a process of ethical training and cultural refinement' according to Jiyuan Yu, 'Virtue: Confucius and Aristotle', *Philosophy East and West*, 48:2 (1998), 323–47, 337.

[51] Ching-I Tu, 'Preface' to *Classics and Interpretations: The Hermeneutic Traditions in Chinese Culture*, ed. Ching-I Tu (London and New York: Routledge, 2000), xi, notes that 'the dominant Confucian hermeneutical regime of late imperial China' influenced not only examination prospects but 'subsequent political success', and that 'in the dominant hermeneutic tradition in Chinese historiography . . . the past is . . . employed as a moral mirror for the present and future times'.

[52] Adheesh A. Sathaye, *Crossing the Lines of Caste: Visvamitra and the Construction of Brahmin Power in Hindu Mythology* (Oxford: Oxford University Press, 2015), 7, states in relation to the case of the mythical figure of Vishvamitra, the only character in Hindu mythology to achieve membership of the Brahmin caste without rebirth, that 'By telling stories . . . Brahmin communities have been able to conceptualize and maintain their own social power throughout Indian cultural history.'

history that can also be found in other traditional civilisations, so much the better for our argument. This finding would only enhance our claim about the importance of the relationship. But we have no space to pursue this question here. Yet even if one believes the terms of contemporary political debate need modifying to include different categories used by non-Western thinkers and communities, this presupposes an understanding of the Western ideas that one is amending or rejecting.

A final absence is that no women philosophers are amongst the main examples. This reflects only the historical accident that the major theorists of categories have been male. It is not because women are less talented at philosophy than men. They have been present in Western philosophy since its early days. Socrates, according to Plato, had not one but two female teachers, Diotima and Aspasia.[53] But women have only enjoyed anything like an equal opportunity to distinguish themselves very lately, and then only in certain parts of the world. The absence of women is also not a denial of the feminist critique of the patriarchal attitudes found in Western thought. On the contrary, such attitudes were particularly noticeable in its ancient representatives and have been far from absent in modern ones.[54]

For example, the view of Aristotle and his followers that the male represented an active principle and that the female was passive was extremely wide-ranging in its implications, affecting education, medicine, politics and much else besides. Like Aristotelian cosmology, Aristotelian biology continues to resonate even now, supplying an example of the persistence of medieval ways of thinking alluded to earlier. Kant and Hegel were likewise by no means free of prejudices about women, although feminists have disagreed on whether Hegel's remarks, in particular, might not amount to more than mere rationalisations of the biases of his own era.[55] Amongst our post-Hegelian thinkers, Nietzsche's views have aroused particular controversy, while again being of interest to feminist thinkers.[56]

---

[53] Plato, *Menexenus*, trans. Paul Ryan, 235e–36a, had Socrates confirm that Aspasia taught him rhetoric. Plato, *Symposium*, trans. Alexander Nehamas and Paul Woodruff, 201d, made Socrates credit his speech on love to Diotima, 'a woman who was wise about many things', and had him go on to rehearse his extended conversation with her on the subject.

[54] Genevieve Lloyd, *The Man of Reason: 'Male' and 'Female' in Western Philosophy*, 2nd edn (London: Routledge, 2004 [1984]), xii, states that 'The connections between the male-female distinction and the philosophical understanding of reason are a contingent feature of western thought, the elusive but real effects of which are still with us.'

[55] See, for example, Kimberly Hutchings and Tuja Pukkinen, eds, *Hegel's Philosophy and Feminist Thought Beyond Antigone?* (New York: Palgrave Macmillan, 2010).

[56] Luce Irigaray, *Marine Lover of Friedrich Nietzsche*, trans. Gillian C. Gill (New York: Columbia University Press, 1991).

Whatever the shortcomings of these authors, though, it is one thing to treat their writings as containing sexist (or racist) elements, and quite another to dismiss their philosophies as inherently sexist (or racist) in their entirety. The view taken here is that while the former position is undeniable, the latter is untenable.[57] So far as philosophical investigations of categories are concerned, whether ancient, modern or contemporary, our position is that while ideas can most certainly be used to suit the interests of one sex, or one racial group, ideas themselves cannot be reduced to reflections of the identities of their authors without rendering all argument ad hominem. We are interested in the permutations of a pattern of ideas to which the gender (or ethnicity) of an author, simply as such, turns out not to be directly relevant, though we shall certainly notice places where these topics appear.

Finally, let us emphasise that the primary aim is to set out the major theories of categories and their connections with knowledge, politics, and history. Doing so helps to explain the background to our vexed contemporary conversations. We are not mainly concerned about establishing any single approach to categories as correct, and we are taking it for granted that all the theories examined are important. The question of which theory is best is of course perfectly legitimate, and there are some impressive contemporary contenders. George Lakoff, for example, treats categories as arising directly from the 'structure of our perceptual-motor experience' and the linguistic capacity for forming 'image schemas [that] that preconceptually structure our experience of functioning in space'. This 'cognitive model' approach doubtless has much to recommend it.[58]

Lakoff is less sure as a guide to the history of categories, however. His claim that 'From the time of Aristotle to the later work of Wittgenstein', categories were regarded as 'well understood and unproblematic' is incorrect. There has not, in fact, been a single account of categories constituting a 'classical theory' against which modern accounts can be measured.[59] So an explanation of the contemporary background to thought about

---

[57] Charles Mills, *The Racial Contract* (New York: Cornell University Press, 1999 [1997]), 16, argues that the contractarian tradition theorised by thinkers such as Locke and Kant was used in practice to restrict the possession of natural freedom and equality to whites as the only human beings enjoying full personhood. But it does not follow from this that all social contract theory is therefore necessarily racist in principle. As Mills himself remarks (127), Whiteness is '*not really a color at all, but a set of power relations*' (emphasis in original).

[58] Lakoff, *Women, Fire, and Dangerous Things*, 372.

[59] Lakoff, *Women, Fire, and Dangerous Things*, 6.

categories needs, also, to correct this kind of mistaken impression of the historical record.

We said that a comprehensive history of categories is not possible in the space available. It is important to underline that there has been, and is, simply no single meaning given to the term 'category'. But what can be done is to set out the major theories in a way that respects their historical context, makes plain their ramifications, relates them to one another, and establishes their enduring importance. Anything like success in pursuing these goals would justify the attempt. Having dealt with these several caveats, we may set out the path we shall follow.

Chapter 1 is devoted to Plato, whose profound realisation was that we make sense of the sensible in terms of the insensible. The subsequent history of Western philosophy has mostly been an exploration of this problem of the nature of the insensible and the work that it does. Plato's theory of Forms, that is to say, was an explanation of our capacity for organising the seen with reference to the unseen. The unseen Forms were Ideas with no temporal or spatial dimensions. They constituted a logical and normative hierarchy that we could know only via the rational part of the self. Mathematical knowledge was an exemplary, but not ultimate, stage in a process that lead to a direct apprehension of the Form of Forms. This was presented in the *Republic* as the Idea of the Good, which is at once rational, religious, and ethical in nature. The tendency was towards an ultimate unity; the Good was also the One. In it, beauty, truth, and justice were all united.

For Plato, all of this constituted esoteric philosophical knowledge – the 'uninitiated' were precisely those who 'refuse to admit that actions and processes and the invisible world in general have any place in reality'.[60] Justice, intelligence, virtue, and the soul were all amongst the invisible things.[61] The famous parable of the cave-dwellers was invented to underline the importance of invisible distinctions. In Plato's story, the prisoners in the cave sit staring at a wall on which they see flickering shadows that they take to be the whole of reality.[62] This was a metaphor for the human condition. Plato was pointing out that, on reflection, the terms in which we comprehend the world, including our judgements about other

---

[60] Plato, *Theatetus*, 156e, trans. M. J. Levett and Myles Burnyeat, in *Plato Complete Works*, ed. John M. Cooper (Indianapolis: Hackett, 1997), p. 173. All references to Plato are to Cooper's edition unless otherwise noted.
[61] Plato, *Sophist*, 248b, trans. Nicholas P. White, in *Works*, p. 269.
[62] Plato, *Republic*, 514a–515c.

people, become puzzling. Even if, for common sense, our use of concepts to comprehend the world goes unremarked, once a certain kind of self-consciousness intervenes, we are driven to investigate them.

This investigation is the task of philosophical knowledge, but this is only one kind of knowledge among many. Knowledge in Plato is classified in terms of how nearly it approaches a comprehension of the Form of the Good. Practical and technical knowledge of making is the least valuable form of knowledge in this respect, because it aims at the production of things and states of affairs in the world of appearances. The world of appearances is not simply to be dismissed, however. It draws on the rational intelligibility of the world of Forms via a relationship of 'participation' that has been much discussed. While Plato considered that those who knew the Forms best were also best qualified to govern, he required more than just knowledge of the Forms from the philosopher-rulers. They were also supposed to have extensive experience of practical affairs. Nevertheless, the study of history was not a part of their education.

Plato's marginalisation of historical knowledge effectively set a precedent for Western philosophy. Yet he had predecessors and contemporaries, notably Herodotus and Thucydides, who wrote works of history (in the broad sense at least) that are still read today. There was, in principle, no reason why Plato could not have turned his attention to the problems associated with historical knowledge. Insofar as Plato was interested in history at all, however, it was not as a form of inquiry, but as a process. The *Republic*, for instance, set out a theory of a repetitive cycle of constitutional types that treated past events as interesting not as individual happenings but as generic, exemplary instances. Even if understanding this kind of cycle is part of the knowledge the philosopher-ruler must possess, the study of any specific iteration of it has no part in their theoretical knowledge of the Forms.

Chapter 2 addresses Aristotle, often viewed as embodying quite an opposite philosophical position to Plato. Famously, in Raphael's 'School of Athens', Plato points to the heavens while Aristotle gestures towards the ground.[63] The truth is more nuanced. Aristotle was frequently critical of Plato's arguments, but he is best understood as a dissident Platonist who shared broadly the same cosmology. The colt may have kicked its mother, as Plato apocryphally complained, but it could not hide its parentage.[64]

---

[63] Raffaello Sanzio da Urbino, 'Scuola di Atene', c. 1509–11, Apostolic Palace, Vatican City.
[64] See Claudius Aelianus, *Various History*, bk iv, ch. 9, trans. Thomas Stanley (London: Thomas Dring, 1665): 'Plato called Aristotle a Colt: What is meant by that name is manifest: a Colt as soon as it is satisfied with the milk of the Dam kicks at her.' Aelian's anecdote was repeated by Diogenes Laertius, *Lives of Eminent Philosophers*, trans. R. D. Hicks, 2 vols (London: William Heinemann, 1959), i.445.

The relationships we find in Aristotle between categories, identity, knowledge, politics and history are often very similar to those in Plato.

Aristotle's introduction of the concept of a category as a technical term may plausibly be interpreted as a critical response to Plato's notion of Forms. If we understand Aristotle's categories as immanent in the phenomena, then one of the implications is that a timeless realm of Ideas is not required to mark the divisions in the world. Yet Aristotle's theory of categories remained connected with the nature of the human being, just as the Forms were for Plato. The categories still play the role of fundamental concepts defining people and things in ways that defied further reduction. For Aristotle, the most fundamental category of all was that of substance, and the most important instances of that category were persons. The individual human being was identifiable as an instance of a primary substance.

Also like Plato, Aristotle distinguished firmly between theoretical and practical knowledge. Manipulating substances to make useful items or achieve certain goals, on the one hand, and contemplating their nature, on the other, were fundamentally different activities. Aristotle did more than Plato to distinguish and codify the requirements of various branches of knowledge, composing separate treatises on many of them. Nevertheless, he followed Plato in thinking in terms of a hierarchy of knowledge that corresponded to gradations of reality. Knowledge continues to conform to a hierarchical arrangement, and metaphysics, or 'first philosophy' as Aristotle sometimes called it, stands at its head because it is knowledge of the nature of the most important kind of substance of all, the divine intellect.

Aristotle's objections to Plato's ideas on government were typically pragmatic rather than principled. The ideal of the philosopher-ruler, for instance, was problematic not because of any disagreement over the inherent superiority of the contemplative life, but because of the difficulty of finding and instituting such a ruling group. Aristotle was more inclined to distinguish the ideally best from the best in the circumstances, hence his willingness to endorse the type of constitution he called polity as best in practice. But on the whole Aristotle shared Plato's aristocratic outlook. Aristotle's greater interest in the varieties of democracy stemmed from the theoretical need to account for the phenomena rather than any especial enthusiasm for popular government. The problem of politics was an instance of the broader disposition of substances in the world, made especially complex by the fact that the kind of substance that could engage in politics possessed the faculty of speech.

In principle, Aristotle's grasp of politics as deliberation about future action under conditions of necessarily imperfect information might have suggested the need for an appropriate means of understanding the domain of human affairs of the sort that Greek historians were then beginning to supply. Moreover, the members of Aristotle's school, if not Aristotle himself, undertook historical research, as witnessed by the work on the *Constitution of Athens* traditionally attributed to Aristotle.[65] Its authorship is now disputed, but even if it was not his own production, it offered an account of the formation of the Athenian constitution distinct from mythical or religious conceptions of the past. It was grounded in primary source evidence rather than hearsay. It was an instance, in other words, of a new kind of orientation towards the past visible in Greek historiography more generally. Yet Aristotle again followed Plato in showing barely any theoretical interest in history as a form of thinking, dismissing it briefly in the *Poetics* as less universal than poetry.[66]

Chapter three deals with Kant, who, thanks to the way in which the history of philosophy subsequently turned out, could still think of himself as modifying Aristotle's account of the categories despite there being more than two millennia between them. As in both Aristotle and Plato, the categories were crucial for understanding selfhood. They were what Kant called *a priori* structures of our consciousness, logically deducible as given in advance from the judgements we make about things. Yet Kant's categories differed from both Platonic Forms and Aristotelian categories in being self-consciously conceived of as parts of an exhaustive 'system', a notion we should be wary of projecting onto philosophy at large.[67] Indeed, in Kant's post-Cartesian philosophy, we find dual systems of categories, one pertaining to the physical and the other to the moral order. But neither set dealt directly with the structure of ultimate reality after the manner of Plato or Aristotle. Kant wanted to limit our knowledge to experience.

At the same time, Kant wanted to preserve as much as possible of the conclusions of the older rationalist metaphysical tradition. Yet he was convinced that attempts to reach conclusions about the nature of reality based on reason alone had necessarily ended in contradiction and

---

[65] See Aristotle, *Constitution of Athens*, in *Aristotle's Politics: Writings from the Complete Works: Politics, Economics, Constitution of Athens*, ed. J. Barnes, intro. M. Lane, trans. Benjamin Jowett (Princeton: Princeton University Press, 2016).

[66] Aristotle, *Poetics*, trans. George Whalley (Montreal and Kingston: McGill-Queens University Press, 1997), 1451b, wrote that 'Poetry is a more speculative and more "serious" business than history: for poetry deals more with universals, history with particulars.'

[67] Leo Catana, 'The Concept "System of Philosophy": The Case of Jacob Brucker's Historiography of Philosophy', *History and Theory*, 44:1 (2005), 72–90.

confusion. We simply did not have access to ultimate reality in the way that either Plato or Aristotle had believed. To use Kant's vocabulary, our knowledge was limited to the phenomenal realm. Within that realm, we could distinguish different domains, such as science, art and common sense; but knowledge of what Kant called the 'noumenal' order, the realm in which we must postulate the existence of our souls and a divine being, was closed to us.

For Kant, the central problem of scientific knowledge was how to bring experience under rules of various kinds, and in particular the rules of mechanics. The categories of the understanding governed the behaviour of the same phenomena described in the formulae of Newtonian physics. Government and morality were supposed to foster an increasing analogue to this ruliness. The categorical imperative which proposed that all right action should serve as a universal principle for others was inspired by this vision. The chief problem of morality and politics was to achieve an orderliness approximating the regularity that our categorial equipment necessarily leads us to discover in nature. This required, in effect, a moralisation of the political order. This was to be driven, however, by institutions rather than persons in the first instance. Kant's philosopher was not a ruler, although an attachment to social hierarchy remained clearly visible.

The moralisation of politics was a progressive task, hence Kant's intense interest in the logic of the historical process. But that process mattered precisely insofar as it was universal and necessary. Kant was proposing a theodicy, a justification of the ways of God to man. Just as, in the individual, we had to assume the existence of a noumenal self in order to secure a motivation for moral conduct, when surveying the historical process as a whole, we must postulate that there was some overall plan at work. History as a form of knowledge devoted to the study of specific episodes in the human past was at best of secondary interest to Kant. While Kant was very exercised by Hume's arguments regarding the lack of a certain foundation for our expectations of physical events, Hume's *History of England* provoked no such philosophical reflection in him.

Chapter 4 examines Hegel, who like Kant aimed to be systematic in his account of categories. But in place of Kant's two quadratic tables, Hegel introduced a vastly expanded circular arrangement of concepts that aimed to incorporate not just Kantian but also ancient thought in a single vast synthesis. So, for instance, the subject, who for Aristotle was a living substance, had to be reconceptualised in modernity under the category of the 'I'. This reconceptualisation held out the prospect of restoring the continuity between appearance and reality that Hegel argued had been lost in the transition from ancient to modern thought.

Categories became dynamic entities or 'moments' of thought forming a vast and continually interacting whole.

In Hegel's view, it made no sense in the last resort to ask whether the categories were transcendental, or in the things, or in ourselves, or indeed were linguistic meanings; all of these answers could be said to be true so far as they went, but the full truth of the system required that it be taken in its totality. All the parts of Hegel's categorial scheme, and the various genres of knowledge that were distinguished from one another by the categorial presuppositions that they made, reciprocally implied one another. There were also no absolute separations to be found in it, whether between appearance and reality, phenomenon and noumenon, subject and object, or thought and language.

At the same time, the system retained distinct phases, within each of which Hegel offered analyses of the relevant conventional forms of knowledge. Each phase retained a hierarchical progression with respect to the degree of rationality that had been reached; but the phases themselves were not part of a hierarchy. Each implied the others. This was a deliberate critique of the Platonic hierarchy of kinds of knowledge. The importance of the metaphor of circularity for the nature of the system as a whole deserves emphasis here. An important interpretation to consider is whether Hegel's stance towards the nature of the Absolute was not, in fact, an ironic one; after all, one can neither ascend nor invert a circle, only move around within it.

The three main phases or divisions were logic, nature, and the human realm of 'Geist'. Geist has a variety of possible translations in English, including 'spirit', 'soul', 'mind', 'subjectivity', and 'consciousness', all of which have different connotations, but there is no disputing that it is to this part of Hegel's system that government belongs. Like Kant, Hegel did not think that philosophical knowledge was a qualification to rule. While hierarchy was necessary to any form of government, Hegel agreed with Kant that it should be institutional rather than personal. Hegel certainly treated the advent of a distinct subjective moment as a characteristic of modernity that ancient thinkers like Plato and Aristotle had not had to reckon with so explicitly; but the solution was to integrate the subject into a broader moral and political order. In all its shifting forms, Geist remained 'the I that is we and the we that is I'.[68]

The fact of historicity was more clearly recognised in Hegel's thought than by any of his predecessors, but his resulting philosophy of history, in

---

[68] Georg Wilhelm Friedrich Hegel, *The Phenomenology of Spirit*, trans. M. Inwood (Oxford: Oxford University Press, 2018), §177, 76.

which world history had consisted in the gradual extension of freedom, was again not oriented towards historical knowledge of specific contingent events. Hegel followed Kant in thinking of history as a theodicy in a sense unknown to Plato or Aristotle. The difference was that for Hegel, unlike Kant (or Karl Marx), the philosophy of history was no guide to the future. We were standing at the end of something, with no idea what would be coming next.

Together these first four chapters introduce four major, quite distinct, theories of categories: as timeless logical concepts in which the world of appearances somehow participates (Plato); as substances, and as properties and kinds of substances (Aristotle); as *a priori* rules for the understanding and for moral life (Kant); and as dynamic, linguistic, moments of a comprehensive system of logic, nature and spirit (Hegel). These chapters also show how their authors persistently connected their respective theories of categories with their accounts of knowledge, politics, and history. Despite major shifts in the conception of categories involved, this pattern of association survived the otherwise great changes in cosmological and theological orientation separating the ancient and the modern worlds.

There were, however, also some substantive continuities in doctrine. There was a persistent emphasis in favour of universal and necessary forms of knowledge. There was also a tendency in the ancient world to favour aristocratic forms of rule by the wise, and in the modern, to prefer Western forms of government to those found elsewhere. Finally, both ancient and modern theorists of categories, thanks to their emphasis on universality, consistently paid little attention to the philosophical problems associated with historical knowledge.

Chapter 5 deals with the first major line of development after Hegel, the response by the fragmentarians to Idealism. Nietzsche, the earliest of the thinkers we shall consider, set the tone in arguing that Kant's system of categories really amounted to a covert imposition of his own religious and moral beliefs. The particular was illegitimately treated as if it were universal. This argument has been repeated by all later critical theorists, as well as post-colonial and post-modern authors. But their critique of Enlightenment thought was often a revision rather than a repudiation of it. For Nietzsche, scepticism about the status of universals did not entail a complete rejection of the concept of categories (or indeed of Enlightenment) so much as a demand for self-consciousness and honesty regarding our use of them. It was important, for example, not to overlook the role of the will in the construction of the self.

Nietzsche has sometimes been treated as a relativist, but based on his own insistence on the importance of truth, it would be better to say that he sought to reconcile the goals of truth and objectivity with the existence of a plurality of perspectives and the historicity of knowledge. This made him resistant to reductive approaches to knowledge, an attitude inherited by Adorno. If any of the fragmentarians espoused a truly relativistic theory of knowledge, it was Foucault in his earlier writings; but even Foucault softened his position as he developed. What has been characteristic of the fragmentarian position, in fact, is not relativism, but a scepticism towards claims that the kind of synthetic analysis of concepts found in Hegel necessarily possessed the universal philosophical and political validity that was claimed.

This scepticism, however, was not simply a rejection of Hegel's thought at large. Adorno was one of the first contemporary thinkers to grasp that Hegel's analysis of identity had serious political ramifications. Categories could be used to classify individuals in deeply harmful ways, reducing them to their attributes, such as their group identity, in a way that de-individualised them or even dehumanised them altogether, and thus legitimated their oppression and even their destruction. Nor was this a merely theoretical risk. It was, Adorno believed, exactly what twentieth-century totalitarian regimes had done. But it was also a tendency in capitalist societies. This diagnosis was again anticipated, albeit from a quasi-aristocratic, anti-democratic standpoint, by Nietzsche.

Adorno's view of modern totalitarianism as the outcome of a long process of historical development was also thoroughly indebted to Hegel. Despite their repudiation of Hegel's optimistic and progressive outlook, the same could be said of Nietzsche and Foucault. For the first time, however, we begin to find in the fragmentarians a more sustained interest in the problem of historical knowledge as well as in the historical process. Historiography was treated with suspicion by Nietzsche in particular because of its allegedly harmful effects, but the increasing prominence of the discipline made it impossible to ignore altogether. For Foucault, a quasi-historiographical method of analysis became his primary approach to the critique that he, like Adorno, regarded as the best mode in which to continue the work of the Enlightenment in modernity by making it more self-critical.

Chapter 6 turns to the subordinationists, who were often tempted to dispose of categories altogether. Placing Heidegger together with the logical empiricists may seem controversial, given their mutual disdain, but the point is to show that, as mutual antitheses, they had a great deal in common. Heidegger argued that theories of categories tended to impose an unnecessary mediation between the self and the world. The logical empiricist complaint was similar. If direct observation of sense data was the priority, a categorial scheme was an obstruction. Both Heidegger and the logical empiricists found that they needed to modify their early agendas, however.

In Heidegger's case the worry was that the original terms in which he had posed the question of the meaning of Being had not been radical enough. The language of categories had still been very prominent in *Being and Time*.[69] Heidegger became more and more worried that the Western pursuit of scientific knowledge in the service of the technological domination of the world was estranging us from our true nature. But describing the nature of Being proved difficult in anything other than metaphorical terms. The logical empiricists, on the other hand, found it hard to sustain the original project of a unified science in the face of the internal diversity of scientific knowledge itself, especially when extended to include the social sciences. The historicity of scientific knowledge and the dependence of the validity of the scientific proposition on its context of reference were issues they were unable to ignore.

In political terms, the emphasis that Heidegger and the logical empiricists placed on a single standpoint, be it Being or science, pulled them towards radicalism. Seen in context, their different choices reflected a struggle between town and country, secularism and religiosity. Heidegger showed terrible political judgement in believing that Hitler and the National Socialists were allies in his own project of rehabilitating the authentic character of the German people. The logical empiricists for their part typically favoured radical socialism or Communism. They regarded themselves as continuators of an optimistic and rationalistic version of the Enlightenment. Heidegger espoused a Romantic and ultimately despairing neo-pagan outlook. But in both cases, they were drawn away from the messy and unexciting compromises associated with parliamentary liberal democracy.

These views spilled over, once more, into attitudes to history. Heidegger took notice of the discipline of history only to dismiss it as rationalist 'historiology' that had nothing to contribute to his own analysis of the essential feature of the historical process, the gradual covering up of the meaning of Being. The logical empiricist interest in history often stemmed from Marxist commitments. Neurath, for instance, thought of history as worth studying for the insights it might offer in the pursuit of the class struggle. Neurath also thought that the influence of historical beliefs on

---

[69] Martin Heidegger, *Being and Time*, trans. John Macquarrie and Edward Robinson (Oxford: Blackwell Publishers Ltd, 2001 [1962]).

political attitudes was sufficiently important to write a lengthy refutation of Oswald Spengler's *Decline of the West*. But like Heidegger, Neurath treated the nature of historical knowledge as a secondary problem. Where it was noticed, it was assimilated to universal social science.

Chapter 7 examines the pluralists, generally the least influential of the three main lines of response we are considering. Nevertheless, Cassirer, Collingwood and Ricoeur were examples of an effort to develop a distinctive position that accepted the Kantian and Hegelian contention that a determinate system of categories of some kind was both possible and desirable. They therefore rejected the fragmentarian view that we were faced with an undefinable proliferation of categories, and the subordinationist desire to get away from categories altogether. Overall, their inclination was consistently to seek a middle ground between the two positions we have already outlined.

The pluralists typically accepted the historicity of the fragmentarian position. It was indeed necessary to recognise that even the most objective and universal forms of knowledge had a history. But they also recognised the need to deal with Heidegger's argument that the structure of the lifeworld could not be adequately comprehended only in scientific terms. Similarly, modern science might not have the unique status that the logical empiricist variety of subordinationism claimed for it, but the pluralists accepted the logical empiricist argument that modern science had forced a revision of the Kantian and Hegelian philosophical standpoints.

The pluralist search for a middle ground manifested itself in political terms in the form of a commitment to the rule of law and parliamentary institutions. Cassirer, Collingwood and Ricoeur all shared a dislike of political extremes. They were all, in one way or another, greatly affected by the Second World War, and were convinced that only a commitment to representative democracy could prevent a resurgence of totalitarianism. They had seen the fragile nature of all political order, resting as it did on the mutable foundations of the human imagination. Hence the intense concern that Ricoeur, for example, displayed for the conservation of memory in the public sphere in the hope that the conflicts and injustices of the past would not be forgotten.

Historical knowledge was key to the pursuit of this goal. One thing that separated the pluralists from the other two groups of thinkers discussed here was their insistence that history must be taken seriously as a way of understanding human experience, and was irreducible to the terms of natural or social scientific thought. Though fragmentarians and subordinationists recognised the phenomenon of historicity, they did not, for the most part, attribute central importance to the philosophical problem of identifying the conditions of history as a distinctive kind of theoretical analysis. The pluralists were the only thinkers who broke decisively with the long-standing habit of approaching the study of the past through universal categories.

To grasp contemporary discourse about categories, then, we must understand not only the changing meanings of the term itself, but its persistent entanglement with questions to do with knowledge, politics and history. Those changing meanings require appreciating the divergent views of Plato, Aristotle, Kant and Hegel. However, it is also important to understand that since Hegel there have been at least three distinct schools of thought on the subject, and to be alive to the ways in which they were responding to what had gone before, as well as to one another. All these considerations make for a formidably abstract and difficult subject. But if we begin at the beginning, and follow these themes as they develop, we may find that, at the end, we have some clearer and more distinct ideas than when we set out.

Part 1:

Categories in Platonic and Aristotelian Thought

1
Plato: Forms as Categories of Ideal Being

This first chapter argues that there are important connections between Plato's theory of Forms, which we shall understand as categories in the sense of fundamental concepts; his theory of knowledge, which was conceived of as ultimately leading to apprehension of a hierarchy of Forms; his views on politics, which treated government as ideally the preserve of the minority capable of this apprehension; and finally, his views on history, which required a knowledge of the cyclical processes at work in order for those responsible for government to be able to best manage the polity. We are interested not simply in the content of Plato's views on these interconnected subjects, but in how and why they are interconnected. Plato's views on all of these subjects helped to establish the habit of treating them as mutually implicated with one another. This is not a necessary pattern, but it has been persistent. This claim can however only be fully substantiated by the argument as a whole.

We must begin by examining the sense in which Plato has a theory of categories. It is true that, unlike Aristotle, the concept of a category is not part of Plato's philosophical vocabulary. But post-Aristotelian commentators both ancient and modern have treated Plato's writings on the Ideas or Forms as a precursor to Aristotle's writings on categories. Ancient writers like Plotinus sought to blend Plato's Forms and Aristotle's categories into a single metaphysical theory.[1] Modern philosophers including A. N. Whitehead and Gilbert Ryle have argued that Plato's investigation of the Forms constitutes a categorial enquiry insofar as he is addressing

---

[1] See Plotinus, *Enneads*, trans. A. H. Armstrong, 7 vols (Cambridge: Harvard University Press, 1989), vi.15: 'we must examine which of the ten [categories] are also there in the intelligible, and if the things there can be brought under one genus with those here below'.

the concepts that we need to make reality intelligible.² There will probably never be consensus on exactly how the Forms should be understood, and the theory itself (if indeed Plato held such a theory, another disputable issue) is generally held to suffer from various difficulties that many modern philosophers have deemed insuperable. Nevertheless, Platonism has remained influential in modernity, including in certain departments of philosophy, logic, and mathematics. The idea of a domain of abstract objects that can ground the truth of our knowledge has retained its appeal.³

For Plato himself, the Forms were at once universal, extra-temporal, normative and definitive. They also comprised a hierarchy, with the Form of the Good at the summit. The value of human knowledge was judged by its relationship to the Forms. Insofar as knowledge related to appearances, and was tied to practical activities such as making, the role of the Forms remained implicit. Craftsmen produced objects that were copies of an original model supplied by the Form in question, but were unaware that this was what they were doing. Practical excellence was consistent with conceptual ignorance. In Plato's story of the cave, most people lived unaware of the role played by the purely conceptual realm of the Forms. Almost all human activity was conducted with no knowledge of our metaphysical condition.

Usually this ignorance did not prevent daily life from going on well enough, although the discovery of the truth of the matter could come as an unwelcome shock.⁴ There was, however, one domain in which Plato thought the prospects for successful conduct would be greatly improved if we were aware of the role that the Forms really played, namely, government. The small minority capable of the abstract cognition required to master first

---

² Alfred North Whitehead, *Adventures of Ideas* (New York, The Free Press, 1967 [1933]), 228, argues that 'Plato's dialogues ... are mainly an endeavour to elicit philosophic categories from a dialectic discussion of the meanings of language.' Gilbert Ryle, 'Plato's *Parmenides* (ii)', *Mind*, ns, 48, no. 191 (1939), 302–25, 316, suggests that a dialogue like *Parmenides* should 'be classified by us as belonging to the same sphere to which belong, for example, Aristotle's theory of Categories, Kant's separation of formal from non-formal concepts'.
³ See, for example, Gottlob Frege, 'Thought', in *The Frege Reader*, ed. Michael Beaney (Oxford: Blackwell, 1997), 325–45, 328: 'A thought is something imperceptible: anything the senses can perceive is excluded from the realm of things for which the question of truth arises.'
⁴ Plato, *Republic*, ed. G. R. F. Ferrari, trans. T. Griffith (Cambridge: Cambridge University Press, 2000), 517a, has Socrates declare that the philosopher returning to the cave will be ridiculed, and may even be killed, for trying to inform its inhabitants about the nature of the upper world that they have visited.

mathematics and then knowledge of the Forms themselves would, partly in virtue of this knowledge, be better suited and most entitled to rule.

Plato's theory of knowledge was thus at the same time effectively a categorisation of persons for political purposes. The division of knowledge into practical and theoretical or contemplative regions runs parallel to the division of society into bronze, silver and gold types. Only those in the gold class were capable of mastering the knowledge of the Forms and thus truly qualified to govern. One way of understanding this theory is as an argument that government cannot be reduced to a formula, but that it included an element of judgement which from a technical point of view remained ineffable.

The philosopher-rulers were distinguished as possessors of knowledge that allowed them to attune themselves to the right moment for action, possessing a sense of the times and of timing which ancient Greek thought called *kairos*.[5] In Plato's account, the philosopher-rulers had so mastered this power of judgement that they possessed an intuitive vision of the right action which rendered debate superfluous. The philosopher-ruler was able to simply see, with something close to unerring accuracy, what was necessary in order to fulfil the requirements of justice in a given situation. In this sense, Plato was arguably a deliberately anti-political thinker. His aim was the elimination of politics, at least insofar as it involved argument and contestation, leaving only legislation and judicial and executive decision intact.

Because the most perfect form of government was liable to change and decay, a complete philosophical understanding of justice required knowledge of the process by which the decline from the ideal occurred.[6] This was a theory of the historical process as applied to government. But it was a theory governed by logical and metaphysical considerations. The number of types of constitution was fixed, and the cycle as a whole reflected our broader cosmological situation, in which humanity was living in a 'time out of joint'.[7] Although Plato was aware of historiography as a genre of writing, he was largely uninterested in it, especially when compared

---

[5] John. E. Smith, 'Time and Qualitative Time', in *Rhetoric and Kairos: Essays in History, Theory, and Praxis*, ed. Phillip Sipiora and James S. Baumlin (New York: SUNY Press, 2002), 46–57, 54, highlights Plato's remark in *Laws*, bk. IV, that 'Chance [*tyche*] and occasion [*kairos*] cooperate with God in the control of all human affairs.'

[6] Plato, *Republic*, 545a–b, had Socrates say that 'the next thing [is] to describe ... in turn the oligarchic character, the democratic, and the tyrannical' in order to be able to 'contrast the most unjust ... with the most just'.

[7] Shakespeare, *Hamlet*, act I, scene V, had Hamlet say 'The time is out of joint' when he discovers that Claudius is his father's murderer.

to, for instance, geometry. Plato's interest in historical processes treated constitutional forms as typical and exemplary. The Athenian democracy was just a case of democracy in general, and the consideration of it in its historical specificity was of marginal interest. In the end, Plato's attitude to history reflected a more general prejudice in favour of the universal and atemporal aspects of our experience.

Categories

Let us start with the objection that Plato did not have a theory of categories. It is true that Plato did not use the term 'category' as a term of philosophical art, and so there is undeniably a sense in which this objection holds. F. M. Cornford, a prominent Plato scholar in the earlier twentieth century, denied that the Forms could be understood in a way that gave them 'the place afterwards occupied by Aristotle's categories'. Cornford was thus against 'calling [the Forms] "categories" at all'. But Cornford also conceded in his very next sentence that 'There may be some sense of that vague and ambiguous word [category] as used by modern philosophers, that might be considered appropriate.'[8]

For a better understanding of what that sense might be, we may turn to the modern philosophers A. N. Whitehead and Gregory Vlastos. Whitehead famously remarked that 'the European philosophical tradition ... consists of a series of footnotes to Plato'.[9] Even to a distinguished Plato scholar like Vlastos, this seemed an 'absurdly inflated estimate of [Plato's] place in European thought'.[10] But Whitehead was not asserting that subsequent philosophers had simply been commentators on Plato. Indeed, Whitehead was sceptical that there was any 'systematic scheme of thought' in Plato's writings. He meant, rather, that Plato has been 'an inexhaustible mine of suggestion', which seems indisputable. But what Whitehead himself found suggestive in Plato was his attempt to identify the categorial conditions of reality, an approach he wanted to adapt for his own philosophy.[11]

---

[8] Francis Macdonald Cornford, *Plato's Theory of Knowledge: The* Theatetus *and the* Sophist *of Plato translated with a running commentary* (London: Kegan Paul, Trench, Trubner; New York: Harcourt, Brace, 1935), 27.

[9] Alfred North Whitehead, *Process and Reality: An Essay in Cosmology. Gifford Lectures Delivered in the University of Edinburgh During the Session 1927–8*, ed. David Ray Griffin and Donald W. Sherburne (New York: The Free Press, 1978 [1929]), 39.

[10] Gregory Vlastos, *Plato's Universe* (USA: Parmenides Publishing, 2005 [1975]), xxv.

[11] Whitehead, *Process and Reality*, 222, argued that 'There are three main categorial conditions which flow from the final nature of things', namely subjective unity, objective identity and objective diversity.

No doubt Whitehead's interpretation belonged to a post-Kantian and post-Hegelian context, but it was actually shared by Vlastos, despite their apparent disagreement over Plato's importance. Vlastos likewise interpreted Plato's philosophy as 'the first ... in Western philosophy' to explore 'the categorial differences between things like Beauty, Justice, Triangularity, and the like, and those individuals, states, events, processes of which such general terms can be predicated'.[12] Vlastos, in other words, was happy to treat Plato's Forms as categories in the sense that they were general terms with an important role in predication. This is good enough for our purposes. We certainly do not claim to provide a definitive solution regarding the nature of the Forms or to the problems arising from the theory. We may content ourselves with setting the Forms in context by recalling some of the circumstances to which they were a response.

Firstly, Plato was reacting to Parmenides' famous statement that 'Being Is', which entailed that only what did not change was truly real.[13] But the consequence of the Parmenidean claim was that the changing world of our ordinary experience was unreal. All relation between our regular perceptions and ultimate reality was severed. Plato's Forms saved the appearances by bridging the gap between the observable phenomena and ultimate reality.[14] This problem was acute in Greek astronomy at the time, but it was also of more general import. Even if truly real being were changeless, sensible existence was what was most important to most people. Most notably, it was this sensible level of reality that had to be reckoned with in dealing with the problem of government.

An important implication is that Plato's dualism was not transcendental in the modern sense; the role of the Forms was precisely to guarantee that reality remained directly accessible to us, or at least to our reason (unlike the Kantian noumena).[15] There was no bar to full knowledge of things as they truly were, at least not if we had the intellectual capacity, and the character required, to work hard enough at achieving this goal.

---

[12] Gregory Vlastos, *Platonic Studies* (Princeton: Princeton University Press, 1973), 74.

[13] Parmenides stated that 'One should both say and think that Being Is; for To Be is possible, and Nothingness is not possible': see Kathleen Freeman, *Ancilla to the Pre-Socratic Philosophers: A Complete Translation of the Fragments in Diels*, Fragmente der Vorsokratiker (Harvard: Harvard University Press, 1948), 43.

[14] The injunction to 'save the appearances' has become apocryphally associated with Plato in connection with the problem of reconciling the so-called 'wandering' motions of some of the heavenly bodies (now recognised as the planets of our solar system) with the claim that their motions followed perfectly circular orbits. See A. Mark Smith, 'Saving the Appearances of the Appearances: The Foundations of Classical Geometrical Optics', *Archive for History of Exact Sciences* 24:2 (1981), 73–99, 73, n. 1.

[15] See Chapter 3, below.

As we shall see in the next chapter, Aristotle agreed that there was a continuity from the sensible to the suprasensible order of things. But although the suprasensible order was accessible to subjectivity, as we would say, the Forms or Ideas were not to be confused with the ideas we find in our individual minds. They had an independent being, which is what the English upper-case capitalisation of the Forms or Ideas is conventionally supposed to indicate.

Secondly, Plato was responding to the elementalism and atomism of the Ionian thinkers, named for the region from which many of them originated. Instead of making ultimate reality changeless and timeless, the Ionian natural philosophers treated it as purely material; reality was built up from the elements, like water or fire. Plato's theory of Forms was a middle way between the Parmenidean and Ionian approaches. We see here how the theory of Forms already begins to bear on questions of knowledge. Modern writers have often treated the Ionians as the first philosophers to adopt a scientific outlook. Sir Karl Popper, for example, argued that they represented a 'Pre-Socratic Enlightenment'.[16] Plato wanted to find room both for a 'scientific' account of nature that could accommodate Ionian atomism and to insist that 'science' was not the final word on reality.

Thirdly, Plato was also responding to Socrates, who tended to approach moral and political problems as definitional questions. Plato's suggestion was that these questions were soluble by reference to the conceptual order to which the Forms belonged. In this way, the Forms also forestalled what we would now call the conceptual relativism of a Sophist like Thrasymachus, who argued in the *Republic* that man was the measure of all things, and that justice was simply the interest of the stronger.[17] The Sophists offered to teach argumentative strategies useful in practical affairs, as, for example, when one found oneself the subject of a *kategoria* and needed to convince a jury of one's innocence. But this might suggest that truth was just whatever one could persuade people to believe. If, however, we can formulate a definition of Justice that conforms to its essential and unchanging nature, and use this to determine whether words and deeds in the sensible world are just, the Sophistic challenge can be rebutted.

The Forms, then, secured our access to reality, established it as more than simply material, and made moral values an integral part of it. There

---

[16] Karl Popper, *The World of Parmenides: Essays on the Presocratic Enlightenment*, ed. Arne F. Petersen with the assistance of Jørgen Mejer (London and New York: Routledge, 1998), 35, argued, for example, that Xenophanes 'anticipated and strongly represented all the main ideas of the European Enlightenment'.

[17] Plato, *Republic*, 338c, had Thrasymachus say 'justice is simply what is good for the stronger'.

were notable problems with the theory, however. Sensible things, including people, were supposedly connected to the Forms by a relation of 'participation'. But ever since Aristotle, the nature of this relation of participation has been problematic.[18] One suggestion was that the relationship is like that of copy to model. The Forms were akin to templates, according to the *Republic*, which used a couch as an example.[19] The human maker of artefacts grasped the Idea of the thing as an archetype of the actual object that they wanted to produce. This suggestion also accorded well with the creation story that Plato provided in the *Timaeus*, where the demiurge or divine craftsman imposed the Forms on the preexisting inchoate stuff of the world, thus subjecting it to rationality and order.[20] The human craftsman was akin to the demiurge in imposing Form onto tangible materials.

While the theory of Forms may be attractive with respect to the explanation of organic life because of its teleological orientation, according to which the natural process of growth can be understood as an attempt to achieve some pre-existing identity (acorns do not turn into pigs, only oak trees), it struggles, especially from a contemporary perspective, with artefacts.[21] Contemporary readers are likely to find implausible the argument that eternal Forms of technological devices like the microprocessor have always been there, simply waiting for us to discover them. Even if one accepts this consequence, it is at the dual cost of violating long-standing philosophical strictures against the multiplication of entities and of permitting currently unknowable Forms, a notion unacceptable in Platonism.

These are not the only serious difficulties. Two others that are often mentioned are the question of the resemblance of the Forms to the phenomena.

---

[18] Aristotle, *Metaphysics*, trans. C. D. C. Reeve (Indianapolis: Hackett, 2016), 987b, wrote that 'What this participation or this imitation of the Forms could *be* . . . [Plato and the Pythagoreans] left an open question.' Emphasis in original.

[19] Plato, *Republic*, 597c–d, trans. Griffith, had Socrates argue that 'either from choice or because there was some necessity for him not to produce more than one couch in the natural order of things, god has made only this one couch' and is 'the true creator of the true couch'. See also Nicholas Denyer, 'Sun and Line: The Role of the Good', in *The Cambridge Companion to Plato's Republic*, ed. G. R. F. Ferrari (Cambridge: Cambridge University Press, 2007), 284–309, 287.

[20] Plato, *Timaeus*, 30c, trans. Donald J. Zeyl, in *Works*, has Timaeus say that 'The god wanted everything to be good and nothing to be bad so far as that was possible, and so he took over all that was visible – not at rest but in discordant and disorderly motion – and brought it from a state of disorder to one of order, because he believed that order was in every way better than disorder . . . he put intelligence in soul, and soul in body, and so he constructed the universe.'

[21] Denyer, 'Sun and Line', 288.

One way of understanding the relationship of participation is that it is a type of similarity. This suggests that the Forms are not classes, but individual archetypes that somehow share in the nature of the appearances. But then is the Form of a triangle itself triangular? Is Justice itself just?[22] Moreover, whether the Forms are classes or archetypes, their existence apparently leaves the way open to an endless regression. The theory of Forms requires a model for the model, or an archetype for the archetype, and so on ad infinitum, which destroys the unique or ultimate character that each Form supposedly possesses.[23] This so-called 'third man' argument was an objection noted by Plato himself, and Aristotle was inclined to regard it as fatal.[24]

Plato was also aware of the objection that if the Forms existed at all, they were unknowable, and had no relation to our experience.[25] Here again reactions have varied. Gilbert Ryle read *Parmenides* as Plato signalling a break with his own theory of Forms that commenced a late 'analytic' or post-metaphysical period.[26] Others have noted that despite the criticisms, 'Parmenides commends Socrates for his interest in Forms and ... announces that Forms are necessary if one is not to destroy thought.'[27] On this view, Plato was subjecting his own concepts to robust scrutiny rather than giving up on them altogether.

---

[22] Nicholas P. White, 'Plato's Metaphysical Epistemology', in *The Cambridge Companion to Plato*, ed. Richard Kraut (Cambridge: Cambridge University Press, 1992), 277–310, 293, writes that 'Plato's argument for the distinctness of Forms does not itself require that the Form of F be in general F, and in view of the oddity of this idea it has understandably seemed to many interpreters better not to attribute it to him. On the other hand there are numerous passages in which he seems to use language by which self-predication is very strongly suggested, including claims to the effect that perceptible objects are "imitations" or "copies" of Forms, which are "paradigms" for them.'

[23] Plato, *Parmenides*, trans. Mary Louise Gill and Paul Ryan, 132a–b, had Parmenides say that 'another form of largeness will make its appearance, which has emerged alongside largeness itself and the things that partake of it, and in turn another over all these, by which all of them will be large. Each of your forms will no longer be one, but unlimited in multitude.'

[24] W. D. Ross, *Aristotle's Metaphysics: A Revised Text with Introduction and Commentary*, 2 vols (Oxford: Clarendon Press, 1975 [1924]), i.195, remarked that Aristotle saw the 'third man' argument as arising from Plato having made the mistake of 'the positing of the Idea as an individual substance outside the particulars and imitated by them'.

[25] Plato, *Parmenides*, trans. Gill and Ryan, 133b, had Parmenides say that 'if the forms are such as we claim they must be, they cannot even be known'.

[26] Ryle, 'Plato's *Parmenides* (ii)', 313, suggested that after writing *Parmenides* Plato had reached a position similar to Bertrand Russell: 'Russell's proof that, in his code-symbolism, ϕ cannot be a value of x in the propositional function ϕx is only another exercise in the same genre as Plato's proof that "Unity" cannot go into the gap in the sentence-frame "... exists or "... does not exist".'

[27] Constance C. Meinwald, 'Good-bye to the Third Man', in *Cambridge Companion to Plato*, 365–98, 372.

Cornford regarded the *Sophist* as a particularly important dialogue because it introduced what he called the 'five Kinds', which served as de facto fundamental categories for Plato.[28] These were Existence, Motion, Rest, Sameness, and Difference.[29] Their identification was only possible via the highest kind of philosophical skill. It is at this point in the text that we find the famous comparison between the dialectician who is 'able to cut up each kind according to its species along its natural joints' and the good butcher who knows how to avoid splintering the bones.[30]

While all things may be said to participate in these five ultimate natural kinds, however, Vlastos noted that the *Timaeus* distinguished those causes 'which possess understanding and thus fashion what is beautiful and good, from those which, when deserted by intelligence, produce only haphazard and disorderly effects every time'.[31] This suggests that there were some further Forms particularly relevant to the intentional actions of people, who in virtue of their rational intelligence were actively capable of good.[32] The Forms discussed in the *Republic*, including the Just, the Beautiful and the Good, belonged to this latter class as ubiquitous considerations in human conduct.[33] They were not only logical substances that enabled definition and thus knowledge.[34] They were norms that supplied an ethical goal or *telos* for existence in the world of appearances.[35]

This discussion of the Forms may seem somewhat abstract, so we may finish this section by underlining that for Plato the Forms were centrally connected to the idea of the self. The rightly ordered soul of the person determined to pursue justice was ruled firmly by the same rational element via which we come to know the Forms. Such a person enjoyed a rational command of both their own character and of their own desires.[36]

---

[28] Cornford, *Plato's Theory of Knowledge*, 274.
[29] Plato, *Sophist*, trans. Nicholas P. White, 254b–255e. Compare Plato, *Timaeus*, trans. Zeyl, 37a: 'the soul is a mixture of the Same, the Different and Being'.
[30] Plato, *Sophist*, 265e.
[31] Plato, *Timaeus*, 46e. See Vlastos, *Platonic Studies*, 154: 'In the *Timaeus* the whole account of man and the world turns on a clear-cut distinction between two kinds of causes.'
[32] Plato, *Timaeus*, 42e, had Timaeus say that 'humans have a twofold nature'.
[33] Plato, *Republic*, 476a–c, 508e.
[34] Thomas A. Blackson, *Inquiry, Forms, and Substances: A Study in Plato's Metaphysics and Epistemology* (Dordrecht: Springer Science+Business Media, 1995), 2, argues that 'The Theory of Forms is the theory that certain essences exist and that they exist as substances, i.e., ontological starting-points.' Blackson also notes that Plato uses the Greek noun *ousia*, typically translated as 'substance', as well as *eidos*, to refer to the Forms or Ideas.
[35] Denyer, 'Sun and Line', 284.
[36] Plato, *Republic*, 441e, had Socrates inquire rhetorically 'Isn't it appropriate for the rational element to rule, because it is wise and takes thought for the entire soul, and appropriate for the spirited element to be subordinate, the ally of the rational element?'

The more that the just person comprehended the nature of Justice, the more a settled path of virtuous conduct opened up for them that would be rewarded in their next incarnation. The Just itself, like all the other Forms, did not change. The just person came increasingly to resemble, though was never wholly identical with, the Form of Justice. Plato wrote that 'those who are capable of grasping what is always the same and unchanging are philosophers'.[37] But to grasp the full import of this statement, we must examine how the Forms related to Plato's account of knowledge at large.

Knowledge

Philosophical knowledge for Plato had an esoteric quality. It stood at the summit of a hierarchy of kinds of human knowledge but was enjoyed only by a few: escapees from the cave were rare. The analogy of the divided line represented it as standing at the peak of a vertical ascent.[38] The main division in this upwards progression was between knowledge of the sensible and of the ideal aspects of reality. Each of these divisions was further subdivided, so that the lowest form of the sensible consisted of illusions. Notoriously, our senses can deceive us. Insofar as our sensible knowledge escaped this danger, however, it permitted us to engage in useful and meaningful ways with the stuff of sensible reality.

From this upper section of the sensible order, the philosopher-ruler in training progressed to the lower region or first stage of intelligible knowledge, comprising the logical objects of mathematics. These were to the Forms what illusions were to the solid realities of sensible experience, insofar as they were a necessary feature of the intelligible world, just as the possibility of illusion was ineliminable in perception. Of course, they were much closer to real being than either perception or its illusions, but they still employed sensible figures in their demonstrations.[39] These sensible figures must be overcome entirely for us to understand the Forms directly, and finally reach the Form of the Good.

The highest form of knowledge for Plato was this unmediated, direct, wordless vision of the true nature of things as ultimately One. It proved a lasting source of inspiration for later mystical thought; Plotinus is a classic

---

[37] Plato, *Republic*, 484b.
[38] Plato, *Republic*, 509d.
[39] Plato, *Republic*, 511a.

example. It also notably influenced the monotheisms.⁴⁰ Yet Socrates was unable to define the Good; he could only make an analogy with the role of the sun as the source of all light in the sensible realm.⁴¹ The invisible conceptual 'light' of the Forms explained how the perceptual world was meaningful for us. Platonic rationalism culminated in a quasi-mystical religious metaphor. This combination of rationalism and religiosity has been an important factor in the enduring appeal of Plato's account of knowledge.

To take just one example, Henry More, writing in seventeenth-century England, argued that Plato's writings supported a view of 'logical and mathematical terms' as 'evidence of intellection that is not dependent on sense impressions'.⁴² But More did not simply want to identify the foundations of mathematics. His argument was that the new Newtonian natural philosophy did not mean the victory of metaphysical materialism. Newtonianism was not necessarily inimical to Christianity, because logic and mathematics testified to the existence of an immaterial domain of reason that still had place for the divine. In Chapter 3 we shall see Kant taking a similar position in the following century.

Yet despite Plato's clear preference for the kinds of knowledge belonging to the upper part of the divided line (which was also the larger part of knowledge), by his own account the great majority of human beings would always remain exclusively concerned with its sensible dimension. The kind of practical knowledge constituting the mainstay of their occupations was essential to the community. Plato, we said, was concerned to save the appearances, and this applied also to common sense and practical knowledge. Moreover, the kind of knowledge associated with government was itself at least partly practical in nature. The philosopher-ruler's vision of the Good was thus a necessary, but not sufficient, condition for ruling the ideal society.

---

⁴⁰ Patrick Grant, *Literature of Mysticism in Western Tradition* (London and Basingstoke: Macmillan Press, 1983), 132, writes that in the Platonic scheme 'the human soul or higher reason is held, uniquely, to participate in the divine principle ... the way of soul's reunion with its source is described ... by Plotinus ... as a progress through a series of grades towards perfection, a scheme which deeply influenced subsequent Christian thought'. It also impacted the Islamic world, returning to Europe in mediated form as part of the Renaissance revival of interest in Platonism: see, for example, Samar Attar, *The Vital Roots of European Enlightenment: Ibn Tufayl's Influence on Modern Western Thought* (Lanham, MD, and Plymouth: Lexington Books, 2007).
⁴¹ Plato, *Republic*, 506d, 508c.
⁴² Alexander Jacob, ed., 'Introduction' to Henry More, *The Immortality of the Soul* (Dordrecht: Martinus Nijhoff, 1987), lxi.

What Plato called *techne* in Greek covered a wide variety of human activities.⁴³ In English, 'art', 'craft' and 'expertise' are all possible translations.⁴⁴ The Greek term occurs hundreds of times in his writings.⁴⁵ *Techne* incorporated both arithmetical computation and all sorts of productive and useful activities such as medicine, navigation, animal husbandry, and farming, without which civilised life could not go on. So far as it went, it was a reliable form of knowledge that was 'recognized, and rewarded, by other members of the community'. It was certifiable, and teachable.⁴⁶ As Gilbert Ryle put it, *techne* was concerned with 'knowing how'.⁴⁷

Here, the political implications of Plato's view of knowledge begin to appear. The classification of knowledge was also unavoidably a classification of people. Human beings could be grouped according to whether they could comprehend the higher levels of knowledge, and institutions should be arranged accordingly. Miles Burnyeat noted that 'one of the tasks of persuasion which Socrates (Plato) undertakes is to get Glaucon (the reader) to accept that the most important kind of knowledge is out of his reach'.⁴⁸ Individuals were not only distinguished by their capacity for rational intellection; they were also simultaneously marked as belonging to a certain social type. Plato's notion of the just society depended crucially on the belief that we could reliably know which persons belonged in which category, resulting in a social order that reflected the natural ordering of the world. Who would be responsible for the selection process, or how it would actually work, were questions largely overlooked.

This belief came out powerfully in the so-called myth of the metals. In this story, Plato divided society into bronze, silver and gold individuals.⁴⁹ The majority belonged to the bronze class of artisans and farmers. The silver types were the 'guardians' who acted as auxiliaries to the philosopher-rulers and were responsible for the defence of the community; the golden members were the philosopher-rulers. Reproducing the gold class was the most important task of the city, and required elaborate arrangements for mating

---

⁴³ Plato, *Statesman*, 258d, trans. C. J. Rowe, 297.
⁴⁴ See Cooper's note to Plato, *Statesman*, 296, n. 7.
⁴⁵ David Roochnik, *Of Art and Wisdom: Plato's Understanding of Techne* (Pennsylvania: Penn State University Press, 1996), 249, counts 675 uses.
⁴⁶ Roochnik, *Art and Wisdom*, 20.
⁴⁷ See Gilbert Ryle, 'Knowing How and Knowing That', *Proceedings of the Aristotelian Society*, New Series, 46 (1945–6), 1–16.
⁴⁸ Miles Burnyeat, 'Platonism and mathematics: a prelude to discussion', in *Explorations in Ancient and Modern Philosophy*, 4 vols (Cambridge: Cambridge University Press, 2012), ii.145–72, 165.
⁴⁹ Plato, *Republic*, 415a.

festivals in which couples were paired up.[50] The production of children was too important for the choice of a partner to be left to the individual, though presumably participants were envisaged as doing their duty willingly.

This myth has offended modern sensibilities. To legitimate the authority of the philosopher-rulers, the citizens were to be told they were all brothers who emerged from the earth together, but that their creator had 'used a mixture of gold in the creation of those of you who were fit to be rulers, which is why they are the most valuable'. This 'grand lie' has been seen, in the light of modern experiences of propaganda and brainwashing, as an incipiently totalitarian device.[51] But Malcolm Schofield has pointed out that the people whom Socrates considered it most important to persuade of the truth of this story were the rulers themselves, because it was the best way to ensure that they, and their silver auxiliaries, would treat the bronze majority with gentleness.[52] This is the absolute inverse of the cynical indoctrination of a population to suit the rulers' own purposes.

Likewise, the mating festivals may seem similar to modern programmes of eugenics. But while Plato wanted talented offspring who would be future servants to the city, he was not trying to eliminate the mentally unfit or socially undesirable, much less purge the city along racial or ethnic lines. All three classes were to consider themselves part of the same fraternity.[53] Moreover, the festivals reflected the fact that Plato did not think the qualities required for membership of the gold ruling class were hereditary. There was room for social mobility in both directions, as bronze or silver parents might have golden children and vice versa. Admittedly, the necessary qualities were considered innate, even if not entirely inherited. In the last resort, if one were not made of the right stuff, one would never reach the required standard. But, unusually for an ancient Greek, Plato thought women could have the qualities required for ruling.

Perhaps the myth's most unattractive feature of all from a modern democratic and egalitarian perspective, however, is the doctrine that there were brute differences in innate capacities that no amount of education or other opportunities could overcome. Modern egalitarian sensibilities are resistant to the suggestion that individuals or groups may differ significantly in their natural capacities, because of the danger that negative forms of discrimination might follow. Plato's association of cognitive abilities with

---

[50] Plato, *Republic*, 459e–460b.
[51] Plato, *Republic*, 414b–c.
[52] See Malcolm Schofield, 'The Noble Lie', in *Cambridge Companion to Plato's Republic*, 138–64.
[53] Plato, *Republic*, 415a.

gender has thus been contentious from this point of view, for example. As Janet Radcliffe Richards has argued, we find it difficult to acknowledge the socially significant differences between men and women, whether cognitive or behavioural, that evolutionary anthropology suggests do exist.[54]

For Radcliffe Richards, any such differences are wrongly assumed to be normative just because they are natural, a confusion which is a good example of a category mistake in the modern Rylean sense of a conflation of two universes of discourse. We still confuse classical, teleological, pre-Darwinian normative ideas of nature with the post-Darwinian evolutionary version of the concept which abandons the idea of nature as containing moral norms. It thus remains very difficult for us to separate acknowledgement of evolutionary differences from value judgements about them. For Plato, however, who considered conformity to (his conception of) nature to be the essence of (his understanding of) justice, the problem simply did not arise.

Those judged to have the required natural potential to become philosopher-rulers were subjected to the most exacting education Plato could devise, lasting until the age of fifty. The question immediately arises, therefore, of where on Plato's divided line the kind of knowledge required for government belonged. Some modern readers have held that Plato treated political knowledge as a *techne* in its entirety.[55] Plato certainly referred to government in those terms, and regarded it as having a practical, procedural element of knowing how to do things. In *Gorgias*, for instance, Socrates recounted how he was laughed at for not knowing how to call for a vote when serving as a member of the *Boule* or Council in Athens.[56] Likewise, in the *Republic*, candidates for the office of the philosopher-ruler, once they had completed a course of five years in dialectic, were to dedicate themselves to active public service between the ages of thirty-five and fifty. In particular, they must 'hold military command'.[57] Action as well as contemplation made the philosopher-ruler.

---

[54] Janet Radcliffe Richards, *Human Nature After Darwin: A Philosophical Introduction* (London and New York: Routledge, 2000), 105, notes a 'feminist anxiety about . . . sociobiological ideas about sex differences' due to the mistaken assumption that if these are true, 'women are forced by their biology into something alarmingly like their traditional role'.

[55] See, for example, Thom Brooks, 'Knowledge and Power in Plato's Political Thought', *International Journal of Philosophical Studies*, 14:1 (2006), 51–77; Vicky Roupa, *Articulations of Nature and Politics in Plato and Hegel* (Cham: Palgrave Macmillan, 2020), 23.

[56] Plato, *Gorgias*, 474a, trans. Donald J. Zeyl.

[57] Plato, *Republic*, 539e.

Yet Plato did not consider practical, technical, procedural knowledge sufficient for ruling. Although he used metaphors of weaving and music-making in *Statesman* to characterise the kind of knowledge required by the ideal king, this knowledge was presented as a form of expert judgement rather than as practical expertise. The dialogue was an immediate sequel to *Sophist*, so that the search for the highest kinds discussed above was followed by a discussion of an exactly analogous problem in the context of government. In defining the ideal statesman, it was again necessary to 'divide the various sorts of knowledge'.[58]

Plato was keen to emphasise that the knowledge required could not be reduced to rules. In modern terms, there was no algorithm for governing. The laws of the city were not sufficient in themselves, because they did not address particulars. It was impossible to make rules that were equally well-suited for all individuals. The judgement of the ideal ruler on the other hand was attuned to singularities and perceived the specific course of action necessary for the whole to flourish. In *Statesman* Plato thus had the leading figure in the dialogue, the Visitor, repeatedly stress the importance of being able to identify the right moment for action.[59]

This, as we noted above, involved the concept of *kairos*.[60] Knowing when to do something, or just as importantly when not to do something, was the most important skill that the ideal ruler must possess. Machiavelli's idea of the prince as a master of *fortuna* was a much later presentation of this same argument.[61] Yet the view of Plato as a Machiavellian realist sensitive to the particularities of situations might seem in tension with the idea of Plato as a rationalist devoted to the universal aspect of knowledge. In particular, the heavy emphasis on the study of geometry in the *Republic* in the training of the philosopher-ruler might suggest that for Plato, government was analogous to a problem in mathematics.

It would, however, be incorrect to think of Plato as claiming that deductive reasoning was directly applicable to the problem of political timing. Plato's rationalism, though real enough, was qualified in two directions. First, as we saw above, at the theoretical level, it was linked to a mystical outlook. Second, it did not lead him to forget the practical management

---

[58] Plato, *Statesman*, 258b, trans. C. J. Rowe.
[59] Plato, *Statesman*, 284e, 305d.
[60] See Chelsea Harry, 'Concerning the Right Time: καιρός in Plato's *Statesman*', *Proceedings of the XXIII World Congress of Philosophy*, 2:2 (2018), 145–51.
[61] Compare Niccolò Machiavelli, *The Prince*, ed. Quentin Skinner and Russell Price, 2nd edn (Cambridge: Cambridge University Press, 2019), 83: 'we are successful when our ways are suited to the times and circumstances, and unsuccessful when they are not'.

of affairs. Thus, in the *Republic* the study of the mathematical kind of hypothetical reasoning was said to have two benefits. First, its abstract quality acted as a propaedeutic for dialectic, leading the soul upwards to even higher questions.[62] But second, it was useful to 'warlike men', suggesting that even if theoretical knowledge were to be distinguished from practical knowledge, it could still have an indirectly practical application.

The knowledge required for government thus spanned both parts of the line, which is why producing its possessors was so much more difficult than either just teaching a *techne* or simply producing an 'armchair' philosopher. It demanded a kind of qualitative judgement steeped in both theory and practice. Certainly, government belonged firmly to the world of changing appearances. Plato remarked that 'practically nothing in human affairs ever remains stable' and so the task of the ideal king became one of, in contemporary parlance, change management.[63] But to master appearances, we require a kind of knowledge that goes beyond the world of appearances. Dialectic supposedly supplied those who have mastered it with the necessary transferable skills. Dialectic, however, was not analogous to a formal mathematical deduction of an ideally best constitution. For Plato there was no single set of rules that was to be absolutely preferred in all times and all places. Insofar as we could approach the ideally best condition of things, it was by ensuring the right kind of people were in charge.

There was, nevertheless, a fundamental sense in which Plato's account of the knowledge of the philosopher ruler, or of the ideal statesman, remained a rationalistic one. Though human affairs were always changing, they did so in accordance with fixed rules. Things here on earth were always striving after an eternal rational pattern, although their incorrigibly flawed material basis prevented them from ever fully conforming to it.[64] Likewise, the task of the ideal king – bringing executive oversight to the legal (judicial), rhetorical (political), and military domains which together comprised the institutions of the polity with the goal of

---

[62] Plato, *Republic*, 525b, had Socrates describe number as 'an essential part of a soldier's education'. In the same passage Socrates told Glaucon that 'our guardian is in fact both a soldier and a philosopher'. We noted above the similarity between Platonic and Confucian ideals, but there is a less commonly observed parallel with the Japanese samurai maxim 'bunbu ichi', or 'pen and sword as one'.

[63] Plato, *Statesman*, 294b.

[64] Plato, *Timaeus*, 39b, had Timaeus say that 'the god kindled ... the Sun ... to bestow upon all ... living things appropriately endowed and taught by the revolution of the Same and the uniform, a share in number'.

maximising the virtues of the different kinds of people living in the city – never changes. The philosopher-ruler's facility with *kairos* in the face of contingency would be impossible without an accompanying theoretical knowledge of the Forms.

Plato's account of the kind of knowledge the philosopher-rulers required suggests another consideration regarding the relationship between the kinds of Forms required for knowledge of human affairs and those involved in knowledge of the natural world discussed above. We saw that, based on the account of the making of the world in the *Timaeus*, the natural and the human worlds were distinct. Yet in Plato's mind they were not fundamentally separate. On the one hand, nature also participated in the Forms, though in an inferior manner. On the other hand, although human beings were made of the same flawed stuff as the rest of the natural world, their detachable rational souls derived their worth from their participation in Goodness and Beauty.[65]

To know nature for Plato was thus equally to know humanity, and to know humanity was likewise to know nature. In the *Timaeus* every soul was given its own star. This idea remains an agreeably poetic notion, but it was taken very literally by ancient astrology and its medieval successors. The motions of the stars were believed to govern, or at least foretell, individual fates, which partly explained the importance of representing their movements mathematically.[66] In the *Timaeus*, living a virtuous life was said to allow one 'to return to his dwelling place in his companion star'.[67] Timaeus warned that being less than virtuous, however, meant that one risked being reincarnated as a woman. This passing piece of chauvinism might seem out of keeping with the argument of the *Republic* that women as well as men could be philosopher-rulers. But in fact, even Socrates still took the view that men were generally better than women at everything.[68] On that note, so out of tune with modern sensibilities, we may turn to the theme of politics.

---

[65] Plato, *Phaedo*, trans. G.M.A. Grube, 100b-d, had Socrates say 'I assume the existence of a Beautiful, itself by itself, of a Good and a Great and all the rest . . . if there is anything beautiful besides the Beautiful itself, it is beautiful for no other reason than that it shares in the Beautiful'.

[66] Peter Adamson, *Philosophy in the Hellenistic and Roman Worlds: A History of Philosophy Without Any Gaps*, vol. 2 (Oxford: Oxford University Press), 199, notes the distinction between 'hard' (deterministic) and 'soft' (predictive) astrology, but points out that there were also astrological sceptics.

[67] Plato, *Timaeus*, 42b.

[68] Plato, *Republic*, 455d, had Glaucon concede that 'If you [Socrates] are saying that one sex is better than the other at practically everything, then you are right.'

Politics

Plato's atypical willingness to entertain a formal role for women in government, despite his belief in their inferiority, may have reflected the fact that his mentor Socrates had acknowledged female teachers.[69] Women philosophers were extremely rare at the time and would thus be likely to have made a powerful impression. The usual fate of women in ancient Athens during Plato's lifetime was a life of domestic sequestration that any independent modern woman would find intolerable.[70] As a result, the idea of the female philosopher-ruler is one of the aspects of Plato's philosophy likely to win contemporary approval. Nevertheless, even if Popper's critique of Plato as a prototype of totalitarian thought must be rejected, we should not forget that on the whole Plato was an inegalitarian elitist whose beliefs generally place him at odds with contemporary democratic values.

The dialogues themselves were frequently critical of democracy, including the Athenian democracy in which Plato lived. In *Gorgias* Socrates made the flat declaration that Athens has had no good politicians. Even Pericles, perhaps the best-known of Athenian democratic statesmen, had corrupted the city by introducing wages for public service.[71] Socrates also uttered the radical claim that he himself was in fact the only true 'politician' in Athens, because he was the only one trying to introduce justice and goodness into the souls of the citizens.[72] Socrates' (possibly fictitious) interlocutor Callicles, represented as a leading citizen in the Athenian democracy, was told bluntly that he was guilty of simply telling the demos whatever it wanted to hear, and of shifting his position whenever his words met with a hostile reception.[73] In Plato's mind, Callicles' conduct was presumably typical of the democratic politician.

---

[69] See the Introduction, n. 53.

[70] Modern scholarship has suggested that women's status changed over the centuries and that by late antiquity, women's education was probably more common: see Edward J. Watts, *Hypatia: The Life and Legend of an Ancient Philosopher* (Oxford: Oxford University Press, 2017), 25. But the exclusion of women from public life was never complete: see Przemysław Siekierka, Krystyna Stebnicka and Aleksander Wolicki, *Women and the Polis: Public Honorific Inscriptions for Women in the Greek Cities from the Late Classical to the Roman Period*, vol. 1 (Berlin and Boston: Walter de Gruyter GmbH, 2021). Nevertheless, in general 'women lived much of their lives' in 'the private sphere': see Beryl Rawson, 'From "Daily life" to "Demography"', in Richard Hawley and Barbara Levick, *Women in Antiquity: New Assessments* (London: Routledge, 1995), 13.

[71] Plato, *Gorgias*, 515e, 517a.

[72] Plato, *Gorgias*, 503b, 521d.

[73] Plato, *Gorgias*, 481c.

Whether Plato was completely opposed to democracy in practice, even if it fell far short of his ideals, has nevertheless been debated. Both the *Laws* and the *Statesman*, two of the later dialogues in which the main interlocutors are not Socrates but unnamed philosophers from Athens and Elea respectively, have been cited as evidence for the view that later in life, Plato was more willing to compromise with the messiness of democracy. Sara Monoson has argued that 'ambivalence' rather than 'unequivocal hostility' best describes Plato's overall attitude to democracy.[74] In further support of this position, one could note that even in the *Republic*, which was devoted to the discussion of the ideally best city, Socrates remarked that democracy was attractive to many because of the freedom of speech and individualistic way of life that it permitted.[75]

Plato never explained why Socrates failed to appear, but one suggestion is that Socrates was associated with a more idealistic view, and his omission signalled a greater realism, in the form of an increased willingness to accept at least a democratic element in the city. This is consistent with the insistence of the Eleatic Stranger that it was 'absolutely vital' for a polity in which 'freedom and friendship applied with good judgment' were to prevail that the constitution should be a combination of monarchy and democracy.[76] As pure constitutional forms go, the democratic option was described as the third best, after benevolent dictatorship and constitutional monarchy.[77] This interpretation also seems consistent with the argument put forward in the *Statesman* by the Visitor or Eleatic Stranger that democracy was the least objectionable of the flawed types of constitution discussed there.[78]

The interpretation of the *Laws* and the *Statesman* is as contentious as anything else in Plato, however, and the debate over Plato's attitude to democracy also raises a more radical problem, analogous to that of attributing a theory of categories to Plato. We saw that Plato can only be said to have a theory of categories in the broad sense of a concern with fundamental concepts. Likewise, labelling Plato a 'political' thinker is tenable only if we conflate 'politics' with 'government'. Plato was in fact concerned to reject the practice of politics understood as a formal, institutionalised process of debate designed to produce decisions concerning the rules and policies that will shape the future of the community. The

---

[74] S. Sara Monoson, *Plato's Democratic Entanglements: Athenian Politics and the Practice of Philosophy* (Princeton: Princeton University Press, 2000), 3.
[75] Plato, *Republic*, 557b.
[76] Plato, *Laws*, trans. Trevor J. Saunders, 694d.
[77] Plato, *Laws*, 710e.
[78] Plato, *Statesman*, 303b: 'if all the types of constitution are . . . uncontrolled, living in a democracy takes the prize, but if they are ordered, life it in it is least liveable'.

point is well noted by F. E. Sparshott, who has correctly described Plato as in this sense an anti-political thinker. For Sparshott, the term 'politics' implied the existence of just that sort of constitutional framework required for regularising and formalising political argument.[79]

Politics, we are suggesting, was not something that Plato thought his ideal city needed to accommodate, because the kind of knowledge that genuine rulers possessed was designed to make it redundant.[80] Based on the discussion of knowledge above, we can say that, at least in *Republic* and *Statesman*, whatever continuity there was with respect to Plato's views on democracy, the two dialogues still displayed a very similar view of the role of dialectical knowledge based on correct distinctions. In both cases, despite the lack of any explicit reference to the Form of the Good in *Statesman*, the kind of knowledge appropriate to ruling was supposed to make political debate, democratic or otherwise, otiose. After all, given the presence of a philosopher-ruler or an ideal king, it ought to be obvious to all concerned who knew best what to do, or at least how best to direct those more immediately in charge of the actual doing. In such a situation, there was no further need for discussion.

Moreover, insofar as the just city reflected the ideal order of things, the emphasis was on unity, understood on the analogy of harmony or correct proportions according to a predetermined ratio. Argument and disagreement of the sort associated with political debate were disruptive forces. Nothing was gained from the city being at odds with itself, any more than disunion within the soul of the individual was beneficial. Justice was an attunement to a single cosmological norm. While Martin Heidegger's declaration that 'the polis lets the totality of beings come . . . into the unconcealedness of its condition' so that 'Between polis and "Being" there is a primordial relation' may be fanciful if taken as a historical claim about the actuality of Athenian life, it arguably captured something of the tendency of Plato's thinking.[81] Plato really was inclined to think that the city should reflect the independent being of natural, normative hierarchical principles of order. He may have wavered on how far it could do so in practice; that it should at least try to do so as far as was possible was not something he ever seriously doubted.

---

[79] F. E. Sparshott, 'Plato as Anti-political Thinker', in Vlastos, ed., *Plato: A Collection of Critical Essays*, 2 vols (London and Basingstoke: Macmillan, 1972 [1971]), ii.174–86, 181.

[80] Christopher Rowe, 'The Place of the *Republic* in Plato's Political Thought', in *The Cambridge Companion to Plato's Republic*, 27–54, 28, writes that 'there seems no good reason in principle why the construction of utopias should not legitimately be seen as a part of political theorizing', but concedes in the same place that 'the *Republic*, which imagines and argues for the possibility of eradicating political conflict altogether, is no truly "political" work'. The corollary is that utopian thinking is apolitical.

[81] Martin Heidegger, *Parmenides*, trans. André Schuwer and Richard Rojcewicz (Bloomington and Indianapolis: Indiana University Press, 1992), 102.

Sparshott argues that the *Laws* was no exception to Plato's anti-political orientation. Although it did make 'a most elaborate set of provisions for the selection of authorities' according to voting procedures that are 'closer to the practice of modern representative government than to that of Plato's own time and place', no place was allotted in the dialogue to 'the actual dynamics of the politicking within the constitutional framework'.[82] Plato was typically suspicious of political rhetoric and associated it with Sophism. It is true that Plato had Socrates say in *Phaedrus* that 'writing speeches is not in itself a shameful thing'.[83] Still, the only speeches that Socrates found acceptable were those that reached the truth, understood as a dialectical grasp of the correct definitions of the objects of discourse.[84]

Plato was no doubt right to distinguish between the truth of a speech and its persuasiveness. But how the terms of this distinction were drawn is important. Sparshott's point about Plato's lack of interest in 'politicking' points to the fact that political decision-making is necessarily undertaken under conditions of imperfect information, because the future is unknown and often unpredictable. This consideration suggests that even constructive political discourse that avoids being simply manipulative and deceitful can never derive its value entirely from its truth, because propositions about the future either have no truth value or their truth value is unknowable.[85] Political discourse cannot escape the weighing of likely consequences in ignorance of actual outcomes. Aristotle, we will see below, accepted this as a feature rather than a defect of political rhetoric. But Plato was committed to assessing political discourse in terms of a hard distinction 'between a dream-image and the reality of what is just and unjust'.[86]

The ideal Platonic community achieved justice not because it was fair, the criterion of justice for much contemporary thought thanks to John Rawls, but because in it everyone occupied their proper place.[87] This view,

---

[82] Sparshott, 'Plato as Anti-political Thinker', 180–1.
[83] Plato, *Phaedrus*, trans. Alexander Nehamas and Paul Woodruff, 258d.
[84] Plato, *Phaedrus*, 260e.
[85] Aristotle would later address this problem of the truth value of propositions about the future directly; see Chapter 2, below.
[86] Plato, *Phaedrus*, 277d–e.
[87] John Rawls, *A Theory of Justice*, revised edn (Harvard: Belknap Press, 1999 [1971]), 9 and n. 3, argued that his conception of justice as fairness was consistent with classical tradition because, for example, it conformed to Aristotle's condemnation of *pleonexia*, or 'gaining some advantage for oneself by seizing what belongs to another' in a manner 'inconsistent with what properly belongs to a person and what is due to him'. But even if this interpretation could be extended to Plato, Rawls did not share the metaphysical considerations that informed Plato's understanding of what was proper to a person. Compare the discussion of the myth of the metals, above.

however, rested on the prior assumption that everything did in fact have a place proper to it. In mathematical terms the Platonic ideal of justice could be expressed as a conformity to a ratio. This mathematical criterion was at the same time an aesthetic standard that applied to music in particular. Justice was analogous to a correct tuning in which the distance between higher and lower conformed to naturally fixed proportions. Hence the exclusion of certain forms of music from the city.[88]

Plato argued that constitutional changes became more likely when the wrong sorts of music disturbed the equilibrium of the different parts of the soul, disordering it and producing disruptive forms of conduct. Certain musical instruments, and certain musical scales, were held to produce almost irresistible stirrings in the soul towards what Plato considered disorderly conduct. The use of the pipes in the orgiastic, Dionysiac, mystery cults was a prime example of the conjunction of an inappropriate type of music with an unruly variety of religious devotion that Plato considered wholly unsuited to a city in which the regulation of procreation was vitally important.

Considering the history of moral panics that have repeatedly been set off in contemporary society by musical change, we may still agree with Plato, though for very different reasons, that 'Changes in styles of music are always politically revolutionary.'[89] The modern world has witnessed repeated moral panics and episodes of political censorship thanks to the emergence of new musical genres; from jazz to rock'n'roll to hip hop, the walls of the city trembled with virtually every passing generation in

---

[88] Plato, *Republic*, 399c, has Socrates say that the ideal city will permit only 'two modes' of music, 'One for adversity and one for freely chosen activity, the modes which will best imitate the voices of the prudent and of the brave in failure and success.'

[89] Plato, *Republic*, 424c. This famous observation has been variously translated. Benjamin Jowett offered 'when modes of music change, the fundamental laws of the State always change with them': see *The Dialogues of Plato Translated into English with Analyses and Introductions by B. Jowett, M.A.*, 5 vols., 3rd edn (Oxford, Oxford University Press, 1931 [1871]), iii.113. However, the use of 'State' anachronistically imports a kind of institution altogether unknown in the ancient world. Allan Bloom's 'never are the ways of music moved without the greatest political laws being moved' is a far more literal rendition: see *The Republic of Plato Translated with Notes and an Interpretation Essay by Allan Bloom* (USA: Basic Books, 1991 [1968]), 102. But the phrase 'political laws' is still misleading unless it is understood as referring to 'the laws of the polity'; Plato did not think the laws of his ideal community were 'political' in the modern sense of being the products of interested contestation and negotiation.

the twentieth century. Plato also extended the criterion of musical exclusion by analogy to other forms of art in a manner likewise redolent with contemporary parallels. Misrepresentations of the gods by the poets or on the stage could have similar effects to the wrong kind of music.[90] In modernity, modern art forms including film, television, and video games have all provoked analogous worries about destructive forms of imitative behaviour undermining social ties.

This theme of social solidarity is very important in considering the Platonic ideal of justice. We should appreciate that Plato regarded the different classes of the community as completely mutually dependent. The philosopher-rulers could not, in the end, live their lives of communal austerity and devote themselves entirely to ruling without a much larger class of persons whose agricultural and manufacturing activities supported them. Likewise, the farmers and artisans needed guidance from those with the appropriate knowledge to ensure that self-destructive tensions did not flare up in their community. These complementarities and dependencies were fully compatible with hierarchy and inequality. Indeed, they were demanded by inequality, which was nothing other than the way in which the differences between human beings expressed themselves. Some were stronger, some were weaker; some were more intelligent, some were less so. None of this, in Plato's mind at least, inhibited the creation of a strong form of communal cohesion in which all classes of society and all individuals cared for one another as best as they were able.

Whether this society represented a practical goal is a perennial question for Plato scholars. Harvey Yunus has suggested that the *Republic* is an example of protreptic rhetoric, in the sense that its arguments are presented 'in such a way that the reader would most be likely to be compelled by them to choose to live in a particular way'.[91] This was far from suggesting that the plan of *kallipolis*, as the ideal city is known in the *Republic*, was itself feasible. Yet Aristotle, who was well-placed to know Plato's intentions, tended to treat the *Republic* as containing at least some proposals that were within the realms of practical possibility, for instance its strongly communal character (a feature that has attracted socialist

---

[90] Plato, *Republic*, trans. Griffith, 604c, had Socrates say that 'the imitative poet sets up a bad regime in the soul of each individual, gratifying the senseless part of it'.

[91] Harvey Yunus, 'The Protreptic Rhetoric of the Republic', in *Cambridge Companion to Plato's Republic*, 1–26, 2.

interpretations in a modern context). Citizens could in principle 'have wives and children and property in common, as Socrates proposes as in the *Republic* of Plato'.[92]

Aristotle was typically critical of Plato's proposals, however. One of his greatest objections was that the *Republic* placed excessive emphasis on unity. He criticised 'the supposition from which the argument of Socrates proceeds [is] that it is best for the whole state to be as unified as possible' on the grounds that 'the nature of the state is to be a plurality'.[93] Perhaps Aristotle did not give enough credit to Plato's acknowledgment of the positive role played by difference and inequality. But in the last resort, Plato's view of government, like his view of the Forms and of knowledge more generally, was still organised around an ascending hierarchy determined by the capacity for a vision of unity. Later neo-Platonic tradition identified the timeless and changeless Form of the Good with the One, and Christian theology followed in treating God as simple (whence the notorious difficulties of Trinitarianism).[94]

Even in the transient world of appearances, the elimination of change was also a Platonic ideal, insofar as it was possible. Hence Plato's considerable admiration for ancient Egypt, which he imagined had come closest of all the actual communities he was familiar with to instituting a permanent frame of government.[95] In reality, of course, ancient Egypt experienced plenty of change, and was far from the immobile kingdom of Plato's imagination. Nevertheless, Plato's vision of Egyptian stability, as we will now see, was revealing of a certain attitude towards historicity.

---

[92] Aristotle, *Politics*, in *Aristotle's Politics: Writings from the Complete Works: Politics, Economics, Constitution of Athens*, ed. J. Barnes, intro. M. Lane, trans. Benjamin Jowett (Princeton: Princeton University Press, 2016), 1261.

[93] Aristotle, *Politics*, 1261a. See also Chapter 2, below.

[94] See Plotinus, *Enneads*, vi.303: 'It is by the one that all beings are beings, both those which are primarily beings and those which are in any sense said to be among beings. For what could anything be if it was not one?' Compare Thomas Aquinas, *On Being and Essence: A Translation and Interpretation*, trans. Joseph Bobik (Notre Dame: University of Notre Dame Press, 2007 [1965]), 63, where God is described as 'that simple substance which is first'.

[95] Plato, *Laws*, 1347e, has the Athenian claim that 'ten thousand years ago (and I'm not speaking loosely: I mean literally ten thousand), paintings and reliefs were produced [in Egypt] that are no better and no worse than those of today, because the same artistic rules were applied in making them', something described as 'a supreme achievement of legislators and statesmen'. The source of the inspiration for the artistic policies set out in the *Republic* may possibly have been this fantasy of pharaohism.

History

Our account of Plato's views on knowledge and politics has made plain that he thought human affairs required separate theoretical and practical treatment, even if they were part of a larger continuum. Socrates, sitting in his cell as a condemned man, remarked that any explanation of how he had come to be there in terms of what we would call physical or material causes would be inadequate.[96] But Socrates did not spend his final hours in trying to understand his fate as an outcome of the events that had shaped the Athenian polity. He wanted, rather, to convince his friends of the immortality of their souls. Moral and theological questions, not historical ones, occupied him.

The idea that Plato was concerned with history at all may thus be thought to need justification. Reputable authority contends that philosophical interest in history only began at a later period, under the influence of Christianity.[97] It is undeniably true that Christianity caused a major reorientation of attitudes towards history, by introducing for the first time a theological perspective centred on the revelation of a future apocalypse at which a last judgement would take place. There was certainly no equivalent of this idea of the historical process in Graeco-Roman antiquity, which tended to regard the present as a decline from an earlier ideal, a process which was itself iterative. But to say that Plato thought of history as altogether irrelevant can be challenged on several grounds.

We should remember that the *Republic* was the first in a trilogy of dialogues. It is referred to in *Timaeus*, which is in turn referred to in *Critias*. The *Republic* introduced a theory of history as a cyclical process in which even the most ideal condition of things was doomed to decay; *Timaeus* related a speculative and mythological natural history which located the contemporary world in a phase of increased cosmological disorder; and *Critias* concluded the trilogy with a mythological account of a war between Athens and Atlantis that supposedly took place thousands of years earlier. Thus, in all three dialogues Plato was concerned with

---

[96] Plato, *Phaedo*, 98e, has Socrates criticise Anaxagoras for identifying Mind with 'air and ether and water . . . sounds and air and hearing', which would lead to saying that he was present in a condemned cell 'because my body consists of bones and sinews', rather than because 'the Athenians decided . . . to condemn me'.

[97] Peter Adamson, *Medieval Philosophy: A History of Philosophy Without any Gaps*, vol. 4 (Oxford: Oxford University Press, 2019), 79, writes that 'Religion put the history into the history of philosophy. The pagans of antiquity by and large saw history as irrelevant to a philosophical understanding of the world.'

both the processes specific to human affairs and with the larger setting of which human history was a reflection.

The human world was explicitly recognised in *Critias* as a distinct problem. Plato had Critias say that 'human life is no easy subject for representation, but is rather one of great difficulty'.[98] In telling his tale, Critias was made to stress the importance of documentary evidence. The authority of his tale was clearly supposed to be enhanced by the claim that it was based on manuscripts of Greek translations from Egyptian sources by the Athenian lawgiver Solon himself.[99] But the ultimate purpose of the narrative seems to have been to inspire contemporary Athenians. For example, according to Critias himself, their distant ancestors were 'the leaders of the rest of the Greek world, which followed them willingly'.[100]

The claim that 'no particular historical event figured importantly' in Plato's world-view can thus be qualified by the observation that the founding of Athens certainly seems to have done so.[101] Moreover, the Athenian founding was of interest not chiefly in its own right but as an instance of a belief on Plato's part in the importance of founding moments generally. The founding of Sparta, and that of Crete, were both specifically mentioned in the *Laws*. But these events were likewise significant not for their own sake but as exemplary cases. The goal was to 'get some idea of what was right and wrong in the way these foundations were established' and if possible, to identify 'what kind of laws are responsible for continued preservation of the features that survive and the ruin of those that collapse' (thus prefiguring Aristotle's interest in cataloguing the Greek constitutions in a way that also investigated the circumstances of their establishment).[102]

Plato was writing at a point where history was still imperfectly recognised as a distinct genre of writing. Aristotle was apparently the first to use the term 'history' to refer to historiography specifically, rather than in the more general sense of a research report still associated with Herodotus.[103]

---

[98] Plato, *Critias*, tr. Diskin Clay, 108e
[99] Plato, *Critias*, 113b. Solon is also represented as discussing Egyptian history and its relation to Greek history in *Timaeus*, 21a.
[100] Plato, *Critias*, 112d.
[101] Adamson, *Medieval Philosophy*, 79.
[102] Plato, *Laws*, 683a.
[103] Christian Meier, 'Historical Answers to Historical Questions: The Origins of History in Ancient Greece', *Arethusa*, 20:1–2 (1987), 41–58, 41. Meier argues that Herodotus's work was continuous with the Ionian tradition of the critical investigation of nature and that his novelty lay in applying this perspective to the explanation of human affairs in fully contingent, long-run, 'multi-subjective' terms.

But the remark given to Critias on what we would call the sociological conditions of historical knowledge suggests that Plato already saw history as a distinct activity: 'it is in the train of Leisure that Mythology and Inquiry into the Past arrive in cities, once they have observed that in the case of some peoples the necessities of life have been secure'.[104] Moreover, while Plato never mentioned his older contemporary Thucydides, several references suggest familiarity with Herodotus's *Histories*, at least at second hand.[105]

Plato's assessment of this emerging genre was in some ways clearly negative. In addition to the presumably unflattering association with mythology just noted, he connected historical discourse with Sophistry, an association that long survived him.[106] To Plato, Athens was a city in which various aspects of the past were commemorated to the point of cliché.[107] In *Greater Hippias*, for instance, Socrates asked Hippias what his Spartan audiences typically enjoyed hearing him speak on, and Hippias replied that although they dislike 'things about stars and movements in the sky', they 'love to hear about ... the genealogies of heroes and men ... and the settlements (how cities were founded in ancient times), and in a word all ancient history'.[108]

Socrates was dismissive of this response, saying to Hippias that 'the Spartans ... use you the way children use old ladies, to tell stories for pleasure'.[109] But as we have established, Plato himself could find interest in genealogies and foundations, so long as they were studied for the correct purposes. The problem with the Sophistic approach was not the interest in history as such, or indeed the subject matter, but the goal of the inquiry. An interest in the history of particular events without

---

[104] Plato, *Critias*, 110a.
[105] Cooper notes that several stories in Plato also appeared in Herodotus's *Histories*: see *Euthydemus* 299e, 738 and n. 23; *Republic* 453d, 1081, n. 5; and *Laws* 694c, 1383, n. 20.
[106] Emily Baragwanath, *Motivation and Narrative in Herodotus* (Oxford: Oxford University Press, 2008), 56, points out that Plutarch accused Herodotus of passing off sophistry as history, but notes that Herodotus may well have considered himself a sophist in a pre-Platonic, non-pejorative, sense, given that historiography was not identified as a distinct genre at the time when he was writing.
[107] Plato, *Lysis*, trans. Stanley Lombardo, 205c, has Ctesippus complain that when Hippothales tries to show his liking for Lysis 'All he can think of to say or write is stuff the whole city goes around singing – poems about Democrates and the boy's grandfather Lysis and all his ancestors, their wealth and their stables and their victories at the Pythian, Isthmian, and Nemean Games in the chariot races and the horseback races. And then he gets into the really ancient history.'
[108] Plato, *Greater Hippias*, trans. Paul Woodruff, 285e.
[109] Ibid. 285e.

a more general aim could only be regarded as an idle pleasure. Yet if history were treated as exemplary, then Plato could attribute to it genuine philosophical value.

Although the *Republic* gave the philosopher-ruler no specific course of instruction in history, the *Laws* treated history as capable of reinforcing the conclusions of philosophy by adding a factual basis to the results of philosophical speculation.[110] Hence Plato's interest in particular examples of constitutions like those of Sparta and Crete. They were relevant to understanding how to manage, and if possible delay, the onset of the ultimately inevitable process of decline from the ideally best form of government outlined in the *Republic*. Fighting this rearguard action, we noted above, was one of the main tasks of philosophic rule.[111] But at some point the effort to maintain the ideally just society would always definitively fail, to be followed by an unavoidable process of socio-political decline as different kinds of regime succeeded one another.

In Plato we thus find an early example of what we would now call a 'speculative philosophy of history', associated in modernity with figures such as Kant and Marx. History understood in this way is a necessary process, typically divided into a series of stages, in which the eventual future destination is already determined, at least in general outline. In Plato's account, timarchy, oligarchy, democracy and tyranny inevitably succeeded one another as conditions gradually approached the limits of misery and abjection for rulers and ruled alike.

Plato regarded this historical process as part of the natural order of things, at least in this phase of the cosmological revolution (in the pre-modern sense of the term relating to circular motion). As Michel Foucault observed, 'in Plato's *The Statesman* the interlocutors recognize that they belong to one of those revolutions of the world in which the world is turning backwards'.[112] The god responsible for directing the rotation of the universe in a direction that ensured a benign relationship between all living things has left his station, and now things have gone into reverse.[113]

---

[110] Plato, *Laws*, 683a–684a, had the Athenian say 'now we can put our thesis on a firmer footing, because it looks as if our study of history has led us to the same conclusion as before. This means we shall carry on our investigation on the basis of the actual facts rather than conjecture.'

[111] See Plato, *Republic*, 545d ff.

[112] See Michel Foucault, 'What is Enlightenment?', in *The Foucault Reader*, ed. Paul Rabinow (New York: Pantheon Books, 1984), 32–50, 33.

[113] See Plato, *Statesman*, 271d, 272e.

Societies were thus like individual organisms; all were fated to die in the end. Plato suggested, however, that this process occurred in a predictable way. He offered the hypothesis that all political change resulted from strife within the ruling group. Thus, for as long as a unified governing class could be preserved, change could be resisted, potentially (as in the Egyptian case) for a very long time. While all life, including human life, was in the last analysis cyclical, proceeding according to mathematical rules, those in charge of a community would do best when they governed in accordance with rather than in ignorance of these animating principles.[114] An important consideration here was that one must know the kind of people one was governing. The analogy between the tripartite structure of the soul of the individual and the three divisions of the city was crucial to the construction of the ideal community in the *Republic*, but it held equally good for all constitutions.

So there was, for instance, a democratic persona that was the corollary of a democratic constitution. Democracy for Plato represented the rule of the poor.[115] It arose once strife in the ruling oligarchy had allowed the poor to rise up and overthrow their rulers. The new constitution was 'full of freedom and freedom of speech', and was thus superficially highly attractive.[116] Democracies were full of variety, and also practised legal equality even amongst unequals, including between the sexes.[117] But democratic citizens were uncritical, 'paying no attention to what kind of life someone led before he entered political life'.

All that a would-be tyrant needed to do was 'to win favour is say he is a friend of the people', promising, as it were, to make Athens great again.[118] Democratic citizens were also spendthrifts, impoverishing themselves by pursuing unnecessary desires that went beyond not only what was necessary for bare life but even for well-being.[119] They were not indifferent to questions of government or even to philosophical ones, but they lacked the self-discipline to properly pursue the kinds of knowledge that ruling and philosophy required. This was because they had no capacity for taking a sustained interest in political questions; their views were dictated by the impulses of the moment.[120]

---

[114] See Cooper's note to Plato, *Republic*, 546b, p. 1158, n. 8, for an explanation of Socrates' remark that there is a 'perfect number' that 'controls better and worse births', and which turns out to be $(3.4.5)^4$ in modern notation.
[115] See Plato, *Republic*, 545d ff.
[116] Plato, *Republic*, 557b.
[117] Plato, *Republic*, 558c, 561e, 563b.
[118] Plato, *Republic*, 558b.
[119] Plato, *Republic*, 559b.
[120] Plato, *Republic*, 559b.

In the end, democracy was destroyed, ironically enough, by its own love of freedom. Authority of any kind was rejected, even the authority necessary to sustain the constitution of the city itself. For example, education in a democracy collapsed because the inherent inequality in the teacher–student relationship was denied: 'In a society of this sort teachers are afraid of their pupils and curry favour with them, Pupils have an equal contempt for their teachers.'[121] The unwillingness of the individual democratic citizen to tolerate restraints or limits of any kind served as the source of divisions within the ruling group, which in this case was the entirety of the citizenry.[122] Democracy thus split into three main factions.

First, there were those who Plato calls its 'fiercest element' which 'does the talking and acting'. These in turn have followers who are known for 'refusing to allow the expression of any other view'. In contemporary terms, according to Plato, the chattering classes become the sponsors of cancel culture. Meanwhile, a second, minority, group emerged that concentrated on making money. A few rich people generated the wealth that sustained the first group; Plato calls them the 'drones' feeding ground' because they were like the bees who made the honey.[123]

Finally, there was the working class, composed neither of the drones nor of the wealthy but of the majority of artisans and farmers. Democracy finally collapsed altogether once the drones incited the majority against the wealthy, and 'there are impeachments, litigation, and lawsuits' on both sides.[124] The response of the majority was to 'set up one single individual who is their own particular champion'.[125] All sides having made themselves the victims of their own personalities, tyranny ensued.

Although Plato did not really take up the question of what followed tyranny, the picture he presented was arguably not an entirely hopeless one, insofar as he was explicit that nature is also capable of renewal. He was silent on the question of whether we may once again establish something close to the ideally best society on the ruins of a tyranny. But he did imply at the start of the discussion that socio-political processes are analogous to natural processes in being circular: 'Both for plants in the ground and for animals above the ground . . . the cycles of begetting for each species complete their revolutions.'[126] There was even a suggestion

---

[121] Plato, *Republic*, 563a.
[122] Plato, *Republic*, 562c.
[123] Plato, *Republic*, 564e.
[124] Plato, *Republic*, 565c.
[125] Plato, *Republic*, 565c.
[126] Plato, *Republic*, 546a.

that at some point the god will return to his post and will institute immortality and agelessness.[127]

This discussion indicates that rather than thinking of historical processes as philosophically unimportant, Plato integrated human history into a broader, speculative and quasi-mythical, natural history. But the question remains of how best to characterise the difference between Plato's view of history and the kind of emerging historical consciousness represented by authors like Herodotus and Thucydides. The issue is an important one. Raymond Geuss has noted that Friedrich Nietzsche believed 'an issue of real philosophical substance' was involved in the choice between a Thucydidean and a Platonic outlook.[128] But it is important to understand exactly what Nietzsche thought was at stake.

It might be tempting to assume that Nietzsche was arguing in favour of a view of historiography as the inversion of the ideal of knowledge contained in the Platonic myth of the cave. Such an image was perfectly possible in Nietzsche's day. Ernst Cassirer interpreted the Roman historian Barthold Niebuhr's remark that writing history was akin to learning to see in the darkness as a vindication of the interest of the cave-life that Plato had dismissed in favour of the sunlight of the Forms.[129] Nor would this be an unreasonable reading of the ancient Greek sources themselves, given Christian Meier's remark that in coming to understand human existence historically, the Greeks were learning to 'endure the perception of contingency'.[130] Meier suggests that Greek historiography made this perception of contingency central, whereas Plato wanted to marginalise it in favour of the universal aspects of existence.

In fact, however, Nietzsche was less interested in the differences between historical and philosophical knowledge that he found in Plato and Thucydides than in their contrasting ethical perspectives. Thucydides seemed to Nietzsche to have a greater sense of the complex realities of

---

[128] Raymond Geuss, 'Thucydides, Nietzsche, and Williams', in *Outside Ethics* (Princeton: Princeton University Press, 2005), 219–33, 219.

[129] Ernst Cassirer, *The Problem of Knowledge: Philosophy, Science, and History since Hegel*, trans. William H. Woglom and Charles W. Hendel (New Haven: Yale University Press, 1950), 229, attributed to Barthold Niebuhr, nineteenth-century German historian of Rome, a view of historical knowledge as the 'opposite' of the ideal of knowledge put forward in Plato's myth of the cave. Cassirer was citing an anecdote in G. P. Gooch, *History and Historians in the Nineteenth Century* (London, New York, and Toronto: Longmans, Green, and Co., 1935), 19, which related that Niebuhr compared the historian 'to a man in a cell whose eyes gradually become so accustomed to the darkness that he can perceive objects which one newly entering not only does not see but declares to be invisible'.

[130] Meier, 'Historical Answers', 50.

moral life than Plato. In other respects, for all Nietzsche's self-proclaimed differences with Plato, as we shall see in more detail below, the conception of history he actually endorsed was not what we might now call analytic historiography, for which everything that happens in human affairs could have been otherwise, but rather, the kind of exemplary and inspirational use of it that Plato himself was demanding.[131]

Indeed, although Plato was writing at a time when historiography was becoming recognised as a distinct genre in a way that permitted a contrast between history and philosophy as distinct genres of thinking, this should not obscure what he and Thucydides had in common. Both were interested, as Geuss also points out, in 'understanding those forms of collective human behaviour that are recurrent and thus comprehensible'.[132] Thucydides was interested in the causes of the war between Athens and Sparta not simply as a historical problem, but also because the same kind of events were bound to recur in the future.[133] As we have established, Plato too thought of historical change in terms of repeatable cycles of events. Likewise, just as Plato regarded the Forms as supplying fixed moral standards, Thucydides thought of his highly detailed narratives of events as illustrating timeless moral truths, such as the dangers of hubris.

In important respects, then, Thucydides and Plato were more alike than treating them as opposing representatives of history and philosophy would suggest. Nietzsche's choice, at least in some respects, was misleading. Thucydides saw history, just as Plato saw philosophy, as a propaedeutic for practical reasoning in politics and morals.[134] Both thinkers were motivated to study historical states of affairs as typical, and not with respect to their individuality.

While Thucydides' explanations of events do engage with particular circumstances, his motivation was supplied at least part by a focus on what was universal, and he was also convinced that he was studying a series of events that were exemplary. In this regard both Thucydides and Plato are more akin to modern social scientists who study n instances of a certain type of phenomenon than either are to modern historians concerned with an individual sequence of events. Plato's claim that all political change was the product of a crisis in a ruling elite is the kind of hypothesis that

---

[131] See Chapter 5, below.
[132] Geuss, *Outside Ethics*, 227.
[133] Thucydides, *History of the Peloponnesian War*, trans. Martin Hammond, intro. P. J. Rhodes (Oxford: Oxford University Press, 2009), 12, wrote that 'what happened ... such is the human condition, will happen again at some time in the same or a similar pattern'.
[134] Guess, *Outside Ethics*, 229.

a modern social scientist would recognise as testable, though of course Plato could not take a statistical approach to its verification.

This understanding of Plato's view of history integrates his views on the understanding of the human past into his broader reflections on categories, knowledge and politics. But it also indicates why it could be so readily integrated with the Christian conception of the past that would succeed it. While Christianity was in one sense a narrative of unique events, so that, in the words of the Nicene creed, there is only 'one Lord Jesus Christ, the only Son of God', the story of the life of Jesus acquired the same inspirational and exemplary functions as the Platonic myth of the Athenian past. Moreover, Platonism and Christianity shared the belief that human history was part of a necessary process. Although in the Christian view, history was a process that would only occur once, rather than being cyclical, as for Platonism, it was still a process in which the main events had to happen just as they did, while everything else could be dismissed as incidental. The incarnation was a condition of salvation, just as decay was a condition for a return to the ideal. Platonism and eschatology turned out to fit very neatly together.

Conclusion

This chapter has argued that Plato's writings connected his discussions of the Forms, which we treated as categories in the sense of fundamental concepts arranged in a unified hierarchy, to his conception of knowledge. The movement from practice to theory culminated in a direct vision of the Good crucial for successful government, which should ideally be conducted exclusively by those who had mastered this dialectic. In turn this involved a view of history as cyclical and exemplary, which ultimately made all government an exercise in delaying the inevitable. We did not argue, however, that these relationships were necessary.

The theory of Forms was Plato's solution to the problem of how we understand the visible in terms of the invisible. But a solution of this kind need not presuppose, for instance, that the Forms or categories must be arranged hierarchically. Even if one were to insist on a hierarchy, one need not put dialectic at the top. One might decide instead that mathematics should have pride of place. Nor is it obvious, even if one opts for dialectics as the highest form of knowledge, that this should be the best qualification to rule. This only follows if we are willing to accept other premises, such as that genuine knowledge consists of self-evident definitions, and that these definitions are required for telling one set of circumstances from another in a way that constitutes good political judgement.

Yet even if the links between Plato's ideas about categories, knowledge, politics and history were in no sense logically necessary, the sum of their relations was anything but a heap. Plato's writings were not simply a set of disparate convictions. They formed a tightly interwoven and distinctive pattern. Together his arguments constituted a 'web of belief', to use Quine's phrase, not because they logically entailed one another, but because, irrespective of their soundness, they could be treated as mutually reinforcing. What we shall see as we move forward is that the connections in Plato between the themes of categories, knowledge, politics and history established a pattern that was important in a formal or structural sense.

It was possible in other words for the content of some or all Plato's positions to be amended or even rejected and for the pattern of association between them to continue to hold good. As we shall show in the next chapter, this was certainly true of Aristotle. Aristotle has lately come to be recognised as closer to Plato in many of his substantive opinions than was once acknowledged. But we shall argue that however he did or did not depart from Plato with respect to particular issues, Aristotle fully shared Plato's habit of connecting the subjects of categories, knowledge, politics and history.

2

Aristotle: Categories as not-Forms, or Substances

This second chapter examines how Aristotle's categories, and in particular the categories of primary and secondary substance, were linked with both his account of the different genres of knowledge and with his political thought. The main source for Aristotle's ideas on categories is the *Categories* itself, a short work with an importance in the history of philosophy inversely proportionate to its length. For centuries, its Latin translation served medieval readers as an introduction to logic and thus by convention to philosophy as a whole.[1] During that period, the *Categories* was one of only two works by Aristotle known to Latin Christendom. The medieval world did not become fully aware of the enormous range of Aristotle's writings until the recovery in the twelfth century of most of the remaining works in the corpus that we have today.[2] But just about everything else about the *Categories* other than its importance has been disputed.[3]

---

[1] In Aristotle, *Categories and De Interpretatione*, trans. J. L. Ackrill (Oxford: Clarendon Press, 2002 [1963]), 69, Ackrill notes that 'In the traditional ordering of Aristotle's works the logical treatises (the Organon) come first. Among the logical treatises the *Categories* and *De Interpretatione* come first, followed by the *Analytics*. This is because the *Categories* deals with terms, the constituents of propositions, the *De Interpretatione* deals with propositions, the constituents of syllogisms, and the *Analytics* deals with syllogisms.' Ackrill also remarks that 'This traditional ordering is systematic, and is therefore not a guide to the actual chronology of the writings.'

[2] The other was *De Interpretatione*. For the transmission and translation into Latin of Aristotle's works (effectively their second recovery in the history of Western thought, since his writings were also lost for an extended period in the Hellenistic era), see Gábor Betegh, 'The Transmission of Ancient Wisdom: Texts, Doxographies, Libraries', in *The Cambridge History of Philosophy in Late Antiquity*, vol. I, ed. Lloyd P. Gerson (Cambridge: Cambridge University Press, 2010), 25–38, and Bernard G. Dod, 'Aristoteles Latinus', in *The Cambridge History of Later Medieval Philosophy From the Rediscovery of Aristotle to the Disintegration of Scholasticism 1100–1600*, ed. Norman Kretzmann, Anthony Kenny and Jan Pinborg, associate ed. Eleonore Stump (Cambridge: Cambridge University Press, 1997 [1982]), 45–79.

[3] Paul Studtmann, 'Aristotle's Categorial Scheme', in *The Oxford Handbook of Aristotle*, ed. Christopher Shields (Oxford: Oxford University Press, 2012), 63–80, 64, writes that

Aristotle's list of ten categories, consisting of 'things said without any combination', raised questions of how many categories there were.[4] But people were definitely included; they came under the heading of primary substances. The individual person was 'called a substance most strictly, primarily, and most of all'. This also opened the question of the nature of categories themselves.[5] Aristotle was explicitly critical in his *Metaphysics* of Plato's arguments concerning the Forms, and we have said that the categories should be understood as 'not-Forms'.[6] Even when Aristotle departed from Plato, he was still responding to him. But the fact that Aristotle was often critical of Plato's arguments should not obscure the significant continuities between them.[7] Aristotle shared Plato's affinity for hierarchy as an organising principle in both knowledge and politics. He likewise shared Plato's belief that the most valuable forms of knowledge were universal, necessary and demonstrative.

A lasting disagreement concerns whether Aristotle's categories were a classification of linguistic terms, or whether they marked divisions in the phenomena themselves.[8] Some notable ancient commentators took the former view.[9] Modern interpreters have tended to read Aristotle as not simply providing a theory of language, because he thought that in dealing with the words, one could deal at the same time with the things

---

'there is hardly any discussion of the *Categories* that either in substance or in emphasis will not appear to some scholar or other as seriously wrongheaded'. The present discussion is doubtless no exception.

[4] Aristotle, *Categories*, 1b.

[5] Aristotle, *Categories*, 2a.

[6] Aristotle, *Metaphysics, Translated With Introduction and Notes By* C.D.C. Reeve (Indianapolis: Hackett Publishing Company, Inc.), 1059b, writes 'that the Forms do not exist is clear'.

[7] Miles Burnyeat, 'Platonism and Mathematics: A Prelude to Discussion', in *Explorations in Ancient and Modern Philosophy*, 4 vols (Cambridge: Cambridge University Press, 2012), ii.145–72, 145, writes that 'Aristotle and Plato agree that the sciences which are central to our understanding of the world are those which study the paradigm cases of being and goodness ... The disagreement between Aristotle and Plato is about where the paradigm cases of being and goodness are to be found: in the hierarchy of natural kinds studied by theology and natural philosophy, or in the hierarchy of abstract structure revealed by mathematics and dialectic.'

[8] Robin Smith, 'Logic', *The Cambridge Companion to Aristotle*, ed. Jonathan Barnes (Cambridge: Cambridge University Press, 1999 [1995]), 27–65, 55–6, points to at least three interpretations of the categories – as types of predicates, as highest genera and as terms for relations.

[9] For example, Porphyry, *On Aristotle Categories*, trans. Steven K. Strange (London: Bloomsbury Academic, 2014 [1992]), 32–3, argued for the view that 'the treatise cannot be about the genera of being nor about things *qua* things at all, but is instead about the words that are used to signify things'.

themselves.[10] Aristotle thus understood the categories as fundamentally connected to knowledge.

All knowledge, whether practical or theoretical, was to do with substances, Aristotle's term for the various entities collectively comprising reality. Human beings were the most important kind of earthly substance, but substances formed a hierarchy, and Aristotle placed a divine being or prime mover at its summit. Like Plato, Aristotle sought a rational, post-Homeric, approach to religion in which the gods were no longer anthropomorphised.[11] Also like Plato, Aristotle thought that human beings could share in the divine nature insofar as they too were rational creatures.

Rational knowledge for Aristotle was thus theoretical knowledge of what was necessary and universal as such. In its most fully developed form this kind of knowledge involved studying the nature of the divine directly, hence its supreme importance.[12] But the demonstrative, mathematical, sciences also counted as rational knowledge. Perhaps less obviously, so did disciplines like biology and physics.

Aristotle believed that they too led back to the underlying causes of things, which did not change, despite sub-lunary variations in the phenomena that resisted explanation on the mathematical model.[13] To the extent that biology studied kinds, like 'humanity', these were understood as secondary substances. These secondary substances were clearly of a different order to individual members of a species, which could differ significantly from one another and were also subject to change and decay. For Aristotle, natural kinds were timeless; no new species could come into existence.[14]

---

[10] Charles H. Kahn, 'Questions and Categories Aristotle's Doctrine of Categories in the Light of Modern Research', in H. Hiż, ed., *Questions* (Dordrecht: Springer, 1978), 227–78, 268, insists that while there is a linguistic dimension to Aristotle's theory, the theory itself was 'not formulated as a theory of linguistic meaning or linguistic structure' alone.

[11] Jonathan Barnes, 'Metaphysics', in *Cambridge Companion to Aristotle*, 66–108, 104, describes Aristotle as having 'a refined view of the gods'.

[12] As Barnes, 'Metaphysics', 66, points out, 'metaphysics' was not Aristotle's own term but was used by later editors to denote the work coming after the study of physics in the Organon. Aristotle himself used several terms, including 'wisdom', 'primary' or 'first' philosophy, and 'theology' for the sort of knowledge he had in mind.

[13] For Aristotle, the moon marked a spatial boundary between substantial kinds; different rules applied to the heavens to those in operation here on earth. R. J. Hankinson, 'Philosophy of Science', in *The Cambridge Companion to Aristotle*, 109–39, 114, notes that the truths of 'Aristotelian natural science . . . tend to hold only for the most part'.

[14] Andrea Falcon, *Aristotle and the Science of Nature: Unity Without Uniformity* (Cambridge: Cambridge University Press, 2005), 28, points out that Aristotle believed it was the sun, acting as a 'remote moving principle' that 'indirectly secures the continuous generation of man from man, and hence the eternal permanence of the species'. David Depew, 'Aristotelian Teleology and Philosophy of Biology in the Darwinian Era', in *The Cambridge*

Despite Aristotle's emphasis on rational, theoretical knowledge, he did not follow Plato in thinking it possible to create a group of people with the kind of rational knowledge that would legitimate their rule over the great majority.[15] But this should not be taken as a principled objection. Aristotle's account of knowledge was just as vertical in its ordering as Plato's, and he was in no doubt that the social order should ideally display a parallel structure. Aristocratic and monarchical rule represented the ideal.[16] But his pragmatic response to the question of 'whether it is more advantageous to be ruled by the best man or by the best laws' was to prefer the latter alternative.[17] It seemed impossible to Aristotle to guarantee good government by force of character alone, however rigorous an education was involved.[18]

In consequence, Aristotle was more concerned to investigate the logic of political action than Plato. Political discourse was its own form of rhetoric, with a structure of argumentation (and a subject-matter) peculiar to it. Where Plato found it difficult not to suspect political speech of being inherently deceptive, Aristotle treated its lack of certainty and its inability to articulate necessary truths as inevitable features of debate and decision-making under unavoidable conditions of ignorance about an indeterminate future.

Aristotle's logical writings considered what we now call the problem of determinism and decided against the position that the future was already fixed. But although Aristotle viewed politics as belonging to a distinctive realm of human affairs in which contingency was ineliminable, he was no more sympathetic to historical knowledge than Plato.[19] We noted previously

---

Companion to Aristotle's Biology, ed. Sophia M. Connell (Cambridge: Cambridge University Press, 2021) 261–79, 267, remarks that although Aristotle's eternal species resembled Platonic Forms in being timeless, 'Aristotle arrives at the eternity of species from the differentiated integrity of sexually reproducing organisms, not from typological thinking'.

[15] Aristotle, *Nicomachean Ethics*, trans. Roger Crisp (Cambridge: Cambridge University Press, 2004 [2000]), 1094a–b, writes that 'Knowledge of the good would seem to be the concern of the most authoritative science, the highest master science. And this is obviously the science of politics, because it lays down which of the sciences there should be in cities, and which each class of person should learn and up to what level.' The difference from Plato is that Aristotle asserted a gap between theory and practice.

[16] Aristotle, *Politics*, in *Aristotle's Politics Writings from the Complete Works Politics Economics Constitution of Athens*, ed. J. Barnes, intro. M. Lane (Princeton: Princeton University Press, 2016), 1289a.

[17] Aristotle, *Politics*, 1286a.

[18] Aristotle, *Politics*, 1287a: 'he who bids the law rule may be deemed to bid God and Reason alone rule, but he who bids man rule adds an element of the beast'.

[19] D. W. Lucas, 'Introduction' to Aristotle, *Poetics*, intro. D. W. Lucas (Oxford: Oxford University Press, 1980 [1968]), 118, comments that Aristotle 'has extraordinarily little to say about history in general' although he mentions Herodotus occasionally.

that in the *Poetics* Aristotle remarked that poetry was more philosophically serious than history because it dealt with universals to a greater extent.[20] In art, one could develop a theme to its logical conclusion in a way not permitted to historiography. The study of the past was important only insofar as it displayed regularities of some kind. As we noted at the outset, the scholastic view that there could be no science of the particular was derived from Aristotle's conviction that 'particulars are limitless and not knowable'.[21]

Yet this view arguably rested on a lacuna in Aristotle's own thinking. In his studies of politics, he went to great lengths to gather information on the constitutions of the various Greek cities.[22] Although Aristotle offered no account of historical knowledge comparable to his philosophical analyses of other disciplines, the techniques of historical research were being practiced in the Lyceum. The *Constitution of Athens*, the sole surviving example of this major effort at comparative analysis, suggests that Aristotle was not content with discovering what the letter of the law happened to be in any given city.[23] He wanted a full account of how the Athenian constitution had come into being, and the terms of the understanding provided can only be described as historical. Athenian history was treated not simply as an instance of a process of constitutional development, but as having its own intelligibility. Nevertheless, Aristotle's treatment of the relations between categories, knowledge and politics gave him to think there were good reasons for marginalising history.

Categories

With Aristotle we encounter the use of the concept of a category as a philosophical term of art for the first time. Despite its extreme brevity, the work known as the *Categories* played a major role in making Aristotle 'the leading thinker of all humanity west of India for twenty centuries'.[24] The full list of the ten categories, or of those 'things said without any

---

[20] See Introduction, n. 66, above.
[21] Aristotle, *On Rhetoric: A Theory of Civic Discourse*, trans. and intro. George A. Kennedy, 2nd edn (New York; Oxford: Oxford University Press, 2007), 1356b. See the Introduction, above.
[22] John J. Keaney, *The Composition of Aristotle's Athenaion Politeia Observation and Explanation* (New York; Oxford: Oxford University Press, 1992), 178, states that a total of 158 constitutions were collected.
[23] Aristotle's direct authorship of the *Athenaion Politeia* is disputed; see below.
[24] Dimitri Gustas, 'The Letter Before the Spirit: Still Editing Aristotle after 2300 Years', in Aafke M. I. van Oppenraay, ed., *The Letter before the Spirit: The Importance of Text Editions for the Study of the Reception of Aristotle* (Leiden and Boston: Brill, 2012), 11.

combination', was as follows: 'substance or quantity or qualification or a relative or where or when or being-in-a-position or having or doing or being-affected'.[25]

The reference to 'things said' immediately takes us back to the question already noted of whether Aristotle was talking about the categories as purely verbal expressions, or whether he had in mind the things to which the words referred, or whether he intended no such distinction. We shall have to explore this question further below. Here let us note simply that the phrase 'without any combination' suggests that whichever of these interpretations is correct, categories had an analytically basic, fundamental status.

We noted above that substance was by far the most important of the categories for Aristotle, and that he closely associated substances with persons. So, using Aristotle's list, we could say of Socrates, for example, not only that he was a primary substance, but that he was unique (quantity); wise (quality); wiser indeed than all other Athenians (relation); and when he was alive, he was typically to be found in Athens (place); perhaps in the gymnasium during the mornings (time); where he could be observed sitting (position); wearing his tunic (state); talking (action); and being disagreed with by his interlocutors (affection). A substance was thus a (relatively) permanent substrate to which changing and even contradictory qualities could be attributed at different times.

Unlike a Platonic Form, which cannot change, a key feature of a primary substance for Aristotle was the capacity to 'receive contraries'.[26] In contemporary terms, this means that the truth of propositions concerning a primary substance can be dependent on their context. A sick person becomes well again; the young person becomes middle-aged, then old, and finally dies. A person cannot at one and the same time be both young and old, except perhaps metaphorically, but they can (and indeed, unless their life is cut short, must) have these mutually exclusive qualities successively, because it is the nature of human beings to first be young, then middle-aged, then old.

We have said that Aristotle's categories were 'not-Forms'. In this sense there is truth to the long-established view that Aristotle was focused on earthly, or as we would say empirical, considerations and Plato on the heavenly or transcendental order. Aristotle's doctrine of substance was oriented towards the objects of ordinary experience, hence their focus on

---

[25] Aristotle, *Categories*, bk 1, ch. 4, 1b.
[26] Aristotle, *Categories*, ch. 5.

persons and their properties.[27] Plato's Forms were abstract concepts for the existence of which Aristotle could see no basis. He declared in his *Metaphysics* that 'of the ways in which we show that there are Forms exist none makes these evident'.[28]

A potential source of confusion lies in the fact that Aristotle also used the term 'substance' to indicate the genus to which the individual thing belongs. The genus was the 'secondary substance'. Socrates was not only a primary substance. As an individual human being, he was also an instance of the secondary substance, 'man'; and he could not be one without being the other. Individuals must belong to kinds; kinds must be instantiated in specific exemplars.

According to Aristotle, the things that were true, and could be said to be true, of Socrates, could not also be true of the secondary substance. 'Man' was not wise, in the gymnasium, talking, and so on. But the secondary substance, or genus, did establish a normative template for the individual. It was the *telos* or end of a human being to develop into a rational creature. The individual person was to be judged by how far they fulfilled this human nature. Individuals may be more or less successful in exemplifying their *telos* as persons and as human beings.

Aristotle's secondary substances, or genera, were no more sensible percepts than a Platonic Form. Aristotle's theory of categories must thus be understood as still engaged in the Platonic project of explaining the visible in terms of the invisible. Rational knowledge in particular did not rest on sensible foundations.[29] Indeed, as Lloyd P. Gerson has emphasised, for an extended period in the history of philosophy, 'Aristotelianism and Platonism were widely studied and written about on the understanding that they were harmonious philosophical systems'.[30]

In the previous chapter we remarked on how Plotinus's *Enneads*, for example, reconciled Plato's account of the purely conceptual, intelligible, domain, identified with the 'highest kinds' in *Sophist*, with Aristotle's list of the categories that shape our comprehension of things in the domain

---

[27] Kahn, 'Questions and Categories', 265, argues that 'Aristotle's doctrine of οὐσία [*ousia*, substance] proposes a "thisworldly" concept of being, a descriptive rather than a revisionary metaphysics . . . oriented towards a commitment to the commonsense ontology implied in everyday talk about ordinary subjects, about "entities" such as men and mammals.'

[28] Aristotle, *Metaphysics*, 990b.

[29] Aristotle, *Posterior Analytics*, trans. Jonathan Barnes, 2nd edn (Oxford: Clarendon Press, 1993), 87b, writes 'You cannot understand anything through perception . . . It is impossible to perceive what is universal and holds in every case.'

[30] Lloyd P. Gerson, *Aristotle and Other Platonists* (Ithaca and London: Cornell University Press, 2005), 2.

of sense-objects.³¹ If Plato and Aristotle were interpreted simply as dealing with different domains of reality, then their theories not only did not clash, they could even be treated as mutually complementary.

Just as Plato had offered no exhaustive enumeration of the Forms, however, Aristotle provided no definite answer to the question of whether there were really exactly ten categories, and if so, why. One of several alternative titles for the *Categories* proposed in the ancient world was *On the Ten Genera*, but the dispute over the number of categories made this contentious.³² Many centuries later, Kant would claim to solve this problem by providing a deduction of the categories showing that they were necessarily divided into four triads, but there was no such deduction in Aristotle. To complicate matters further, Aristotle gave alternative lists of categories elsewhere in his writings.³³

This inconsistency has unsurprisingly generated conflicting interpretations. As Franz Brentano noted, in the *Metaphysics* Aristotle seemed to suggest the categories can be further analysed into just three kinds.³⁴ The medieval nominalist William of Ockham had long before suggested an even more radical reduction to just two.³⁵ Worse still, so far as the number

---

[31] Plotinus, *Enneads*, trans. A. H. Armstrong, 7 vols (Cambridge: Harvard University Press, 1989), vi.179, wrote that 'the way in which we think about substance . . . might accord with the thought of Plato'.

[32] Porphyry, *On Aristotle Categories*, 31.

[33] Aristotle appears never to have arrived at a definitive set of categories, though as Robin Smith, 'Logic', 57, notes, substance, quantity and quality occurred consistently. Aristotle, *Topics Books I and VIII with Excerpts from Related Texts*, trans. Robin Smith (Oxford: Clarendon Press, 1997), 103b, is the other place exactly ten categories were listed. Aristotle, *Posterior Analytics*, 83b, listed nine categories. Aristotle, *Metaphysics Books Γ, Δ, and E*, trans. Christopher Kirwan, 2nd edn (Oxford: Clarendon Press, 1993), provided slightly different lists of seven or eight categories at 1003b and 1017a, the first of which introduces the idea that 'even what is not *is* a thing that is not' (emphasis in original). Both lists replace *ousia* ('substance') with *ti esti* ('what it is') notes Paul Studtmann, *The Foundations of Aristotle's Categorial Scheme* (Wisconsin: Marquette University Press, 2008), 8. Aristotle, *Aristotle's Metaphysics Books M and N*, trans. Julia Annas (Oxford: Clarendon Press, 2003 [1976]), 1089b, wrote that 'there can be many objects or many qualities . . . some of them being objects, some characteristics, some relatives', suggesting that the ten categories could indeed be reduced still further to a classification of just three main types.

[34] Franz Brentano, *On the Several Senses of Being in Aristotle*, ed. and trans. Rolf George (Berkeley; Los Angeles; London: University of California Press, 1975), 99, read *Metaphysics* 1089b as arguing that 'the total domain of the being of the categories is divided into three classes'. But Studtmann, *Foundations of Aristotle's Categorial Scheme*, 8, reads the same passage as listing not three but four categories.

[35] Marilyn McCord Adams, *William Ockham*, 2 vols (Indiana: University of Notre Dame Press, 1987), i.121: 'Ockham . . . insists that all really inherent accidents fall under the common genus quality and all subjects of inherence under the common genus substance.'

of categories was concerned, the later sections of the *Categories* featured discussions of what have become known from Latin translations as the post-praedicamenta, a series of important concepts following the initial list of categories that arguably still deserved inclusion.[36]

The fact that the *Categories* begins not by listing the ten categories themselves but with a discussion of homonyms, synonyms and paronyms encouraged the interpretation that it was dealing with words rather than things.[37] Because Aristotle's argument moved so quickly from an analysis of parts of speech to a classification of the most basic entities and states of affairs in the world, either reading was defensible. In late antiquity, Porphyry was convinced that the *Categories* was a book 'about the words that are used to signify things'.[38] To a medieval thinker like John Duns Scotus, who insisted that the universal terms represented by the genera or the secondary substances had no more than a conceptual or linguistic reality, it seemed obvious that Porphyry's view was correct. Logic was not a 'science of the real' but of speech only.[39]

Against these ancient and medieval readings, modern scholarship has generally taken the view that 'predication, as Aristotle conceives it, is in the first instance an ontological relation, and only secondarily and derivatively a linguistic matter'.[40] Understood in this way, Peter Hacker has argued, Aristotle's theory of categories still offers a sound philosophical account of common-sense thinking.[41] Aristotle has also found renewed admirers amongst contemporary philosophers who endorse an immanent realism about universals.[42]

On the other hand, contemporary nominalism is often traced back to Ockham's criticisms of Aristotelian realism in the medieval era. Stemming from the Latin word 'nomen', meaning 'name', nominalism became the philosophical term for those holding that universal terms have no

---

[36] Aristotle, *Categories*, chs 10–15, identified the post-praedicamenta as opposites, contraries, priority, simultaneity, change, and having or possession.
[37] Aristotle, *Categories*, ch. 1.
[38] Porphyry, *On Aristotle Categories*, 33.
[39] John Duns Scotus, *Questions on Aristotle's Categories*, trans. Lloyd A. Newton (Washington DC: Catholic University Press, 2014), 42.
[40] Wolfgang-Rainer Mann, *The Discovery of Things: Aristotle's Categories and their Context* (Princeton: Princeton University Press, 2000), 23.
[41] P. M. S. Hacker, 'Substance: Things and Stuffs', *Proceedings of the Aristotelian Society, Supplementary Volumes*, 78 (2004), 41–63, 56.
[42] David Armstrong, *A Theory of Universals*, 2 vols (Cambridge: Cambridge University Press, 1978), ii.75, notes that he has also 'described my position on universals as "Aristotelian"'; Ruth Millikan, *Language, Thought, and Other Biological Categories: New Foundations for Realism* (Cambridge, MA, and London: MIT Press, 1984), 11, calls her theory 'close to Aristotelian realism'.

reality beyond our own words and ideas. Nominalism has been powerfully appealing to some modern analytical philosophers. W. V. O Quine, for example, endorsed nominalism's commitment to ontological parsimony, seeing it as a presupposition of modern scientific knowledge.[43]

Indeed, despite a twentieth-century revival in Aristotle's reputation, the emergence of modern thought in general is only properly intelligible in the context of an effort to be 'non-Aristotle'.[44] Richard Sorabji has stressed that the 'Aristotle' whom modernity attacked was partly the creation of the very free interpretations of ancient and medieval commentators who sometimes attributed to Aristotle positions that were the reverse of ones he actually held (making him, for example, into a believer in a created universe in order to conform with Christian teaching).[45] Nevertheless, this attack was so successful that by the later nineteenth century, Aristotle had become a synonym for ignorance and confusion for those wanting to think of themselves as modern. His ideas were deemed so obviously wrong that they were barely worth refuting. No one sought to define themselves against Aristotle in the way that Popper felt the need to define himself against Plato, for example.

This dismissal extended to Aristotle's *Categories*. It looked to modern writers as if Aristotle were unable to tell logic from grammar. To an early twentieth-century critic such as Fritz Mauthner, for instance, Aristotle had confused 'the categories of the spoken sentence' in his own ancient Greek language with 'necessary and generally valid categories of thought'.[46] The question of whether Aristotle had confused the particularities of the ancient Greek outlook with what was genuinely universal in thought has prompted a number of comparisons of Aristotle's list of categories with categories in other languages. Clearly, some vital questions arise here, including not only whether languages differ in their use of categories and possibly in their structures of thought, but also whether categories can even be said to be universal features of language and thought at all.

The first question requires a recognition that the standard terms of grammatical analysis are themselves subject to considerations of

---

[43] See, for example, Nelson Goodman and W. V. Quine, 'Steps Toward a Constructive Nominalism', *Journal of Symbolic Logic*, 12:4 (1947), 105–22.

[44] John Aubrey, 'Thomas Hobbes', in *'Brief Lives', chiefly of Contemporaries, set down by John Aubrey, between the Years 1669 & 1696*, ed. Andrew Clark, 2 vols (Oxford: Clarendon Press, 1898), i.357, reported that Hobbes described Aristotle as 'the worst Teacher that ever was . . . a Countrey-fellow that could live in the world [would be] as good'. See also the Introduction, n. 43, above.

[45] Richard Sorabji, 'The Ancient Commentators on Aristotle', in *Aristotle Transformed: The Ancient Commentators and their Influence*, ed. Richard Sorabji (Ithaca: Cornell University Press, 1990), 1–30, 25.

[46] Fritz Mauthner, *Aristotle*, trans. Charles D. Gordon (New York: McClure, Phillips & Co., 1907), 75.

historicity and cultural particularity. Basic concepts like 'noun' and 'verb' were once taken as universal features of all languages, but in modern linguistics even this has been subject to qualification.[47] Nevertheless, distinctions between parts of speech that are functionally equivalent to the distinction between nouns and verbs in Indo-European languages do seem to be universal across all languages.[48] To that extent, all language, ancient or modern, really does display a categorial structure. But even if categoriality is universal in principle, the questions of which universals are present in any given language and how they are used remain. Increasingly, this has become an empirical matter.

With respect to Aristotle, Robert Wardy has examined the partial translation of Porphyry's *Isagoge* which included the *Categories* published in Chinese by the Jesuit Francisco Furtado and the Chinese astronomer Li Chih-tsao during the late Ming era (1631).[49] The Jesuits, deeply immersed in scholastic thought, regarded knowledge of Aristotle's *Categories* as essential for teaching Christian theology to Chinese intellectuals. As a result, Wardy notes, 'In the [*ming li t'an*, or the theory of names] we have . . . a rendering into Chinese of that very philosophical text which has been castigated as the classic instance of inflating quite parochial linguistic traits into general features of reality itself.'[50] Yet Wardy argues that although Chinese readers would often have found the text odd, they would not have found it either nonsensical or incomprehensible. The real problem was one of context. A Chinese reader lacking a broader knowledge of Western theology and philosophy within which to locate the *Categories* would probably have found its ideas difficult to grasp; but the issue was not with the translation itself. 'The language is lucid: it is the thought which is so fearsomely obscure.'[51]

---

[47] Peter Siemund, 'Universals and Variation: An Introduction', in *Linguistic Universals*, ed. Peter Siemund (Berlin; New York: Walter de Gruyter GmbH & Co., 2011), 1–20, 1, writes that 'Linguistic universals are highly theory dependent and can hardly be discussed outside a specific model or framework.'

[48] Paolo Ramat, 'How Universal are Linguistic Categories', in *Universals of Language Today*, ed. Sergio Scalise, Elisabetta Magni and Antonietta Bisetto (New York: Springer Science + Business Media B.V., 2009), 1–12, 3, writes that 'If we understand the Aristotelian terms *hypokeímenon* and *katēgoroúmenon* (Lat. *subjectum* and *praedicatum* respectively) not in the grammatical meaning they acquired in the Western grammatical tradition but, in a functional sentence perspective, as "topic" and "comment", or "theme" and "rheme", we may affirm that they do constitute the universal basic sentence structure, the essential part for the semantic interpretation of the sentence.'

[49] Robert Wardy, *Aristotle in China Language, Categories and Translation* (Cambridge: Cambridge University Press, 2003).

[50] Wardy, *Aristotle in China*, 70.

[51] Wardy, *Aristotle in China*, 115.

When it came to translating the terms for the ten categories themselves, Wardy argues that in at least some cases, the Chinese rendition of Greek terms was actually closer, grammatically speaking, to the original Greek than Latin could manage. For example, rendering *poson* and *poion*, 'quantity' and 'quality', as *chi ho che* and *ho ssu che* did a better job, in Wardy's view, of capturing the fact that the Greek words used by Aristotle were 'either indefinite adjectives or interrogatives'.[51] In fact, according to Wardy, in the Chinese translation of the *Categories*, 'crucial distinctions – such as those between ... primary and secondary substances, and between these and accidents both general and particular – are perfectly conveyed'.[53] The Chinese translation reflected a 'reading of the *Categories* as moving effortlessly from words to the world'.[54]

In sum, Wardy found 'no evidence that Aristotle ... could not make the transition from fourth-century BCE Greek ... to seventeenth-century Chinese'.[55] Wardy did concede a weak version of relativism, according to which the grammar of a language may have some impact on our thinking: he suggested that perhaps 'Greek's rich variety of moods *mildly* improved the chances that modal logic would develop'.[56] But an important conclusion that follows from Wardy's study of the sinicisation of Aristotle is that a weak version of relativism and universalism are not necessarily incompatible.[57] The precise categorial make-up of the Greek and Chinese languages may vary; but given that all languages employ some categorial scheme, categorial concepts available in one language can still be successfully translated into another. Aristotle's categories may have had a peculiarly Greek flavour, but they performed a universal function.

Knowledge

Although the *Categories* once served as the gateway to logic, 'logic', like 'metaphysics', was not Aristotle's own term.[58] His conception of 'logic' was both broader and narrower than the contemporary conception of it as the discrimination of valid arguments.[59] Although a work like the *Prior*

---

[52] Wardy, *Aristotle in China*, 132.
[53] Wardy, *Aristotle in China*, 150.
[54] Wardy, *Aristotle in China*, 151.
[55] Wardy, *Aristotle in China*, 152.
[56] Wardy, *Aristotle in China*, 132. Emphasis in original.
[57] Ramat, 'How Universal are Linguistic Categories', 3, agrees, writing that 'relativism and universalism in language theories ... are not irreconcilable' if we concentrate on 'inductively drawing universal conclusions from the observation of real language facts'.
[58] Smith, 'Logic', 28, notes that 'Aristotle has no word for logic as a whole'.
[59] Susan Haack, *Philosophy of Logics* (Cambridge: Cambridge University Press, 1978), 1, writes that 'A central concern of logic is to discriminate valid from invalid arguments.'

Analytics can be treated in hindsight as marking 'the beginning of formal logic' in a modern sense, because it identifies different forms of syllogism, the six books of the Organon also dealt extensively with informal reasoning or dialectic.[60] Moreover, the Organon also included a great deal of what we would now simply call philosophy. The *Posterior Analytics* in particular set out a conception of the requirements for knowledge also applicable to Aristotle's treatment of the natural sciences and metaphysics, and even ethics and politics.[61] These divisions were in turn conventional. Aristotle himself never provided a definitive ordering of his works, and we cannot treat them as comprising a finished system in the manner that Kant or Hegel later intended.

There was, nonetheless, a close connection between categories and knowledge for Aristotle. The nature of the connection is neatly summarised by Peter Hacker's remark that for Aristotle, 'if we want to know not what [a thing] is like, but *what it is*, we must be told, by specification of a secondary substance, what kind of thing it is'.[62] A world composed of substances of different types required kinds of knowledge appropriate to them.[63] Aristotle himself gave a condensed summary of these kinds in his discussion of the 'virtues of thought' in his *Nicomachean Ethics*. The virtue specific to thought was truth, and Aristotle enumerated 'five ways in which the soul arrives at truth by affirmation or denial'. These were 'skill, scientific knowledge, practical wisdom, wisdom, and intellect'.[64] The Greek words Aristotle used for the different kinds of knowledge

---

[60] See Gisela Striker, 'Introduction' to Aristotle, *Prior Analytics Book I*, trans. Gisela Striker (Oxford: Clarendon Press, 2009), xi. Robin Smith, 'Logic', 29, even argues for the inclusion of the *Rhetoric* as a seventh book in the logical writings on the grounds that 'its theory of oratory rests on the dialectical theory in the *Topics*'.

[61] For example, Aristotle, *Posterior Analytics*, 71b, claims that 'demonstrative understanding ... must proceed from items which are true and primitive and immediate and more familiar than and prior to and explanatory of the conclusions'.

[62] Hacker, 'Substance', 62. Emphasis in original.

[63] Miles Burnyeat, 'Aristotle on Understanding Knowledge', in *Explorations in Ancient and Modern Philosophy*, ii.115–44, ii.115, points out that Aristotle's discussion of knowledge offers both 'a theory of the structure of a science' understood as 'an account of the conditions for a proposition to belong to a body of systematic knowledge', on the one hand, and 'an account of the cognitive state of the individual' who can be said to know; a theory of knowledge, in other words, that includes the knower as well as the known.

[64] See Aristotle, *Nicomachean Ethics*, 1139a–b. As Martha Nussbaum, *The Fragility of Goodness*, rev. edn (Cambridge: Cambridge University Press, 2001 [1986]), 444, n. 11, observes, these distinctions could overlap: it is 'not uncommon for [Aristotle] to use a word in both a wide and a narrow sense – both for the genus and for one of its subspecies' so that, for example, a *techne* could also be an example of an *episteme*, rather than being itself a distinct genus.

in this connection are *techne, episteme, phronesis, sophia* and *nous*.⁶⁵ We may thus treat the states of the soul associated with affirming or denying the truth of propositions as corresponding to a classification of types of knowledge.

Aristotle's account of the knowledge associated with *techne* was very close to Plato's. Both thinkers treated it as the domain of practical knowledge and activity. In the *Metaphysics*, Aristotle stated that someone was competent in a *techne* 'when, from many intelligible objects belonging to experience, one universal supposition about similar things comes about'.⁶⁶ Such a person was not only able to make or do certain things requiring specific skills, but as a result of their deep engagement with a particular activity, had developed expert classificatory judgement. The expert had a good eye for the quality of the kinds of things they themselves were skilled at making, or of the animals that they bred. More abstractly, their judgement could subsume a certain range of phenomena under a universal. Hence, Aristotle said that 'experience is knowledge of particulars, whereas craft knowledge is of universals, and actions and productions are all concerned with particulars'.⁶⁷ This capacity for judgement, we saw, was also a feature of Plato's account. Being able to captain a ship involved being able to reliably make successful decisions about what kinds of action to take in which types of circumstances, for example.⁶⁸

Like Plato, however, Aristotle thought that while mastering a *techne* allowed someone to reliably get good results in, and be a good judge of, a particular field, it was mostly concerned with making rather than doing: its competence in judgement was restricted to a given craft. Thus, also like Plato, Aristotle believed there was an additional need for a kind of practical wisdom peculiar to action at large, one that involved knowing not only how to choose successfully in consequentialist terms, but also how to choose the good. Aristotle's *Ethics* asserted that there was a natural hierarchy of goals in human life determined by our rational nature, rendering some activities inherently more worthwhile than others.⁶⁹ Hence the

---

[65] See Aristotle, *Nicomachean Ethics*, trans. H. Rackham (Cambridge, MA: Harvard University Press; London: William Heinemann Ltd, 1956 [1926]), 332.

[66] Aristotle, *Metaphysics*, trans. Reeve, 981a.

[67] Aristotle, *Metaphysics*, trans. Reeve, 981a.

[68] Compare Plato, *Republic*, ed. G. R. F. Ferrari, trans. T. Griffith (Cambridge: Cambridge University Press, 2000), 360e–361a: 'A really good ship's captain or doctor, for example, can distinguish in the exercise of his skill between what is not feasible and what is feasible.'

[69] Aristotle, *Nicomachean Ethics*, 1094a, writes 'the end of the master science is more worthy of choice than the ends of the subordinate sciences, since these latter ends are pursued also for the sake of the former'.

importance of *phronesis*, which in modern English is sometimes rendered as practical wisdom in pursuing our goals.[70]

Cleverness in reliably achieving our ends was important for Aristotle, but that was not all there was to the virtue of *phronesis*, however; its possessor must also be a good judge of which ends were worthy to begin with.[71] The person who displayed this virtue knew how to live well for themselves. But knowledge of how the whole community could live well was even more valuable: 'while the good of an individual is a desirable thing, what is good for a people or for cities is a nobler and more godlike thing'.[72] The implication was that the exercise of the political virtues was not reducible to a *techne*, just as Plato had insisted. But Aristotle differed from Plato in making the 'science' of politics entirely a matter of the practical exercise of *phronesis*.[73]

The difference from Plato's emphasis on the *kairos* of the philosopher-ruler was a subtle one, because like *phronesis*, *kairos* was supposed to involve good judgement regarding the best course of action. Like Plato, Aristotle drew a firm distinction between the practical domain to which *techne* and *phronesis* belonged, and theoretical contemplation. He declared that 'of theoretical science the end is truth, whereas of practical science it is function'.[74] Also like Plato, Aristotle was in no doubt as to which of the two was ultimately more valuable. But although theoretical knowledge was 'extraordinary, wonderful, abstruse', even 'godlike', it was also 'useless', in the sense that it was not interested in 'human goods'.[75] Aristotle in effect maintained his own version of Plato's doctrine of the divided line, and at least the most fully developed forms of *episteme*, *sophia* and *nous* all fell on the theoretical side of it. The difference was that Aristotle did not think it was possible to apply the knowledge gained from theoretical contemplation directly to life in the cave, so to say. There was no straight

---

[70] Christopher Gill, 'In What Sense are Ancient Ethical Norms Universal', in Christopher Gill, ed., *Virtue, Norms, and Objectivity: Issues in Ancient and Modern Ethics* (Oxford: Oxford University Press, 2005), 20, describes the *phronimos* as someone who 'combines practical wisdom with good ethical motivation, in terms of accurate "perception" of the right course of action in specific situations'.

[71] Aristotle, *Nicomachean Ethics*, 1145a, declares that 'rational choice will not be correct in the absence of either practical wisdom or virtue'.

[72] Aristotle, *Nicomachean Ethics*, 1094b.

[73] Aristotle, *Nicomachean Ethics*, 1141b, treats both 'political science' and 'practical wisdom' as having to do with legislation and policy: neither is a purely contemplative or theoretical affair.

[74] Aristotle, *Metaphysics*, trans. Reeve, 993b.

[75] Aristotle, *Nicomachean Ethics*, 1141b.

road back from theory to practice, where political action belonged; philosophers and politicians were distinct characters for him.

For Aristotle, one could say, the kind of theoretical knowledge that he predominantly associated with *episteme*, conventionally translated by the English word 'science', was, unlike for Plato, irrelevant to politics. We noted that Aristotle drew a fundamental distinction between kinds of knowledge that deal with things that are 'in the same state always ... of necessity' and things which are in a certain state 'for the most part'.[76] In modern terms, we too distinguish between necessity and contingency, and assign them to different kinds of study. But the difference between ancient and modern science is not simply a distinction between the truths of demonstrative reasoning and those discovered by observation and experiment. The grounds of the ancient and modern distinction between rational and empirical knowledge are also different.

Aristotle's divisions of knowledge were rooted in and were supposed to reflect his cosmology.[77] Like Plato, he believed in carving nature at its joints.[78] The inherited Greek common-sense belief was that the universe was like a person in being alive and intelligent. Aristotle, like Plato, was trying to give this conviction a rational basis. Hence, Aristotle described metaphysics in particular as getting to 'the truth of the ancient and truly traditional theories' which claimed that there was 'something immortal and divine among the things that have movement, having movement of such a sort that there is no limit to it, but rather it is the limit of the others'.[79]

In one way or another, then, all theoretical knowledge falling within the category of *episteme* dealt at least in part with what was necessary and eternal, physics and biology no less than geometry. The distinction between those things which are 'necessary, without qualification' and 'eternal', and those subject to 'coming to be and passing away' overlapped with the division of the supposedly perfectly spherical universe into sublunary and supra-lunary regions already noted.[80] Here on earth, because things were made of the grossest materials, they naturally gravitated

---

[76] Aristotle, *Metaphysics*, trans. Kirwan, 1026b.

[77] Aristotle, *Metaphysics*, trans. Kirwan, 1004a, wrote 'that which is divides directly into genera; hence the disciplines too will follow these'.

[78] See Chapter 1, n. 94.

[79] Aristotle, *De Caelo*, trans. C. D. C. Reeve (Indianapolis: Hackett Publishing Company, 2020), 248a.

[80] Compare Aristotle, *Nicomachean Ethics*, 1139b, and Aristotle, *Physics Books I and II, translated with an Introduction, Commentary, Note on Recent Work, and Revised Bibliography by William Charlton* (Oxford: Oxford University Press, 1992 [1970]), 196a.

towards the centre of the world, and change and motion were the rule. As we noted, biology and a great part of physics were concerned with these earthly phenomena. This may explain the discrepancy often remarked on between Aristotle's ideal type of science as demonstrative, and his own scientific practice in his writings on physics and biology, where syllogisms were conspicuously absent.[81] Matter resisted reason; its subjection to form was always imperfect.

Beyond the moon, where the heavenly bodies resided, scientific knowledge (in Aristotle's sense of the term) was dealing with the supra-lunary part of the universe, which was made of purer stuff. At the circumference of this sphere was the eternal, unmoved mover itself. The perfectly circular astronomical paths supposedly followed by the heavenly bodies lead out to it. They were thus amongst the most important objects of geometry, which abstracts lines and numbers from things and considers them in purely conceptual terms.[82] Metaphysics, the 'most ruling and most leading' of all the sciences, was spatially as well as conceptually continuous with physics and geometry; the study of what was most rational was also the study of what was furthest from the earth.[83] Physics studied a living, divine, intelligent universe; metaphysics studied the unmoved mover that governed it.[84] Aristotle's account of the soul, or as we should say, his psychology, was in turn integrated with both his physics and his metaphysics.

---

[81] R. J. Hankinson, 'Philosophy of Science', 113, remarks that 'one can trawl the whole of Aristotle's considerable scientific oeuvre without netting a single instance of a fully worked-out syllogism'. Orna Harari, *Knowledge and Demonstration Aristotle's Posterior Analytics* (Dordrecht, Boston and London: Kluwer Academic Publishers, 2004), 87, likewise observes that 'the prominence that Aristotle ascribes to syllogistic reasoning in the *Posterior Analytics* does not find expression in his physical or biological writings'.

[82] Aristotle, *Physics*, trans. Charlton, 193b, writes that 'Both the student of nature and the mathematician deal with [planes, solids, lengths, and points]; but the mathematician does not consider them as boundaries of natural bodies . . . they are separable in thought from change, and it makes no difference; no error results.'

[83] Aristotle, *Metaphysics*, trans. Reeve, 996b.

[84] The question of whether Aristotle thought that the unmoved mover moved is contentious. For example, Richard Dien Winfield, *Conceiving Nature After Aristotle, Kant, and Hegel: The Philosopher's Guide to the Universe* (Cham: Palgrave Macmillan, 2017), 166, argues that because Aristotle held nothing could impart motion to itself, the unmoved mover was likewise motionless. But there is reason to think that Aristotle's unmoved mover was 'unmoved' not because it was still, but rather because it was unlike anything else in being entirely self-moved: see n. 79, above. Since, however, the unmoved mover was pure form, it was indeed unmoved in any spatial sense, and the idea of it having a 'location' at the edge of the substantial universe presumably also should not be taken literally. Its 'movements' were, rather, a metaphor for its thoughts of itself, meaning that its circular 'motion' was likewise purely ideal or logical.

Just like Plato (and later, Hegel), Aristotle saw human beings as the most rational earthly features of a universe that was itself inherently rational.[85]

In Plato's *Timaeus*, the demiurge was said to have made the human soul and left the rest of the task to the lesser gods; and in the *Republic* Socrates encouraged a belief in the reincarnation of the soul.[86] Aristotle likewise suggested that there was a rational element to the human soul that could potentially survive death insofar as it was detachable from its gross material substrate.[87] Nevertheless, some of Aristotle's most significant departures from Plato were cosmological. His introduction of a pure 'fifth element' of aether, an addition to the traditional theory of the four elements of earth, air, fire, and water, and his insistence that Plato was eccentric in treating the universe as having a beginning in time, were two particularly important instances.[88]

With respect to the ranking of the various sciences falling within the category of *episteme*, there was no argument that philosophy was the most important for Aristotle, as it had been for Plato, though how he thought of the relationships between those sciences ranking below it can be debated. He is sometimes said to have favoured the formal, mathematical sciences. Robin Smith, for example, argues that 'Aristotle's model for a science was the mathematical disciplines of arithmetic and geometry'.[89] When Aristotle wanted to emphasise the superior status of metaphysicians, however, he remarked that 'there is someone still further above the

---

[85] Circular motion was also important in Plato. *Timaeus*, trans. Zeyl, 34b, described the universe as 'turning continuously in the same place, spinning around upon itself'.

[86] Plato, *Timaeus*, trans. Zeyl, 42d, has Timaeus say that the divine maker 'handed over to the young gods the task of weaving mortal bodies'; *Republic*, trans. Griffith, 608d, had Socrates say that 'our soul is immortal . . . it never dies'.

[87] Aristotle, *De Anima Books II and III (With Passages from Book I)*, trans. D. W. Hamlyn (Oxford: Clarendon Press, 2002 [1968]), 430a, asserted that there is a part of our intellect that was 'distinct, unaffected, and unmixed, being in essence activity' and that 'this alone is immortal and eternal'.

[88] See Aristotle, *Physics Books III and IV, Translated with Introduction and Notes by Edward Hussey* (Oxford: Clarendon Press, 1993 [1983]), 212b: 'the earth is in the water, the water in the air, the air in the ether, and the ether in the world, but the world is no longer in anything else'; and Aristotle, *Physics Book VIII, Translated with a Commentary by Daniel W. Graham* (New York: Oxford University Press, 1999), 251b: 'Plato alone generates time. For he says that it is coeval with the heaven, and that the heaven has come to be.' Aristotle's view later caused problems for the Christian doctrine of creation. Thomas Aquinas, *Summa Theologiae*, Q. 46, viii.71, was forced to claim that Aristotle's arguments were 'limited to countering the reasons put forward by the ancients for a beginning to the world in ways veritably out of the question'.

[89] Robin Smith, 'Logic', 47.

student of nature', possibly implying that the natural philosopher was second only to the metaphysician, and in any case giving natural philosophy a very elevated status.[90] This could be read as putting natural philosophers before mathematicians.

As we saw, however, physics and biology were also considered by Aristotle to be sciences of what is rational and necessary, just like mathematics. It was just that 'the mode of demonstration and of necessity is different in natural science and the theoretical sciences'.[91] But it was not a defect of biology or physics as compared to geometry that they dealt with efficient causes whereas mathematicians did not; this simply reflected the nature of their respective objects. Every science had its own advantages and disadvantages, and each was valuable for different reasons.[92] There was a notable openness to Aristotle's handling of the *episteme*.[93] While they clearly ranked above the practical arts and below metaphysics, their internal ranking was not something he emphasised very strongly.

Each science had its own province, however, and it was vital not to confuse them on pain of error: 'you cannot prove anything by crossing from another kind – e.g. something geometrical by arithmetic'.[94] No science, moreover, made the investigation of its own presuppositions its chief concern.[95] There was an important distinction between the kind of knowledge involved in the various *episteme* and the conditions of that knowledge.[96] For example, mathematicians made use of numbers,

---

[90] Aristotle, *Metaphysics*, trans. Kirwan, 1005a.
[91] Aristotle, *On the Parts of Animals*, trans. James G. Lennox (Oxford: Clarendon Press, 2004 [2001]), 640a.
[92] Aristotle, *Parts of Animals*, trans. Lennox, 644b, wrote 'Each study has its attractions.'
[93] According to James G. Lennox, *Aristotle on Inquiry: Erotetic Frameworks and Domain-Specific Norms* (Cambridge: Cambridge University Press, 2021), 18, 'the *Posterior Analytics* ... tells us that ultimately we are seeking answers to four intimately related questions: "Is there an S (or P)?," "What is S (or P)?," "Does P belong to all S?," and "Why does P belong to all S?" Knowing, from the start, that one's goal is achieving answers to these questions is important. But if S is (say) Soul, your inquiry will be governed by very different norms than if S is Plane Figure, The Good Life, or Animal Locomotion.'
[94] Aristotle, *Posterior Analytics*, trans. Barnes, 75a.
[95] Aristotle, *Metaphysics*, trans. Kirwan, 1005a, argued that 'none of those who conduct specialized investigations endeavour to say anything about [axioms], as to whether or not they are true'. Aristotle did allow that 'some students of nature' paid attention to their own assumptions, but only as a secondary consideration.
[96] Aristotle, *Posterior Analytics*, trans. Barnes, 72b: 'We assert that not all understanding is demonstrative: rather, in the case of immediate items understanding is indemonstrable.'

but doing so did not require reflecting on what kinds of things numbers were. As Aristotle remarked in the *Metaphysics*, it was not the business of the mathematician but the philosopher 'to go through puzzles about the *matter* of the objects of mathematics'.[97]

This is why Aristotle believed that 'there is not only understanding but also some principle of understanding by which we get to know the definitions'.[98] This was *nous*, the capacity to recognise first principles not only as useful and thus as fit to serve as immediate premises, but as themselves true.[99] It is sometimes translated as 'intuition', though it must be taken as rational rather than sensible in nature.[100] It may be compared to the purely theoretical aspect of the kind of judgement that Plato's philosopher-ruler was supposed to develop as part of their education in *kairos*. The need for explicit demonstration was supplanted by a correct, direct vision of the nature of things.

Those with *nous* have developed a faculty of rational intuition that is higher even than scientific knowledge.[101] But *nous*, as Stephen Menn points out, was also the term Aristotle used to describe the essence of the unmoved mover. God for Aristotle was simply intellectual virtue existing by itself, the Good unmediated. We, by contrast, could *have nous* as a virtue, but we could never *be* it. In categorial terms, *nous* could never be our substance, only one of our attributes. Nevertheless, to the degree that we did have it as a virtue, we were god-like, participating in the very same knowledge as the divine.[102]

Unlike Plato, however, Aristotle did not think that enjoying a vision of the Good conferred any special authority with respect to practical, political matters. It seems that he did not even think of *nous* as the very highest form of knowledge. This place was occupied by *sophia*, which was 'scientific knowledge, combined with intellect'.[103] Metaphysics was the

---

[97] Aristotle, *Metaphysics*, trans. Reeve, 1059b.
[98] Aristotle, *Posterior Analytics*, trans. Barnes, 72b.
[99] Aristotle, *Metaphysics*, trans. Kirwan, 1005b, cited the principle of non-contradiction as 'the firmest of all principles'.
[100] See Barnes, 'Commentary' to Aristotle, *Posterior Analytics*, 259.
[101] Aristotle, *Posterior Analytics*, 100b, writes that 'since nothing apart from comprehension can be truer than understanding, there will be comprehension of the principles' (translating *nous* as 'comprehension' and *episteme* as 'understanding'.)
[102] Stephen Menn, 'Aristotle and Plato on God as Nous and as the Good', *Review of Metaphysics*, 45:3 (1992), 543–73, 569: 'the virtue the god is is the same as the virtue we have or participate in: when we intellectually-perceive what the god perceives (namely, the god himself), we possess the very same intellectual virtue which the god possesses, that is, the same science specified by the same content'.
[103] Aristotle, *Nicomachean Ethics*, 1141a.

highest science of all in virtue of this synthesis of *episteme* and *nous*. It was 'scientific knowledge of the most honourable matters'.[104] These highest objects were described as consisting in pure mind, with the unmoved mover being the highest object of all.

Ultimate reality for Aristotle, its first principle, consisted purely of thought thinking itself: 'in the case of those things which have no matter, that which thinks and that which is thought are the same; for contemplative knowledge and that which is known in that way are the same'.[105] The divine for Aristotle turned out to be nothing other than the complete reflexivity of thought: '*Itself*, therefore, is what it thinks . . . and its thinking is a thinking of thinking.'[106] This understanding of the divine, which resembled Plato's Form of the Good in being timeless, normative, and ideal, would prove powerfully appealing to later Idealists. Hegel's consideration of the nature of the Absolute Idea, we shall see, was heavily influenced by Aristotle.

Aristotle's conception of *sophia* also explains why he believed theoretical contemplation offered the ideally best kind of life for a human being. *Sophia*, or the kind of knowledge that metaphysics offered, came nearest to emulating divinity, for when doing philosophy, our thinking was itself a thinking on thinking, and the difference between ourselves and the divine came closest to being eliminated. The divine, as we noted in discussing nous, was the primary substance par excellence. Substance for Aristotle was separate, at its limits, from material stuff.

Aristotle believed our rational aspect was not material to begin with. In metaphysical contemplation, for Aristotle, as for Plato, we came closest to a quasi-mystical, religious, union with the divine. But Aristotle departed from Plato in distinguishing this 'best science' from 'political science, or practical wisdom'.[107] *Sophia*, 'since it is not concerned with any process of coming into being, will not consider any of the things that make a human being happy'.[108] Politics, on the other hand, was concerned with nothing else.

---

[104] Aristotle, *Nicomachean Ethics*, 1141a.
[105] Aristotle, *De Anima*, 429b.
[106] Aristotle, *Metaphysics*, trans. Judson, 1074b. Emphasis in original. Judson argues (326–7) that the most plausible interpretation of what Aristotle meant by thought thinking itself is that 'the subject of divine thinking has some determinate content which is of the same general type as the content of some high-level human thinking; it is *of itself* because it is in some way constituted by this content'. Emphasis in original.
[107] Aristotle, *Nicomachean Ethics*, 1141a, wrote that 'It would be absurd for someone to think that political science or practical wisdom is the best science, unless human beings are the best thing in the cosmos.'
[108] Aristotle, *Nicomachean Ethics*, 1143b.

Politics

Aristotle described metaphysics as so superior to the other forms of knowledge that they, 'like ... handmaidens', should never try to contradict it.[109] The analogy, which was intended to convey Aristotle's belief in the superiority of metaphysics to all other disciplines, rested on the inferior position of women and slaves in Greek society (though women were not natural slaves).[110] It was, in the modern sense, a political one. Just as the hierarchy of the sciences rested on the analogy of slavery, the position of the unmoved mover at the head of the hierarchy of being was conceived in similarly 'political' terms. To emphasise the unmoved mover's role as the supplier of a single standard of order, Aristotle quoted a line given to Ulysses in Homer's *Illiad*: 'To have many rulers is not good: let there be one ruler.'[111] When Ulysses uttered these words in the poem, he had just been persuaded by the goddess Minerva to remain at Troy. With her voice still ringing in his ears, he sets about beating those of his soldiers who protested at this sudden alteration to their plans. Ulysses accompanied his blows with a verbal reminder that monarchy was divinely ordained by Zeus.

For Aristotle, then, there was a clear and mutually reinforcing element to these parallel hierarchies: knowledge was hierarchically ordered in relation to the divine by analogy with politics, and an earthly political hierarchy in its turn was divinely ordained according to religious and mythical tradition. Despite questioning the provisions Plato made for the ideal city in the *Republic*, and making no attempt in his own writings on politics to construct such an ideal community, Aristotle agreed with Plato that in principle 'a wise person should prescribe, not be prescribed to, and should be obeyed by the less wise, not obey someone else'.[112] The issue here was who should count as the wise man in this context, since possession of *nous* and *sophia*, as we have established, would not be relevant.

Indeed, we might have to reckon without any wise men in politics at all. Where we find ourselves dealing with a situation 'where men are alike and equal', Aristotle remarked, it was 'neither expedient nor just that one man should be lord of all'.[113] In the absence of individuals of clearly

---

[109] Aristotle, *Metaphysics*, trans. Reeve, 997a.
[110] Aristotle, *Politics*, 1252b, wrote that 'nature has distinguished between the female and the slave'.
[111] Aristotle, *Metaphysics*, trans. Judson, 1076a. Emphasis in original. Compare Homer, *Illiad*, bk 2, ll. 204–5.
[112] Aristotle, *Metaphysics*, trans. Reeve, 982a.
[113] Aristotle, *Politics*, 1288a.

superior wisdom, it was better that authority be shared. But this did not make Aristotle an unqualified enthusiast for democracy, despite his interest in classifying its varieties. While he distinguished half-a-dozen different types of democracy, he showed a clear preference for that variety in which people of 'quality', by which he meant people who enjoy 'freedom, wealth, education, [and] good birth', were in charge.[114] Equality in Aristotle's sense did not exclude relative superiority, only limiting cases like that of the Platonic philosopher-ruler.

Like Plato, Aristotle argued that there was a tendency for democracy to favour the expropriation of the rich by the poor. He too considered it prone to demagoguery. These developments needed to be guarded against by ensuring that a democracy was run by the right kind of people, and that in it, the rule of law rather than numerical superiority prevailed.[115] Aristotelian democracy was also entirely compatible with slavery, the exclusion of women and colonial ventures. Although in practice Aristotle eschewed the possibility of an ideal state constructed on Platonic lines in which a specially educated ruling class of militarily trained intellectuals lived communally, he still sought to reconcile democracy with the entitlement of the well-born and the rich.[116] Citizens should not have to provide for their own daily wants.[117] In a modern context we might compare Aristotle with a liberal like J. S. Mill, who likewise wanted to preserve an element of hierarchy in a democratic context.[118]

What separated Aristotle from Plato, then, was less their views on democracy, which Plato also recognised was not without its attractions, than Aristotle's acceptance of politics as an activity with a unique and specifiable structure. Where Plato's inclination was to try and make politics redundant, Aristotle accepted politics as a necessary feature of both oligarchical and democratic regimes. Moreover, he did not see politics as reducible to any other form of activity or relationship. He separated

---

[114] Aristotle, *Politics*, 1296a.
[115] Aristotle, *Politics*, 1281b, stated 'laws, when good, should be supreme'.
[116] Aristotle, *Politics*, 1283a.
[117] Aristotle, *Politics*, 1269a.
[118] J. S. Mill, *Considerations on Representative Government*, in *Essays on Politics and Society: Collected Works of John Stuart Mill*, vol. XIX, ed. J. M. Robson, intro. Alexander Brady, 33 vols (Toronto and Buffalo: University of Toronto Press, 1977), xix.475, 499, suggested that 'individual mental superiority' might justify 'two or more votes' for the professionally successful, as against one for the ordinary individual, and worried (like Plato) that paying politicians would make holding office 'an object of desire to adventurers of a low class'.

it both from *techne* and other kinds of practical wisdom, arguing that it involved a genuinely distinctive form of action and an equally distinctive kind of reasoning to be set alongside demonstration and dialectic. The political domain presupposed both genuine agency and a world that was at least partially tractable.

Aristotle distinguished the political relationship between citizens from several other kinds, beginning with slavery. Slavery was a 'despotic' relationship and quite literally one of ownership and domination, though Aristotle argued that it could be legitimated by an alleged incapacity of the so-called 'natural' slave for self-government.[119] But it was also the antithesis of the relationship between free and equal people that defined citizenship. The political relation was likewise distinct from familial, conjugal and paternal, relationships, both of which were in Aristotle's eyes relationships of inequality, though to a lesser degree than slavery.[120] Aristotle's belief in the inequality of the sexes prohibited women from being full citizens, even if Athenian women were freer than in other ancient Greek cities.[121]

Contemporary liberal democracy endorses full equality of status for men and women as citizens. But the modern liberal would still agree with Aristotle in distinguishing citizenship from 'economic' relationship.[122] Aristotle's attitude to purely economically focused activity, or the 'art of getting wealth', as he called it, was equivocal. By Aristotle's day, the Greek city-states had become fully fledged money economies, trading widely with the Mediterranean world to which they belonged. But even though Aristotle thought a certain limited amount of property was necessary to the household, he did not approve of business for profit.[123] Indeed, he argued that making money for its own sake was an unnatural activity because it was inherently interminable.[124] The only *telos* of money was more money.

---

[119] Aristotle, *Politics*, 1254a, argued that 'from the hour of their birth, some are marked out for subjection . . . he who participates in reason enough to apprehend, but not to have, is a slave by nature'.
[120] Aristotle, *Politics*, 1255b, stated that 'The rule of a household is a monarchy.'
[121] Josiah Ober, *The Athenian Revolution Essays on Ancient Greek Democracy and Political Theory* (Princeton: Princeton University Press, 1996), 181.
[122] Ober, *Athenian Revolution*, ch. 11, 'The Polis as a Society: Aristotle, John Rawls, and the Athenian Social Contract', argues that, given the ancient context, Athens constituted a well-ordered society in Rawlsian terms, prioritising political liberty and limiting inequality within fair bounds (as then understood).
[123] Aristotle, *Politics*, 1253b, declared 'Property is a part of the household, and the art of acquiring property is part of the art of managing the household; for no man can live well, or indeed live at all, unless he is provided with necessaries.'
[124] Aristotle, *Politics*, 1257b, wrote that in trade, 'coin is the unit of exchange and the limit of it. And there is no bound to the riches which spring from this art of wealth-getting'.

Aristotle's criticism of business is in sharp contrast with modernity. Where Aristotle found money-making taken as an end in itself as literally a perverted activity, for Hobbes it was simply a reflection of the nature of human life. The ceaseless, restless, pursuit of one desire after another was the hallmark of the human condition.[125] But Aristotle was not denying that this side to life existed: he accepted economic exchange as a necessary condition of *polis*-life and was only claiming that limitless accumulation ought not to dominate it.[126]

Characterised positively, a polity was 'a partnership of citizens in a constitution'; an association of people living according to a shared set of rules.[127] This implied a certain level of mutual concern. When Aristotle remarked that 'to secure gentle treatment for the poor is not an easy thing, since a ruling class is not always humane', the implication was that there ought to be such treatment.[128] The relationship of friendship and equity with which Aristotle identified citizenship was also a pluralistic one. Whatever kind of unity partnership in a constitution involved, it did not eliminate difference. Aristotle explicitly contradicted Socrates' claim that the more unified a polity was, the better, saying that 'a state is . . . made up . . . of different kinds of men; for similars do not constitute a state. It is not like a military alliance'.[129] The Spartans, so admired by Plato, erred in treating citizenship as identical with comradeship.[130]

Unity was not to be identified with uniformity, and Plato's suggestion that ownership of property for his governing class should be collectivised was likely to be counter-productive. It would tend to erode the sense of individual responsibility.[131] Aristotle granted that Plato had proposed such measures out of a sense of benevolence towards his fellow human beings but portrayed his own stance as the more realistic one. 'In framing an ideal we may assume what we wish, but should avoid impossibilities.'[132] This outlook imposed definite limits on what Aristotle thought one should expect from the kind of friendship involved in citizenship. Disagreement

---

[125] See Hobbes, *Leviathan*, ed. Richard Tuck (Cambridge: Cambridge University Press, 2003 [1991]), bk 1, ch. 11, 70: 'I put for a generall inclination of all mankind, a perpetuall and restlesse desire of Power after power, that ceaseth onely in Death.'

[126] Aristotle, *Politics*, 1257b, acknowledged that 'the art of getting wealth' appropriate to assuring a sufficiency for the household still involved the use of money.

[127] Aristotle, *Politics*, 1276b.

[128] Aristotle, *Politics*, 1297b.

[129] Aristotle, *Politics*, 1261a.

[130] Aristotle, *Politics*, 1271b, argued 'the whole [Spartan] constitution has regard to one part of excellence only – the excellence of the soldier, which gives victory in war'.

[131] Aristotle, *Politics*, argued 'that which is common to the greatest number has the least care bestowed upon it'.

[132] Aristotle, *Politics*, 1265a.

was unavoidable. But Aristotle emphasised the contrary of friendship was not hatred but enmity. We might be angry with our political enemies, but they were still people for us. Hatred, in contrast, was purely of types. To really hate someone, Aristotle argued, we must categorise them as simply an instance of a kind.[133]

Aristotle's point about the distinctive nature of political reasoning stemmed from his belief that our very substance was political for the same reason that it was rational. Our rationality was due to our capacity for speech, and so we were fated to politics for the same reason that we could be said to be doomed to rationality. Politics was an inescapable consequence of the fact that we could talk, and thus were able to project future possibilities in a way that no other creature could. But because the future was uncertain, and because different groups (like rich and poor) approached it with different goals in mind, potentially destabilising disagreements were inevitable.

Politics attempted to cope with this situation by doing two things: firstly, crafting legislation, and secondly, deliberating over or carrying out a particular course of action. The difference was that between universals and particulars, and as usual for Aristotle the universal was superior.[134] Political deliberation, which involved responding to particular circumstances, was essential in its own way; but it was legislation that established the general rules that the community lived by. The value of the rules was to be judged, firstly, by how far they encouraged good habits and a virtuous character in the citizens, and secondly, by the prospect they offered of long-term stability irrespective of the particular type of constitution.[135]

The kind of practical wisdom associated with 'political science', on the other hand, was centrally concerned with future contingencies. It was concerned with things that were not yet and which could be otherwise, and so were instances of 'coming into being'. Political action, insofar as it consisted of deciding on and pursuing a specific policy, or in executive decision about how to put legislation into practice, was the part of government that came closest to being a *techne*: 'only people exhibiting

---

[133] Aristotle, *Rhetoric*, 1382a, argued 'anger is always concerned with particulars, directed, for example, at Callias or Socrates, while hate is directed also at types (everyone hates the thief and the sycophant)'.

[134] Aristotle, *Nicomachean Ethics*, trans. Crisp, 1141b, declared 'that which co-ordinates is legislative science'.

[135] Aristotle, *Nicomachean Ethics*, trans. Crisp, 1103b, wrote 'legislators make the citizens good by habituating them'; Aristotle, *Politics*, 1320a, argued that a legislator 'must not think the truly democratical or oligarchical measure to be that which will give the greatest amount of democracy or oligarchy, but that which will make them last longest'.

this kind of practical wisdom . . . are said to participate in politics: they are the only ones who practise politics in the way that craftsmen practice'.[136]

In the standard arrangement of Aristotle's works, the *Rhetoric* was given the title *Techne rhetorike*.[137] It identified a kind of discourse distinct from other non-demonstrative forms, including the forensic speech of the lawyer which sought to establish guilt or innocence in relation to past events.[138] More specifically, political discourse as a branch of rhetoric was 'like some offshoot of dialectic and ethical studies'.[139] Unlike demonstrative reasoning, it contained an inextricable element of uncertainty. It was simply impossible to prove a political argument in the same way as a logical or a geometrical one. One of the implications was that reasonable people could disagree, and so political discourse must always seek to persuade.

Where Plato tended to see persuasion as necessarily duplicitous, for Aristotle it was a necessary feature of the distinctive logical structure of political discourse, which he called 'enthymemic' reasoning. An enthymemic argument was 'a deduction from likelihoods or signs'.[140] Some 'signs' inevitably go together or succeed one another, as when we walk outside and see puddles everywhere, and so can reliably infer that it must have rained. But other signs, in particular those relating to human action rather than natural phenomena like precipitation, may be less certain.[141]

To use a modern example, a politician sweating on television may look untrustworthy, but not everyone who sweats on television is trying to deceive us. Some signs, therefore, relate to 'probabilities', things that are 'for the most part thus and thus'. Likelihoods were common-sense understandings of how things usually occur that likewise lack demonstrative certainty. But this lack of certainty did not mean that all politicians were engaged in the kind of self-interested deception that Aristotle, like Plato, thought sophistry was sometimes guilty of.[142] For Aristotle, the probabilistic

---

[136] Aristotle, *Nicomachean Ethics*, 1141b.
[137] Kennedy, 'Introduction' to Aristotle, *Rhetoric*, xiv.
[138] Aristotle, *Rhetoric*, 1358b, writes: 'A member of a democratic assembly is an example of one judging about future happenings, a juror an example of one judging the past.'
[139] Aristotle, *Rhetoric*, 1356a.
[140] Aristotle, *Prior Analytics*, trans. Robin Smith (Indianapolis: Hackett Publishing, 1989), 70a.
[141] Aristotle, *Prior Analytics*, 70a, gives the example that pregnant women (supposedly) typically look pale, but a woman can look pale without being pregnant.
[142] Aristotle, *Rhetoric*, 1355a, 1359b, acknowledges a similarity between sophistry and political rhetoric, but also argues 'humans have a natural disposition for the true and to a large extent hit on the truth'.

character of political discourse was not a defect but an inherent, ineliminable, feature of discourse concerning what rules to make and what action to take in the face of uncertainty.

Aristotle was also clear about the content of political discourse. There were five main subjects: 'finances, war and peace, national defense, imports and exports, and the framing of laws'.[143] Whether modernity has added any additional topics is something to ponder. In recognition of the importance of identity politics, the topic of citizenship itself might be a possible candidate. But Aristotle already knew that the question of who counted as a (full) citizen was itself political, and that even in his own time different answers were possible.[144] He could perhaps have included that topic under the heading of 'legislation' broadly construed, given that citizenship was defined by legal rights and obligations. One might also ask whether contemporary environmental concerns constitute a separate subject, or whether they too could fall under one or more of Aristotle's original five headings – perhaps under national defence, for instance. The main point, however, is that Aristotle supplied criteria for what counted as a 'political' subject that were sufficiently broad to be useful without being indiscriminate.

Perhaps the most important feature of Aristotle's account of politics, though, was his view of it as a meaningful activity, capable of changing the course of events. On some theories of the nature of the world, politics effectively becomes insignificant. For example, if the course of human affairs has a necessary direction or is predetermined, it is hard to understand how the decisions resulting from our deliberations can alter the unfolding future. We may act under the illusion that we are making a difference to how things would otherwise have turned out, but we are self-deceived; our actions are at best contributing to shaping the form the future must take anyway. Aristotle rejected any such position. His teleological understanding of human nature and of reality at large was not in contradiction with distinguishing voluntary from involuntary action.[145]

If anything, free action was most in accord with the natural ends of human beings, because the natural end of a human being was to be a rational creature, and we would normally freely choose the most rational

---

[143] Aristotle, *Rhetoric*, 1359b.
[144] Aristotle, *Politics*,1274b, wrote that 'we must begin by asking, Who is the citizen, and what is the meaning of the term?'
[145] Aristotle, *Nicomachean Ethics*, 1111a, argued that 'what is voluntary would seem to be what has its first principle in the person himself when he knows the particular circumstances of the action'.

course of action open to us. Freedom, nature and reason, on this view, ideally coincided. Yet even if the hierarchical order of the universe naturally culminated with the absolutely free and rational necessary being, in the sub-lunary world, contingency and necessity co-existed. Our political deliberations could play a vital role in determining our fates, and so one might have expected that the study of past human affairs would be a major theoretical concern for Aristotle. But, at least officially speaking, his philosophy was no more interested the theory of historical knowledge than Plato had been.

History

Hannah Arendt suggested that for Aristotle, 'The chief characteristic of this specifically human life, whose appearance and disappearance constitute worldly events, is that it is itself always full of events which ultimately can be told as a story, [or] establish a biography.'[146] But although this view of human life might be implied by Aristotle's conception of political deliberation as engaging with the contingencies the world throws up, he never developed it theoretically. The events of an individual human life, like the subject-matter of political deliberation, were related as a series of particulars; one thing after another.[147] He thought that there could be no science of history for similar reasons. The ideal type of knowledge took the universal and the necessary for its objects; it had no space for the flow of events of which narratives of the kind Arendt had in mind were composed.

Certainly, like Plato, Aristotle drew a fundamental distinction between natural happenings and human actions. The difference, however, was not simply the presence of contingency. In his logical writings, Aristotle distinguished what was possible but not actual from what was actual but not necessary, and both of these statuses from the necessarily impossible and the necessarily existent.[148] But he also made clear that contingency could be a feature of 'natural events', as well as 'events due to habit'. The difference was that in nature, contingent events were exceptions to the rule; but in human affairs, contingency itself was the rule, because 'nature does not belong to these in the same way'.[149] Contingency in the context

---

[146] Hannah Arendt, *The Human Condition*, 2nd edn (Chicago and London: University of Chicago Press, 1998 [1958]), 97.
[147] Aristotle, *Metaphysics*, trans. Kirwan, 1027a.
[148] See the table in Aristotle, *De Interpretatione*, 62.
[149] Aristotle, *On Memory*, trans. Richard Sorabji (Providence: Brown University Press, 1972), 452a.

of nature was 'what occurs, but not always nor of necessity nor for the most part'. This species of accident, in other words, might have no further explanation beyond pure chance.[150] But in the human realm, where habit was a factor, there were things that could not be understood as necessary, but that were also not mere accidents. An artefact like a house did not occur at random, but nor had it simply grown like a plant from a seed.

To explain artefacts, Aristotle employed the concept of a final cause: the house had come into being in accordance with a design. The account in the *Metaphysics* distinguished four different types of causation.[151] In English, these are normally rendered as efficient, material, formal, and final causes. Typically for Aristotle, they formed an ascending hierarchy in that order, with the final cause or *telos* at the summit. The first was what we would call the physical (kinetic) cause, the work of the builders; the material cause accounted for the different stuffs involved in whatever process or event we were considering, like the stones or planks from which the house was made; formal causes had to do with the different shapes or structures involved in and resulting from it, the plan of this particular house; and the final cause or *telos* was the desired goal, creating a dwelling.

As with Plato, however, human life, despite its artefactual component, was not absolutely divorced from the natural order. Aristotle likewise saw an important analogy between human action and nature in the sense that nature itself acted with intelligence. The universe as a whole was nature's artefact, and human beings had been made with a final cause in mind: their purpose was to contribute to the realisation of rationality in the universe. Animal growth occurred 'as if they were handicrafted'.[152] Even animal sense-perception was knowledge of a kind, but 'the most practically-wise of the animals is the human'.[153]

The most characteristically human way of exercising that wisdom was by engaging in political action, but political action was not simply a process of making. Aristotle was careful to distinguish politics from the kind of *techne* associated with artefactual production. Admittedly, even in house-building, there was no escape from contingency: 'one who produces a house does not produce all the things which coincide in the house

---

[150] Aristotle, *Metaphysics*, trans. Reeve, 1064b–1065a.
[151] See Aristotle, *Metaphysics*, trans. Kirwan, 1013a–b.
[152] Aristotle, *Generation of Animals*, 743b, in *Generation of Animals & History of Animals I, Parts of Animals I*, trans. C. D. C. Reeve (Indianapolis: Hackett Publishing Company, Inc., 2019).
[153] Aristotle, *Generation of Animals*, 744a.

that is coming to be, for they are infinite'.¹⁵⁴ But house-building could still be reduced to a generic art. Politics could not, which was why it required a special kind of wisdom.

Despite this awareness of the importance of contingent, unique, unpredictable events in a political context, Aristotle's prioritisation of the universal and the necessary ensured that giving a theoretical account of history did not interest him. The realm of human affairs was full of 'items which are true and are the case but which can also be otherwise', but 'understanding cannot be concerned with these'. All such studies were disbarred from claiming the title of 'science', because they were not demonstrative. They were relegated by Aristotle to the status of 'opinion', or 'a proposition which is immediate and not necessary'.¹⁵⁵ Aristotle made clear in the *Metaphysics* that 'no discipline deals with the coincidental'.¹⁵⁶

This attitude proved to be consequential for Christian thought. Medieval thinkers wanting to incorporate theology into the Aristotelian schema of knowledge could use the *Metaphysics* to substantiate the claim that the study of God was likewise a demonstrative science, indeed by far the most important of such sciences. Even when the association between science and rational demonstration was lost, the attractions of certainty and necessity remained. Modern philosophers of science may have departed from Aristotle in other respects, but they have often agreed with him in thinking that only truly certain and necessary knowledge really deserved the name.¹⁵⁷

The *Poetics* did identify historiography as a species of writing distinct from poetry, but only to underline that poetry dealt with universal questions while history was interested in particulars.¹⁵⁸ The crucial difference between them was that while history 'tells what has happened', poetry was concerned with 'the sort of things that *can* happen'.¹⁵⁹ Whereas poetry showed us 'the sort of things that according to likelihood and necessity a certain kind of person tends to say or do', history could only deal with 'particulars ... what Alcibiades [for example] [actually] did or what happened to him'.¹⁶⁰ Certain historical events might have poetic value

---

¹⁵⁴ Aristotle, *Metaphysics*, trans. Kirwan, 1026b.
¹⁵⁵ Aristotle, *Posterior Analytics*, 88b–89a.
¹⁵⁶ Aristotle, *Metaphysics*, trans. Kirwan, 1027a.
¹⁵⁷ See Peter Adamson, *Medieval Philosophy A History of Philosophy Without Any Gaps, Volume 4* (Oxford: Oxford University Press, 2019), 141, 320.
¹⁵⁸ See p. 71, above.
¹⁵⁹ Aristotle, *Poetics*, trans. George Whalley (Montreal and Kingston: McGill-Queens University Press, 1997), 1451b.
¹⁶⁰ Aristotle, *Poetics*, 1451b.

because they happened to illustrate the kind of universal truths expressed in poetry, but this was incidental.

Aristotle's position was thus close to that of Thucydides, who found the Peloponnesian war interesting because it was exemplary. Quite consistently, when Aristotle did discuss the analysis of historical events in theoretical terms, he approached the problem via his conception of scientific reasoning. In the *Posterior Analytics*, for example, he discussed the question 'Why did the Persian war come upon the Athenians?' His answer was 'Because they attacked Sardis with the Eretrians.' But the way in which Aristotle supported this explanation underlines the difference from a historian like Herodotus. Aristotle continued 'War A, being first to attack B, Athenians C. B holds of C (being first to attack holds of the Athenians), and A holds of B (men make war on those who have first wronged them).'

This, however, was not intended as a specific explanation of an individual event. Aristotle continued: 'Therefore A holds of B (being warred upon holds of those who first began), and this – B – of the Athenians (they first began it). Therefore here too the explanation, what initiated the change, is a middle term.'[161] Aristotle explained the Persian war as typical of the *kind* of thing that was likely to happen in the circumstances. Historical events were amenable to a kind of quasi-algebraic substitution where the letters stood for types of events like war, unprovoked raiding and generic groups of victims.

The point is not that Aristotle was wrong to think in this way, but rather that he favoured explaining the past by subsuming particular events under universal kinds. What Aristotle's account explained was not the Persian war in its specificity, but the Persian war as an instance of a certain type of event, 'war' as such. Like Plato, when Aristotle considered past events, he tended to do so in what we would call social-scientific rather than historical terms. The upshot was that history in the sense of an understanding of an individual event or passage of events had no official place in Aristotle's philosophical account of the main branches of science, which were limited to natural philosophy, logic and ethics.[162]

Yet Aristotle, or at least his school, was nevertheless familiar with a distinctively historical form of thinking. The work we now call the *Constitution of Athens* was traditionally ascribed to Aristotle, but

---

[161] Aristotle, *Posterior Analytics*, 94a–b.
[162] Aristotle, *Topics*, trans. Robin Smith, 105b, wrote 'In outline, there are three classes of premisses and problems. Some premisses are ethical, some are scientific, and some are logical.'

P. J. Rhodes, author of a thorough modern study, has declared against Aristotle's personal authorship.[163] The question may never be settled decisively.[164] Even Rhodes accepts, however, that the work is indubitably a product of Aristotle's Lyceum; that it was composed in the late 330s or 320s BCE, when Aristotle was still alive; and that Aristotle's project of studying the constitutions of the various Greek cities is the most likely reason for its existence. As Rhodes also notes, moreover, the 'interest and importance' of the work do not depend on the question of authorship.[165] At the very least, it is evidence for the existence of historical analysis within the Lyceum.

As its title suggests, the work was a study of the Athenian constitution as Aristotle knew it. Its development was set in the context of a discussion of Athenian history, especially political history, from the time of Solon. Importantly, this history was not treated in generic terms (even if it was ultimately intended for use in a larger project), nor did it make use of teleological explanation.[166] The Athenian constitution was not treated simply as an instance of a democratic *type* of constitution. Nor was it presented as having a telos in the same way we saw Aristotle had discussed the example of a house in his Metaphysics.

The Athenian constitution had no architect or designer; its form was the product of contingent responses to contingent circumstances, not a plan. It was represented purely as the product of the vicissitudes of past politics. The genesis of the city's constitution was explained exclusively via the actions of identifiable individuals and the unfolding of specific passages of events. It is true that its current state was represented as the product of a series of changes in the Athenian system of government, first from tyranny to democracy, and then to oligarchy. But this continuum of events differed from the ideal, cyclical, theory set out in the *Republic* not simply in the order of the constitutional changes it described, but in not presenting those changes as instances of a necessary or typical pattern.[167]

---

[163] See P. J. Rhodes, 'Introduction' to Aristotle, *The Athenian Constitution* (London: Penguin, 2002 [1984]).

[164] John J. Keaney, *The Composition of Aristotle's Athenaion Politeia Observation and Explanation* (Oxford: Oxford University Press, 1992), 14, argues against Rhodes that textual evidence combined with ancient tradition allows 'no other conclusion except that Aristotle himself was the author'.

[165] P. J. Rhodes, *A Commentary on the Aristotelian Athenaion Politeia* (Oxford: Clarendon Press, 1985 [1981]), 63.

[166] P. J. Rhodes, *Commentary*, 8.

[167] Aristotle, *The Athenian Constitution*, 95. Aristotle, however, still shared Plato's general view that 'human affairs are a cycle', based on his idea of time as measured by circular motion: see *Physics*, 223b.

Whoever wrote the *Constitution of Athens* understood the importance of evidence. In discussing the challenges that Aristeides faced in governing, for example, facts and figures were given particular to the condition of Athens: this was a city with 'six thousand jurymen, one thousand six hundred archers and also one thousand two hundred cavalry, five hundred members of the Council, five hundred guardians of the docks, and also fifty watchmen'.[168] These facts were not offered as an illustration of a general rule, for instance that governing large cities was difficult; they were supposed to elucidate the circumstances peculiar to Athens.

There was also explicit use of what we would now call primary source materials. When relating the overthrow of the tyranny of the Thirty and the reconciliation of the main democratic factions, the document setting out the terms and conditions of the peace agreement was quoted directly.[169] Historical works were treated as engaged in mutual criticism: in assessing the reputation of controversial figures in Athens, it was made clear that the views of various historians had been consulted.[170] There was, in other words, an awareness that historical explanations have a reflexive dimension, insofar as they necessarily refer to other, similar, explanations to which they are critically related.

The Constitution of Athens certainly did not conform in all respects to modern historical practice. At least as it has come down to us, it lacks a critical apparatus. It also often failed to identify its sources. But the kind of thinking on display was unmistakably historical nonetheless. Athenian politics was presented as belonging to a ceaseless flow of events without invoking any overall plan or intention. For example, internal developments in Athenian politics were repeatedly understood as caused by external wars and other contingent events. The famous naval battle of Salamis of 480 BCE, in which Athens participated in a decisive Greek victory against the Persians, was singled out as a key event that tipped power in favour of the democratic faction. The Athenian generals had given up hope of fighting on, but the Boule or Council organised a fighting fund that crewed the necessary ships and so was able to take credit

---

[168] Aristotle, *The Athenian Constitution*, 75.
[169] Aristotle, *Athenian Constitution*, 109, 111.
[170] Aristotle, *Athenian Constitution*, 85. F. R. Ankersmit, *Meaning, Truth, and Reference in Historical Interpretation* (Leuven: Leuven University Press licensed by Cornell University Press, 2012), 71, observes that historical knowledge grows because 'historical writing addresses the same topic over and over again'.

for the success. Yet the author explains that the money for the ships was itself only available because of the recent discovery of profitable mines at Maroneia.[171]

We may compare this way of thinking about the actual battle of Salamis with the well-known logical puzzle of the sea-battle in *De Interpretatione*, where Aristotle dealt with the problem of future contingency. In a famous passage, he wrote that 'it is necessary for there to be or not to be a sea-battle tomorrow; but it is not necessary for a sea-battle to take place tomorrow, nor for one not to take place – though it is necessary for one to take place or not to take place'.[172] He made this statement in the context of an argument about the truth of propositions: 'if it is necessary, for every affirmation and negation either about universals spoken of universally or about particulars, that one of the opposites be true and the other false', then it seems to follow that 'nothing of what happens is as chance has it, but everything is and happens of necessity'.[173]

In fact, Aristotle found this strongly deterministic thesis absurd. Arthur Danto has argued that while Aristotle believed that for at least some forms of scientific reasoning there were general propositions which could be 'true (or false) independently of the time at which they may be asserted', he excluded propositions about tensed sentences from this class.[174] As Danto put it, 'sentences regarding the future, in Aristotle's analysis, are not true: they are not true, and they are not false'. They simply lacked a truth value, reflecting his belief that the future is open for us.[175] The account of the battle of Salamis given in the *Constitution of Athens* was consistent with this view that Aristotle rejected the idea that statements about the future must have a truth value.

Aristotle's logical writings thus confirmed his view of the realm of human affairs as one in which 'what will be has an origin both in deliberation and in action, and that, in general, in things that are not always actual there is the possibility of being and of not being'.[176] This realm was,

---

[171] Aristotle, *Athenian Constitution*, 69, 71.
[172] Aristotle, *De Interpretatione*, 19a.
[173] Aristotle, *De Interpretatione*, 18b.
[174] A. C. Danto, *Analytical Philosophy of History* (New York: Cambridge University Press, 1965), 198.
[175] Danto, *Analytical Philosophy of History*, 197. Danto's view was not unprecedented; according to Susan Haack, *Philosophy of Logics*, 206, Polish logician Jan Łukasiewicz argued that a third value of 'indeterminate' or 'possible' had to be taken by future contingent statements, since these were neither true nor false.
[176] Aristotle, *De Interpretatione*, trans. Ackrill, ch. 9, 19a.

for him, precisely the temporal setting of political action, where there were genuine alternatives: 'both possibilities are open, both being and not being'. A phenomenon like the constitution of Athens was a product of this human realm. It was the product of a distinctive world of human affairs defined by its historicity. Yet Aristotle never gave detailed attention to the kind of knowledge concerned with the past of 'the things that may possibly be or not be', despite his recognition of this distinctively human realm of action in the face of contingency, and despite, moreover, the presence of such studies in his own school.

Conclusion

This chapter has argued Aristotle's conception of a category, and in particular his notion of substance, were connected first to his view of knowledge as the study of substances of one kind or another, and then to his conception of politics as the most important activity of the most important kind of substance, human beings. We also saw that despite having the conceptual materials at his disposal to theorise the understanding of the past doings of human substances as a distinctive kind of knowledge, the priority he gave to necessary, universal, rational, demonstrative forms of knowledge led him instead to treat historical study as of marginal philosophical interest.

In his neglect of history, as in much else, Aristotle was broadly similar to Plato. His categories, despite their sub-lunary location and reference, still served as fundamental concepts. At least some of them (the secondary substances that constituted species) also shared the timelessness of the Forms. The categories, like the Forms, were invisibles that told us about what there is. In turn, the different types of knowledge available to us conformed to these specifications.

That there were also major differences between Plato and Aristotle is nonetheless indisputable. Aristotle unequivocally denied the reality of Plato's Forms on the grounds that they involved an incoherent proliferation of entities for the being of which there was no good evidence. The very stuff of reality was also differently constituted for Plato than for Aristotle; Plato did not posit the supra-lunary element of the aether, to mention just one major difference.

Nevertheless, knowledge for both thinkers remained hierarchical, and both preferred a correspondingly hierarchical, aristocratic political order that reflected the status of philosophical contemplation as the ideally best life. Aristotle's objections to Plato's *kallipolis* were more to do with the feasibility of its design rather than the intrinsic desirability of the rule of the best elements of society.

Aristotle, conscious of the distinction between the ideally best and the best in the circumstances, was however more willing to accept political diversity than Plato.[177] He eschewed Plato's blanket condemnations of Athenian politics. Perhaps more importantly, Aristotle was more willing to accept politics itself. For Aristotle, politics was a distinctive activity with its own logic that Plato (who would have preferred to do without it altogether) did not specify with the same care, though both recognised the importance of some uncodifiable kind of judgement or wisdom in ruling.

Distinguishing political relations from family or conjugal or tribal or market relations, Aristotle identified politics as an activity in which we, the chief members of the category of rational substances, engaged in talk designed to make rules for ourselves and to decide on courses of action in the face of inevitable uncertainty regarding an indeterminate future. Politics thus liberated us from natural necessity, unlike any other beings we know of.

Aristotle's writings on politics, together with those on ethics and rhetoric, drove his later twentieth-century rehabilitation. As theories of action, valuation and discourse, they were less obviously subject to supersession than his scientific and logical works. The revival of Aristotelian ethics was perhaps most pronounced.[178] But although the decline in Aristotle's reputation was precipitous it was, by historical standards, brief, given that he was previously forgotten for centuries.

Indeed, though we tend to think of the early modern and Enlightenment periods as decisively rejecting Aristotle, this is true mostly in hindsight. Thinkers like Descartes or Hobbes who wanted to break with the Aristotelian framework were, in their own time, exceptions. Aristotle's thought continued to enjoy the status of orthodoxy in some fields, including logic and biology, well into the nineteenth century. This status was powerfully supported by the continuing importance of Aristotelian ideas in the received thinking of the Christian churches, both Catholic and Protestant, which have retained considerable power as social institutions in the twenty-first century.

At the level of assumption, some of Aristotelianism's key ideas, such as the normativity of nature, likewise linger on.[179] It should not be surprising,

---

[177] Aristotle, *Politics*, 1288b, argued that 'the best is often unattainable, and therefore the true legislator and statesman ought to be acquainted, not only with that which is best in the abstract, but also with that which is best relatively to circumstances'.

[178] Martha Nussbaum, *Creating Capabilities: The Human Development Approach* (Cambridge, MA, and London: The Belknap Press, 2011), 125, writes that 'The earliest and most important Western historical source for the Capabilities Approach is . . . the political and ethical thought of Aristotle.'

[179] See Janet Radcliffe Richards, *Human Nature After Darwin: A Philosophical Introduction* (London and New York: Routledge, 2000).

therefore, that in the late eighteenth century even a self-consciously innovative thinker like Immanuel Kant still presented his own theory of categories as a revision of Aristotle. But Kant also preserved the associations that we have shown were present in both Plato and Aristotle between categories, however conceived, and knowledge and politics; and he likewise maintained the tradition of marginalising history as a form of knowledge.

Part 2:

Categories in Modernity: Kant and Hegel

3

Kant: The Categorial A *Priori*

This third chapter argues for a continuity between Kant's thought and the classical tradition with respect to the association between categories, knowledge and politics. After Aristotle, Kant is the thinker most closely associated with a theory of categories.[1] Kant himself claimed that his own theory of categories was a more satisfactory version of Aristotle's.[2] Likewise, Kant's philosophy was a self-conscious modification of Platonism.[3] The three critiques of pure reason, practical reason and judgement that comprised Kant's system – what he called his 'critical philosophy' – addressed the three Platonic virtues of truth, goodness and beauty, in that order. But Kant thought that classical Platonism was no longer possible, precisely because, as the *Critique of Pure Reason* tried to show, all our objective knowledge of empirical truth was mediated by categorial structures that determined our subjective experience.

Kant called his own philosophy 'critical' because he claimed that unlike traditional metaphysics, it was self-conscious about its own limitations.[4] Kant himself regarded his theory as an achievement on the level of Copernicus's proposal of a heliocentric model for the solar system.

---

[1] Michael Marder, *Political Categories: Thinking Beyond Concepts* (New York: Columbia University Press, 2019), 34, writes that Kant and Aristotle are 'the unrivaled masters of the categories in Western philosophy'.

[2] Alain Badiou, *Theoretical Writings*, ed. and trans. Ray Brassier and Albert Toscano (London and New York: Continuum, 2005 [2004]), 186, writes that 'it is the completion of the Aristotelian project that allows for the completion of the Kantian one'.

[3] Immanuel Kant, *Critique of Pure Reason*, trans. and ed. Paul Guyer and Allen M. Wood (Cambridge: Cambridge University Press, 1998), 396, wrote that 'the lofty language that served [Plato] . . . is surely quite susceptible of a milder interpretation, and one that accords better with the nature of things'. The intended inference was presumably that the critical philosophy was just such a milder interpretation.

[4] Kant, *Critique of Pure Reason*, 119, defined dogmatism as the 'procedure of pure reason, without an antecedent critique of its own capacity'.

Copernicus had suggested the earth orbited the sun rather than vice versa; Kant's theory of categories made objective reality depend not on features of the external world but on the workings of our own minds.⁵ Kant's attribution of this central role to subjectivity in the constitution of reality was indeed a radical move, the consequences of which are still reverberating. If it is an exaggeration to say that all modern thought treating categories as integral to knowledge descends from Kant, it is a forgivable one.

Thus, although Kant sought new arguments with which to support traditional positions, his philosophy turned out to be a notable waypoint in the breakdown of the ancient-medieval complex of ideas rooted in Platonism and Aristotelianism. Kant's seemingly abstract account of the relationship between categories and knowledge had profound implications for both religion and politics. In the critical philosophy, we could no more claim genuine knowledge of God than we could of a transcendental order of Platonic Forms.⁶ But since both royal and ecclesiastical authority traditionally rested on claims to such knowledge, Kant's position was potentially deeply subversive. He was saying, in effect, that these claims had no basis in fact. Yet subversion was not Kant's intention. He made obedience to authority a moral duty regardless.⁷ Likewise, although we could have no genuine knowledge of God, belief in God remained a practical necessity for sustaining morality.⁸ Kant was philosophically radical, but at the same time, notably conservative in his moral and political thinking.

Kant, we might say, would have been a traditional rationalist and Platonist if his conclusions about the conditions of scientific and metaphysical knowledge had not made it impossible. Yet Kant's moral positions

---

⁵ See Kant, *Critique of Pure Reason*, 110: 'Up to now it has been assumed that all our cognition must conform to the objects . . . let us once try whether we do not get farther with the problems of metaphysics by assuming that the objects must conform to our cognition . . . This would be just like the first thoughts of Copernicus, who, when he did not make good progress in the explanation of the celestial motions if he assumed that the entire celestial host revolves around the observer, tried to see if he might not have greater success if he made the observer revolve and left the stars at rest.'

⁶ Kant, *Critique of Pure Reason*, 563–82, 'Transcendental Doctrine of the Elements', pt 2, div. 2, bk 2, ch. 3, devoted considerable discussion to showing that none of the traditional metaphysical proofs of the existence of God, including the ontological argument, can be made to work.

⁷ Immanuel Kant, *Critique of Practical Reason*, in *Practical Philosophy*, trans. and ed. Mary J. Gregor (Cambridge: Cambridge University Press, 1999 [1996]), 133–271, 204, argued that practical reason presented the pure moral law to us for 'obedience'.

⁸ Kant, *Critique of Practical Reason*, 139, asserted that the possibility of the existence of God was proven by the reality of human freedom.

remained close to Platonic and Christian tradition. There was no contradiction in believing that we possessed a timeless, or to use Kant's term, 'noumenal' self that could survive us after death, even if we could not actually know this was the case.[9] This self was characterised by its capacity for free will, enabling conduct that would ideally be as rational and universal in its adherence to the moral law as the causal interactions of empirical things according to physical laws. Such conduct, moreover, should remain firmly subject to the legally constituted authorities. Rational criticism of public authority went hand in hand with a duty of obedience and the observance of social and political hierarchy.[10]

Finally, Kant's emphasis on the rational and the universal lead him, like Plato and Aristotle, to marginalise historical knowledge. Certainly, Christianity had very different ideas about the nature of the historical process. History, all Christians agreed, was a progress towards salvation, even if there was plenty of disagreement over the details. This belief was reflected in Kant's philosophy by the replacement of the cosmological cycles found in Plato with a process tending in the direction of the realisation of the good. Kant wrote of a universal history with a cosmopolitan aim that would culminate in a peaceful international federation of states. But this view was not the product of critical historiography. It was derived, rather, from Kant's conviction that the practical certainty of the freedom of the noumenal self also gave us reason to believe in a divine intelligence with a teleological purpose for the world, namely the actualisation of the good.[11] While Kant did not ignore historical knowledge, he subordinated it to moral, theological and philosophical treatments of the past.

Categories

Kant's critical philosophy does not contain one set of categories, but two. *The Critique of Pure Reason* deals with the categories of the understanding, and the *Critique of Practical Reason* presents the categories of

---

[9] Kant, *Critique of Practical Reason*, 140, treated immortality as necessary condition of the moral will.
[10] Immanuel Kant, 'An Answer to the Question: What is Enlightenment?', in *Practical Philosophy*, 11–22, 22, summed up his position as '*Argue as much as you will and about what you will; only obey!*' (Italics in original).
[11] Immanuel Kant, 'Idea for a Universal History with a Cosmopolitan Aim', trans. Allen W. Wood, in *Anthropology, History, Education*, ed. Günter Zöller and Robert B. Louden (Cambridge: Cambridge University Press, 2007), 107–20, 107, wrote that 'History . . . allows us to hope . . . that . . . the play of the freedom of the human will in the large . . . can be recognized as a steadily progressing though slow development.'

freedom.¹² The categories of the understanding have attracted by far the most attention, however. The understanding was Kant's term for the faculty that related the different elements of our sensory experience to one another, enabling both a unified sense of self and a coherent experience of the world. The categories of the understanding allowed Kant to answer Hume's argument that our experience gave us no grounds to believe that there was any rational necessity to causal relations.¹³

For Hume, although in practice we have no reason to believe that the sun won't come up tomorrow, we also have no theoretical grounds for saying that it must.¹⁴ Kant's argument that the categories supplied the required theoretical necessity seemed to provide a philosophical foundation for the Newtonian natural sciences he so admired. This made him particularly attractive in the second half of the nineteenth century as the appeal of Hegelian natural philosophy waned. In that era, Kant's credibility was also enhanced by his own writings on natural philosophy, which included some important conjectures regarding what we would now call astrophysics.¹⁵ Even when Kant's critical philosophy was undermined by developments in geometry and physics in the later 1800s, the logical empiricists, the first generation of modern 'analytical' philosophers, inherited Kant's project of providing a philosophical guarantee for the certainty of scientific knowledge.

The categories of the understanding belonged to what Kant called the 'transcendental doctrine of elements'. By the 'elements' he meant the fundamental constituents of our experience that provided it with its logical foundations and defined its scope in advance. They were not to be treated

---

[12] For the tables of categories of the understanding and of freedom respectively see Kant, *Critique of Pure Reason*, 212; and Kant, *Critique of Practical Reason*, 193–4.

[13] See Nelson Goodman, *Fact, Fiction, and Forecast*, 4th edn (Cambridge, MA: Harvard University Press, 1983 [1954]), for an important modern treatment of the so-called 'problem of induction'.

[14] David Hume, *A Treatise of Human Nature A Critical Edition*, ed. David Fate Norton and Mary J. Norton, 2 vols (Oxford: Oxford University Press, 2007), i.86, wrote that 'One wou'd appear ridiculous, who wou'd say, that 'tis only probable the sun will rise to-morrow, or that all men must dye; tho tis plain we have no further assurance of these facts, than what experience affords us.'

[15] Immanuel Kant, 'Universal Natural History and Theory of the Heavens, or Essay on the Constitution and the Mechanical Origin of the Whole Universe According to Newtonian Principles', in *Natural Science*, ed. Eric Watkins, trans. Lewis White Beck, Jeffrey B. Edwards, Olaf Reinhardt, Martin Schönfeld and Eric Watkins (Cambridge: Cambridge University Press, 2012), 182–308, advanced what is now called the nebular hypothesis, which Watkins describes (186) as the view that 'our solar system formed over time out of a nebulous expanse of original matters endowed with different specific densities'.

as filtering or screening our experience, but as making it possible. It was this argument that the categories were conditions of the possibility of an experiencing subject that prompted Kant's comparison of himself with Copernicus. But Kant's categories were not therefore 'subjective', in the sense of expressing a personal viewpoint. The categories were, rather, the universal grounds that made subjective or personal viewpoints possible.

Kant's theory of categories at least has in common with Aristotle's that it was contentious from the outset. As Paul Guyer remarks, the first reviewers of the *Critique of Pure Reason* found Kant's argument for the deduction of the categories so confusing that he rewrote that section of the book, but 'the attempt in the second edition to remove the obscurity that had shrouded the Deduction in the first did not succeed'.[16] Kant's deduction of the categories was partly based, like Aristotle's, on our use of predication; it aimed to delimit what could meaningfully be said of something. But, as Guyer also rightly emphasises, showing that our judgements were empirical evidence for an implicit categorial structure was not enough for Kant. His argument was that the use of the categories of the understanding was logically necessitated if our experience were to take the form that it did. It is this debate that has never been conclusively settled.

Kant's final arrangement of the categories of the understanding was emblematic of the intricacies and complexities of the critical philosophy at large. Rather than the simple list provided by Aristotle, Kant argued for a fixed total of twelve categories themselves grouped under the four headings of quantity, quality, relation and modality.[17] These headings were not themselves strictly categories, and their status was left undefined. We also have to talk of groups of categories as in some cases the concepts involved were pairs, rather than individual. They were unity, plurality and totality (quantity); reality, negation and limitation (quality); substance and accident, cause and effect, and reciprocity (relation); possible or impossible, existent or non-existent, and contingent or necessary (modality). Within each of these triads, the third member was supposedly to be derived from the first two.[18]

Moreover, the four main groups were themselves further subdivided into two pairs. The first two groups were said to be 'mathematical', and

---

[16] Paul Guyer, 'The Deduction of the Categories: The Metaphysical and Transcendental Deductions', in *The Cambridge Companion to Kant's Critique of Pure Reason*, ed. Paul Guyer (Cambridge: Cambridge University Press, 2010), 118–50, 119.
[17] Kant, *Critique of Pure Reason*, 212.
[18] Hegel's dialectical approach was influenced by Kant's treatment of the categories of the understanding: see Chapter 4, below.

the second two were 'dynamical'. The difference is that the 'mathematical' categories of quantity and quality could be used for both purely rational and empirical purposes, whereas the 'dynamical' ones of modality and relation were restricted to structuring empirical presentations. Geometrical, mathematical, objects had the purely rational qualities of being countable and measurable, and possessed abstract properties such as shape, whereas only those things we experience through our senses could be said to exist dynamically and to be subject to the laws of cause and effect. But both mathematical, ideal and dynamical, empirical objects were understood in terms of a pre-given categorial structure.

It is difficult to know how seriously to take Kant's claim that he adopted the term 'categories' for the components of this intricate structure because his own philosophical aims were 'basically identical' with Aristotle's. But it is easy to agree with him that his approach was 'very distant from [Aristotle's] in execution'.[19] In an era when official censorship and sanctions for religious deviations remained a real threat, Kant may simply have been exploiting the continued prestige of scholastic thought to minimise the novel and controversial aspects of his own claims. Kant's qualifications suggest that he should not be taken entirely at face value. For example, he argued that while Aristotle provided a list of 'pure elementary concepts', it had not been 'worked out according to rules' and was thus no better than 'a hint for future enquirers'.[20]

It is nonetheless possible to compare Kant's list to Aristotle's. Notably, Kant retained substance, which he made the first of his categories of relation. Yet where Aristotle's categories had individuated substances, for Kant, substances and their properties belonged exclusively to a homogeneous physical order.[21] Persons were substances only to the extent that they were thingly. Substance were still bearers of properties, but the properties were restricted to those of material objects conceived exclusively as bodies interacting causally with one another.

---

[19] Kant, *Critique of Pure Reason*, 212.

[20] Immanuel Kant, *Prolegomena to any future metaphysics that will be able to come forward as science*, in *Theoretical Philosophy after 1781*, ed. Henry Allison and Peter Heath, trans. Gary Hatfield, Michael Friedman, Henry Allison and Peter Heath (Cambridge: Cambridge University Press, 2002), 30–169, 115.

[21] Richard Dien Winfield, *Conceiving Nature After Aristotle, Kant, and Hegel: The Philosopher's Guide to the Universe* (Cham: Palgrave Macmillan, 2017), 64, puts it concisely: Kant's categories 'do not specify types of objects. Instead of determining different natures or forms of things, the categories specify the different possible ways in which representations can be necessarily connected so as to convey some objective relation that applies to any object of possible experience. Rather than placing objects into a hierarchy of genus and species [as in Aristotle], these categories determine connections that objects must exhibit, no matter what they are.'

Aristotelian categories such as 'having' and 'doing', which treated substances as agents, were thus altogether omitted from Kant's categories of the understanding, whereas one might say 'being-affected' was retained, at least implicitly, insofar it overlapped with efficient causation. Other important Aristotelian categories, notably quantity, quality and relation, were no longer strictly categories at all for Kant, but meta-headings. As for Kant's meta-heading of modality, this had not been part of Aristotle's original list of categories at all; but its inclusion was nonetheless clearly continuous with key Aristotelian concerns. As we saw, Aristotle gave considerable attention to problems of modality in his discussions of possibility, actuality and necessity.

Looking only at the table of categories, one might also conclude that Aristotle's inclusion of the categories of time and place, the 'where' and the 'when' pertaining to substances, had been altogether omitted. But this would be to overlook Kant's argument that the categories operated on objects necessarily conceived as extended in space and persisting in time. Kant referred to this as the transcendental aesthetic, where 'aesthetic' had to do with the five senses rather than with beauty. In order to judge whether we were seeing one thing or many, for example, as we did when we applied one of the categories of quantity, we must presuppose that what we were experiencing was both located outside us and had duration.

Kant's argument that space and time were structural features of our experience thus gave time a more fundamental role than it had for Aristotle.[22] For Aristotle, time as such was simply a measure of change, even if he recognised the constitutive role of temporality in human existence in other contexts.[23] Space and time, however, were not features of an independent reality for Kant any more than the categories themselves. They were what Kant called the forms of the outer and the inner sense, respectively.

There was an important parallel with Plato here, insofar as Kant maintained a significant gap between appearance and ultimate reality. Our knowledge of existent things was necessarily a knowledge of them

---

[22] This move proved redolent with unintended philosophical consequences. Martin Heidegger, *Being and Time*, trans. John Macquarrie and Edward Robinson (Oxford: Blackwell Publishers Ltd, 2001 [1962]), 416, related his argument that '*The existential-temporal condition for the possibility of the world lies in the fact that temporality, as an ecstatical unity, has something like a horizon*' directly to the *Critique of Pure Reason*. Emphasis in original.

[23] Aristotle, *Physics Books III and IV, Translated with Introduction and Notes by Edward Hussey* (Oxford: Clarendon Press, 1993 [1983]), 219b, defined time as 'a number of change in respect of the before and after'. Compare Aristotle, *On Rhetoric*, trans. Kennedy, 1389b, where the old were said to 'assert nothing with certainty' as a result of 'having lived for many years'.

in time and space; but this knowledge was nevertheless of appearances only, because all our experience was shaped, as Kant would say, *a priori* – in logical advance of any possible encounter with the world. But unlike Plato, Kant treated being as a realm that was closed to us. Regarding what things might be like without our sensory and conceptual apparatus, we could have no idea. Even science could not tell us.

Here Kant's distinction between synthetic and analytic propositions and *a posteriori* and *a priori* judgements became relevant. Knowledge claims were classifiable according to whether they depended on something beyond themselves, such as experience (and thus were synthetic), or were true simply by logical definition (and thus analytic). Likewise, knowledge claims were true either purely on the basis of rational argument (*a priori*) or were founded on experience (*a posteriori*). This yielded four possibilities: knowledge could be analytic but either *a priori* or *a posteriori*, and the same was true of synthetic propositions.

The class of synthetic *a priori* propositions struck Kant as particularly difficult to account for. Such statements did not rely on experience for their truth, but were not simply true by definition, either. Kant treated both mathematical and moral propositions as synthetic *a priori* claims.[24] To explain how they were possible, Kant argued that mathematical propositions were grounded in the forms of space and time that supplied these formal sciences with ideal units of extension and duration. In the moral case, they rested on rational analysis of our practical experience. In this respect, however, Kant was firmly anti-Platonic: either the objects of both mathematical and moral propositions were not features of independent reality, or if they were, they were necessarily unverifiable.

Subsequent developments suggested that Kant's account was flawed. The discovery in the later nineteenth century of alternative geometries broke the link between the three-dimensional space of our experience and the space of Euclidean geometry, which became only one possible geometry amongst many.[25] This development lies largely beyond our remit, but

---

[24] Kant, *Critique of Pure Reason*, 146, argued that mathematics contained synthetic *a priori* propositions; Immanuel Kant, *Religion Within the Boundaries of Mere Reason*, in *Religion and Rational Theology*, ed. and trans. Allen W. Wood and George di Giovanni (Cambridge: Cambridge University Press: 1996), 39–215, 59, asserted that 'The proposition, "There is a God, hence there is a highest good in the world," if it is to proceed (as proposition of faith) simply from morality, is a synthetic *a priori* proposition.'

[25] Gary Carl Hatfield, *The Natural and the Normative: Theories of Spatial Perception from Kant to Helmholtz* (Cambridge, MA: MIT Press, 1990), 223, writes that the German physicist Hermann von Helmholtz, who sought to demonstrate empirically that physical space was non-Euclidean, 'chalked up Kant's belief in the necessity of Euclid's axioms to the simple fact that ... Euclid's was the only available geometry when Kant wrote.'

it does indicate that Kant tended to conflate the spatio-temporal and categorial foundations of our ordinary experience with time and space as they figured in the theoretical foundations of the natural sciences. This identification effectively restricted experience in terms of the categories of the understanding to sensations that could be organised in causally necessary terms. Experience in terms of moral valuations, in other words, had no place within the categories of the understanding.

This had implications for Kant's notion of the self. There were in fact at least three ways in which Kant dealt with the self or the 'I'. Firstly, there must be a formal subject of experience. According to Kant's faculty psychology, the imagination did the work of unifying sensible presentations of objects with the categories of the understanding to yield what he called 'the unity of apperception' or a single set of percepts that the subject, in knowing itself, knew to be its own.[26] To describe this unified perception of the world, Kant coined the term *Weltanschauung* or 'world-view', which would enjoy a long subsequent history. But in Kant's original use of the term, a 'world-view' was a formal conception, constrained entirely to the physical, empirical order.[27] It could not explain our nature as free agents.

So, secondly, Kant argued for a reasonable belief in (though not an objective knowledge of) a timeless noumenal self, possessing a free will that acted as an empirical cause.[28] This free will functioned as a *deus ex machina* in the world of empirical appearances, pursuing its noumenal ends via interventions in series of causally governed events. Furthermore, Kant claimed that this empirically mysterious but pragmatically undeniable experience of selfhood legitimated belief in (though not knowledge of) the immortality of the soul and the existence of a divine being. This timeless noumenal self was, however, no more contentful or embedded in a context than its formal apperceptual counterpart.

To bridge the gap between these first two ideas, Kant employed a third concept of the self, understood in terms of human nature.[29] He made this 'anthropological' self the bearer of what we think of as ordinary lived experience, subject to historicity and figuring in social and political life.

---

[26] Kant, *Critique of Pure Reason*, 238, writes that '**The unity of apperception in relation to the synthesis of the imagination is the understanding.**' Bolding in original.

[27] Kant, *Critique of Judgment*, 138. David K. Naugle, *Worldview: The History of a Concept* (Michigan: Wm. B. Eerdmans Publishing, 2002), 59, argues that 'for Kant the word *Weltanschauung* means simply the sense perception of the world'. Emphasis in original. See also n. 133, below.

[28] Kant, *Critique of Practical Reason*, 179, writes that 'we could *defend* the *thought* of a freely acting cause, when we apply this to a being in the sensible world, only insofar as this being is also regarded on the other side as a noumenon'. Emphasis in original.

[29] See, for example, Kant, *Religion Within the Boundaries*, pt 1, 'Concerning the Indwelling of the Evil Principle Alongside the Good, or, Of Radical Evil in Human Nature'.

But this self was simply a brute fact that Kant's formal system struggled to find a place for. The empirical realm was supposedly restricted entirely to physical causation. Insofar as the teleological, organic, processes by which living organisms grew and reproduced were included in it, any knowledge of them must likewise be explicable in causal terms. Here too Kant's philosophy was contradicted by later developments. Lacking the benefit of Charles Darwin's theory of natural selection or any knowledge of molecular DNA, he confessed he did not see how growth and reproduction could ever be made scientifically intelligible.[30]

Kant's mistakes regarding biology or mathematics are no more to be held against him than Aristotle's. What is relevant here is that on the one hand, he devised a categorial framework that struggled to account theoretically for persons as historical selves, yet on the other hand, was very much concerned in practice with just this aspect of experience. As we remarked above, Kant believed that it was in history that the good would realised, if at all.[31] The reason for the lacuna lay in the dualistic framework that Kant had inherited from Cartesianism, which had reduced substance to only two categories fundamentally different in kind from one another, mind and matter.[32] Material substance obeyed purely mechanical laws; mind, identified chiefly with rationality, was located altogether outside or beyond the physical order of being. As we observed, although Kant retained Aristotle's category of substance, the *Critique of Pure Reason* identified it exclusively with physical objects.[33]

Kant did still deal with substances in Aristotle's 'primary' sense of the term, namely human beings who were moral agents, in the *Critique of Practical Reason*. There, he developed a table of the categories of freedom. But the structures of the tables of categories in the critiques of pure and practical reason were designed as mirror images of one another.[34] The

---

[30] Immanuel Kant, *Critique of the Power of Judgment*, ed. Paul Guyer, trans. Paul Guyer and Eric Matthews (Cambridge: Cambridge University Press, 2000), 278, insisted that 'absolutely no human reason . . . can ever hope to understand the generation of even a little blade of grass from merely mechanical causes'.

[31] See Kant, 'Idea for a Universal History', and n. 11, above.

[32] René Descartes, *Meditations on First Philosophy*, in *The Philosophical Writings of Descartes*, trans. John Cottingham, Robert Stoothoff and Dugald Murdoch, 3 vols (Cambridge: Cambridge University Press, 1995 [1984]), ii.9, defended the view that 'all the things that we clearly and distinctly conceive of as different substances (as we do in the case of mind and body) are in fact substances which are really distinct one from the other'.

[33] Winfield, *Conceiving Nature*, 66, remarks that matter was not one of the formal elements of experience for Kant and was only known empirically, in keeping with the distinction between critical and metaphysical philosophy discussed below.

[34] See Ralf M. Bader, 'Kant and the Categories of Freedom', *British Journal for the History of Philosophy*, 17:4 (2009), 799–820.

harmony of the arrangement between the two groups of categories indicated a deliberate parallelism between the operations of the natural and moral orders. In both cases, experience was necessarily rule-governed, and the source of the rules, whether physical or moral, lay in the subject, not the object. It is we who give the rules to nature for its necessity; it is we who supply the rules of morality that ought to govern the operation of our free will. The categorial rules in both cases were universal and timeless.

As Ralf Bader has shown, this equivalence applied, for example, to the three categories of modality, by which we understand whether something is possible, actual, or necessary. For the understanding, the categories of modality allowed us to rule out some things as impossible in advance of experience, such as, for instance, the same thing being in two places at once. Most fundamentally, they established some existences as necessary and others as contingent. When the categories of modality were considered with respect to our free will, what is possible or impossible took the form of what was permitted and what was forbidden to us. They allowed us to know our duties and also the kinds of things we must not do. Finally, they established a distinction between duties which were always applicable, and a category of 'imperfect duty' which could vary with the circumstances – the moral counterpart of physical contingency.

The moral equivalent of substance in the table of the categories of freedom was the relation to personality which as Bader puts it was understood in the first instance as a 'sensibly conditioned . . . ordering of desires'.[35] Insofar as the self was conditioned by sensible desires, however, Kant regarded it as both pathological and unfree. Behaviour determined by empirical considerations of any kind was not distinct from animal existence, morally speaking. For Kant, genuine moral personality must be entirely impersonal, since the categorical imperative indicated just what any rational individual would do.

For Aristotle, in contrast, the category of substance was not restricted to bodies purely insofar as they figured in a chain of causal interactions or were impelled by desire. Substances were subject to efficient causation, but actions done from passion belonged to the same continuum as actions understood as final causes. The difference between the sub- and supra-lunary worlds we noticed in Aristotle was one of degree, not of kind. Aristotelian substance involved an inextricable blending and shading into one another of (what we would call) mind and matter; Kant's physico-empirical and noumenal orders strictly separated them. This is why Kant struggled to accommodate social and political experience within the framework of his system.

[35] Bader, 'Kant and the Categories of Freedom', 813.

Aristotle's category of 'being in a position' brings out the difference clearly. For Aristotle a substance could be something that was sitting or standing. But 'sitting' lacked any place in the categories of the understanding for Kant. How we could recognise someone as 'sitting' in purely physical terms was mysterious. When Kant used the example of deciding to stand up in the *Critique of Pure Reason*, he presented it as a free action not determined by natural causes and thus as a complete break in the chain of causation of appearance.[36] Standing up may be physically and temporally continuous with what went before, but in relation to previously having been sitting, it was an 'absolute beginning'.

Aristotle would have found this odd. Sitting happened in continuity with purposes that were just as much properties of the substance constituting the embodied individual as its location in time and space. Like Socrates, who did not think his presence in a condemned cell was explicable in terms of material causes, Aristotle believed something other than physical causation explained a substantial change in position.[37] But rather than being an intervention of a noumenal will in an utterly distinct physical order, as for Kant, the change made sense for Aristotle as a sign of the purposes of a rational substance in a world of substances. Kant's philosophy arguably made accommodating both the phenomenon of historicity and a theory of historical knowledge even more difficult than it had been in the ancient world.

Kant fully shared the emphasis on what was timeless, universal, necessary and rational in knowledge and experience that we saw militated against a philosophical interest in historical knowledge for Plato and Aristotle. Although Kant gave reason a much-reduced role so far as its ability to arrive at metaphysical truths was concerned, he preserved reason's critical role as the source of a single overarching account of the grounds of theoretical and practical knowledge. The gap between the phenomenal and the noumenal orders could still be bridged by reference to 'the standpoint of the highest concept'.[38] This 'universal and true

---

[36] Kant, *Critique of Pure Reason*, 488, argued that 'If (for example) I am now entirely free, and get up from my chair without the necessarily determining influence of natural causes, then in this occurrence, along with its natural consequences to infinity, there begins an absolutely new series, even though as far as time is concerned this occurrence is only the continuation of a previous series. For this decision and deed do not lie within the succession of merely natural effects and are not a mere continuation of them.'

[37] See Chapter 1, n. 96, above.

[38] Kant, *Critique of Pure Reason*, 599.

horizon' ensured a unified conceptual hierarchy. It was what Kant called, acknowledging Plato, an 'ideal of reason'.[39]

But Kant also acknowledged what he called the 'incalculable gulf fixed between the domain of the concept of nature, as the sensible, and the domain of the concept of freedom, as the supersensible'.[40] The argument that it was reasonable to believe a divine intelligence was responsible both for the law-governed natural order, and for endowing the human beings belonging to it with the free will required to progress towards the realisation of the good via the gradual implementation of the rational moral law, connected Kant's whole system. But if that vital link were absent, we would be left simply with 'a multiplicity of points', each of which 'must be able to be given to infinity'.[41] As we shall see, the perspectivism characteristic of nineteenth-century historicist thought embraced precisely those consequences that Kant wanted to forestall.[42]

Kant's response to Hume was not only intended to give scientific knowledge a certain foundation; he also wanted to establish the limits of scientific knowledge in order to preserve scope for religious belief.[43] Likewise, philosophical knowledge should be confined to the reflexive study of its own limits rather than to metaphysical investigations of the nature of reality. Kant re-interpreted the history of Western philosophy as a series of categorial confusions that began in ancient Greece (a narrative that Hegel and Heidegger, amongst others, would likewise later employ).[44] Metaphysics had imagined itself capable of the kind of knowledge claims that were properly the preserve of empirical science. Only Kant's own critical philosophy had avoided this conflation of the

---

[39] Kant, *Critique of Pure Reason*, 551, wrote that 'What is an ideal to us, was to **Plato an idea in the divine understanding**, an individual object in that understanding's pure intuition, the most perfect thing of each species of possible beings and the original ground of all its copies in appearance.' Emphasis in original. Compare *Critique of Practical Reason*, 253, where Kant argued that 'it is only by this deduction [of the categories] that we can be prevented from taking them [i.e. the categories], with Plato, to be innate and basing on them extravagant pretensions and theories of the supersensible to which we can see no end, thereby making theology a magic lantern of chimeras'.

[40] Kant, *Critique of Judgment*, 63.

[41] Kant, *Critique of Pure Reason*, 599.

[42] Nietzsche's writings on categories argued that reality lacked any final unity, and that there was only a multiplicity of perspectives to be reckoned with. See Chapter 5, below.

[43] Kant, *Critique of Pure Reason*, 117, wrote 'I had to deny **knowledge** in order to make room for **faith**.' Emphasis in original.

[44] Kant, *Critique of Pure Reason*, 702–4.

philosophical and scientific standpoints by stripping traditional metaphysics of its pretensions.

Kant's categorial theory also prefigured the argument which became a commonplace in twentieth-century philosophy of language that category mistakes were confusions of types of propositions. He compared the identification of the categories with compiling a grammar, and remarked that the two tasks were very closely related.[45] Wittgenstein's famous mid-twentieth-century description in the *Philosophical Investigations* of the task of philosophy as 'showing the fly the way out of the fly-bottle' (by which he meant that our philosophical difficulties would mostly be dispelled if we realised that the questions we were asking were the product of what we could call a confusion of genres) was a lineal descendent of Kant's late eighteenth-century effort to dispel the confusions of metaphysicians who took the illusions to which reason was supposedly naturally prone for reality (he described them as chasing soap bubbles).[46] The roots of the 'linguistic turn' are already visible in Kantian categorial theory.

Knowledge

Just as in Plato and Aristotle, Kant's categorial scheme was directly connected to his delineation of the different departments of knowledge. In that delineation, the divisions of knowledge familiar from ancient thought remained broadly recognisable. Philosophy, logic, and the various sciences still constituted the domain of theoretical knowledge, which was firmly separated from the practical sphere. But their status changed radically. Under the influence of Christianity, Kant inverted classical priorities, making conformity to the moral law in the practical domain our most urgent concern, while relegating traditional metaphysics to the status of illusion.

Kant's critical philosophy was thus instrumental in bringing about a fundamental change in the hierarchical ordering of knowledge employed by Plato and Aristotle in which metaphysics occupied pride of place.

---

[45] Kant, *Prolegomena*, 115, wrote that 'To pick out from ordinary cognition the concepts that are not based on any particular experience and yet are present in all cognition from experience . . . required no greater reflection or more insight than to cull from a language rules for the actual use of words in general, and so to compile the elements for a grammar (and in fact both investigations are very closely related to one another).'

[46] Ludwig Wittgenstein, *Philosophical Investigations*, trans. G. E. M. Anscombe, P. M. S. Hacker and Joachim Schulte, 4th edn, rev. P. M. S. Hacker and Joachim Schulte (Oxford: Blackwell Publishing Ltd, 2009 [1953]), §310, 110ᵉ, writes 'What is your aim in philosophy? To show the fly the way out of the fly-bottle.'

Science became firmly distinct from the metaphysical natural philosophy that the medieval world inherited from Aristotle. Science now became identified with the task of stating the rules governing causal interactions between empirical phenomena in a fully quantifiable, algebraically expressible, way. Scientific phenomena also underwent a fundamental change in character. Elementally distinct substances whose interactions were explained by their natural affinities became materially homogeneous units in a causal series. Moreover, scientific knowledge and moral value belonged to altogether different orders of being, a scheme deliberately to prevent both scientific and philosophical rationality from trespassing onto the practical terrain of moral judgement.

One element of classical knowledge that survived in Kant's philosophy relatively unscathed, however, was logic. In the 1780s it was still generally believed that traditional Aristotelian logic had perfected our knowledge of the universally valid rules of formal reasoning. Kant himself declared that Aristotle had given logic the form of a 'finished and complete' science, a belief that Gottlob Frege and others later exposed as incorrect (but that modern historians of logic would also say under-rated later classical and medieval contributions).[47] Kant thought that the judgements we made on the basis of our informal use of these logical rules supplied the necessary material for the deduction of the categories, although he left room for doubt over how exactly our judgements and the categories were related.[48]

Unlike logic, mathematical thinking could hardly be treated, in the aftermath of the invention of calculus, as a perfected science. Yet Kant did think that like logic, mathematics was tied to the structure of the subject. Where logic formalised the rules of inference from which the categories were derived, mathematics gave formal expression to our intuitions of space and time. The role of intuition was important because the objects of mathematical knowledge were not given in experience. What the geometer worked with, Kant stressed, was not an empirical representation of a triangle, but the concept of a triangle.[49] A geometrical figure presupposed a shape, and as such was linked to our capacity for intuitions of space, but it did not presuppose that the geometer must then be experiencing any actual shape. Number, likewise, presupposed the possibility of series, but not that the mathematician was counting empirical objects. Space and time were structural features of the subject.

---

[47] Kant, *Critique of Pure Reason*, 106.
[48] Manley Thompson, 'Unity, Plurality, and Totality as Kantian Categories', *The Monist*, 72:2 (1989), 168–89.
[49] Kant, *Critique of Pure Reason*, 108, credited ancient Greek geometers with the insight that their discipline was grounded in the *a priori* structure of their own subjectivity.

Like Kant's theory of logic, his philosophy of mathematics was later criticised by Frege in particular for what the nineteenth century dubbed 'psychologism'.[50] The question of whether Kant had tied mathematics to the structure of consciousness in an unnecessary way proved to be an early phase of a long-running debate over what would become known as mathematical intuitionism.[51] Kant's critics argued that physical and mathematical space no longer needed to be conceived as necessarily limited to three dimensions on the analogy of our ordinary experience. Yet Kant's larger philosophical strategy still contributed to setting the philosophical and scientific agenda, even for his critics.[52]

Kant's argument was that a failure to recognise the limits to reason had misled Plato into thinking of the Forms as 'archetypes of the things themselves, and not, like the categories, merely the key to possible experiences'.[53] Insofar as they had endorsed Platonism, subsequent philosophers had inevitably fallen into one or more of four contradictions, which Kant called 'antinomies'. For example, traditional metaphysics had relied purely on rational argument when attempting to resolve such questions as whether the world did or did not have a beginning in time, or whether the universe was limited in size. Likewise, the questions of whether things were infinitely divisible; whether we have free will or all our actions are determined by a prior causal series; and whether or not there is an absolutely necessary being (a God) were problems that perforce arose but inevitably proved insoluble by reason alone.

These 'antinomies of pure reason' were necessarily tetradic because philosophical thought was always constrained, even unawares, by the tetrad of the categories of the understanding. In particular, the ideas of a world, of freedom, of God and of immortality were derived by extending the categories connected with the concept of a series beyond experience: 'the transcendental ideas will really be nothing except categories extended to the unconditioned'.[54] The idea of a world implied an absolutely unified

---

[50] Martin Kusch, *Psychologism: A Case Study in the Sociology of Philosophical Knowledge* (London: Routledge, 1995), esp. ch. 3, 'Psychologism Refuted?'

[51] Kant's intuitionist position has defenders as well as critics. See Janet Folina, 'Poincaré's Circularity Arguments for Mathematical Intuition', in *The Kantian Legacy in Nineteenth-Century Science*, ed. Michael Friedman and Alfred Nordmann (Cambridge, MA: MIT Press, 2006), 275–93.

[52] Michael Friedman, *Reconsidering Logical Positivism* (Cambridge: Cambridge University Press, 1999), argues that early twentieth-century logical empiricism continued the Kantian tradition insofar as it accepted that knowledge was relative to a framework of some kind. See also Chapter 6, below.

[53] Kant, *Critique of Pure Reason*, 395.

[54] Kant, *Critique of Pure Reason*, 461.

whole impossible in experience, which was only ever of parts or aspects of things. Freedom was the power of initiating an absolute first beginning lying outside the chain of empirical causality. God was both the first cause and the paradigm of moral order; and immortality was the idea of a self not limited by a temporal series.

The ideas associated with the antinomies did not lead to contradictions, however, if they were not taken to be empirical facts. Kant's position here was subtle. The noumena were not simply the obverse of the phenomena. Claiming this would involve claiming that we knew something about things in themselves. Strictly, we could not even know that there was a noumenal order of reality, much less what it contained. Kant's approach resembled the equivocal 'negative way' of medieval theologians who argued that although God was essentially unknowable, we could at least be sure that none of the predicates appropriate to the things in this world were applicable to the divine.[55] But this argument from ignorance nevertheless seemingly yielded positive knowledge. If it could be said that God was not in space and time, for instance, we have arguably learnt something about the nature of the divinity.

Rather like negative theology, Kant's account of philosophy gave with one hand only to take back with the other, regaining for rationalism what had been conceded to empiricism. Kant remarked that 'the philosopher's spiritual flight, which considers the physical copies in the world order, and then ascends to their architectonic connection according to ends, i.e., ideas, is an endeavor that deserves respect and imitation'.[56] This passage clearly alluded to the escape of Plato's philosopher from the cave in the *Republic*. Though the status of rationalistic metaphysics had changed, its goals remained intact. Philosophy could at least show that the ideas of freedom, God, and immortality were not contradictory, and even that these ideas were a practical necessity for morality. In fact, the philosophical ideas of reason could do more; though they could not supply scientific knowledge directly, they could provide what Kant called regulative ideals for scientific inquiry.

Kant argued, for example, that science treated the necessary laws governing physical phenomena as all part of the same unified system, but that this was a scientific assumption rather than a discovery. Indeed, it was not

---

[55] D. M. MacKinnon, 'Kant's Philosophy of Religion', *Philosophy*, 50:192 (1975), 131–44, 141, argues that Kant belongs in the tradition of negative theology. For an overview of that tradition (which does not include Kant), see William Franke, ed., *On What Cannot Be Said: Apophatic Discourses In Philosophy, Religion, Literature, And the Arts*, 2 vols (Notre Dame: University of Notre Dame Press, 2014 [2007]).

[56] Kant, *Critique of Pure Reason*, 398.

the sort of thing that science could possibly discover. Another subtlety of Kant's argument was that while the critical philosophy could tell us that physical nature must be law-governed thanks to the *a priori* foundations of our experience, the specific form that those laws took could not be known in the absence of experience. We could know *a priori* that motion obeyed physical laws, but not, for instance, that $f=ma$. Newton's laws of motion were thus genuine scientific discoveries. The discovery of the philosophical foundations of specific scientific laws of this kind was the task of an entirely separate metaphysics of natural science, a specialised application of the critical philosophy.[57]

Critical philosophy explained how science could go beyond experience in treating nature as a systematic unified whole. Moreover, this 'principle of the empirical use of reason' inexorably led back to 'the idea of a most real being as the supreme cause'.[58] This was the other aspect of Kant's answer to Hume in establishing a necessary basis for causal relations for the natural sciences. The claim that causal relations could be shown to be universal and necessary rather than merely dependable regularities was not only a way of rebutting empiricism. It was also intended to have theological ramifications. Nor was this argument limited to the physical sciences. It applied equally to the scientific study of the natural world, as the *Critique of Judgment* explained.

Judgement, unlike understanding or reason, had no associated categories. Rather, it was the faculty responsible for the application of the rules that the categories made possible, and from which the categories had originally been derived. As Kant put it, judgement subsumed the particular under the universal.[59] This work was entirely on the side of the subject. When we judged that the various parts of a living organism had purposes or functions, in the first instance we did not assert that anything other than physical causes were at work. The idea that all the different parts of a plant or animal necessarily worked together to ensure its growth and reproduction did not prove that living creatures were products of intelligent design. Even the idea that nature constituted a single system of ends

[57] Immanuel Kant, *Metaphysical Foundations of Natural Science*, in *Theoretical Philosophy after 1781*, 171–270, 190, argued that while the deduction of the categories in the *Critique of Pure Reason* established the 'principles of the possibility of experience in general', this was 'not the solution to the problem **how** experience is now possible by means of these categories'. It was this latter problem that the *Metaphysical Foundations of Natural Science* was supposed to solve. Emphasis in original.
[58] Kant, *Critique of Pure Reason*, 577.
[59] Kant, *Critique of Judgment*, 66–7, wrote 'If the universal (the rule, the principle, the law), is given, then the power of judgment . . . subsumes the particular under it.'

did not do that. These ideas served biology in the same way that the idea that the laws of nature belonged to a single unified system served physics. They were simply regulative assumptions that allowed us to extend natural science to organic nature.[60]

Kant nevertheless argued that the ideas that individual creatures and even nature as a whole were the products of intelligent design did not form a contradiction. Reason naturally suggested to us the idea of a first cause, but this only yielded the idea of God as some overwhelming physical power, as yet lacking in moral qualities. The idea of a benevolent creator required the further idea of nature as purposive; but we had already found such purposiveness in our own capacity for free action. Reason again suggested that the only explanation for our having this natural capacity was the existence of a divine being whose will was that we should realise the moral law in the world.

This was Kant's moral 'proof' of the existence of God. It was not supposed to be a demonstrative proof in the same manner as the ontological argument that God's perfection necessarily entailed His existence. Kant insisted that 'Being is obviously not a real predicate', by which he meant that existence was not equivalent to a property like colour or shape. Put another way, Kant's argument that 'every existential proposition is synthetic' meant that we could not deduce the existence of anything, even God, simply by logical argument.[61] What Kant thought he had supplied, in other words, was not a logical proof of God's existence, but grounds for a practical conviction of it.[62]

Kant further supported his proof by a consideration of judgements of beauty that again displayed his rationalist and universalist preferences in knowledge. In a contemporary context, when someone says that the beauty of a work of art is subjective, they mean that it is a matter of opinion. What is beautiful to one person is not so to another. For Kant, however, judgements about beauty, or as he called them, judgements of taste, were supposed to apply universally. The person who judged something beautiful was also necessarily claiming that it ought to be beautiful

---

[60] Kant, *Critique of Judgment*, 250, argued that it is via 'the idea of the whole of nature as a system in accordance with the rule of ends' that 'we acquire . . . a guideline for extending natural science in accordance with another principle'.

[61] Kant, *Critique of Pure Reason*, 566–7.

[62] Kant, *Critique of Judgment*, 316, wrote 'This moral argument is not meant to provide any objectively valid proof of the existence of God, nor meant to prove to the doubter that there is a God; rather, it is meant to prove that if his moral thinking is to be consistent, he must include the assumption of this proposition among the maxims of his practical reason.'

for others, too.[63] Kant recognised that different people may find different things agreeable, including works of art and much else besides. We find different food and clothing to our liking. We vary in who we find amusing or attractive. But none of these preferences constituted genuine judgements of taste, to Kant's way of thinking.

For Kant, an aesthetic judgement (and here the word did have the modern meaning of having to do with beauty) was no more 'subjective', in the sense of being purely personal, than a judgement that two events were causally related. But he found this situation puzzling, since an aesthetic judgement that something was beautiful, just like a teleological judgement of natural purposiveness, seemed to be entirely on the side of the subject. The feeling of beauty that was aroused in us, in other words, was not objectively a property of whatever had provoked it. What was actually going on, according to Kant, was that our imagination and our understanding were brought into a satisfying relation to one another in response to the form of the object in question. It was this free play of our own faculties that was responsible for the feeling of pleasure beauty aroused. So, my judgement that something was beautiful was in effect a claim that it would cause your imagination and understanding to interact in an identical way were you to apprehend the form of the same object.

This focus on the formal qualities of the beautiful object was important for Kant because he wanted to insist on the disinterested character of the judgement of beauty. If we found something simply pleasurable with respect to the sensations it provoked, then our sensible, embodied desires were in play. We had an interest in whatever aroused pleasure in us and to that extent we were concerned with instrumental considerations of happiness. We wanted to consume a delicious meal or enjoy the touch of our beloved. But judgements of beauty were supposedly unrelated to sensual pleasure. They rested on the general idea of lawfulness, without our bringing the object under any particular law in the way that making use of the categories of the understanding would require.[64]

This was the great difference between artistic genius and scientific brilliance, according to Kant. The person who discovered a scientific law could

---

[63] Kant, *Critique of Judgment*, 168–9, argued that a judgement of taste occurred when 'merely from one's own feeling of pleasure in an object independent of its concept', a person 'judges this pleasure, as attached to the representation of the same object in **every other subject**, *a priori*'. Emphasis in original.

[64] Kant, *Critique of Judgment*, 125, wrote that 'only a lawfulness without law and a subjective correspondence of the imagination to the understanding without an objective one – where the representation is related to a determinate concept of an object – are consistent with the free lawfulness of the understanding'.

teach it to someone else, but the great artist could at most give rise to a style or school; their work was necessarily purely individual. Nevertheless, in its general lawfulness, universality, and disinterestedness, beauty for Kant was 'the symbol of the morally good'.[65] Just like teleological judgements of nature, aesthetic judgements of beauty (which were most authentically applied directly to nature, because Kant, like Plato, saw the art of painting as mimetic) lead us ultimately to the idea of a divine author of the moral law. This argument was the last step in the account of the various forms of knowledge delineated by the critical philosophy. Kant wove together logical, mathematical, philosophical, scientific, aesthetic, and moral experience into a single tightly integrated account of the genres of knowledge.

We should also note the limits to this account. We observed that so far as science was concerned, the critical philosophy demonstrated that necessary causal relations were a feature of our experience, but that the precise form of those relations could only be known via empirical investigation. Exactly the same was true of our moral duties. The critique of practical reason could establish that the principle of morality was that we should always act in a way that could serve as a rule for others in the same situation, but it could not provide a ground for the specific duties we actually do have. That was the preserve of the metaphysics of morals.

The question of how to ensure that people could actually be educated into moral conduct Kant termed 'anthropology'. This was the study of how to actually bring about 'the subjective conditions in human nature that hinder men or help them in *fulfilling* the laws of a metaphysics of morals'.[66] At its simplest, anthropology comprised a catechism in which teachers put questions to their students concerning virtue. The assumption, naturally, was that the teacher already knew the right answers. Kant was happy, in his own lectures, to supply some illustrations. 'Young man! Deny yourself gratifications', Kant told his students, noting that this was a precept of Stoic morality – albeit one that even he thought could be taken too far if not also tempered with some Epicurean happiness.[67] Indeed, Kant's practical philosophy, with its intense focus on the importance of inner virtue, shows

---

[65] Kant, *Critique of Judgment*, 227.
[66] Immanuel Kant, *The Metaphysics of Morals*, in *Practical Philosophy*, 353–603, 372.
[67] Immanuel Kant, *Anthropology From a Pragmatic Point of View*, in *Anthropology, History, and Education*, 227–429, 275. Kant, *Critique of Practical Reason*, 209, cautioned that an unchecked Stoicism could produce '*moral enthusiasm*' or as we would say, fanaticism, and recommended (229) that we combine 'virtue and happiness together'. Kant always insisted that Stoicism needed not only Epicurean but Christian doctrine to complete it; but Lara Denis, 'Kant's Conception of Virtue', in *The Cambridge Companion to Kant and Modern Philosophy*, ed. Paul Guyer (Cambridge: Cambridge University Press, 2006), 505–37, 526, argues that Kant nonetheless still preferred Stoicism to Epicureanism.

the influence of the neo-Stoic revival that began during the Renaissance and endured well into Victorian times.[68]

Kant's anthropology also revealed the extent to which his substantive moral opinions were bound up with prevailing social and political conditions. For example, Kant was a believer in innate differences between male and female character, and considered women less suited for intellectual pursuits such as science or, indeed, history. 'A woman ... who conducts thorough disputations about mechanics might as well also wear a beard', and 'In history [women] will not fill their heads with battles nor in geography with fortresses, for it suits them just as little to reek of gunpowder as it suits men to reek of musk.'[69] His opinions on race were similar. Though Kant considered humanity a single species (a question which was then still in dispute), he acknowledged four basic racial types, on the grounds of the persistence of ethnic characteristics across generations.[70] These distinctions were not merely to do with appearances. That members of the white race were inherently intellectually superior to black people seemed if anything even more obvious to Kant than that men were naturally cleverer than women.[71]

Kant's views on gender and race were erroneous prejudices, yet their nature as prejudices deserves further comment. They were the products of the continuing influence of a way of thinking about human nature familiar from Plato and Aristotle, according to which the substantial

---

[68] Christopher Brooke, *Philosophic Pride Stoicism and Political Thought from Lipsius to Rousseau* (Princeton: Princeton University Press, 2012), 204, argues that Kant's emphasis on moral autonomy was developed under the influence of Jean-Jacques Rousseau, himself inspired by Stoicism. The broad compatibility of Kant's moral thought with Stoicism is generally agreed upon. Allen W. Wood, 'The Supreme Principle of Morality', in *The Cambridge Companion to Kant and Modern Philosophy*, 372, writes that Stoicism could be 'framed in terms that are compatible with understanding morality as grounded on a categorical imperative'.

[69] Immanuel Kant, *Observations on the Feeling of the Beautiful and Sublime*, in *Anthropology, History, and Education*, 18–62, 41.

[70] Immanuel Kant, *Of the Different Races of Human Beings*, in *Anthropology, History, and Education*, 82–97, 87, wrote that 'one is only compelled to assume four races of the human species in order to be able to derive from these all the easily distinguishable and self-perpetuating differences'.

[71] Kant, *Observations on the Feeling of the Beautiful and Sublime*, 59, citing David Hume as an authority, wrote 'not a single [Negro] has ever been found who has accomplished something great in art or science or shown any other praiseworthy quality'. Taken literally, this claim was empirically false even at the time. Anton Wilhelm Amo, born in what is now Cameroon, taught philosophy in Germany at the universities of Halle and Jena in the 1730s and 1740s. See Stephen Menn and Justin E. H. Smith, eds, *Anton Wilhelm Amo's Philosophical Dissertations on Mind and Body* (Oxford: Oxford University Press, 2020).

essence of a thing determined its peculiar characteristics.[72] Kant's critical philosophy carefully avoided making claims to objective empirical knowledge about the teleological basis of either moral or physical phenomena. But his anthropology lay outside the scope of the critical philosophy, and so there he was less guarded, and sometimes entirely uncritical (in the modern sense) in his views. Put another way, Kant's approach to dealing with the categorial foundations of experience was in tension with his treatment of the classifications of social and political life. Kant's rational political ideals tended in an egalitarian direction, but co-existed in his thought with a traditional substantialist categorial hierarchy.

Finally, historical knowledge occupied the same kind of marginal position for Kant that it had for Plato and Aristotle. Kant was perfectly aware of the existence of what he called the 'historical sciences', but treated them as devoted to the study of the sensible order of actions determined by the same kinds of desires that drove the behaviour of all animal creatures. In human beings, these were pathological. In history, empirically considered, we were dealing with 'the oppression of domination' and 'the barbarism of war'. The lesson of history at this level was that the human being was hard at work on 'the destruction of his own species'.[73] As we shall see, it was a different matter when history was considered from a philosophical point of view.

Politics

The *Critique of Pure Reason* was initially received by contemporary readers as a contribution to theology.[74] But that also made it a political work. The conclusion of the critical philosophy that we could not claim to know there was a divine being had political implications. The established authorities regarded such views as subversive, and Kant fell foul of the Prussian censors over the orthodoxy of his religious opinions in

---

[72] Kant still treated Herodotus as an authority. See Kant, *Of the Different Races of Human Beings*, 91–2.
[73] Kant, *Critique of Judgment*, 227.
[74] Karl Leonhard Reinhold, *Letters on the Kantian Philosophy*, ed. Karl Ameriks, trans. James Hebbeler (Cambridge: Cambridge University Press, 2005 [1790]), 20, ix, which Ameriks describes as 'arguably the most influential work ever written concerning Kant', asserted that the importance of the *Critique of Pure Reason* was that it 'demonstrates from the essence of practical reason the necessity of a moral faith in God's existence. Consequently it compels naturalists to abandon, in favor of a rational faith, their ungrounded claims to knowledge, and supernaturalists to accept their faith from reason.'

later life.⁷⁵ But the first *Critique* was political in another sense also. Just as Kant acknowledged Plato's ideas as an inspiration for the categories, so long as they were not taken as things in themselves, he singled out the *Republic* as a guide in politics. The Platonic ideal as Kant understood it was 'A constitution providing for the greatest human freedom according to laws that permit the freedom of each to exist together with that of others (not one providing for the greatest happiness, since that would follow of itself).' It did not matter if this could not be perfectly realised; it was 'at least a necessary idea'.⁷⁶

Whether Kant's interpretation of the *Republic* was faithful to the Greek context is doubtless debatable. For example, he ignored the hierarchical ordering crucial to Plato's conception of the ideal type of government. But Kant did preserve Plato's rationalism. The ultimate goal of political life, in Kant's view, was 'a sovereignty in which reason alone shall have power'.⁷⁷ In detail, certainly, Kant did not follow Plato. He did not, for instance, attempt to argue that philosopher-rulers should be in charge.⁷⁸ Indeed, unlike either Plato or Aristotle, Kant did not believe in the legitimacy of natural aristocracy of any kind. He was fully persuaded by the rightness of the French revolutionary decision to do away with inherited inequalities of status. Although hereditary nobility persisted in Prussia, Kant rejected the idea that it belonged in an ideally just constitution, because membership bore no relation to merit.⁷⁹

Nevertheless, Kant's rationalism did prompt him to preserve a quasi-Platonic natural hierarchy in practice. We saw that the various departments of knowledge were correlated with the faculties of the knowing subject, namely understanding, judgement, and reason. In Kant's view these also composed a hierarchy that ought to be reflected in social organisation. So, for example, when it came to decision-making, the civil servant needed only understanding, whereas the officer needed judgement, and the general needed reason.⁸⁰ The ordinary bureaucrat

---

⁷⁵ See Allen W. Wood, 'Rational Theology, Moral Faith, and Religion', in *The Cambridge Companion to Kant*, ed. Paul Guyer (Cambridge: Cambridge University Press, 1992), 394–416, 397.

⁷⁶ Kant, *Critique of Pure Reason*, 397.

⁷⁷ Kant, *Critique of Judgment*, 301

⁷⁸ Immanuel Kant, 'Toward Perpetual Peace: A Philosophical Project', in *Practical Philosophy*, trans. Mary J. Gregor, 311–51, 337, did, though, make the consultation of philosophers 'by states armed for war' a 'secret article' in 'negotiations of public right', which might be taken as further evidence of some residual Platonic yearnings.

⁷⁹ Kant, *Metaphysics of Morals*, 471, declared that 'an *hereditary* nobility is a rank that precedes merit and also provides no basis to hope for merit, and is thus a thought-entity without any reality'. Emphasis in original.

⁸⁰ Kant, *Anthropology From a Pragmatic Point of View*, 305.

only had to be capable of grasping instructions and carrying them out, whereas the officer must decide on whether a particular case falls under one or another of the relevant rules, and instruct his subordinates accordingly; but the person in overall charge must be able to identify the relevant rules in the first place. A hierarchy of intellectual ability remained a feature of the organisation of the state.

In politics, as in knowledge, Kant was thus a very conservative radical. Despite his sympathy with the principles of 1789, his endorsement of liberty and equality was compatible with a highly stratified society in which different ranks of people should occupy positions reflecting their intellectual achievements. He happily spoke of the majority of the population as 'the rabble' and 'the masses'.[81] In Kant's political thought, an intense moral idealism shaped by Jean-Jacques Rousseau was constantly wrestling with a bleak scepticism that owed a great deal to Thomas Hobbes. On the one hand he looked forward to a future in which a cosmopolitan federation of states would make war ever more unlikely, each having realised the perfect form of political constitution.[82] On the other hand, he declared that 'the human being is an *animal which*, when it lives among others of its species, *has need of a master*'.[83]

One of Kant's best-known remarks is that 'out of such crooked wood as the human being is made, nothing entirely straight can be fabricated'.[84] But the apparent contradiction between political idealism and scepticism was dissolved in the same way as that associated with the antinomies of the critical philosophy. The cosmopolitan federation of states was a guiding ideal even though it had no basis in our knowledge of fact, and since the discouraging facts in no way made it contradictory to believe in its possibility, we ought to act as if realising it were indeed possible regardless.[85]

Ideally speaking, both government and morality would be as rule-governed as the objects of the physical order. We noted the equivalence between the tables of the categories of the understanding and those of practical reason. The moral ideal for Kant was subjects whose motions consisted entirely of freely willed rational actions in accordance with the moral law. In the first instance, our natural right to freedom, which Kant declared was simply innate, obliged us to leave the state of nature and

---

[81] Kant, *Anthropology From a Pragmatic Point of View*, 315, 327.
[82] Kant, 'Idea for a Universal History', 117–18.
[83] Kant, 'Idea for a Universal History', 113.
[84] Kant, 'Idea for a Universal History', 46.
[85] Hans Vaihinger, *The Philosophy of 'As If': A System of the Theoretical, Practical and Religious Fictions of Mankind* (London: Routledge, 2000 [1925]), argued that this notion of the useful fiction was the leitmotif of Kant's philosophy and could be extended to all areas of human thought and activity.

establish a common authority. All should be able to enjoy their freedom, limited only by the condition that they did not interfere with that of others. In keeping with contractarian tradition, Kant argued that one of the main functions of the state was to transform ad hoc possession into the secure legal institution of property.[86]

Real property played a particularly important role in Kant's philosophy of government, and was the analogue of the category of substance. In relation to it, all other forms of property were mere predicates.[87] But the laws governing the freedom to acquire and own property were also only one instance of the principle of popular sovereignty at work. Kant argued that there was a 'general will corresponding *a priori*' to the idea of common ownership of all things from which the right of private ownership was ultimately derived.[88] This general will, however, also served as the basis of 'all rights of individuals' in the civil condition.[89] The people were the supreme original authority.

Though this reference to the general will sounds Rousseauian, Kant did not share Rousseau's view that the citizens must represent themselves directly in the legislative assembly in order for sovereignty to be legitimate. The 'right of supreme legislation' must be exercised in accordance with the 'collective will' of the people but was not wielded by the people themselves; or at least, not in their entirety.[90] Kant excluded from full citizenship, and thus from the right to vote on legislation, anyone in a dependent situation. Those who lacked 'civil personality' included all women, servants and in general anyone 'under the direction or protection of other individuals'.[91] Moreover, the law, once made, was administered and adjudicated by executive and judicial authorities who, even if elected, could not be opposed. Kant followed Hobbes in treating all resistance to established authority as contradicting the goal of making the civil condition a permanent establishment.[92]

---

[86] Kant, *Metaphysics of Morals*, 414, writes that 'What is called a right to a thing is only that right someone has against a person who is in possession of it in common with all others (in the civil condition).'

[87] Kant, *Metaphysics of Morals*, 414, writes 'Just as in a theoretical sense accidents cannot exist apart from a substance, so in a practical sense no one can have what is movable on a piece of land as his own unless he is assumed to be already in rightful possession of the land.'

[88] Kant, *Metaphysics of Morals*, 404.

[89] Kant, *Metaphysics of Morals*, 481.

[90] Kant, *Metaphysics of Morals*, 481.

[91] Kant, *Metaphysics of Morals*, 458.

[92] Kant, *Metaphysics of Morals*, 505, wrote that 'even though [a rightful] constitution may be afflicted with great defects and gross faults and be in need eventually of important improvements, it is still absolutely unpermitted and culpable to resist it'.

Obedience to the law, which could legitimately coerce and punish in accordance with its rational ends, was not just a legal obligation but a moral duty.[93]

Kant could take this position because both law and morality were for him expressions of rationality. The categorical imperative that everyone should 'So act that the maxim of your will could always hold at the same time as a principle in a giving of universal law' was for Kant at once a legal, moral, and religious principle.[94] The goal of the civil condition was the total rationalisation of law, morality and faith. The categorical imperative applied when voting on legislation and to all other uses of civil personality; in respect of one's private moral conduct; and to one's performance of one's religious duties.

This was a self-conscious refinement of the so-called golden rule, Jesus's command that 'all things whatsoever ye would that men should do to you, do ye even so to them'.[95] But as originally formulated, this principle might admit of exceptions, because it could be interpreted as making reference to self-interest. For Kant, though, genuine moral judgements, like judgements of the beautiful, were necessarily disinterested.

In defining Enlightenment as *'the human being's emergence from his self-incurred minority'*, the most important issue for Kant was the ability to choose one's religious confession.[96] But he once again separated the empirical or historical expression of religion from its ideal, rational component in a radical way. The various Christian churches (and indeed all other faiths) were only imperfect expressions of a rational moral ideal. Perhaps the most important function of government was to provide us with the security to pursue the 'endless progress towards holiness' that Kant associated with rational religion.[97] Jesus was, on this view, the categorical imperative incarnate: he was the absolutely morally exemplary human being who must serve as a guiding ideal for us.[98] Kant reinterpreted the words of Jesus as the command to 'Do your duty from no other incentive except the unmediated appreciation of duty itself.'[99]

---

[93] Kant, *Religion Within the Boundaries*, 60, stated 'the command: Obey authority! is also a moral one'.
[94] Kant, *Critique of Practical Reason*, 164.
[95] Matthew, 7:12. See also Immanuel Kant, *Groundwork of the Metaphysics of Morals*, in *Practical Philosophy*, 39–108, 80 and n.
[96] Kant, 'What is Enlightenment?', in *Practical Philosophy*, 17. Emphasis in original.
[97] Kant, *Religion Within the Boundaries*, 91.
[98] Kant, *Religion Within the Boundaries*, 104.
[99] Kant, *Religion Within the Boundaries*, 182.

Kant's reading of Scripture thus required extracting the rational essence of Christianity from its empirical manifestation. This involved a very free approach to interpretation, which Kant justified by the goal of creating 'better human beings'.[100] Those pursuing Kantian rational religion constituted a separate ethical community that amounted to the true 'church' within the state. Simply obeying the law from convenience or self-interest did not make one morally good. One must obey simply from duty alone. This is what the truly religious did, and so they constituted an 'association of human beings merely under the laws of virtue'.[101] This association in principle needed no actual, empirical expression at all. Although it presupposed political community, it was by no means necessarily co-extensive with it.

The distinction Kant was drawing was reminiscent, though he did not explicitly make the parallel, of the contrast in St Augustine between the City of God and the City of Man. For Augustine, the earthly church necessarily included some who would not be saved. They only pursued religion by observing its external forms in the hope of furthering their own interests. The genuine members of the City of God were the ones who displayed true piety without hope of any reward, at least in this life.[102] For Kant, likewise, a great deal of so-called religion as it was actually practised had nothing to do with the true sense of the term.

Kant knew this argument might be read as condemning the established religious authorities, and thus as politically subversive, so he attempted to forestall these worries. One issue was that members of a religious community might reject earthly government since they no longer felt any need of it. Kant's statement that a truly moral person, of the kind that the religious person was supposed to exemplify, did not 'need ... another being above him in order that he recognize his duty' might suggest this.[103]

Kant denied that this was an anarchistic view, because the truly moral person would follow existing law simply out of their own sense of duty.[104]

---

[100] Kant, *Religion Within the Boundaries*, 143.
[101] Kant, *Religion Within the Boundaries*, 130.
[102] Saint Augustine, *The City of God, Books I–VII*, trans. Demetrius B. Zema and Gerald G. Walsh (Washington DC: Catholic University of America Press, 1962 [1950]), 71–2, wrote that 'the City of God itself, so long as it is a wayfarer on earth, harbors within its ranks a number of those who, though externally associated in the common bond of the sacraments, will not be associated in the eternal felicity of the saints'.
[103] Kant, *Religion Within the Boundaries*, 57.
[104] Kant, *Religion Within the Boundaries*, 151, wrote that 'equality springs from true freedom, yet without anarchy, for each indeed obeys the law (not the statutory one) which he has prescribed for himself, yet must regard it at the same time as the will of the world ruler as revealed to him'.

Another worry was that members of this ethical community would believe that they had a special status as one of the elect, and would become arrogant. In response, Kant cautioned against thinking that simply trying to behave well was any kind of mark of distinction. He repeatedly warned the reader against the 'madness of enthusiasm', or what we would now call religious fanaticism.[105]

Kant did, however, look forward to the possibility that this ethical community would one day include everyone. The result of reducing Christianity to its moral essentials and rejecting everything else either as irrational dogma, or at best necessary for the persistence of institutional religion insofar as it was a desirable aid to the maintenance of the ethical community, was a kind of syncretism. Insofar as religions other than Christianity were genuine religions, they necessarily shared the same rational core.[106]

Kant's 'concept of an ethical community', he was explicit, 'always refers to the ideal of a totality of human beings'. Moreover, this ethical community rested on 'consensus'. All rational people necessarily agreed with one another. The 'absolute ethical whole' was distinguished by perfect accord on all moral questions.[107] If it were ever fully realised, the various institutional churches or other religious bodies would have ceased to exist. It was Kant's stated view that 'in the end religion will gradually be freed of all empirical grounds of determination'.[108]

Kant's prediction of what we might call the withering away of the Church, and its replacement by a 'cosmopolitan moral community' united by 'the moral disposition of brotherly love', antedated Marx's hope for the eventual withering away of the state under Communism by many decades. Yet it rested on the same belief, that rational people can come to universal agreement.[109] This emphasis on consensus is key to appreciating Kant's rationalism. It explains why, though he was acutely concerned with government as a way of enabling morality and religion, he sided with Plato rather than Aristotle on the topic of political deliberation. For Plato, we saw, there were two kinds of political discourse, Sophistical rhetoric and what we might call authentic discourse. Rhetoric was deceptive and served only to manipulate the unwary. The

---

[105] Kant, *Religion Within the Boundaries*, 96, 136, 158, 193, 215.
[106] Kant, *Religion Within the Boundaries*, 140.
[107] Kant, *Religion Within the Boundaries*, 131.
[108] Kant, *Religion Within the Boundaries*, 151.
[109] Kant, *Religion Within the Boundaries*, 214. Compare Frederick Engels, *Principles of Communism* (Peking: Foreign Languages Press, 1977), 12, which made Communism rest on 'the common utilization of all instruments of production and the distribution of all products according to common agreement', and looked forward to a situation in which 'the public power will lose its political character'.

philosopher-ruler, it seems, supposedly employed a kind of discourse free of rhetoric's misleading qualities.

Kant reproduced this Platonic distinction. He insisted, on the one hand, that 'the art of the orator (*ars oratoria*), as the art of using the weakness of people for one's own purposes (however well-intentioned or even really good these may be) is not worthy of any respect at all'. Yet he defended 'the *vir bonus dicendi peritus*, the speaker without art but full of vigor, as Cicero would have him'.[110] The issue here was not simply whether political discourse was open to abuse; it obviously was. The question was more fundamental. It related to the very possibility of artless political discourse, which Aristotle had argued the conditions of politics rendered impossible.

Artless discourse for Kant was synonymous with purely rational discourse, the outcome of which, if sincerely undertaken by the parties involved, would be consensus. Kant's preference for consensus reflected the influence not just of Platonic metaphysical rationalism but also of Christian theology. God's 'speech' (metaphorically speaking, of course, since God could not be said to talk in the same sense as a person) was not only the source of the creation of the world but also the manifestation of an absolutely rational will. Some of the most influential modern theories of political discourse, such as Jürgen Habermas's theory of communicative rationality in which the outcome of the ideal speech situation is likewise consensus, are secular descendants of this way of thinking.[111]

A danger for all such theories, insofar as they become practical assumptions, is that those with whom one disagrees must be morally reprehensible and acting in bad faith. Kant's writings, to be fair, avoided this danger. He was too acutely conscious of the risk of persecution by the authorities for his own progressive views to become self-righteous. Having compared himself with Copernicus in the *Critique of Pure Reason*, in *Religion Within the Limits of Mere Reason Alone* Kant drew an implicit comparison between his own situation and the fate of another famous astronomer, Galileo. In Galileo's time the theological authorities had sought to 'humble the pride of the sciences', and the same danger was now present again.[112] Kant defended himself against possible censure with the declaration that he had no wish 'to modify [the] public doctrines' of theology. The arguments

---

[110] Kant, *Critique of Judgment*, 205. Emphasis in original.
[111] Jürgen Habermas, *The Theory of Communicative Action*, trans. Thomas McCarthy, 2 vols (Boston: Beacon Press, 1984–7 [1981]), ii.399, writes that 'The theory of communicative action aims at the moment of unconditionality that, with criticisable validity claims, is built into the conditions of processes of consensus formation.'
[112] Kant, *Religion Within the Boundaries*, 61.

he was presenting in the public sphere were esoteric, for a small, educated audience only, and hence harmless.[113]

Kant devoted himself to setting limits to public authority that he believed would protect the liberty of all. Hence his insistence that although this authority was rooted ultimately in land, the sovereign was not the direct owner of the citizens living on it.[114] Whereas a European monarch traditionally possessed large estates that belonged to them personally, Kant's sovereign owned nothing itself. Its authority was conditional, in keeping with the argument that the constitution of legitimate government should be regarded as if there had been an original contract created by a general will. Kantian sovereignty was ideally devoid of self-interest (another position later reproduced in Marx's conception of public authority under Communism.) Though established authority must be obeyed, that authority was itself under an obligation 'to change the kind of government gradually and continually so that it harmonizes ... with the only constitution that accords with right, that of a pure republic'.[115] This process, which Kant believed was already ongoing, explains a great deal of his thought on history.

History

In the *Critique of Pure Reason*, time was the form of the inner sense. It was a part of the transcendental aesthetic through which our sensible experience became available for categorial ordering and imaginative synthesis, resulting in a knowing subject. What is perhaps not so obvious are the theological and historical implications of this way of treating time. But they were profound. By making time a constitutive feature of the subject, Kant was continuing the Platonic view of time as purely a property of appearances and ultimately unreal. In the context of Christian belief, moreover, such a view had ramifications for how one conceived of salvation in the form of an afterlife. Any notion of a heaven in which there was personal immortality became a metaphor at best, since we could not understand how a life lived in time could figure in an exclusively noumenal order of being.[116]

---

[113] Kant, *Religion Within the Boundaries*, 61.
[114] Kant, *Metaphysics of Morals*, 466, wrote that 'The people, the multitude of subjects ... belong to [the sovereign] (they are his people). But they belong to him not as if he owned them (by a right to things); they instead belong to him as their supreme commander.'
[115] Kant, *Metaphysics of Morals*, 480.
[116] Immanuel Kant, 'The End of All Things', in *Religion and Rational Theology*, trans. and ed. Allen W. Wood and George di Giovanni (Cambridge: Cambridge University Press, 2001 [1996]), 217–31, 221.

This conception of time also had implications for Kant's understanding of the historical process. Though Kant did not say so explicitly in the first *Critique*, his declaration that time has only one dimension implied that he was thinking of time in Newtonian terms as a series of identical units. But Kant did not clearly distinguish this physical time from time experienced in terms of what Heidegger later called its three 'ecstases', past, present and future.[117] Kant could perhaps have treated the former as a condition of the latter, so that past, present and future were purely empirical rather than *a priori* notions. At any rate, this was what Heidegger later took Kant to have done; he argued that Kant's order of priority should be reversed, so that the time of the ecstases rather than physical time was the more fundamental notion. But for Kant himself, the consequence was that we knew time only as succession. History, empirically speaking, was simply an earlier phase of a physical series relative to the present.

By the same token, however, history could not then be apocalyptic. Kant's belief that there was nothing contradictory in believing that history was the realisation of a divine plan to unite humanity into a single ethical if not political community was an argument for, as he called it, '*philosophical chiliasm*'.[118] It was intended to oppose the view that we were part of an accelerating decline into evil and 'the Last Day and the destruction of the world are knocking at the door'.[119] We could not possibly claim that the end of days was at hand based on any empirical knowledge we could have, and so the usual antinomic solution applied. If we had to choose between believing things were getting worse or that they were getting better, it was more rational to believe the latter, because it was at least not inconsistent with our moral duty to always act in accordance with the principles of universal right.

Thus, Kant's theory of history, his 'Idea for a Universal History with a Cosmopolitan Aim', was a theodicy and not just a theory of the historical process. But it was also a philosophical theory. It was not as a historian but as a philosopher that Kant wanted to 'discover an *aim of nature* in this nonsensical course of things human'.[120] Making yet another comparison with a famous astronomer, Kant likened the philosopher of history to Kepler, 'who subjected the eccentric paths of the planets in an

---

[117] Heidegger, *Being and Time*, 377, stated that 'We . . . call the phenomena of the future, the character of having been, and the Present, the "*ecstases*" of temporality.' Emphasis in original.
[118] Kant, *Religion Within the Boundaries*, 81. Emphasis in original.
[119] Kant, *Religion Within the Boundaries*, 69.
[120] Kant, 'Idea for Universal History', 109.

unexpected way to determinate laws'.[121] Though Kant talked about history as an aspect of nature, he wanted to discern 'the ordering of a wise creator' behind its operations.[122] In those operations it was often hard to discern progress. But in an argument that would be echoed by both Hegel and Marx, Kant attempted to show that progress resulted from the clash of antagonist forces. 'Nature has therefore once again used the incompatibility of human beings ... as a means to seek out in their unavoidable *antagonism* a condition of tranquillity and safety.'[123]

This thesis had little basis in empirical fact, as Kant himself admitted.[124] But then the domain of history, which Kant called senseless, or lacking in meaning, was so precisely because it was nothing other than the domain of the sensible, or purely empirical sensation. When in the first *Critique* Kant wrote of 'historical' knowledge (*cognitio ex datis*) he meant by it exactly what John Locke had meant in referring to the 'Historical, plain method' in the *Essay Concerning Human Understanding*.[125] 'Historical' knowledge here was not primarily knowledge of the past in the first instance, but rather empirical knowledge gained through the senses, to be contrasted with rational knowledge (*cognitio ex principiis*).

This explains why, though Kant was perfectly aware of history's existence as a branch of scholarship, it held little interest for him. The analysis of a series of past events understood neither in terms of its moral significance nor with respect to its contribution to a universal process was philosophically unimportant. History could not qualify as a science in the strict sense, because science was ideally apodictic, just as in classical tradition.[126] Purely 'historical' knowledge of events lacked the requisite certainty. It was exclusively empirical, without the *a priori* component that gave science its necessary character.

At most, history could play a role as a study of applied morality. It could serve the goals of Kant's metaphysics of morals and his pragmatic anthropology, which in combination addressed the problems of establishing our

---

[121] Kant, 'Idea for Universal History', 109.
[122] Kant, 'Idea for Universal History', 112.
[123] Kant, 'Idea for Universal History', 114. Emphasis in original.
[124] Kant, 'Idea for Universal History', 116, wrote that 'It all depends on whether experience reveals something of such a course as nature's aim. I say: it reveals *a little*.' Emphasis in original.
[125] Kant, *Critique of Pure Reason*, 693. Compare John Locke, An *Essay Concerning Human Understanding*, ed. Peter H. Nidditch (Oxford: Clarendon Press, 1975), 44.
[126] Kant, *Metaphysical Foundations of Natural Science*, 184, argued that 'What can be called proper science is only that whose certainty is apodictic; cognition that can contain mere empirical certainty is only knowledge improperly so-called.'

actual duties were and realising a more moral world in practice. 'A *history* is composed pragmatically when it makes us *prudent*, that is, instructs the world how it can look after its advantage better than, or at least as well as, the world of earlier times.'[127] But unless historical knowledge could serve some edifying moral purpose, it had little value, even though it could serve as 'an excellent means for exercising the understanding in judgment'.[128] Quite consistently, the context in which Kant showed most interest in historical study, other than the improvement of morals, was in relation to religion.

In Kant's late work on the *Conflict of the Faculties*, the main theme was the relation of philosophy to the three 'higher' faculties or disciplines that had dominated the universities since medieval times: specifically, theology, law and medicine. Although Kant's critical philosophy was concerned with the theoretical differences between various types of thinking, here he was addressing their institutional dimension. The faculties concerned were not intellectual or psychological, but departmental. Kant associated them with our eternal, civil, and bodily well-being respectively, so that together they comprised a comprehensive scheme of human welfare. As such, their teachings fell under the purview of government. This why they were described as 'higher'; insofar as they were concerned with public teaching, they rested on government-sanctioned authority.[129]

The corollary was that these traditional disciplines were not 'higher' than philosophy because they were more rational. In fact, only the philosophy faculty possessed the rationality that could identify the truth and logic at work in what Kant considered the otherwise purely empirical fields of revealed religion, civil statutes and what we would now call public health. The discussion of the relationship between the faculties of philosophy and theology occupied by far the largest portion of the text, more than the essays on law and medicine combined. Again, however, the focus was not the *a priori* categorial structures of such knowledge, but what would now be called the sociology and the politics of knowledge. Kant wanted to settle the respective roles of philosophical and religious discourse in the public sphere.

To that end, Kant distinguished between the philosophy faculty and what he called 'pure philosophy'. The philosophy faculty was much

---

[127] Kant, *Groundwork of the Metaphysics of Morals*, 69 n.
[128] Immanuel Kant, 'Lectures on Pedagogy', in *Anthropology, History, Education*, 434–85, 462.
[129] Immanuel Kant, *The Conflict of the Faculties*, in *Religion and Rational Theology*, 233–327, 248, wrote that 'a faculty is considered higher only if its teachings – both as to their content and the way they are expounded to the public – interest the government itself.'

broader in scope than pure philosophy. Kant declared that it 'consists of two departments: a department of *historical cognition* (including history, geography, philology and the humanities, along with all the empirical knowledge contained in the natural sciences), and a department of *pure rational cognition* (pure mathematics and pure philosophy, the metaphysics of nature and of morals)'.[130] Here too Kant was thinking of 'historical' knowledge as signifying any kind of empirical study, including but not restricted to the study of the past, which is why he could make 'history' a sub-species of 'historical cognition'.

What we would now call biology was thus also a species of history, but of 'natural history', conventionally distinguished from both 'sacred' and 'civil' history. Sacred history was the history of the Jews and of Jesus Christ and had the status of revealed truth; civil history was the recorded history of humanity, which in practice tended to mean ancient and modern European history (though European interest in the histories of other parts of the world was increasing rapidly by Kant's day). Subsequent changes in meaning have created pitfalls for the modern reader used to more restricted conceptions of both philosophy and history.

Nevertheless, in the *Conflict*, Kant did engage with historical knowledge in the sense of historiography perhaps more closely than anywhere else in his writings. He addressed the 'Grundsätzen der Geschichtslehren', or principles of historical knowledge. So, for example, as part of his discussion of the 'Philosophical Principles of Scriptural Exegesis for Settling the Conflict' he insisted that the principles of historical interpretation must be rational.[131] By this he meant, for instance, that history considered as a philosophical or theoretical means of analysis must insist that a text be interpreted as consistent with itself, and reports of physically impossible events could not be taken as literally true.[132] But applying logic and evidence to the analysis of the text of the New Testament would lead to doubt being cast on the authenticity of its miracles, like the reality of the resurrection.

For Kant, this was no threat to true religion, because he distinguished between the historical and rational elements of Christianity. The resurrection could be safely regarded as a symbolic representation of a moral truth. The fact that it had never actually happened was no threat to faith – when

---

[130] Kant, *The Conflict of the Faculties*, 256. Emphasis in original.

[131] For example, Kant, *The Conflict of the Faculties*, 267, argued that 'Action must be represented as issuing from the human being's own use of his moral powers, not as an effect [resulting] from the influence of an external, higher cause.'

[132] Kant, *The Conflict of the Faculties*, 266–7, asserted that reports of events like demonic possession in the Bible need not be accepted as factual even if their author believed them.

correctly understood. But the potential effects of a failure by the public to make this distinction between moral truth and historical reality did concern Kant. This category mistake, in the modern sense, was consequential because it had the potential to undermine moral behaviour. People might conclude that if Christianity were not literally true then there was no reason to pursue moral improvement. But it also committed Kant to distinguishing between ways of speaking and acting that were valid in the apostles' times and Christian doctrine itself.[133]

By 'valid' here Kant meant something like 'practically efficacious' rather than logically coherent, but his view still entailed that words and actions must be understood against the background in which they were originally uttered. While this was not a strong version of relativism, because Kant was still prepared to fall back on the idea that religion was 'one, universal, and necessary', it implied the need for something like the concept of a world-view in a very different, contentful, sense to the one in which Kant himself had originally used the term.[134]

This in turn presumed a kind of historical analysis devoted to the investigation of such world-views that was distinct from the search for rational moral truth. Kant clearly distinguished historical analysis from Biblical theology which treated the empirical events of the Bible as revealed truths and thus foundations for dogma. Nor did he think of historiography as identical with philosophical theology, the identification of the universal moral truths that could be extracted from Christianity. Finally, historiography was also distinct from the pursuit of universal history, which was philosophical rather than historical.

Yet Kant's acknowledgement of a distinctive set of 'Grundsätzen der Geschichtslehren' never prompted him to state what these principles of historical inquiry were. While there was scope in principle in Kant's philosophy to incorporate an analytic of historical reason, therefore, just as there had been scope in Plato and Aristotle for a philosophical consideration of the premises involved in history as a distinctive form of knowledge of human affairs, Kant, in keeping with the classical tradition of concentration on the necessary and the universal, never pursued it.

Kant's neglect of the issue was for different reasons than either Plato and Aristotle, however, for whom cyclical and generic approaches to understanding the past were uppermost. The great disparity in this respect

---

[133] Kant, *The Conflict of the Faculties*, 263, wrote that 'we can accept [the apostles' method of teaching] as valid in relation to the way of thinking in the apostles' times . . . not as a part of doctrine itself'.

[134] Kant, *The Conflict of the Faculties*, 272. Compare n. 27, above.

between the temporal horizons of pagan and Christian culture must be acknowledged.[135] If ancient thought contained any apocalyptic dimension, the end of the world was only a prelude to a new beginning, just as death preceded reincarnation for the individual. But the result, the marginalisation of historical knowledge, remained the same.

The status of Kant's philosophy of history as a theodicy and not any kind of empirical analysis of the historical process is especially worth emphasising considering its subsequent fortunes. The League of Nations and the United Nations were partly inspired by the Kantian ideal of 'perpetual peace'.[136] In the later twentieth century, Kant remained 'a source of insight, policy, and hope' for modern liberals interested in international relations. Yet he has been interpreted as if his argument applied to historical actuality.[137]

The observation that modern democratic states have not gone to war with one another, for instance, has been treated as a kind of empirical proof of Kant's arguments. But for Kant himself, it could be no such thing. The twentieth-century liberal reading of Kant typically ignored its theological status. Its defenders could reply that Kant's argument can be tested empirically without invoking his broader philosophical and theological assumptions. But the worry remains that the secular ideal of history as empirically progressive necessarily invokes an assumption to which it is no longer entitled, that there is a 'good principle' which is at work 'unnoticed to the human eye yet constantly advancing'.[138] Replacing salvation with variables quantifying material well-being as the standard of progress does not address this issue.

A further problem with Kant's conception of history was that his distinction between phenomenal and noumenal reality made it difficult to accommodate the idea of the self as a historical agent. This problem is visible in the declaration that 'To look for the temporal origin of free actions as free (as though they were natural effects) is ... a contradiction.'[139] To understand why Kant said this, we can revisit the two examples he gave involving a house. In the first *Critique*, perhaps inspired by Aristotle's

---

[135] Reinhart Koselleck, *Futures Past On the Semantics of Historical Time*, trans. Keith Tribe (New York: Columbia University Press, 2004 [1979]), especially ch. 14 '"Space of Experience" and "Horizon of Expectation": Two Historical Categories', 256–75.
[136] Carl J. Friedrich, 'The Ideology of the United Nations Charter and the Philosophy of Peace of Immanuel Kant 1795–1945', *Journal of Politics*, 9:1 (1947), 10–30.
[137] Michael W. Doyle, 'Kant, Liberal Legacies, and Foreign Affairs', *Philosophy and Public Affairs*, 12:3 (1983), 205–35, 206.
[138] Kant, *Religion Within the Boundaries*, 153.
[139] Kant, *Religion Within the Boundaries*, 86.

Metaphysics, Kant remarked that we can never see the whole house at once.[140] The house as we experience it is rather a series of appearances, literally presenting different sides to us as we walk around it. The idea of something's being a whole is one of those non-empirical ideas that reason supplies to us in terms of which we can make sense of our experience.

The problem that Kant's account never addressed was how we knew that what we were seeing was a house at all. It was not clear, in other words, how, based purely on the content of my unified visual field conceived as a synthesis of spatio-temporal presentations with the relations supplied by the categories, the formal 'I' of the categories of the understanding could identify one part of that field as a view of (part of) a house. Kant had assumed that we had the idea of a house; but this idea was no more purely empirical than the idea of a whole. The idea of a house, which Heidegger would later call 'equipment for residing', must be an expression of the ideas of a particular culture or world-view.[141] Yet although Kant made use of this idea of a world-view in relation to Biblical criticism, he never developed it theoretically.

In the third *Critique*, in contrast, Kant described the house as being the cause of the rent.[142] But here the problem ran in the other direction. We were not dealing with the kind of efficient causation that is the preserve of the 'I' of the categories of the understanding, but rather with the final causes associated with the categories of freedom; the realisation of ends. But it is not clear what relation a noumenal 'I', supposedly concerned only with the realisation of its free will in the form of rational action, could have to 'rent'. The noumenal self was, after all, not essentially embodied.

Kant was clear, like Descartes and Rousseau, that there was a radical separation between body and soul.[143] Nevertheless, he was well aware that in reality we exist as embodied selves; hence his introduction of an anthropological dimension to his thought, to capture the historical and social world that fell between two phenomenal and noumenal stools. But the kind of knowledge involved in explaining how these selves had come to be living in houses or paying rent did not seem worth investigating. At most, what mattered was that the houses had legitimate owners and the rent was genuinely owed.[144]

---

[140] Kant, *Critique of Pure Reason*, 305–6. Compare Chapter 2, above.

[141] Heidegger, *Being and Time*, 98.

[142] Kant, *Critique of Judgment*, 245.

[143] Jean-Jacques Rousseau, *Emile, or On Education*, trans. Allan Bloom (USA: Basic Books, 1979), 279–80, wrote that 'I need only know that matter is extended and divisible in order to be sure that it cannot think . . . my will is independent of my senses.'

[144] Kant, *Metaphysics of Morals*, 472.

The terms of Kant's division between the categories of the understanding and the categories of freedom thus effectively guaranteed a relative neglect of historical knowledge. Kant's conception of freedom as entirely noumenal ensured his interest in the explanation of human action was exclusively moral and religious, in terms of its tendency to further the good or perpetuate evil. It was moreover an ahistorical interest, since moral action, which was synonymous with free and rational action, was atemporal. Originating in a noumenal realm, it began, literally, from outside history.

The distinction passed through to Kant's arrangement of knowledge, where objective empirical knowledge was restricted to knowledge of what was necessary and scientific. It also affected Kant's treatment of government, where whatever could not be treated in universal terms (the actual activity of politics) was likewise pushed to one side. As a result, historical knowledge was marginalised. It was one form of what Kant called 'the hell of self-cognition' that his philosophy managed to avoid.[145]

Conclusion

Although Kant's theory of categories would prove transformative, Kant was, and understood himself as, a philosophical continuator of the classical tradition. But in order to preserve the Platonic and rationalist approach that formed his own point of departure, some radical reformulation was required. Metaphysics was put at the service of practical reason, and the remainder of philosophy became critical, transformed from a search for knowledge of ultimate reality into the reflexive examination of the conditions of its own possibility. The emphasis on practical reason stemmed from a conviction of the importance of the conservation of religious values in the face of the Newtonian revolution in physics and the sceptical challenge posed by Hume.

The solution to these challenges was the theory of categories itself. The categories structured our knowledge but also limited it, thus opening the possibility of regions of experience that were not strictly subject to knowledge claims, but were nonetheless vitally important for human life, especially for our values. In particular, scientific knowledge was put on an objective footing, but its challenge to religion was defused. Indeed, one of Kant's claims was that the guiding ideals of religion could play an important role in giving overall unity to scientific thought. Those ideals, after all, shared the rational and universal quality of scientific knowledge; just not its empirical component.

[145] Kant, *Metaphysics of Morals*, 562.

Rationality and universality were the key themes of morality as well as religion for Kant, to the point where the two became synonyms. The core of both moral and religious principles was their generalisability. But this argument rested ultimately on a conception of the self as a noumenal entity, utterly separate from the physical and bodily order of reality, endowed with a freedom that was the primary postulate of practical reason. This radical freedom could not be understood, only presupposed. The worry for subsequent generations would be that if there were no such self, there could be no such morality. This, we shall see, was more or less Nietzsche's position.

Kant's emphasis on rationality and universality also led him, in various ways, to marginalise both politics and history. With respect to the philosophy of government and the nature of the historical process he had plenty to say. But Kant gave little consideration to politics as Aristotle had presented it, as deliberation over action under conditions of uncertainty, and as a formalised arena for disputation over the rules by which society should function. Kant's belief that rationality mandated consensus necessarily marginalised any conception of politics to which disagreement was integral.

The emphasis on rationality necessarily also pushed to the margins any consideration of historical knowledge, since it retained the classical stress on universality and necessity. History understood as knowledge of events that could have been otherwise held little interest for Kant. He was concerned with the historical process only insofar as it held out hope for the future creation of a cosmopolitan federation of states and a universal ethical community. His main aim was providing an alternative narrative to that of apocalyptic theology.

It is true that Kant thought history as a distinctive discipline could provide a foundation for religion; but the logic of historical inquiry was at best a peripheral concern for him. It is an irony of the history of philosophy that it was Kant's categorial approach, and his clear separation of a phenomenal realm of nature from a noumenal realm of freedom, which provided the starting points from which a later generation of neo-Kantian thinkers would construct a philosophical account of historical epistemology.[146]

Overall, then, in Kant the pattern in which we are interested held good. As in Plato and Aristotle, categories, knowledge and politics were connected, albeit in a very different way. Though Kant's categories did

---

[146] See, for example, Alan Kim, 'Neo-Kantian Ideas of History', in Nicolas De Warren and Andrea Staiti, eds, *New Approaches to Neo-Kantianism* (Cambridge: Cambridge University Press, 2015), 39–58.

the same general job as Plato's Forms and Aristotle's categories of explaining the visible in terms of the invisible, they were conceived, and worked, very differently. Neither Plato nor Aristotle made the Forms or categories features of the structure of subjectivity itself. Nevertheless, in other respects, Kant continued the emphasis on universality and necessity in ancient thought which, though it entailed significant alterations in the hierarchy of knowledge, ensured that the marginal status given to history in ancient philosophy was carried over into the context of modernity. Much the same can be said of Hegel.

4
Hegel: The Dialectical Dynamics of Categories

This fourth chapter argues that, like Kant, Hegel preserved the relationship between categories, knowledge, and politics first found in Plato and Aristotle. It suggests, moreover, that just as Aristotle cannot be understood without Plato, Hegel cannot be understood without Kant.[1] Aristotle had objected to the completely transcendental status of Plato's Forms and treated his categories as immanent in things; Hegel's criticism of Kant's categories was that they left the noumena absolutely cut off from the phenomena, instead of yielding an integrated whole. Hegel thus played Aristotle to Kant's Plato not merely by analogy but in a substantive way to which the theory of categories was central.

Indeed, Hegel's whole system, including the *Science of Logic*, was explicitly presented as a system of categories.[2] He even declared that 'all education reduces to the distinction of categories'.[3] But these categories were neither purely transcendental, as for Plato, nor exclusively subjective, as for Kant. Nor were they limited to a list of ten, as in Aristotle, or to two triadically structured tetrads, as in Kant's critical philosophy. Instead,

---

[1] Robert Pippin, 'Hegel and Category Theory', *Review of Metaphysics*, 43:4 (1990), 839–48, 843, argues that Hegel must be understood as 'still adhering . . . to the Kantian strategy on how to establish basic or fundamental components of any conceptual scheme (or rules for any possibly objective judgment about determinate objects)'.

[2] Terry Pinkard, *Hegel's Dialectic: The Explanation of Possibility* (Philadelphia: Temple University Press, 1988), 6, writes that the key to understanding Hegel's philosophy is to realise that he 'always begins with some basic category, shows how it conflicts with an equally basic category, and then offers a speculative explanation using some new category or set of categories to show how the conflict is only apparent'.

[3] Georg Wilhelm Friedrich Hegel, *Hegel's Philosophy of Nature, Being Part Two of The Encyclopedia of The Philosophical Sciences (1830), Translated From Nicolin and Pöggler's Edition (1959) and From the Zusätze in Michelet's Text (1847)*, trans. A. V. Miller (Oxford: Clarendon Press, 2004 [1970]), 11.

Hegel conceived his entire philosophy as a triadic system. Its three major divisions were logic, or the analysis of categories in the abstract; nature, or the physical and organic instantiation of categories; and spirit or mind (*Geist*), in which we find a specifically human and increasingly self-conscious expression of categories. This system was also circular; each one of its divisions implied both the others.[4]

Hegel broke with Kant in several other ways too. Unlike Kant's critical philosophy, his system was not arranged in terms of a psychology of the faculties. Certainly, Hegel acknowledged differences between ordinary sense-perception, scientific understanding, and rational philosophical thought, but these were not only to be explained as different orientations of the knowing subject. Since the subject or self was always involved in a mutually constitutive relationship with an objective reality, the divisions of Hegel's philosophy applied equally to both sides of that relationship.

The knowing subject did retain a special status, though. In the *Phenomenology of Spirit*, Hegel referred to the subject or the 'I' simply as *die Kategorie*: the category. The *Phenomenology* described the progression of this subject towards what Hegel called 'Absolute Knowing'. What Hegel intended by the term 'Absolute Knowing' is contentious and has often been construed in ways that are obscure; we shall argue that it meant simply the subject's full comprehension of its own categorial historicity.[5]

Such self-consciousness about our use of categories was the exception rather than the rule, however. Categories for Hegel frequently played the role of assumptions or presuppositions. But Hegel did not always clearly separate his philosophical identification of these categorial conditions of a particular form of knowledge from his efforts at their emendation. This was evident, for instance in his philosophy of nature, which has often been received as a confused and badly executed philosophy of science.[6] But this arguably mistakes Hegel's enterprise. Where Kant had argued that philosophy could do no more than provide a categorial foundation for the necessity of natural scientific explanation, Hegel was arguing that the categories of physics, chemistry, and biology did not fully capture the

---

[4] M. J. Inwood, *Hegel* (London: Routledge & Kegan Paul, 1983), 71, writes that for Hegel 'the categories involved in any one science, or area of science ... are ... bounded by the categories of other sciences or areas of science, and ... flow or spill over into one another'.

[5] Rebecca Comay and Frank Ruda, *The Dash – The Other Side of Absolute Knowing* (Cambridge, MA: MIT Press, 2018), 4, argue that 'Absolute knowing ... marks the point where experience turns into an experience of the impossibility of experience.'

[6] Sir Karl Popper, *Conjectures and Refutations* (New York and London: Basic Books, 1962), 332, writes that 'the futility of views which [Hegel] held within the field of the natural sciences was – at least for natural scientists – only too obvious'.

logical structure of the natural world. Philosophy had a positive contribution to make to our knowledge of the natural order.⁷

Another Hegelian departure from Kant was the dynamic nature of the categories. An analysis of any given category showed that it necessarily entailed a transformation into another, distinct, and perhaps even opposing, category. This was true of the categories involved in Hegel's philosophy of government, for example. The modern state had three distinct parts, which Hegel called 'moments' to signify that they continually transitioned into one another. The family, civil society and the legal order together made up the modern state. But the nature of that state, just like the nature of the modern individual, could only be understood in terms of its own development. Historicity was integral to Hegel's categorial theory in a way that it was not to the categories of the understanding and of freedom in Kant.⁸

Yet Hegel, like Kant, continued to marginalise historical knowledge in favour of a theodicic interpretation of historical progress. The historical process made sense as the progressive realisation of freedom in accordance with a divine plan. In this process, great historical figures who embodied the current phase of spirit's development played a disproportionate role. But unlike Kant or Marx, Hegel was describing something he believed had already happened. We stood at the end of what, at least in conceptual terms, was a completed process.

Whatever one makes of Hegel, his ideas, as Michel Foucault observed, have continued to dominate modern thought.⁹ Certainly, the assessment of Hegel's legacy has often been negative. Hegel's reputation, like Aristotle's, has fluctuated wildly in modernity. When Hegel died in 1831 his dominance of German philosophy was unchallenged, though the next generation, including Karl Marx, increasingly tried to reject him. But the Anglophone

---

⁷ John W. Burbidge, *Real Process: How Logic and Chemistry Combine in Hegel's Philosophy of Nature* (Toronto, Buffalo and London: University of Toronto Press, 1996), 4, argues that Hegel clearly distinguished 'second-order reflection on natural science and natural phenomena' and philosophical comprehension of nature 'according to logical principles'.

⁸ Dario Perinetti, 'History, Concepts, and Normativity in Hegel', in *Hegel's Theory of the Subject*, ed. David Gray Carlson (Basingstoke and New York: Palgrave Macmillan, 2005), 60–72, 60, writes that 'Hegel's . . . originality lies in the attempt to come to terms with the "logic" of human historical existence.'

⁹ Michel Foucault, 'The Order of Discourse', in *Untying the Text: A Post-Structuralist Reader*, ed. Robert Young (Boston and London: Routledge and Kegan Paul, 1981), 48–78, 74, wrote that 'our entire epoch . . . is trying to escape from Hegel'. In this inaugural lecture, Foucault explicitly acknowledged his indebtedness to the French Hegel scholar Jean Hyppolite, translator of G. W. F. Hegel, *La Phénoménologie de l'esprit*, 2 vols (Paris: Aubier, 1941).

world took Hegel up just as the Germanic one was repudiating him, until the early twentieth century, when new movements like pragmatism and logical empiricism seemed to sweep him decisively aside.

The analytical tradition which dominated subsequent twentieth-century Anglo-American philosophy came into existence, one could say, partly as an effort to be 'not-Hegel'. Consequently, for much of the twentieth century, Hegel was 'the very model of how *not* to do philosophy'.[10] By the early twenty-first century, however, even analytical philosophers had begun to take him seriously once more.[11] Hegel's theory of categories as set out in the *Science of Logic* has been crucial to this re-engagement.[12]

Categories

Categories for Plato were transcendental entities giving form to material existence and intelligibility to moral experience; for Aristotle they were properties and classes either inhering in or arising from the primary substances encountered in the world; and for Kant they constituted logical derivations from the judgements implied in our practical and theoretical knowledge of the world. Hegel's concept of categories supposedly included all these previous theories, while also being dynamic and linguistic. In the *Phenomenology of Spirit*, Hegel defined a category as a 'self-sublating opposition'.[13] Categories, in other words, contained inherent contradictions that set them into (logical) motion and generated further categories as a result.[14]

---

[10] Frederick C. Beiser, 'Introduction: The Puzzling Hegel Renaissance', in *The Cambridge Companion to Hegel and Nineteenth-Century Philosophy*, ed. Frederick C. Beiser (Cambridge: Cambridge University Press, 2008), 1–14, 1.

[11] See, for example, Tom Rockmore, *Hegel, Idealism, and Analytic Philosophy* (New Haven and London: Yale University Press, 2005); Paul Redding, *Analytic Philosophy and the Return of Hegelian Thought* (Cambridge: Cambridge University Press, 2007); and Angelica Nuzzo, ed., *Hegel and the Analytic Tradition* (London and New York: Continuum International, 2010).

[12] David Gray Carlson, 'Introduction', in *Hegel's Theory of the Subject*, xi, notes that contemporary Hegel scholarship puts Hegel's *Science of Logic* 'at the very center of Hegel's philosophy'.

[13] Georg Wilhelm Friedrich Hegel, *The Phenomenology of Spirit*, trans. M. Inwood (Oxford: Oxford University Press, 2018), §177, 76, §344, 139. Subsequent references are to Inwood's translation unless otherwise noted. G. W. F. Hegel, *The Phenomenology of Spirit*, trans. A. V. Miller (Oxford: Oxford University Press, 1977), 209, gives 'self-superseding antithesis'.

[14] The term 'Phenomenology' was used in Kant, *Metaphysical Foundations of Natural Science*, 191, to refer to the foundation of the appearance of specifically physical motion in the categories of the understanding. Hegel presumably appropriated the term to suggest that spirit also 'moves', in the sense of undergoing a series of conceptual transformations.

In the *Phenomenology*, which claimed to follow the development of consciousness to full self-awareness, so-called Absolute Knowing, the term *die Kategorie* first appeared in a discussion of Descartes's notion of the self as the cogito, or pure thinking substance. Although it also occurred in other contexts, Hegel mainly used it as a term for the 'I' and the changes it underwent. Hegel presented *die Kategorie* as initially simple self-identity, the most simple sense of oneself as oneself. 'Reason appealed to the self-consciousness of each and every consciousness: "*I am I*, my object and essence is *I*."'[15]

Hegel called the 'I' at this phase of its development 'the simple *category*' because it attempted to unify external reality and self-consciousness within itself as a single undifferentiated whole.[16] But this proved a failure. The result was the 'I' taking on a new appearance as 'a *plurality* of categories'.[17] This in effect characterised the change that Hegel believed had happened between Descartes and Kant; the self as a simple substance was replaced by the categorially generated unity of apperception.

Since, however, the *Phenomenology* supposedly described a logical rather than a chronological development, the recognition by the Kantian understanding that 'it is a *law of appearance itself*' preceded the advent of *die Kategorie* in Hegel's argument.[18] The understanding did not yet know that it was also describing itself in identifying the rules to which appearances necessarily conformed.[19] For Hegel, although Kant's arrangement of the categories of the understanding in a tetrad of triads was an advance on Descartes's undifferentiated 'I', Kant's transcendental deduction, which inferred the categories from our judgements about objects, was still an inadequate approach. Hegel indignantly described what he regarded as Kant's derivation of the categories in a contingent manner as 'an outrage on Science'.[20] As necessary determinations of being, the Kantian categories should have been shown to be essential features of both the 'I' and its objects.

Hegel revised Kant's claim that subjectivity was responsible for the terms of the constitution of our external reality by arguing that the relation was bi-directional. Both the object and subject terms were always categorially constituted in a way that ensured they were necessarily mutually implicated. Hegel also included under the object term the existence

---

[15] Hegel, *Phenomenology of Spirit*, §234, 96. Emphasis in original.
[16] Hegel, *Phenomenology of Spirit*, §235, 97. Emphasis in original.
[17] Hegel, *Phenomenology of Spirit*, §235, 97. Emphasis in original.
[18] Hegel, *Phenomenology of Spirit*, §156, 67. Emphasis in original.
[19] Hegel, *Phenomenology of Spirit*, §163, 70, argued that 'consciousness ... although it seems to be occupied with something else ... is in fact preoccupied only with itself'.
[20] Hegel, *Phenomenology of Spirit*, §235, 97.

of other 'I's in a way that Kant did not. We saw that Kant's critical philosophy had struggled to answer the question of how the categories of the understanding and of freedom jointly yielded the experience of being a human being: they restricted the self either to knowledge of physical objects or to a noumenal good will. For Hegel, the answer was the existence of other 'I's. Others were the only means to the full realisation of my own individuality.[21]

Die Kategorie initially took pleasure in 'the consciousness of its actualization in a consciousness which appears as independent'. But it sought to complete this identification by assimilating the other to itself in an 'intuition of the unity of the two independent self-consciousnesses'.[22] This relationship functioned similarly to that between lord and bondsman, which preceded the first appearance of die Kategorie. But whereas in the struggle between lord and bondsman, both parties had simply participated unwittingly in this dynamic conflict, now its terms and conditions began to become objects to self-consciousness.[23] Thus commenced a process in which self-consciousness apprehended itself as inherently rational, creating the possibility of forms of individuality that did not rely on the subjugation of the other.

Reason as the category of the 'I' gave itself content in pursuing some purpose. But this presupposed its engagement with a broader reality inhabited by others who were likewise actors with purposes of their own that could potentially become shared ends. An important phase of the 'I''s development was its 'being-for-another'.[24] Whereas the 'I' first attempted to realise its individuality by attempting to assimilate the other, in the next phase, its recognition of its fundamentally social character, it found itself entirely absorbed into its community. Hegel here had the political culture of the ancient world in mind, which he believed had sublimated the individual in just this fashion.[25] Hegel argued that this resulted in latent ethical conflicts in ancient Greek culture which explained the development of the tragic drama.[26] Hegel's idea of a Weltanschauung or world-view effectively adopted

---

[21] See Robert Pippin, Hegel on Self-Consciousness, Desire and Death in the Phenomenology of Spirit (Princeton: Princeton University Press, 2011), especially ch. 2.
[22] Hegel, Phenomenology of Spirit, §362, 145.
[23] Hegel, Phenomenology of Spirit, §363.
[24] Hegel, Phenomenology of Spirit, §394, 157, wrote that 'purpose and Being-in-itself have proved to be the same thing as Being for another and the actuality found before it'. Emphasis in original.
[25] Hegel, Phenomenology of Spirit, §436, 172, wrote that 'Ethical self-consciousness is immediately one with the essence through the universality of its Self.' Emphasis in original.
[26] This view informed Hegel's interpretation of Sophocles' Antigone, for instance. See Hegel, Phenomenology of Spirit, §457.

Kant's later notion of a world-view as a contentful cultural perspective rather than the earlier Kantian conception of it as restricted to our formally integrated sense perception of the world.[27]

Modernity, unlike ancient culture, allowed *die Kategorie* to participate in an ethical order without being subsumed by it, and thus marked the final transition from Reason to Spirit or '*Geist*'. The definition we noted earlier of Geist as the 'I that is We, and We that is I' entailed at least two things.[28] The first clause treated the self as internally differentiated. We all had multiple aspects to our identity. This was not least because the self always gained part of its identity from the collectivity to which it belonged. The different aspects of our identities as individuals also reflected the social roles that defined us, as family members, workers, and citizens. The second clause indicated that the 'we', or the social whole, possessed a certain unity. This social whole, which for Hegel was the nation, had a corporate personality distinct from the individual 'I's composing it.

Already in ancient culture the 'I' that spirit knew itself to be could no longer be thought of abstractly, but was consciously embodied as either male or female.[29] But whatever the gender of the 'I', it was only fully realised through speech, the condition of individual personality.[30] Hegel in effect agreed with Aristotle that speech was the distinctive characteristic of the human being.[31] The universal 'I' could only individuate itself by giving voice to itself in conversation with similarly dependent others. In doing so, we became real at once to ourselves and for others.

Strictly speaking, though, what was realised was not individual subjects, but inter-subjectivity. Hegel made clear that speech was not a monologue but a dialogue. For Hegel there was, so to say, no such thing

---

[27] For example, Georg Wilhelm Friedrich Hegel, *Phänomenologie des Geistes* (Hamburg: Felix Meiner Verlag, 1988), §599, 442, wrote explicitly of 'Die moralische Weltanschauung'.

[28] See the Introduction, above.

[29] Hegel, *Phenomenology of Spirit*, §461, 182, wrote that 'The universal ethical essences . . . have . . . the man and the woman for their natural Self and the activating individuality.'

[30] Hegel, *Phenomenology of Spirit*, §508, 203, wrote that 'language is the *Being-there* of the pure Self as Self; in it, the *singularity* of self-consciousness, a singularity that is *for itself*, comes as such into existence, so that it is *for others*. Otherwise the *I*, as *this pure* I, is not *there*.' Emphasis in the original.

[31] Aristotle, *Politics*, in *Aristotle's Politics: Writings from the Complete Works: Politics, Economics, Constitution of Athens*, ed. J. Barnes, intro. M. Lane (Princeton: Princeton University Press, 2016), trans. Benjamin Jowett, 1253a, wrote 'that man is more of a political animal than bees or any other gregarious animals is evident . . . man is the only animal who has the gift of speech'.

as a private language.³² Two speakers were required for Spirit to realise itself.³³ There was a deliberate echo here of the Biblical verse 'For where two or three are gathered together in My name, I am there in the midst of them.'³⁴

The final mention of *die Kategorie* in the *Phenomenology* occurred in the discussion of the tension between reason and faith.³⁵ Hegel treated religion as the penultimate stage in the development of rational self-consciousness, just before *die Kategorie* assumed the form of Absolute Knowing. But though reason was a more developed form of spirit than religion, it failed to understand that its criticisms of religion were also true of itself. The Enlightenment argument that the idea of a God or absolute Being was simply religion's own creation, for instance, failed to recognise that Enlightenment was likewise 'a creation of consciousness'.³⁶ Faith and reason were the obverse of one another rather than simply opposed. Like Kant, Hegel assimilated Christianity to his own philosophy at the expense of orthodoxy.³⁷

Hegel's last reference to *die Kategorie* identified it with the 'absolute Notion', or *der absolute Begriff*, that is to say, with Absolute Knowing. In the discussion of religion, the incarnation of Jesus was treated as an exemplary instance of the process in which Spirit fully becomes a self.³⁸ This was the same process that we have witnessed *die Kategorie* undergoing all along. Understood from the standpoint of faith, we are all spirit made flesh.³⁹ In the fullest development of religious belief, the idea of a divine Being was itself 'raised to a Self'. Yet this Christian spiritualisation of the self was

---

[32] Ludwig Wittgenstein, *Philosophical Investigations*, trans. G. E. M. Anscombe, P. M. S. Hacker and Joachim Schulte, 4th edn, rev. P. M. S. Hacker and Joachim Schulte (Oxford: Blackwell Publishing, 2009 [1953]), 101ᵉ, argued that a private language would be one that 'no one else understands'.

[33] Hegel, *Phenomenology of Spirit*, §509.

[34] Matthew, 18:20 (King James version).

[35] Hegel, *Phenomenology of Spirit*, §548.

[36] Hegel, *Phenomenology of Spirit*, §549, 219, wrote that 'Enlightenment thereby declares faith to be error and fiction with respect to the same thing as enlightenment is.'

[37] Inwood, 'Commentary', *Phenomenology of Spirit*, 336–7, argues that Hegel regards God as incomplete without the world and as requiring human beings to complete His own self-realisation, both ideas that contradicted the traditional belief in God's perfection common to both Catholic and Protestant theology.

[38] Hegel, *Phenomenology of Spirit*, trans. Inwood, §532, 213, alluded to Jesus in referring to the transformation of Spirit into 'an *actual*, *self-sacrificing* absolute essence . . . a *Self*, but a transitory Self'. Emphasis in original.

[39] Hegel, *Phenomenology of Spirit*, §758, 299, wrote that the religious Spirit 'has become a *simple* positive Self, just as the actual Spirit as such in the unhappy consciousness became just this *simple* self-conscious negativity'.

only a prelude to the revelation, so to say, of Absolute Knowing's true character. Even the most developed form of Christianity, Hegel made clear, was arrested at the stage of 'representation'.[40]

The fully realised form of Absolute Knowing or *der absolute Begriff* turned out to be that it was just 'comprehended History'; *die begriffne Geschichte*.[41] *Die Kategorie*, or the 'I', in its complete development, was identical with the self-consciousness of its own historicity. Hegel's argument was that we have achieved absolute knowledge to the extent that we know how we have become who we are, in the broadest sense of that statement. The *Phenomenology of Spirit* was an analysis of the stages or *Gestaltungen* through which phenomenal knowledge passed on the way to this discovery. Consciousness, self-consciousness, reason and religion were all *Gestaltungen*, and so were their various internal phases or, as Hegel called them, 'moments' (*Momenten*).

For Hegel, one must always understand the nature of *die Kategorie*, at any rate prior to its attainment of Absolute Knowing, as relative to the stage that the development of consciousness had reached. The same was true of the various types of knowledge, such as the natural sciences or psychology. These too were either embedded in, or were themselves, stages in a progression. But whatever we say about the *Gestaltungen* as 'categories' applies only to the *Phenomenology of Spirit*. That work represented the introduction to Hegel's philosophical system, not the system itself. In the *Science of Logic*, the outcome of the *Phenomenology* was presupposed.

The *Logic* was, at the highest level, the study of just three categories: 'Being', supposedly the simplest of all categories; 'Essence', or the substantial hidden natures of things not intelligible from their initial appearances; and 'The Concept', or the dialectical product of the previous two categories. It culminated in the Absolute Idea. Like Absolute Knowing, this sounds grandiose, but a much more modest reading is possible, in which the Absolute Idea referred simply to our knowledge of the process via which thinking came to grasp its own categorial terms and conditions.[42] Hegel's account

---

[40] Hegel, *Phenomenology of Spirit*, §787, 310. Miller's translation prefers 'picture-thinking' to 'representation' as a translation for 'die Vorstellung', which perhaps carries rather more pejorative connotations in English than Hegel intended.

[41] Hegel, *Phenomenology of Spirit*, §808, 321.

[42] Georg Wilhelm Friedrich Hegel, *The Science of Logic*, trans. George di Giovanni (Cambridge: Cambridge University Press, 2010), 753: 'the concept ... in the science of logic finds the highest concept of itself, the pure concept conceptually comprehending itself'. The similarity with Aristotle's conception of the unmoved mover as thought thinking itself is not coincidental.

of this process could be described as anti-materialist, because it entailed that thought was not reducible to a physical foundation. Yet Hegel also rejected a binary opposition between matter and mind, or phenomenon and noumenon. Nature and mind were joined by logic as the three main mutually dependent elements of his system. The system could also be read as an exercise in the philosophy of language. Di Giovanni interprets the *Science of Logic* as announcing, well over a century before Ludwig Wittgenstein and Jacques Derrida, that 'There is no exit from language.'[43]

Hegel certainly argued that 'The forms of thought are first set out and stored in human *language*.'[44] Like Kant, he saw himself as following Aristotle as a theorist of categories. But Hegel's praise was more unqualified. Aristotle's status as 'the first to undertake' the description of 'the forms of logic' was hailed as 'an infinite merit . . . that must fill us with the highest admiration for the power of his genius'.[45] Nevertheless, the overall goal of the *Science of Logic* was not at variance with Kant's critical philosophy. Like Kant, Hegel insisted that we must not confuse reason, which dealt with pure concepts, with the relations restricted to finite things addressed by the understanding: 'The true critique of the categories and of reason is just this: to acquaint cognition with this distinction and to prevent it from applying to God the determinations and the relations of the finite.'[46]

The *Logic* was thus the study of pure abstractions. It began with 'Being' because this was purportedly the purest and most basic of all concepts. Existence as such was the simplest possible starting point.[47] In Aristotelian terms, we could say that Hegel was presenting Being as the conceptual equivalent of a substance absolutely devoid of qualities: there were no further categories applicable to it. But to know only that something 'is', Hegel argued, was to find that we were altogether ignorant of it. 'Being' thus turned out to be an empty concept; yet that very discovery made it possible to derive the contrary of Being, Nothing, from Being itself.

Nothing, like Being, was abstract self-identity, utterly lacking in any content to differentiate it.[48] We find, then, that Being has turned out not

---

[43] Di Giovanni, 'Introduction' to Hegel, *Science of Logic*, xxxiv.
[44] Hegel, *Science of Logic*, 12. Emphasis in original.
[45] Hegel, *Science of Logic*, 525.
[46] Hegel, *Science of Logic*, 66.
[47] Hegel, *Science of Logic*, 59, began the discussion of being simply by saying 'Being, pure being – without further determination'.
[48] Hegel, *Science of Logic*, 59, described nothingness as 'simple equality with itself, complete emptiness, complete absence of determination and content; lack of all distinction within'.

to be empty after all. What was purportedly the simplest starting point has turned out to involve the kind of conceptual presupposition or entailment we had sought to eliminate. Moreover, in this very derivation of Nothing from Being there was a logical transition that yielded a third concept, Becoming. Becoming was produced by the very change from Being to Nothing. This kind of dialectical argument was typical of the *Logic* as a whole and is a good illustration of why Hegel's approach to philosophy has been so divisive.

Hegel's justification for this manner of arguing was that the conceptual order operated according to distinctive rules that were not reducible to those of either propositional (Aristotelian) logic or common sense. In the *Phenomenology*, for example, he made an analogy between the abstraction of universality and the status of death. Death marked the end of individuality in human life; it was a return to the insubstantial universal. Living reality was always a synthesis of the universal and the particular in the individual. An individual human being could not be just an 'I', a simple substance. They were necessarily a particular person with a name and a history. If we studied the 'I' in isolation, then in concentrating on this universal concept, we necessarily lost direct contact with our lived experience.

We might compare Hegel's view of conceptual analysis to lepidoptery. A living butterfly is typically on the wing. To study it requires capturing it and fixing it, which also means killing it. But a dead butterfly is not fully a butterfly any longer, any more than a dead body is a person, although much can still be learnt from anatomising a corpse. Hence Hegel's characterisation of conceptual analysis as the demanding effort 'to hold fast what is dead'.[49] Modern philosophy, Hegel argued, had the task of analysing a categorially structured subjectivity that had not seemed problematic to ancient thought.[50]

In Hegel's eyes, Platonism in particular had concentrated too heavily on the universal. Plato had tended to ignore 'the side of tangibility and of sensuous self-externality' because he had believed that 'it is only in the concept that something has actuality, and to the extent that it is different from its concept, it ceases to be actual and is a nullity'.[51] Hegel's Absolute

---

[49] Hegel, *Phenomenology*, §32, 16.
[50] Hegel, *Science of Logic*, 21, wrote that compared to Plato the modern philosopher 'is confronted by a profounder principle, a more difficult subject matter and a material of greater compass'.
[51] Hegel, *Science of Logic*, 30.

Idealism is thus seriously misunderstood if it is identified with Platonism. In fact, Hegel's system was a deliberate *inversion* of the Platonic analogy for philosophy as an escape from the darkness of the cave. In contrast to the Platonic account, in which the philosopher escaped from the cave into the light of the sun, for Hegel the philosopher must enter a 'realm of shadows'. The region of pure concepts from which all reference to sensation and representation had been removed was not true reality, as it was for Plato, but at best an abstract aspect of it.[52]

Hegel described the *Science of Logic* as an explicit departure from 'the former *metaphysics* which was supposed to be the scientific edifice of the world as constructed by *thoughts* alone'.[53] Against both Plato and Kant, Hegel defended the view that thought was not to be conceived of as transcendental or noumenal. Already in the *Phenomenology* Hegel had remarked that 'The supersensible is . . . *appearance* as *appearance*.'[54] That is, in inhabiting the apparently perceptually straightforward and uncomplicated world of ordinary experience, common sense was typically unconscious of the extra-sensible categorial mediation on which its normal apprehension of the world rested. But this did not mean for Hegel, any more than it did for Kant, that reality was 'subjective' in the sense of being just whatever the individual self-consciousness judged it to be.

For Hegel, this idea of subjectivity as the self wilfully imposing a conception of reality onto a world that stood over and against it entailed a standpoint from which subject and object were opposed to one another. As we saw in the *Phenomenology*, however, that standpoint was only a moment in the development of consciousness, and was gradually abandoned. In the *Logic*, Hegel explained fully developed subjectivity by saying that it was objectivity that had become self-aware.[55] We may think of this process, once again, in theological terms. If we remember that Hegel was putting forward a version of the Aristotelian concept of God as thought thinking itself, then we may think of the movement of the subjective part of the logic, which culminated in the Absolute Idea, as a series of phases via which we increasingly participated in this divine kind of self-knowledge.

---

[52] Hegel, *Science of Logic*, 37, wrote that 'The system of logic is the realm of shadows, the world of simple essentialities, freed of all sensuous concretion. To study this science, to dwell and to labor in this realm of shadows, is the absolute culture and discipline of consciousness.'
[53] Hegel, *Science of Logic*, 42.
[54] Hegel, *Phenomenology of Spirit*, §147, 62. Emphasis in original.
[55] Hegel, *Science of Logic*, 516.

But if we ask in what knowledge of the Absolute Idea ultimately consisted, it was, as David Carlson has argued, that 'Self-destruction is the only thing that truly is.'⁵⁶ God, or reality, which is to say the world and the categories through which it is constituted and comprehended, was nothing more than the intelligible process of its own continuous creative self-immolation. The *Science of Logic* was intended as a mirror of this reality. In it, Hegel argued that we repeatedly go through the process of analysing the structure of a category, only to find that the category itself was unravelled by our doing so.

The process was saved from being an exercise in mere repetitive futility, however, by our own growing awareness of what was happening; our discovery of the different patterns that unfolded as we followed them out; and our enhanced appreciation of the larger relations between these patterns. The conclusion of Hegel's doctrine of categories in the *Logic*, then, was that a category just was its own self-cancelling movement, like the 'I' of the *Phenomenology*. As Carlson remarks, 'The only thing that endures is self-erasing system.'⁵⁷ The resemblance to Heraclitus was not coincidental.⁵⁸

Knowledge

While Hegel agreed with Kant that knowledge was categorially structured, in detail his approach differed significantly. For one thing, while Hegel's analysis still distinguished different faculties on the side of the subject like reason and understanding, these no longer constituted the main organising divisions of his philosophy. The various genres of knowledge themselves were also conceived differently. For instance, Hegel followed Kant in retaining a special position for philosophy, but rejected Kant's distinction between critical philosophy and metaphysics because it separated experience from ultimate reality. Instead, Hegel wanted to reinvigorate classical metaphysics by making philosophical reasoning as reflexive as possible, thus incorporating the subjective dimension of epistemology highlighted in Kant's theory of categories. But this revival entailed abandoning the traditional hierarchical approach to knowledge that we saw was common to Plato and Aristotle.

In contrast to Plato's divided line, Hegel used the image of a circle for thought. Yet even though the circumference of a circle was composed in

---

⁵⁶ David Gray Carlson, *A Commentary to Hegel's Science of Logic* (Basingstoke and New York: Palgrave Macmillan, 2007), 606.
⁵⁷ Carlson, *Commentary*, 607.
⁵⁸ Hegel, *Science of Logic*, 60, wrote of 'the profound Heraclitus [who] proposed the ... total concept of becoming and said: *being is no more than nothing*; or also, all *flows*, that is, all is *becoming*'. Emphasis in original.

mathematical terms of ideal points all equally equidistant from the same fixed centre, the figure could still accommodate hierarchy of a kind.[59] Since Hegel's circle was segmented in developmental fashion, within each portion there was still scope for a movement from simplicity to complexity. Nevertheless, all areas falling within the circle were equally necessary. Moreover, this mathematical metaphor of the circle was not definitive; mathematics was, rather, one of its sections.

A more appropriate image for Hegel's circle, although it is not his own, might be the ensō of Zen Buddhism, in which the beginning is thickly brushed but the stroke gradually tails off into insubstantiality, so that the final section is altogether absent. As Carlson observes, since Hegel's system aimed to include everything, it had to include the element of lack or incompleteness.[60] Such a circle can expand indefinitely to include ever-finer detail and ever-more complex analysis; there is no requirement that it must ever be complete, even when it has already been grasped in outline.[61]

This circular conception of thought had implications for any conventional conception of knowledge positing an absolute separation of subject from object. For Hegel, the *Logic* no longer counted as 'knowledge' in this sense, because it had overcome the kind of absolute distinctions that were assumed in both common sense and scientific understanding.[62] Knowledge was not reducible to a property of a knowing subject confronting an objective world, but an analysis of concepts in their inter-relatedness. The subject-object distinction was itself a relation generated by the operations of dialectical logic.

Hegel likewise gave propositional logic in the Aristotelian sense more fundamental roots in his dialectical logic. Like Kant, he treated this derivation of the concepts needed for ordinary reasoning as a timeless affair. The 'movements' involved were purely logical transformations. Time only arose in the Hegelian system in the philosophy of nature.[63]

---

[59] Hegel, *Science of Logic*, 170, wrote that 'The circle ... is based solely on the *equality* of the distance of all its possible points from a center point'. Emphasis in original.

[60] Carlson, *Commentary*, 596.

[61] On Carlson's view of Hegel, therefore, Alain Badiou, *Theoretical Writings*, ed. and trans. Ray Brassier and Alberto Toscano (London and New York: Continuum, 2005 [2004]), 221, is mistaken when he writes that 'whereas we locate the starting point of a transcendental theory of worlds in the statement "There is no Whole," Hegel guarantees the inception of the dialectical odyssey by positing that "There is nothing but the Whole."' The aim of Hegel's positing of nothing but the Whole, or pure Being, was to show that it immediately undermined itself, just as the goal of Hegel's subsequent account of essence was to demonstrate that what was essential to essence was its non-being.

[62] Carlson, *Commentary*, 10.

[63] Carlson, *Commentary*, 17, n. 27, notes that 'time is not an official category' in the *Science of Logic*.

But Hegel departed radically from Kant in arguing that the philosophical standpoint could go beyond empirical, phenomenal reality and still offer genuine knowledge. For Hegel, the conceptual interconnections of the logic that philosophy made plain were quite literally the mind of God on display.[64] The contrast with Kant's unknowable noumenal deity could not be greater.

Hegel could thus easily be accused of having simply fallen back into pre-Kantian metaphysical error. But he expressed irritation with his critics over just this issue: 'all too often . . . have I been confronted by opponents incapable of the simple consideration that their opinions and objections imply categories which are presuppositions and themselves in need of being criticized first before they are put to use'.[65] The goal of Hegel's philosophy was to make us fully self-aware regarding the presuppositions of our knowledge.

Under normal conditions, however, 'the use of thought determinations . . . is unconscious'.[66] We typically just make use of, rather than examine, our concepts. As Hegel puts it, 'thought determinations . . . instinctively and unconsciously pervade our spirit everywhere – and remain non-objectified and unnoticed even when they enter language'.[67] In this respect, Hegel was entirely in agreement with Plato's characterisation of ordinary consciousness as unaware of its own situation.

Yet it was these very categories that Hegel considered the source of our rationality, at least implicitly. Human beings were naturally logical and rational creatures precisely because life is inescapably 'a matter of making use of the thought determinations'.[68] By default, however, we remained tangled in our own net: 'when thought is an instinctive activity', we are simply 'caught up in the web of its categories'.[69] This use of the metaphor of the web to stand for a set of inter-connected social or logical categories

---

[64] Hegel, *Science of Logic*, 'Introduction', 29, wrote 'this content *is the exposition of God as he is in his eternal essence before the creation of nature and of a finite spirit*'. Emphasis in original.

[65] Hegel, *Science of Logic*, 20. Hegel wrote of presuppositions as 'Voraussetzungen' in German: see Georg Wilhelm Friedrich Hegel, *Wissenschaft der Logik. Erster Band. Die Objektive Logik. Erstes Buch. Das Sein* (Hamburg: Felix Meiner Verlag, 1999), 29.

[66] Hegel, *Science of Logic*, 15.

[67] Hegel, *Science of Logic*, 19.

[68] Hegel, *Science of Logic*, 14, wrote that 'From the honor of being contemplated for their own sake, such determinations are debased to the position of serving in the creation and exchange of ideas required for the hustle and bustle of social life.' The determinations are 'Kategorien' in German. See Hegel, *Wissenschaft der Logik*, 15.

[69] Hegel, *Science of Logic*, 17.

later became a feature of what are normally taken to be distinct, even opposing, philosophies. It occurs in the hermeneutic tradition represented by Wilhelm Dilthey; in later analytical philosophers like W. V. O. Quine; and in critical theory, as in Jürgen Habermas.[70]

For Hegel, Kant's account of knowledge had never completely escaped the standpoint of common sense. Common sense presupposed an absolute separation of subject and object; so did the Kantian theory of the understanding as the source of natural scientific knowledge grounded in sense experience and structured by *a priori* categories. For both common sense and natural science, understood in Kantian terms, 'truth rests on sensuous reality' and 'thoughts are *only* thoughts'.[71] But Hegel did not want to simply contradict Kant's view. He did not want to say, for instance, that truth has no relation to the appearances that constituted sensible reality, or that abstract thought was the whole of reality. The presupposition of an absolute separation of subject and object associated with sense experience was a necessary stage in the development of consciousness towards self-consciousness.

Similarly, our scientific knowledge of nature was also a distinct moment of reality. Neither could replace the other; but nor could either replace philosophical knowledge. Kant's solution to the problem of showing why the relationships science identified in nature were necessary was philosophically inadequate from Hegel's point of view because it located that necessity in the subject. What needed to be demonstrated, for Hegel, was that necessity was inherent in the very stuff of nature itself. Explaining nature in Kantian physicalist terms entailed a gap between appearance and reality, or between things and thought.

Another issue for Hegel was that our lived experience of nature was one of singular variety, and the Newtonian explanation of nature had introduced a universality not visible in the things as we experienced

---

[70] Wilhelm Dilthey, *Introduction to the Human Sciences*, ed. Rudolf A. Makkreel and Fritjhof Rodi (Princeton: Princeton University Press, 1989), 207, wrote that 'historical critique destroyed the web of legends, myths, and fables used by the theocratic theory of society to link social institutions with the will of God'; W. V. Quine, *Quiddities: An Intermittently Philosophical Dictionary* (Cambridge, MA: Belknap Press, 1987), 161, wrote that in 'the method . . . which John Stuart Mill called concomitant variation [an] intricate web of hypotheses is devised'; Jürgen Habermas, *Knowledge and Human Interests*, trans. Jeremy Shapiro (Boston: Beacon Press, 1971 [1968]), 279, writes that 'The institutional framework of the system of social labor serves the organization of labor in co-operation and the division of labor and in the distribution of goods . . . this web of communicative action also serves functional needs of the system of social labor.'

[71] Hegel, *Science of Logic*, 25. Emphasis in original.

them. The certainty of the laws of nature only emerged in a process of abstraction that departed from the original goal of explaining the things themselves. But science, Hegel argued, was supposed to deal with nature as it really was, and not to impose itself on it. For science to remain true to its original intent, we must posit that nature itself already contained a latent conceptual element, or moment, as he called it.

Nature was thus already incipiently the vehicle of the rational universal that developed first in purely conceptual form in the logic before actualising itself in space and time, eventually becoming self-consciousness as spirit.[72] Science, unbeknownst to itself, was a process of investigating and of extracting from nature the ideas that were already latent in it. The task of the philosopher was then to explicate the logic of these ideas. But this was not a replacement for the work of the natural sciences.

Hegel occasionally let frustration get the better of him, asking rhetorically 'When will science ever become aware of the nature of the metaphysical categories it employs and base its reasoning on the Notion of the thing'?[73] But for physical science to abandon its categories in this manner really would have rendered it indistinguishable from the philosophy of nature. More usually, Hegel treated science as an independent activity that provided philosophers of nature with their materials. Of course, Hegel's enterprise of interpreting the significance of scientific results for use in a philosophy of nature has never gained widespread acceptance, although there has been a revival of contemporary interest.[74] But Hegel himself saw no problem in treating the philosophy of nature as entitled to interpret, though not to overturn, scientific results by explaining them as necessary. It took up 'the material which physics has prepared for it empirically, at the point to which physics has brought it, and reconstitutes it, so that experience is not its final warrant'.[75]

Importantly, however, Hegel's argument that the absolute distinction between subject and object in knowledge was philosophically unsustainable had no direct consequences for either common sense or scientific

---

[72] Richard Dien Winfield, *Conceiving Nature After Aristotle, Kant, and Hegel: The Philosopher's Guide to the Universe* (Cham: Palgrave Macmillan, 2017), 9, writes that Hegel's philosophy of nature 'conceives nature such that . . . living intelligence can make its appearance in the world', something that a Kantian mechanist philosophy of science struggled to accommodate.

[73] Hegel, *Philosophy of Nature*, §270, 68.

[74] See, for example, Alison Stone, *Petrified Intelligence: Nature in Hegel's Philosophy* (New York: SUNY Press, 2005).

[75] Hegel, *Philosophy of Nature*, §246, 10.

knowledge. Both could legitimately presuppose a distinction between subject and object, so long as it was not asserted dogmatically. What made this qualification difficult to appreciate was that Hegel often failed to distinguish clearly between the task of identifying the distinctive categorial assumptions of the various forms of knowledge, on the one hand, and their philosophical criticism on the other. Hegel's analysis of infinitesimal calculus proved particularly contentious. His argument that the idea of an immeasurably small number was philosophically incoherent because the property of measurability was intrinsic to quantity found few supporters.

Since it was still generally accepted in the early nineteenth century that Newton had given a definitive account of physical reality, Hegel's argument was not well-received. Michael Perry argues that 'the way in which Hegel criticizes Newton . . . has done more than anything else to prejudice his own reputation'.[76] The later nineteenth-century neo-Kantian reaction against Hegel's philosophy was motivated partly by Hegel's supposed misunderstandings of Newton, and Hegel's mathematical writings continued to mar his reputation into the twentieth century.

Bertrand Russell, for example, declared that his early devotion to Hegel's philosophy of mathematics had resulted in his writing 'unmitigated rubbish'.[77] Nevertheless, some modern scholars would disagree with Inwood that 'Hegel's hostility to Newton is one of those embarrassing facts about him that we just have to accept'.[78] Hegel's critique of Newtonianism has been seen as anticipating the concepts underlying the theories of relativity and quantum mechanics that would only be developed in physics in the twentieth century.[79]

Moreover, there was common ground between Hegel and Newton. Newton had believed, just like Hegel, that the new mechanical philosophy did not capture the full truth of nature's operations. Hence Newton's interest in alchemy, which has often seemed incongruous with his scientific

---

[76] See Michael John Petry, 'Foreword' to *Hegel and Newtonianism*, ed. Michael John Petry (Dordrecht: Kluwer Academic Publishers, 1993), xi–xiv, xi.
[77] Bertrand Russell, *My Philosophical Development* (London: Routledge, 1997 [1959]), 32.
[78] Inwood, 'Commentary', *Phenomenology of Spirit*, 388.
[79] See Carlson, *Commentary*, 17–18: 'In quantum mechanics, the collapse of the wave function is a well-known example of the incompatibility of stasis and movement . . . a phenomenon cannot "be" and be perceived or measured at the same time. Such a principle is present in Becoming. It moves and yet it does not move. We cannot focus on these moments simultaneously.' See also Winfield, *Conceiving Nature*, 311: 'Hegel's commencement of physical processes with light anticipates Einstein's theories of special and general relativity as well as quantum "mechanics."'

work to modern scholars.[80] In Newton's lifetime, though, the newer sense of 'natural philosophy' represented by the mechanical physics that he pioneered was still not clearly distinguished from the older medieval philosophy of nature based in the Aristotelian theory of elemental substances with distinct natures.

It was this view that Hegel's philosophy of nature espoused.[81] Hegel's natural philosophy was a late effort to reconcile the ancient-medieval substantialist theory of the four elements with modern science. Hence Hegel's remark that in nature the dialectic assumed a quadratic form.[82] In keeping with the classical and Christian tradition that gave rise to it, Hegel's philosophy of nature also differed from later philosophy of science in being theological. Indeed, the philosophy of nature and theology simply described the same thing from different points of view. Hegel asserted that

> The divine Idea is just this: to disclose itself, to posit this Other outside itself and to take it back again into itself, in order to be subjectivity and Spirit. The Philosophy of Nature itself belongs to this path of return; for it is that which overcomes the division between Nature and Spirit and assures to Spirit the knowledge of its essence in Nature.[83]

As in medieval thought, the book of nature and the book of God carried the same message.

Aristotle's account of the soul employed a teleological hierarchy in which we progressed from vegetable through animal to distinctively human forms, with some significant qualities of the earlier forms being retained in the later.[84] Hegel's version of this claim was that 'Mind has

---

[80] Hegel and Newton would likely have disagreed most deeply over an issue having little to do with physics. Whereas Hegel's entire philosophy was Trinitarian in design, Newton inclined to Arianism and thus regarded Trinitarianism as a post-Biblical doctrinal error that made worshipping Christ as God into an idolatrous act. See Richard S. Westfall, *Never at Rest: A Biography of Isaac Newton* (Cambridge: Cambridge University Press, 2010 [1980]), 314–15.

[81] Terry Pinkard, *Hegel's Naturalism: Mind, Nature, and the Final Ends of Life* (Oxford: Oxford University Press, 2012), 17, describes it as a 'disenchanted Aristotelian naturalism'.

[82] Hegel, *Philosophy of Nature*, §248, 19, wrote 'In Nature, as the otherness [of the Idea], there also occur the square or the tetrad, for example, the four Elements, the four colours, etc.'

[83] Hegel, *Philosophy of Nature*, §247, 14.

[84] Aristotle, *De Anima Books II and III*, trans. D. W. Hamlyn, 413b, wrote that 'We speak of as nutritive that part of the soul in which even plants share; all animals clearly have the sense of touch.'

come into being as the truth of nature.'[85] He remained faithful to the Aristotelian idea that the human soul participated in divinity in virtue of its rationality. Everything, from being in its simplest form, to human self-conscious subjectivity, was permeated by rationality to a greater or lesser degree. The philosophy of nature began with the abstract principles of mechanics (of the sort described by Kant), before moving to physical and chemical bodies, and culminating in the organic realm.

This raises the other main modern criticism respecting Hegel's philosophy of nature: his treatment of evolution. Hegel argued that for the philosophy of nature, the evolutionary hypothesis was irrelevant. He is thus sometimes held, even by sympathetic critics such as Stephen Houlgate, to have believed 'contra Darwin – that species emerge fully formed and fixed'.[86] We saw that Aristotle regarded species as eternal, and Hegel likewise held that the development of the genus was not a temporal process. But Houlgate's statement equivocates between temporal and logical processes.

As Janet Radcliffe Richards observes, Hegel's era lacked not the idea of evolution, but a plausible causal mechanism for it, something only supplied by Charles Darwin's theory of natural selection.[87] Hegel knew how evolution was supposed to have occurred, temporally speaking:

> The way of evolution, which starts from the imperfect and formless, is as follows: at first there was the liquid element and aqueous forms of life, and from the water there evolved plants, polyps, molluscs, and finally fishes; then from the fishes were evolved the land animals, and finally from the land animals came man.[88]

Hegel did not reject the claim that there had been such a temporal process. But just as in the *Phenomenology of Spirit*, he denied that a logical progression must always follow temporal developments in empirically observable nature. Hegel thought the philosophy of nature, like all philosophy, was *sub specie aeternitatis*. Since all temporal processes were subject to contingency, the biological processes by which species developed were not always a good

---

[85] G. W. F. Hegel, *Hegel's Philosophy of Mind, Translated from the 1830 Edition, together with the Zusätze by W. Wallace and A. V. Miller, Revised with an Introduction by M. J. Inwood* (Oxford: Oxford University Press, 2010 [2007]), §388, 29.
[86] Stephen Houlgate, *An Introduction to Hegel: Freedom, Truth and History* (Oxford: Blackwell, 2005), 174.
[87] Janet Radcliffe Richards, *Human Nature After Darwin: A Philosophical Introduction* (London and New York: Routledge, 2000), 185.
[88] Hegel, *Philosophy of Nature*, §249, 21.

guide to the rational grounds of the teleological necessity these processes instantiated. The important point, however, is that if Hegel's philosophy of nature did reject evolution, it did *not* do so insofar as evolution was a finding of empirical, biological science.

In other words, Hegel rejected evolution *only* as an ultimate explanation of the rational necessity of the concepts it embodied, like genus and species. Houlgate's observation that 'Hegel's systematic philosophical interest in rational distinctions between animal species (and in comparative anatomy) does not justify [his] anti-evolutionary position, but is in fact quite compatible with the idea that species evolved from one another' is thus slightly off.[89] It is correct to say that Hegel's interest in the difference between species was rational rather than empirical, but wrong to think that Hegel considered his argument incompatible with evolution empirically considered.

Hegel even made some positive use of the empirical concept of evolution himself. For example, he wrote that 'Matter . . . negates itself as an untrue existence and from this negation emerges a higher existence . . . Evolution is thus also an involution, in that matter interiorizes itself to become life.'[90] At the very least, he left open the biological fact of the matter so far as the temporal process was concerned, and at the empirical level, made no objection to evolution. Moreover, Hegel's argument that it was impossible to find definite boundaries to species in nature was consistent with Charles Darwin's later view that the notion of a species is inherently vague.[91] As in the case of Newtonian physics, then, whether or not one is ultimately sympathetic to Hegel's position, it was more complex than has often been recognised.

For Hegel, mind emerged in literally organic fashion from nature. Hegel was insistent that 'There is simply no out-and-out Other for the mind.'[92] We could know nature scientifically, in the last resort, because we were already in it and of it; we were as much part of nature as anything

---

[89] Houlgate, *An Introduction to Hegel*, 174. In fairness, Stephen Houlgate, 'Introduction', *Hegel and the Philosophy of Nature*, ed. Stephen Houlgate (Albany: SUNY Press, 1998), xi–xxvii, xxii, acknowledges that it is also possible to argue that 'Hegel's dialectical philosophy is in fact profoundly *evolutionary* in character and indeed anticipates certain modern biological concepts.' Emphasis in original.

[90] Hegel, *Philosophy of Nature*, §251, 26.

[91] Jody Hey, *Genes, Categories, and Species: The Evolutionary and Cognitive Causes of the Species Problem* (Oxford: Oxford University Press, 2001), 5, notes 'our persistent and awkward shortage of consensus' over what a species is. Disconcertingly, neither philosophers nor scientists currently agree on a definition of the term 'species'.

[92] Hegel, *Philosophy of Mind*, §377, 3.

else. Nevertheless, the mind in its full development constituted a distinctive area of inquiry. Whereas Hegel's discussions of the natural sciences of chemistry, physics, and biology were chiefly found in the philosophy of nature, the sciences of anthropology and psychology, or what we would now call the social sciences, belonged to the philosophy of subjective spirit. Hegel's treatment of the arts and the humanities was rather more diffuse. They too belonged to this third part of the system, though, so that world history, for example, was included in the *Encyclopedia* under the more general heading of ethical life.[93] But history, and for that matter art, also received extended separate consideration elsewhere.[94]

There were important similarities between Hegel's account of the disciplines devoted specifically to the study of human beings and his account of scientific knowledge. For instance, Hegel disliked ancient atomistic philosophy not just because of its materialism but because he found the analogous conception of society as composed of absolutely discrete individuals objectionable. The notion that individuality of any kind, whether natural or social, could ever be absolute struck Hegel as absurd.

In physical terms, the concept of a single thing was incoherent. The very concept of a self-identical thing necessarily implied its difference from other things.[95] The obverse of this argument was that any attribution of identity was necessarily exclusionary or partial. In saying that something had a certain quality, for example, we were forced to temporarily neglect the fact that it also had indefinitely many other qualities, and also that other things may have the same quality.[96] The predication of traditional logic, on Hegel's view, was not so much wrong as partial in its operations.

This, however, was also true socially. The idea that there could be just one human being was similarly incoherent. The discrete embodiment of human beings did not make them absolutely separate, whether linguistically, ethically or legally. People, like things, enjoyed their identities in virtue of their relationships. No individual, though, could be reduced

---

[93] Hegel, *Philosophy of Mind*, §§548–52.
[94] Georg Wilhelm Friedrich Hegel, *The Philosophy of History*, trans. J. Sibree (Kitchener: Batoche Books, 2001); Georg Wilhelm Friedrich Hegel, *Aesthetics Lectures on Fine Art*, trans. T. M. Knox, 2 vols (Oxford: Clarendon Press, 1988 [1975]).
[95] Hegel, *Science of Logic*, trans. Di Giovanni, 87, wrote that 'The individual refers to itself by setting limits to every other; but these limits are therefore also the limits of its self; they are references to the other; the individual's existence is not in the individual.'
[96] Hegel, *Science of Logic*, trans. Di Giovanni, 67, argued that 'Judgment joins subject and object in a connection of identity; abstraction is therefore made from the fact that the subject has yet more determinacies than the predicate has, just as that the predicate is wider than the subject.'

to just a single relation or role. Everyone was necessarily possessed of a pluralistic identity and played a variety of roles. Any other account of individuality was ruled out by the conception of 'Spirit' discussed above. Knowledge of the social world had to account for both the necessity and the limitations of individuality. This abstract point also held significant implications for political life.

Politics

Hegel's *Philosophy of Right*, like the rest of his writings, was an exposition of categories. Indeed, his political philosophy was presented as a deduction from the single category of 'right'. Like 'Geist', no single English word captures all the connotations of '*das Recht*'. The term is both legal and moral in its extension. '*Recht*', or 'right', in Hegel's sense, supposedly contained within itself the categories that supplied the three main divisions of the work, namely abstract right, morality, and ethical life. However, the concept of *die Kategorie*, which played a major role in the *Phenomenology* as standing for the 'I', was not used. Hegel did not explain its absence, though it presumably remained presupposed by the more developed concepts of the self that he considered. He was now dealing with persons capable of property ownership and of citizenship. But in a broader sense, the vocabulary of categories was still present. The opening sections of the *Philosophy of Right* were concerned, for example, with the logical categories of subjectivity and objectivity.[97]

In general, then, Hegel's ideas about categories and knowledge were reflected in his arguments about government and politics. Karl Popper was one of those who endorsed this view, albeit in negative form. It was Hegel's 'oracular philosophy' that made him 'the father of modern ... totalitarianism'.[98] Popper described Hegel as 'a mouthpiece of the reaction against the French revolution' and placed him with Plato as one of the most formidable enemies of the 'open society'.[99] For Popper, writing

---

[97] Georg Wilhelm Friedrich Hegel, *Elements of the Philosophy of Right*, ed. Allen W. Wood, trans. H. B. Nisbet (Cambridge: Cambridge University Press, 2003 [1991]), 56. In the German text, Hegel typically used nouns like 'die Bestimmung' or 'die Gattung', that can be translated by a variety of English words including 'determination' or 'genre', but his intention was clearly to distinguish types of concepts and their logic, as elsewhere. To say that Hegel is concerned with 'categories' in the broad sense in these passages thus does no violence to his meaning.

[98] Sir Karl Popper, *The Open Society and its Enemies: New One-Volume Edition With a new Introduction by Alan Ryan and an Essay by E. H. Gombrich* (Princeton and Oxford: Princeton University Press, 1994), 237.

[99] Popper, *Open Society*, 16.

in the mid-twentieth century, Hegel was 'the first official philosopher of Prussianism' who ushered in a modern return to tribalism in the form of the worship of the nation-state. But the later twentieth-century reassessment of Hegel extended to his political philosophy. Charles Taylor, for example, declared Popper's claim that Hegel had endorsed 'Prussia as the fullest realisation of the modern state [was] based on lamentable historical ignorance'.[100] Taylor argued that in fact the *Philosophy of Right* had articulated a theory that insisted on scope for the individual conscience, and for freedom of choice.

Since Popper associated the openness that characterised civilised society with the defence of scientific knowledge, we may note that Hegel gave a spirited defence of Galileo against Papal persecution in the *Philosophy of Right*.[101] This suggests that Taylor was correct that Hegel's thought was neither oracular nor totalitarian. The state, Hegel argued, should be on the side of scientific truth and must stand firmly against superstition and dogmatism. We noted that the *Science of Logic* was the study of the categories that composed the mind of God, and this theological dimension likewise permeated Hegel's political thought. So, when Hegel described the state as 'divine', he did not mean that it should be the object of uncritical adulation, but that it was an expression of truth and rationality.[102]

Yet the state was not simply a church in disguise for Hegel. As the most developed form of rationality, it was firmly separate from religion. Hegel thought that the state could accommodate a plurality of confessions, an acknowledgement of the fact that in his own day there were a variety of Protestant churches in existence. But it retained final jurisdiction over religious doctrine. Though Hegel suggested the state should require that people belong to a church, he did not insist strongly on the point, other than to make plain (and here he agreed with Kant) that the choice of confession was a matter strictly for the individual.[103] Consistently with the viewpoint of the *Phenomenology of Spirit*, religion was a stage on the way to Absolute Knowing, not the last word in thinking. In Hegel's theory of the state, there was no necessary conflict between science and religion.[104] The clash between the Enlightenment spirit and the forces of faith that culminated

---

[100] Charles Taylor, *Hegel* (Cambridge: Cambridge University Press, 1999 [1975]), 425.
[101] Hegel, *Philosophy of Right*, §270, 300.
[102] Hegel, *Philosophy of Right*, §270, 292.
[103] Hegel, *Philosophy of Right*, §270, 295, wrote that 'since religion is that moment which integrates the state at the deepest level of the disposition [of its citizens], the state ought even to require all its citizens to belong to such a community – but to any community they please, for the state can have no say in the content [of religious belief] in so far as this relates to the internal dimension of representational thought'.
[104] Hegel, *Philosophy of Right*, §360, 380.

in the French revolution, Hegel had argued in the *Phenomenology of Spirit*, had been due ultimately to a shared lack of self-understanding, both sides failing to see what each had in common with the other.[105]

In making this claim about the proper relationship between science and religion Hegel did not think of himself as constructing a template for an ideal state, as he thought Plato's *Republic* had tried to do.[106] Hegel argued that a theory of the state 'must distance itself as far as possible from any attempt to construct *a state as it ought to be*'.[107] At this level of conceptual analysis, at least, the state did not contain within itself any conflict between science and religion when correctly understood. This is different from arguing that there ought not be any such conflict (though Hegel would probably also have endorsed this position too). The constitutional form described in the *Philosophy of Right* was not, in other words, a construction blueprint. Philosophy as Hegel conceived it was supposedly incapable of '*issuing instructions* on how the world ought to be'.[108]

Even at the level of theoretical principle, it is difficult to interpret Hegel's theory as illiberal. Like Aristotle, Hegel understood the state as logically prior to the family or to society and the market in the sense that it was a condition of the possibility of the existence of these institutions. That, however, did not imply authoritarian central direction of any kind. Hegel criticised Plato for having suggested in the *Republic* that people should 'have their tasks assigned to them by the authorities'. In modernity, this would not do: 'subjective freedom, which must be respected, requires freedom of choice on the part of individuals'.[109]

Far from endorsing a modern version of allegedly Platonic totalitarianism, as in Popper's account, Hegel's political philosophy was an attempt to deal with the realisation that, as Taylor neatly put it, 'we cannot go home again'.[110] Modern individualistic subjectivity was incompatible with a literal revival of the kind of community that Hegel himself associated with the ancient Greek city-state, whether or not one considers that as a totalitarian model. This concern with subjectivity explains why property

---

[105] Hegel, *Phenomenology*, §575, 230, argued that the apparent victory which constituted the outcome of the Enlightenment's struggle with faith only resulted in its internalisation of the conflict.

[106] Hegel, *Philosophy of Right*, 'Preface', 20, described Plato's *Republic* as 'the embodiment of nothing other than the nature of Greek ethics' in which the rational concept of the state was still only latent.

[107] Hegel, *Philosophy of Right*, 'Preface', 21.

[108] Hegel, *Philosophy of Right*, 'Preface', 23.

[109] Hegel, *Philosophy of Right*, §262, 285.

[110] Taylor, *Hegel*, 443.

was a key feature of Hegel's discussion of 'abstract right', even though from a chronological standpoint property was preceded by other institutions such as the family that came later in the argument.[111] Being able to say 'mine' contributed to a person's sense of self, because they could find their own will expressed in the world in the form of possession of an object. Yet the statement could not simply be an act of self-assertion. Saying 'mine' implied a system of rules involving reciprocal recognition of ownership in which the subject was a participant, and in which, furthermore, this ownership was an expression of 'Right'.

'Right' was identified with 'any existence at all which is the *existence of the free will*' and 'is therefore in general freedom, as Idea'.[112] The free will was both moral and rational, as it was for Kant. Hegel shared Kant's goal of making the moral world as rule-governed after its own fashion as the natural world. The difference, put in Kantian terms, was that Hegel saw the noumenal order as integral to the phenomenal rather than as sharply distinct from it. But both Kant and Hegel held that one could not be said to be free if one's deeds were the unreflective expressions of natural impulses. Freedom could not be identified with simply doing as one pleased.[113] Freedom for Hegel, correctly understood, entailed the reciprocal recognition of individual subjectivity and the universal or collective subjectivity of the community as a whole.

As Taylor points out, Hegel was no democrat.[114] Also like Kant, the principle that all adults should have an individual voice in public affairs in the form of an electoral vote was one that Hegel explicitly repudiated. To the extent that Hegel thought the concept of the state entailed representation at all, it was on a corporate basis. 'Men must relate to the polity not as individuals, but through their membership in the articulated components of the society'.[115] Hegel also argued that the idea of the state involved an hereditary quasi-aristocratic element. Members of this landed estate were released from the need to earn a living thanks to their inherited property, and were thus free to devote themselves to public affairs.

Again like Kant, however, and in contrast to ancient tradition, Hegel found no natural ground for authority. Superior rationality conferred no

---

[111] Hegel, *Philosophy of Right*, §32.
[112] Hegel, *Philosophy of Right*, §29, 58.
[113] Hegel, *Philosophy of Right*, §15, 48, wrote that to say that 'freedom in general consists in *being able to do as one pleases* . . . can only be taken to indicate a complete lack of intellectual culture'.
[114] Taylor, *Hegel*, 445.
[115] Taylor, *Hegel*, 446.

title simply as such. Despite Hegel's belief that human beings were not equal in respect of their natural abilities, the offices of government had to be open to talents. Contra Popper, Hegel, like Kant, was making a significant break with the Platonic version of the link between categories, knowledge and politics. For Hegel, the kind of reason that should rule was not the possession of an elite group of individuals but was now associated with collective wisdom, in which, in the end, all participated, whether formally or informally. While Hegel may still have thought that the best ought to govern, he was clear that he did not mean this in the same sense as Plato.[116]

Hegel's belief in corporate representation reflected his more general philosophical position that individuality was not absolute. Individuals necessarily had their own moral ideas about right and wrong, but these had to be worked out in the context of a larger ethical life in which family, civil society and the state itself all figured. We should construe Hegel's remarks about the 'organic state' in this light.[117] The idea was intended to convey the state's dynamic capacity for integrating difference without eliminating it. The 'organic' state was not a homogeneous amoebic blob, but a highly articulated entity. We can think of Hegel's use of the term as a late effort to employ the ancient and medieval metaphor of the body politic, updated to absorb the modern anatomical knowledge of his day.[118]

Individuals, families, corporations, and the various parts of government all combined to create a whole. But this whole was not 'natural' in the same way as a plant or an animal. For Hegel, human subjectivity was precisely a differentiation of oneself from the rest of the world considered zoologically. The modern state, and in particular its legal and constitutional order comprising a system of rules, was the work of rational inter-subjectivity, understood as *Geist* in action. As Stephen Bosworth agues, even the presence of a monarch was a rational requirement. The monarch symbolised the necessity of the moment of individual will or decision in the state in a formal sense.[119] But Hegel's emphasis on the organic and legal character of

---

[116] Hegel, *Philosophy of History*, 469, 476.

[117] For example, Georg Wilhelm Friedrich Hegel, *Grundlinien der Philosophie des Rechts Oder Naturrecht und Staatswissenschafl im Grundrisse Mit Hegels eigenhändigen Notizen und den mündlichen Zusätzen* (Frankfurt: Suhrkamp Verlag, 1970), §46, 108, referred to 'der vernünftige Organismus des Staats'. But Hegel, *Philosophy of History*, 465, explicitly repudiated the idea of the state as a substantial organic unity.

[118] Hegel, *Philosophy of Right*, §309.

[119] Hegel, *Philosophy of Right*, §280. See Stephen C. Bosworth, *Hegel's Political Philosophy: The Test Case of Constitutional Monarchy* (Abingdon and New York: Routledge, 2020 [1991]).

the state did not mean he expected it to be free of internal conflict. The *Philosophy of Right* made plain that the *Phenomenology of Spirit*'s abstract treatment of the dialectic of the struggle for recognition would be played out temporally in modern history.

There has been no single more important analysis of what we now call identity politics than the account of the interaction between lord and bondsman in the *Phenomenology of Spirit*. It has influenced subsequent understandings of, at least, class, sex and race. So far as class is concerned, before Marx, Hegel discerned the problems modern industrial society was storing up for itself by generating an impoverished underclass that would be at odds with the rest of society. He also foresaw that capitalism would 'attempt to solve this problem by finding overseas markets and by colonization'.[120] As Taylor argued, one reason why Hegel was not a liberal in a modern sense was precisely that he rejected the coming world of market-oriented liberalism, which he regarded as rooted in British approaches to political economy.

Relations between citizens of Hegel's state were characterised by *Sittlichkeit*. This was a non-instrumental ethical relationship between fellow members of the community that could not be reduced to the market relations characteristic of capitalism. The individual could not be understood exclusively as a utility maximiser related to other individuals only in terms of contracts entered into via the market. The pursuit of rational, calculable self-interest was undeniably one aspect of individuality, but if taken for the whole, it would generate alienation of the sort that Marx would complain of in the 1840s.[121] This was also why

---

[120] Taylor, *Hegel*, 436.
[121] Hegel, *Philosophy of Right*, trans. H. B. Nisbet, §66. Hegel, *Philosophie des Rechts*, §66, used 'Entäusserung' for alienation. It was inherent in *Geist* or Spirit that a gap may open up between its inner and outer worlds, so that 'what the spirit is only *in itself* may differ from what it is *for itself*' (ibid., trans. H. B. Nisbet; emphasis in original). Hegel gave the examples of slavery and serfdom as examples of situations in which alienation could occur; but he also considered being prohibited from property ownership as a condition of alienation, a point on which Marx would potentially have differed. Marx and Engels, *The Communist Party Manifesto with Related Documents*, trans. Samuel Moore, ed. John E. Toews, 2nd edn (Boston: Bedford/St Martin's, 2018 [1999]), 77, wrote that 'The distinguishing feature of Communism is not the abolition of property generally, but the abolition of bourgeois property.' Marcello Musto, ed., *Karl Marx's Writings on Alienation* (Cham: Palgrave Macmillan, 2021), 7, notes that although in the writings first published in 1932 as the *Economic and Philosophical Manuscripts* Marx also used 'Entäusserung', he drew a more specific connection than Hegel to alienation as a function of 'wage labour and the transformation of labour products into objects standing opposed to producers'.

Hegel repeatedly rejected Kant's view that the state could be founded on a contract of any kind.[122] To view the state as a contract represented a conceptual confusion of the state with civil society.

Hegel's undemocratic liberalism did not therefore prevent him from giving considerable attention to the question of welfare. His appreciation of the impersonal nature of the new market economy led him to conclude that poverty could have structural causes. People could be poor through no fault of their own, and so 'civil society is obliged to feed its members'.[123] Hegel saw the potential for what Marx called the immiseration of the proletariat and the formation of a revolutionary class consciousness, though unlike Marx, he viewed this development in a thoroughly negative light rather than as the prelude to the creation of an ideal Communist society.

Hegel feared that the creation of a 'rabble' composed of the alienated poor could destroy the modern state from within.[124] To counteract it, the mass of the population should be actively involved in participating in the life of the state in an organised way, and not simply be the passive subjects of government. This partly explained the importance Hegel gave to both the family and the various corporate estates. In addition to their positive roles in providing individuals with developed identities and meaningful occupations, they were also bulwarks against the class struggle.

The struggle for recognition has also been read as applicable to gender relations, as it was, for example, by Simone de Beauvoir.[125] It is easy to dismiss Hegel as an example of patriarchal sexism. Modern feminist critics can point to Hegel's statement that 'The difference between man and woman is the difference between animal and plant', which attributes to women a demeaning vegetable quality.[126] But as with Kant, it is important to appreciate the source of Hegel's prejudices. These were, again, Aristotelian. The traditional patriarchal view maintained by Aristotle was that the male was active and the female passive. This theory, like Kant's essentialist view of race, was derived from a metaphysical principle that applied to everything from the workings of reproduction to the structure of social order.

Also like Kant, Hegel was sexist enough to think that women were 'not made for activities which demand a universal faculty such as the

---

[122] Hegel, *Philosophy of Right*, §§75, 100, 258.
[123] Hegel, *Philosophy of Right*, §240.
[124] Hegel, *Philosophy of Right*, §244.
[125] Simone de Beauvoir, *The Second Sex*, trans. Constance Borde and Sheila Malovany-Chevallier, intro. Judith Thurman (New York: Vintage Books, 2010 [1949]), 60, wrote that in modern society 'sexual opposition increases rather than abates when the individuality of organisms asserts itself. The male finds more and more ways to use the forces of which he is master; the female feels her subjugation more and more.'
[126] Hegel, *Philosophy of Right*, §166.

more advanced sciences [and] philosophy'.[127] Yet Hegel did assert that women as well as men shared in the modern form of subjectivity, even if they were naturally suited for different roles. Although Hegel did not accord women full equality, restricting their economic and political participation, he unquestionably regarded them as self-determining people with legal rights and an ethical existence of their own. His analysis of the tragic character of Antigone in the *Phenomenology of Spirit* made this clear.[128] Women were definitely not destined simply for the use and gratification of men. The choices of modern women on issues like marriage had to be unequivocally respected.[129]

The final issue that has become closely associated with the master-slave relationship is race. Frantz Fanon presented the anti-colonial struggle in racial terms informed by Hegel.[130] Susan Buck-Morss argues that the relationship was not purely conceptual. Hegel was, according to Buck-Morss, the first philosopher to take seriously 'the deterritoralized, world market of the European colonial system'.[131] That system, she observes, was significantly dependent upon African slavery for its profits and productivity, but the practice of slavery was glaringly at odds with the universal principles articulated in the revolutions against the eighteenth-century feudal and monarchical status quo. Buck-Morss suggests that the Haitian revolution, which was widely reported in Europe, including in publications Hegel is known to have read, was a likely source for the account of the master-slave dialectic in the *Phenomenology*.[132] The revolted slaves who took seriously the values of the French revolution exemplified the dialectic in action.

---

[127] Hegel, *Philosophy of Right*, §§165–6.
[128] Hegel, *Phenomenology of Spirit*, §475, 190, called women 'the eternal irony of the commonwealth' because they naturally preferred their own values and interests, especially family, to the rational universal of the state. The root of Sophocles' tragic drama, according to Hegel (§470), was that Antigone put her own conscience regarding her duty to her brother before the law. In Hegel's account, this kind of attitude was crucial to the collapse of the group-oriented form of spirit found in the ancient polis, which implicitly made women the harbingers of the subjective moment in modern individualism.
[129] Hegel, *Philosophy of Right*, §§162.
[130] Frantz Fanon, *Black Skin, White Masks*, trans. Charles Lam Markmann (London: Pluto Press, 1986 [1952]), 217, wrote in a section on 'The Negro and Hegel' that 'There is not an open conflict between white and black. One day the White Master, *without conflict*, recognized the Negro slave. But the former slave wants to *make himself recognized*.' Emphasis in original, with paragraphs omitted.
[131] Susan Buck-Morss, *Hegel, Haiti, and Universal History* (Pittsburgh: University of Pittsburgh Press, 2009), 8, 10.
[132] Buck-Morss, *Hegel and Haiti*, 49, suggests that 'the idea for the dialectic of lordship and bondage came to Hegel in Jena in the years 1803–5 from reading the press-journals and newspapers'.

This reading is at odds, as Buck-Morss recognises, with Hegel's racist remarks about black Africans in the *Encylopedia* and the argument in the *Philosophy of History* that Africa was mostly of no significance for the dialectic of world history. She explains the discrepancy by arguing that a younger, more radical Hegel welcomed the assertion of the universal principles of freedom in a way that his older more conservative self no longer endorsed. Although Hegel's racism, like his sexism, was patronising rather than abusive or hateful, his observations were often ill-informed even by the standards of his day.[133] The remark that 'Negroes are to be regarded as a nation of children who remain immersed in their uninterested and indifferent naïveté. They are sold, and let themselves be sold, without any reflection on whether this is right or not' only showed that Cicero's ancient observation that 'There is nothing so absurd but some philosopher has said it' still held good in the modern world.[134]

Despite Hegel's racism, he did not endorse slavery in any form, which has made it possible to appropriate him for studies of contemporary black culture.[135] The *Philosophy of Right* made Hegel's general position on slavery clear: 'The alleged justification of *slavery* ... and all *historical* views on the right of slavery and lordship, depend on regarding the human being simply as a *natural being* [*Naturwesen*]'.[136] Slavery involved treating people as if they were things, and even if those people were somehow inferior, as Hegel erroneously believed Africans were, this was still wrong. Notwithstanding Hegel's general admiration for Aristotle, he did not share Aristotle's belief in natural slavery. His remark that the very status of being a slave 'violated the concept of the human being' was an unqualified condemnation.[137] Slavery had no place in the concept of the state described in the *Philosophy of Right*. Its members were persons capable of owning property; they could not be property themselves.

For Marx, the necessary outcome of the class struggle was an international union of workers that transcended the state. Hegel, however, was convinced that the state would remain the fundamental unit of international politics.

---

[133] See Robert Bernasconi, 'Hegel at the Court of the Ashanti', in Andrew Benjamin, ed., *Hegel After Derrida* (London: Routledge, 1998), 41–63.

[134] Hegel, *Philosophy of Mind*, trans. Wallace and Miller, rev. Inwood, §389; Cicero, *De Divinatione*, ed. Arthur Stanley Pease (Urbana: University of Illinois, 1920), bk 2, ch. 119, 544.

[135] For example, Jim Vernon, *Hip Hop, Hegel, and the Art of Emancipation: Let's Get Free* (Cham: Springer Nature, 2018), applies Hegel's claim that art creates community and provides a liberatory impetus to the new musical culture emerging in 1970s New York City.

[136] Hegel, *Philosophy of Right*, §57, 86–7. Emphasis in original.

[137] Hegel, *Philosophy of Right*, §2.

States could have a moral relationship to one another, and European states in particular were a 'family' because their laws and customs were all expressions of a single idea of the modern state.[138] But this was not a formal union, and Hegel was sceptical about the viability of Kant's idea for a cosmopolitan federation of republican states. Hegel argued that such a federation would be forced to rely on goodwill, because there could be no genuine sovereign in such an association. This did not make such a federation impossible, but it would remain 'tainted with contingency'.[139]

Federated or otherwise, there was also a clear distinction between the family of European states and other communities that had not reached the same stage in the development of spirit. European states were entitled to treat them as 'barbarians'.[140] Hegel's attitude here was typical of much nineteenth-century liberal opinion. John Stuart Mill, for instance, later expressed similar views in justification of British imperialism.[141] But Hegel's confident distinction between civilised and uncivilised peoples was not a license to exterminate those considered barbarians.

The best evidence for Popper's critique of Hegel is his remarks on war and violence. Hegel scholars disagree on whether or not Hegel thought war was absolutely necessary.[142] What cannot be denied, though, is that Hegel regarded violence, both at the individual level and as organised warfare, as an existential proving-ground. In his account of the struggle between lord and bondsman, he argued that 'the two self-consciousnesses . . . *prove* themselves and each other through a life-and-death combat . . . it is only through staking one's life that freedom is established'.[143] As Inwood points out, this did not mean that death must actually occur as a result of the struggle; it was the willingness to take the risk that mattered.[144]

---

[138] Hegel, *Philosophy of Right*, §339.
[139] Hegel, *Philosophy of Right*, §333.
[140] Hegel, *Philosophy of Right*, §351.
[141] J. S. Mill, *Considerations on Representative Government*, in *Essays on Politics and Society: Collected Works of John Stuart Mill*, vol. XIX, ed. J. M. Robson, intro. Alexander Brady, 33 vols (Toronto and Buffalo: University of Toronto Press, 1977), 387, wrote that 'A rude people, though in some degree alive to the benefits of civilized society, may be unable to practise the forbearances which it demands . . . In such a case, a civilized government, to be really advantageous to them, will require to be in a considerable degree despotic.'
[142] Taylor, *Hegel*, 448, says that for Hegel 'war has necessarily to occur'; Houlgate, 'Introduction' to Georg Wilhelm Friedrich Hegel, *Outlines of the Philosophy of Right*, trans. T. M. Knox, rev. Stephen Houlgate (Oxford: Oxford University Press, 2008 [1952]), xxxii, says that although Hegel rejects the Kantian notion of a federation of cosmopolitan states, 'This is not to say that war is absolutely inevitable.'
[143] Hegel, *Phenomenology of Spirit*, §187. Emphasis in original.
[144] Inwood, *Phenomenology of Spirit*, 'Commentary', 399.

But Hegel did regard war, like the individual struggle for recognition, as a confrontation with the inescapable realities of mortality and finitude. War exposed fundamental ethical truths about the rootedness of identity in community that peacetime tended to obscure.[145]

Given Germany's role in the two world wars of the twentieth century, Hegel's acceptance, if not active endorsement, of war should not be glossed over. His remarks on this topic made him exploitable by later, more aggressively nationalistic and militaristic, voices.[146] That said, Hegel was a stranger to the modern experience of 'total' war. Contemporary ideas of war have been shaped by the twentieth century, in which the bombing of civilian populations became routine and the very idea of a declaration of war increasingly antiquated. For Hegel, 'war' still meant a limited and legal condition that could be fought somewhat humanely. He was adamant that 'war should on no account be waged either on internal institutions and the peace of family and private life, or on private individuals'.[147]

War for Hegel did not prevent states from continuing to recognise one another, and moreover was an inherently temporary state of affairs. His conception of war was shaped by the French revolution and the Napoleonic wars, in which massed armies faced one another on a battlefield in short engagements lasting a few days at most, and the most powerful weapons were cannons, not world-ending nuclear bombs. The kind of genocidal war that Hitler launched in 1939, in the aftermath of which Popper wrote his critique of Hegel, lay altogether outside Hegel's horizons.[148] Nevertheless, in Hegel's philosophy of history, war was one aspect of the state's participation in the unfolding of the world-spirit.

---

[145] Hegel, *Philosophy of Right*, §324, wrote that 'War is that condition in which the vanity of temporal things [*Dinge*] and temporal goods – which tends at other times to be merely a pious phrase – takes on a serious significance.' Emphasis in original.

[146] See Andreas Grossman, 'German neo-Hegelianism and a plea for another Hegel', in *The Impact of Idealism: The Legacy of Post-Kantian German Thought*, vol. II, *Historical, Social and Political Thought*, ed. John Walker (Cambridge: Cambridge University Press, 2013), 232–59.

[147] Hegel, *Philosophy of Right*, §338.

[148] John Keane, *Violence and Democracy* (Cambridge: Cambridge University Press, 2004), 16, writes that 'In matters of violence the twentieth century proved to be the worst ever ... It was also a century in which the burdens of war weighed ever more heavily on civilians ... During the 1914–18 war, civilians comprised one-twentieth of the victims. During the 1939–45 war, that proportion rose to two-thirds; these days, perhaps nine-tenths of the victims of war are civilians.'

History

In Hegel's *Encyclopedia*, world history was the final moment in the dialectical development of the state. It was the destiny of the state, like the individual, to be one amongst others. But since world history was a moment of the state, and the state was a derivation from the category of right, world history was likewise necessarily the realisation of right. It comprised the movement of freedom westwards from Asia and its gradual extension through the Greek, Roman and medieval eras until freedom was fully realised in modernity. Hegel's theory of the historical process, like Kant's, was in that respect progressive, and so a departure from Platonic and Aristotelian models. There was, though, an important difference from Kant's approach, namely that Hegel's theory was progressive but not predictive. Though Hegel is rightly considered a teleological thinker, as James Kreines observes, there is an important distinction to be made between immanent teleology and external teleology.[149]

In external teleology, the end is given. We can think of Christian apocalyptic theology as an external teleology in this sense. God's plan is determined in advance and its ultimate outcome is revealed to us, even if the details are obscure. Hegel's philosophy of history was likewise explicitly a theodicy, a justification of the ways of God to man.[150] To the extent that Hegel's theory fitted the model of an external teleology in which the end was given in advance, it was already completed. The end of history did not lie in the future, as in Kant's anticipation of a future of cosmopolitan states, or indeed Marx's Communist vision. Freedom had already been achieved. The evidence lay in the French revolutionary proclamation of universal freedom and equality that Hegel believed Napoleon had first stabilised and then exported to the rest of Europe via military conquest.

Thus, Hegel did not think of himself making a *prediction* in saying the end of history was freedom, but as describing something that had *already*

---

[149] See James Kreines, 'Hegel: The Reality and Priority of Immanent Teleology', in Jeffrey K. McDonough, ed., *Teleology: A History* (Oxford: Oxford University Press, 2020), 219–48.

[150] Georg Wilhelm Friedrich Hegel, *Philosophy of History*, trans. J. Sibree (Kitchener, ON: Batoche Books, 2001), 29, wrote that 'Our mode of treating the subject is, in this aspect, a Theodicaea – a justification of the ways of God . . . so that the ill that is found in the World may be comprehended, and the thinking Spirit reconciled with the fact of the existence of evil.'

happened.[151] This was consistent with thinking that the working out of the implications of universal freedom remained ongoing. That there could be no further development of freedom in European history in a logical sense did not preclude temporal events from continuing. But we cannot know how these will unfold. Hegel, as we saw, thought of philosophy as only wise in hindsight, hence his remark that 'The owl of Minerva begins its flight only at the onset of dusk.'[152]

Hegel's dominant conception of teleology, however (as the image of the owl of Minerva suggests), was immanent. Things developed according to their own inner necessity, but what form this development would take could not be known in advance. With purely logical categories this was not an issue, because rational analysis was sufficient to exhibit all the connections between them, but when temporality entered the picture, as it did in the later parts of the system, it brought with it an unpredictability and contingency that made the future unforeseeable, at least in detail. Hegel's philosophy of history thus left room for the presence of genuine novelty, at least beyond Europe. What his *Philosophy of History* had to say about the progress of freedom, Hegel made clear, applied only to what he called 'old Europe'. Like Alexis de Tocqueville, Hegel expected America to be 'the land of the future, where, in the ages that lie before us, the burden of the World's History shall reveal itself'.[153]

But that was as specific a prediction as Hegel was prepared to make. An important implication is that Popper's association of Hegel with *predictive* historicist thought was as unsound as his charge of totalitarianism.[154] Popper defined historicism as 'an approach to the social sciences which assumes that *historical prediction* is their principal aim'.[155] Popper offered a variety of arguments to show that this was an impossible goal, in contrast to the truly predictive natural sciences. For example, since human history was a single instance of a process, it was not suitable for the kind of generalisable hypothesis testing associated with the natural sciences.[156] But even if Popper's arguments were sound, they did not apply to Hegel, who

---

[151] Jean-Paul Sartre, *Critique of Dialectical Reason*, vol. 1, *Theory of Practical Ensembles*, ed. Jonathan Rée, trans. Alan Sheridan Smith (London: Version, 2004 [1960]), 23, wrote that 'Hegel took himself to be at the beginning of the end of History, that is to say, at that moment of Truth which is death.'
[152] Hegel, *Philosophy of Right*, trans. H. B. Nisbet, 'Preface'.
[153] Hegel, *Philosophy of History*, 104.
[154] Sir Karl Popper, *The Poverty of Historicism*, 3rd edn (New York: Harper and Row, 1964 [1957]), viii, complained of the 'persistent and pernicious influence [of historicist thought] upon the philosophy of society and of politics, from Heraclitus and Plato to Hegel and Marx'.
[155] Popper, *Poverty of Historicism*, 3. Emphasis in original.
[156] Popper, *Poverty of Historicism*, 109.

unlike Kant and Marx, claimed neither rational nor scientific insight into the *future* course of human history.

Popper's definition of historicism is also a potential source of confusion because historicism has another meaning: 'the tendency to regard historical development as the most basic aspect of human existence'.[157] In this sense, Hegel *was* a historicist, at least with respect to that part of his system which fell outside his logic. As we saw, Hegel treated categories, knowledge and politics as fundamentally developmental and dynamic. In the *Philosophy of Nature*, Hegel declared that 'All revolutions, in the sciences no less than in world history, originate solely from the fact that Spirit . . . has changed its categories.'[158]

The similarity with Thomas Kuhn's notion of a 'paradigm shift' is striking, although it is less anachronistic to say that Kuhn's idea resembles Hegel's. *The Structure of Scientific Revolutions* in fact made no reference to Hegel, taking its philosophical inspiration rather from the later Wittgenstein.[159] The conceptual similarity was thus not the result of any direct influence, but the result of a widespread acceptance after Hegel, and to a significant extent because of Hegel, of the idea that in order to understand thought, we must understand it in its context.

But Hegel's historicism, as Arthur Danto argued in *Analytical Philosophy of History*, was compatible with presentism.[160] The point of Hegel's philosophy of history was to make manifest to his contemporary audience their world-historical position. This was very different to a concern with the historical investigation of past events that did not treat them in terms of their present relevance.[161] Hegel himself was well aware of this difference,

---

[157] See the *Oxford English Dictionary*. Ankersmit, *Meaning, Truth, and Reference*, 1, describes historicism as 'the view that the nature of a thing lies in its history'.

[158] Hegel, *Philosophy of Nature*, §246.

[159] Thomas S. Kuhn, *The Structure of Scientific Revolutions*, 3rd edn (Chicago: University of Chicago Press, 1996 [1962]), 62, wrote that 'all discoveries from which new sorts of phenomena emerge . . . include . . . the consequent change of paradigm categories and procedures'.

[160] Danto, *Analytical Philosophy of History*, 14.

[161] While the orientations to the past found in Hegel's speculative philosophy of history and in historiography are clearly distinct in principle, individual historians sometimes conflated the two. For example, although a historian like Leopold von Ranke rejected presentism and moralism as inappropriate attitudes to the past so far as historiography was concerned, and insisted on not going beyond what the empirical evidence would support in establishing the course of past events, he nevertheless agreed with Hegel that God was operative in history, and that the ultimate aim was to grasp history as a unified whole. See Peter Novick, *That Noble Dream: The 'Objectivity Question' and the American Historical Profession* (Cambridge: Cambridge University Press, 1988), 28, who notes that 'German historians saw Ranke as the antithesis of a non-philosophical empiricism, while American historians venerated him for being precisely what he was not.'

and explicitly criticised the historian who narrated events 'in the contingent way in which he finds them, in their unrelated and thoughtless particularity'.¹⁶² It was his philosophy of history that supplied a 'determinate aim and view by which to select, arrange and assess events'. Yet leading historians of the day did not share Hegel's view that historical events must remain unrelated to one another in the absence of a philosophy of history that revealed their inner logical necessity. For an historian of ancient Rome like Barthold Niebuhr, for example, contingency and particularity did not entail unintelligibility for historiography but were intrinsic to it.¹⁶³

Hegel, though, had no real interest in the variety of pastness uniquely associated with historical knowledge, precisely because his notion of historicity continued to seek the universal in the particular. Aristotle had preferred poetry as more philosophical than history for exactly this reason, that it was more capable of identifying the universal aspect of events. Here, as so often, Hegel was a faithful Aristotelian, saying that 'It was an unerring sense that led to the banishment of such portrayals of the particular, and the gleaning of its traits [from historical writing], into the *novel*.'

In modern literature it may be 'good taste to combine the portrayal of the inessential, particular side of life with an inessential material, such as the novel takes from private events and subjective passions'.¹⁶⁴ But if there is no overall meaning to the historical process that we can identify in philosophical terms, Hegel's reasoning is not sound. Even taken on its own terms, as Inwood notes, Hegel's approach suffered from the fundamental problem that it 'provides no clear criterion for deciding where necessity ends and contingency begins, nor is it always clear where he locates the boundary between them'.¹⁶⁵

This problem exposed Hegel's discussion of world history to the justifiable charge of arbitrariness in its exclusion of entire regions. His treatment of Africa has become particularly notorious in this regard.¹⁶⁶ Hegel was convinced, however, that some regions of the world were simply unhistorical, and that in modernity the universal world-spirit had been at work mainly

---

¹⁶² Hegel, *Philosophy of Mind*, trans. Wallace and Miller, rev. Inwood, §549.
¹⁶³ Barthold Niebuhr wrote: 'I am an historian, for I can make a complete picture from several fragments, and I know where the parts are missing and how to fill them up.' Quoted in G. P. Gooch, *History and Historians in the Nineteenth Century* (London, New York and Toronto: Longmans, Green, and Co., 1935), 19. In other words, Niebhur's claim to a kind of knowledge that could relate particulars to make them parts of an intelligible whole made no mention of necessity or universality.
¹⁶⁴ Hegel, *Philosophy of Mind*, §549.
¹⁶⁵ Inwood, *Phenomenology of Spirit*, 'Commentary', 361.
¹⁶⁶ See Buck-Morss, *Hegel and Haiti*, especially 'Part Two: Universal History', 87ff.

in Europe. Certain heroic or world-historical individuals like Robespierre or Napoleon were its primary agents (a view which has understandably invited reduction of Hegel's position to a so-called 'great man' theory of history.) Those belonging to this type need not be at all aware of it. In making himself the first, de facto, emperor of Rome, Julius Caesar was 'contending for the maintenance of his position, honour, and safety'. But the effect of his actions was to bring into being 'an independently necessary feature in the history of Rome and the world' in the form of the Roman Empire.[167]

Here we see how the dichotomy in the *Phenomenology* between the subject's understanding of its situation and what was actually going on remained at work in Hegel's account of world history. Hegel's account of the world-historical individual as obtaining 'their vocation ... from a concealed fount – one which has not attained to phenomenal, present existence' but 'from that inner Spirit, still hidden beneath the surface, which, impinging on the outer world as on a shell, bursts it in pieces' opened the way for both Marxist and Freudian theories. But in Hegel himself we may see this distinction between outer actions and their inner meaning as a philosophical recasting of a very old theological argument that there was a fundamental difference between our perception of events and God's apprehension of them.[168]

The gap between subjective and objective understandings of a situation also became fundamental to all later critical and psychoanalytic thought. No doubt there may really be such a gap. But the failure of the individual to appreciate their larger context is not, as such, evidence for Marxist or Freudian theory any more than it is for a strictly Hegelian view. Nevertheless, in modernity, Hegel's statement in the *Philosophy of History* that 'man's existence centres in his head, i.e., in Thought, inspired by which he builds up the world of reality', has been so widely accepted that the only remaining disputes are over its implications.[169]

Conclusion

Hegel's writings sustained the pattern of connecting categories, knowledge and politics, and if anything intensified it by radically transforming it.

---

[167] Hegel, *Philosophy of History*, 44.
[168] Saint Augustine, *The City of God, Books VIII–XVI*, trans. Gerald G. Walsh and Grace Monahan (WashingtonDC: Catholic University of America Press, 2008 [1952]), bk 12, ch. 20, 281, writes that 'the ages, as they remain in the unchanging wisdom of God, are the efficient cause of the ages as they pass in the course of history'.
[169] Hegel, *Philosophy of History*, 467.

Categories themselves remained constitutive of subjectivity, as in Kant, but in addition now became dialectical, dynamic and developmental concepts. Knowledge was no longer so closely associated with particular faculties, but with a pluralistic set of groupings of categories, and the traditional hierarchy of knowledge was replaced by an image of circularity. Even if philosophical reason retained a certain priority as the only way to fully analyse the logic of categories, this was not a Platonic justification for placing philosophers in charge of the political order.

Yet Hegel also preserved the pattern of marginalising historical knowledge understood as the explanation of contingency. His historicism favoured an explanation of the historical process in terms of universal rational necessity. As with Kant, this was supposed to be a comforting vision compatible with Christian belief; there was some meaning to be found amidst the horror that contemplating the human past could provoke. But Hegel's theodicic account of the rational necessity of Providence was widely, even if mistakenly, received as a prediction.

Terry Pinkard remarks that 'the great anxiety for all modern philosophers is that no matter how many new paths they take, they will find . . . Hegel waiting at the end of each of them, smiling'.[170] But Pinkard was paraphrasing Foucault, who had previously raised the possibility that 'our resources against him are a ruse which he is using against us, and at the end of which he is waiting for us'.[171] This idea that there have been multiple pathways in modern thought, all of which lead back to Hegel, helps to explain why Foucault thought, as we noted earlier, that modernity had typically sought to define itself against Hegel.

Foucault believed that, on the one hand, work in both 'logic and epistemology' (with which we may identify the Anglo-American analytical tradition) and, on the other, the thought that descended from 'Marx and Nietzsche' (which we may treat as a proxy for twentieth-century so-called continental European thought) were equally defined by their efforts to be, as it were, 'not-Hegel'. But Foucault also had in mind the very nature of Hegel's philosophy which, as we saw, culminated in the Absolute Idea.

Hegel's concept of concept of Absolute Knowing, we noted, could be interpreted in a variety of ways. It could mean a grand optimistic vision heralding a new era of reconciliation in the modern world that the *Phenomenology* declared had arrived. In the summary presented in the *Philosophy of Right*, the Oriental world was originally 'inwardly

---

[170] Terry Pinkard, *Hegel: A Biography* (Cambridge: Cambridge University Press, 2000), xi.
[171] Michael Foucault, 'The Order of Discourse', 74.

undivided' in an unreflective fashion.¹⁷² The Greek world had ended in the collapse of this undivided unity. Its emphasis on the collective aspect of community values was increasingly experienced as unduly repressive towards individual subjectivity (as in the case of Antigone.) But Roman culture had ended up at the opposite extreme, privileging the individual over the universal moment of community. Christianity was the means by which this imbalance would be overcome and the self would be reunited with society. The latest stage of the modern, Germanic, world had completed the resolution of this new synthesis between the particular individual and the universal community. Spirit now explicitly 'grasps the principle of the unity of the divine and human nature' so that 'the reconciliation of the objective truth and freedom' with 'self-consciousness and subjectivity' could take place.¹⁷³

This reading proved highly consequential. Marx's version, in which class conflict would finally be ended, inspired forcible attempts at the creation of a new kind of human being and a new kind society that put an end to imperial rule but also proved deadly to tens of millions in Russia, China and elsewhere in the first half of the twentieth century. But Hegel also inspired later twentieth-century triumphal neo-liberal claims of the 'end of history' in which Western liberal democracy was presented as the ideal norm of government. The destructive consequences for Iraq and Afghanistan were significant, even if not on the same scale as for China and Russia. Francis Fukuyama's *End of History*, self-consciously Hegelian in inspiration, became a symbol of this liberal internalisation of Hegel's vision.¹⁷⁴

There is, though, another way to read Hegel's philosophy of history. As we achieve the standpoint of Absolute Knowing at the end of the *Phenomenology*, the problem arises of how to reconcile this position with the fact that 'philosophy is always capable of further specialisation'.¹⁷⁵ Absolute Knowing, in other words, doesn't mean the last word has been said, just as the realisation of freedom doesn't mean things will cease happening. Rather, we have gained an understanding of the necessary reflexivity of subjectivity and of the inherently mediated subject-object relation from which there is no retreat, but that is still capable of literally infinite

---

¹⁷² Hegel, *Philosophy of Right*, §355.
¹⁷³ Hegel, *Philosophy of Right*, §358.
¹⁷⁴ See Francis Fukuyama, *The End of History and the Last Man* (New York: The Free Press, 1992). Despite the image of the work created by its reception, Fukuyama himself never endorsed a naïve Western triumphalism, writing (332) that 'Modern thought raises no barriers to a future nihilistic war against liberal democracy on the part of those brought up in its bosom.'
¹⁷⁵ Hegel, *Philosophy of Right*, trans. H. B. Nisbet, §216.

further elaboration. We will never be done with this process for as long as there are human beings. Rather than a belief in a final ideal condition of things, then, Hegel's argument was that we simply have nowhere left to go, conceptually speaking, once we have achieved a true self-awareness of our situation. But this self-awareness solved nothing in any practical sense.

The deeply ironic message of Hegel's philosophy of history as the story of the progress of freedom, on this reading, was that history ultimately lacks a punchline. We have found that we are liberated to – ourselves.[176] We reach the 'end of history' only to discover that there is no 'there' there, and that now we must simply cope with the endless flow of events. The only difference is that we are now able to engage in rational self-criticism of our self-understandings and our actions; to take a third-personal view of ourselves seen in terms of our own historicity. Whereas earlier cultures had only myth to guide them, we can also employ reason, in the form of law and science, to navigate the world. When deliberating about what to do, we can thus enjoy what the Stoics sought, rational knowledge of what is, and what is not, up to us. But just because we can now do this does not mean that we will actually seize the opportunity.

What could be called the ironic reading of Hegel's philosophy of history thus makes him a proponent of a kind of reconciliation that accepted the Romantic narrative of the disenchantment of the world, a concept famously taken up Max Weber, and turned it back on itself.[177] The absence of the gods from the world was taken in Romantic thought to be an irretrievable loss, and in a sense, as Taylor argued, Hegel thought that it was. But it also opened the way to new, and more rational, forms of freedom and subjectivity; it did not have to be a purely negative event, but offered its own form of emancipation. On this view, the irony of post-Hegelian modern history would be that it missed Hegel's irony; the twentieth century was not in fact disenchanted in this Hegelian sense.[178]

---

[176] Hegel can be read as articulating an 'existential' sentiment that goes back at least to Pascal ('The eternal silence of these infinite spaces terrifies me') and would be taken up by Nietzsche ('Man Alone with Himself'). Compare Blaise Pascal, *Pensées and Other Writings*, trans. Honor Levi (Oxford: Oxford University Press, 1999 [1995]), 73, no. 233, and Friedrich Nietzsche, *Human, All Too Human: A Book for Free Spirits*, trans. R. J. Hollingdale (Cambridge: Cambridge University Press, 2007 [1986]), ch. 9, 'Man Alone With Himself'.

[177] See Sara Lyons, 'The Disenchantment/Re-enchantment of the World: Aesthetics, Secularisation, and the Gods of Greece from Friedrich Schiller to Walter Pater', *Modern Language Review*, 109:4 (2014), 873–95, for Max Weber's derivation of the concept of disenchantment from Friedrich Schiller.

[178] See Jason A. Josephson-Storm, *The Myth of Disenchantment* (Chicago: University of Chicago Press, 2017) for a critique of the idea that modernity underwent a process of disenchantment as understood by the Romantics and Weber.

Despite secularisation, understood as the decline in traditional forms of Christian belief, Western modernity still entertained various stories about itself as impelled towards some final destination. This persistent 'religious' consciousness that did not know itself to be such kept trying to force the process in destructive ways.[179]

There is no consensus on which of these readings of Hegel is correct. Perhaps the truth is that Hegel himself equivocated. He was at once the last great neo-Scholastic thinker, still conceiving of the world as intelligible rational substance, and the herald of a modernity characterised by infinite linguistic and conceptual reflexivity. His synthetic philosophy, which wanted to unite all previous thought into a single system, remained riven with internal ambiguities. Hegel was trying to say novel things in a traditional vocabulary that could not contain the resulting tensions.

It is not least because Hegel can plausibly be read in more than one way that he enjoyed a revival beginning in the late twentieth century. In the remaining chapters we will argue that insofar as modern thought has been, as Foucault suggested, a series of responses to Hegel, it has taken one of the following forms: denying the possibility of a categorially unified account of thought of the sort Hegel offered; restoring a single privileged perspective that somehow avoided the difficulties of historicity that Hegel had raised; and exploiting the categorial conditions of thought and action as the basis for an epistemological and political pluralism.

---

[179] The literature on disenchantment can be seen as an extension of the scepticism towards the concept of secularisation which was already being questioned in the mid-twentieth century: see Hans Blumenberg, *The Legitimacy of the Modern Age: Studies in Contemporary German Social Thought*, trans. Robert M. Wallace (Cambridge, MA: MIT Press, 1999 [1966]).

Part 3:
Contemporary Theories of Categories

5
Fragmentarians: The Categorial Kaleidoscope

In framing modern thought as a set of responses to Hegel, the first variety, to be examined in this fifth chapter, may be called the philosophy of the fragment. Fragmentation became a well-recognised trope in modernity thanks to Romanticism.[1] For Romantic art, for instance, the mutilated Greek statue missing arms or a head became a symbol of a lost wholeness and beauty located in the past. The aesthetic equivalent of this artistic trope was exemplified in the young Nietzsche's argument in *The Birth of Tragedy from the Spirit of Music* that the ancient Greeks had achieved a cultural synthesis forgotten in modernity.[2] Its philosophical corollary was a scepticism towards the unifying claims of categorial schemes and a belief in the lack of a definitive perspective that we shall call a 'fragmentarian' style of thought.[3]

In a posthumously published early essay 'On Truth and Lie in an Extra-moral Sense', Nietzsche described the world as 'the infinitely refracted echo' of language.[4] This metaphor was a negative version of the argument

---

[1] Linda Nochlin, *The Body In Pieces: The Fragment As A Metaphor Of Modernity* (New York: Thames & Hudson, 1994).
[2] Friedrich Nietzsche, *The Birth of Tragedy out of the Spirit of Music*, in *The Birth of Tragedy and Other Writings*, ed. Raymond Geuss and Ronald Speirs, trans. Ronald Speirs (Cambridge: Cambridge University Press, 2007 [1999]), 1–116, 18, wrote that in Dionysiac celebrations 'nature, alienated, inimical, or subjugated, celebrates once more her festival of reconciliation with her lost son, humankind'. In a preface to a second edition of *The Birth of Tragedy* entitled 'An Attempt at Self-Criticism', in *The Birth of Tragedy*, 3–12, 11, Nietzsche repudiated a Romantic interpretation of the work but still admitted that his language had been open to misreading.
[3] 'Fragmentarian' is a neologism, but the use of the idea of the fragment as a metaphor for modernity is well-established; see n. 1, above.
[4] Friedrich Nietzsche, 'On Truth and Lie in an Extra-moral Sense', in *Writings from the Early Notebooks*, ed. Raymond Geuss and Alexander Nehamas, trans. Ladislaus Löb (Cambridge: Cambridge University Press, 2010 [2009]), 253–64, 259.

we saw Kant make, that since we can never directly encounter the world in its totality, the idea of the world as a whole was not derivable from experience. For Nietzsche, the lack of an empirical basis for totality meant that its use as a regulative ideal should be abandoned, as should Kant's view of the self as a synthesis of categories. Despite a scepticism towards categories that formed part of a more general rejection of Idealism, though, Nietzsche never abandoned their critique. He transmitted this equivocal attitude to subsequent generations.

In the twentieth century, Theodore Adorno and Michel Foucault followed the path Nietzsche had opened. Adorno's declared goal in *Negative Dialectics* was 'a philosophy in fragment form', a rejection of the systematic approach taken by Kant and Hegel.[5] Foucault declared in *The Order of Things* that the coherence of our experience of the world was not 'determined by an *a priori* and necessary concatenation'.[6] Their related expressions of scepticism about categories were related to worries about knowledge. These concerned the claims made for science in particular, although the issue was less the truth of scientific knowledge than its status as the sole valid model of all knowledge.

For Nietzsche, for example, science was an important, but not exhaustive, approach to understanding the world: 'a higher culture must give to man a double-brain ... one for the perceptions of science, the other for those of non-science'.[7] But in general, Nietzsche and his heirs regarded a systematic account of the different genres of knowledge, even if possible, as less important than understanding how knowledge was put to use. Their questioning of the overall unity of knowledge, and the denial that there was one form of knowledge which was definitive, amounted to a pragmatic perspectivalism that should be distinguished from relativism.

Nietzsche, Adorno and Foucault all believed that the failure to acknowledge the inescapability of perspectivalism in knowledge had been politically consequential, though they agreed more in adopting a critical stance towards the existing order than about what should replace it. In *Thus Spoke Zarathustra*, Nietzsche had the prophetic figure of Zarathustra describe the state as 'the coldest of cold monsters', but he also expressed scepticism towards revolution, while favouring a natural

---

[5] Thedore W. Adorno, *Negative Dialectics*, trans. E. B. Ashton (New York: Continuum International, 2007 [1966]), 28.

[6] Michel Foucault, *The Order of Things: An Archaeology of the Human Sciences* (London and New York: Routledge, 2005 [1966]), xxi.

[7] Friedrich Nietzsche, *Human, All Too Human: A Book for Free Spirits*, trans. R. J. Hollingdale (Cambridge: Cambridge University Press, 2007 [1986]), ch. 5, sec. 251, 119.

aristocracy of intellectual and artistic talent.⁸ Adorno's philosophy extended Nietzsche's criticism of Kant's categories of the understanding in a political direction: 'the transcendental subject can be deciphered as a society unaware of itself'.⁹

For Adorno, traditional political authority had been unaware of the oppressive implications of the use of universalistic abstractions. Here, Adorno was indebted to Hegel's philosophy of identity. In the *Science of Logic*, as we saw, Hegel had argued that exclusion was a condition of identity.¹⁰ In asserting that a thing has a certain property, we overlook its other properties. Hegel did not think this was problematic as such, at least if we remained alert to how we were using the concept. Identity in one form or another was a necessary condition of thinking. But Adorno argued that identity could become problematic if used reductively in a political context.

The logic of totalitarianism, for Adorno, was precisely to impose universal categories on individuals to reduce them to a generic identity. At the limit, this intellectual and rhetorical manoeuvre legitimated genocide. Foucault inherited these concerns about the use of language to classify and categorise individuals for purposes of political control. Yet in exposing these issues, all three thinkers regarded themselves as continuing a revised, more sceptical, version of a progressive Enlightenment project.

All three thinkers also emphasised a self-consciousness about the historicity of thought that motivated them to argue that categories must be understood in terms of their genesis and use. But this did not produce a greater interest in historical knowledge as such. Nietzsche declared history was valuable only insofar as it served the needs of 'life'.¹¹ Adorno, despite his general suspicion of universal categories, made a self-conscious attempt to pursue a speculative philosophy of history in a Hegelian style.¹² Foucault, whose genealogical approach to history was acknowledgedly indebted to Nietzsche, likewise thought of his work as having a presentist orientation.¹³

---

⁸ Friedrich Nietzsche, *Thus Spoke Zarathustra: A Book for All and None*, ed. Adrian del Caro and Robert B. Pippin, trans. Adrian Del Caro (Cambridge: Cambridge University Press, 2006), 34.
⁹ Adorno, *Negative Dialectics*, 177.
¹⁰ See Chapter 4, above, especially n. 95 and n. 96.
¹¹ See Friedrich Nietzsche, 'On the Uses and Disadvantages of History for Life', in *Untimely Meditations*, ed. Daniel Breazeale, trans. R. J. Hollingdale (Cambridge: Cambridge University Press, 2007 [1997]), 57–123.
¹² See Theodore W. Adorno, *History and Freedom Lectures, 1964–65*, ed. Rolf Tiedemann, trans. Rodney Livingstone (Cambridge and Malden, MA: Polity Press, 2006).
¹³ Michel Foucault, *Archaeology of Knowledge*, trans. A. M. Sheridan Smith (Abingdon: Routledge, 2002 [1969]), 225, wrote that the aim of an archaeology of knowledge was to bring out 'the difference of our present'.

In a negative way, then, this strand of modern thought maintained the pattern of association we have observed thus far, not just between categories, knowledge and politics, but with respect to the marginalisation of historical thought. Of the three, it was Foucault who came closest to breaking with this pattern.

Categories

Kant's impact on Nietzsche is unmistakeable. In an early unpublished essay titled 'On Truth and Lie in an Extra-moral Sense', Nietzsche wrote that 'All that we know about [laws of nature] is what we add to them . . . these representations are produced in us and out of us by ourselves with the same necessity as the spider spins its web.'[14] For Kant, the categories of the understanding both gave scientific knowledge a necessary foundation and preserved room for religious faith by limiting science to knowledge of the phenomenal order. But Kant was read, probably against his intentions, as treating the categories as a screen or filter occluding reality rather than as conditions of access to it. Thus, Hegel wrote that according to Kant, 'we place thoughts as a medium between us and the things, in the sense that this medium, instead of joining us with such things, would rather cut us off from them'.[15]

Nietzsche sided with Hegel's reading. Kant's critical philosophy encouraged a scepticism toward the self, for instance, because the 'I' was 'a synthesis that only gets *produced* through thought itself'.[16] The self was mere appearance. Nietzsche agreed with Kant that the idea of the soul as a substance in the classical sense belonged to a pre-Cartesian, pre-Kantian metaphysics that must be rejected.[17] Where he disagreed was over the nature of the connection of the 'I' to an embodied will, treated by Kant as mere animal impulse. Nietzsche's empirical and psychological account accepted that willing involved actual bodily sensations and emotions, but rejected the Kantian noumenal self at the same time.[18]

---

[14] Nietzsche, 'On Truth and Lie', 261. Nietzsche later explicitly acknowledged his use of 'Kantian formulations' in his early work: see 'An Attempt at Self-Criticism', 10.

[15] Hegel, *Science of Logic*, 16.

[16] Friedrich Nietzsche, *Beyond Good and Evil: Prelude to a Philosophy of the Future*, ed. Rolf-Peter Horstmann and Judith Norman, trans. Judith Norman (Cambridge: Cambridge University Press, 2002 [2001]), pt 3, sec. 54, 49. Emphasis in original.

[17] Nietzsche, *Beyond Good and Evil*, pt 1, sec. 17, 17, argued that 'It is . . . a falsification of the facts to say that the subject "I" is the condition of the predicate "think."'

[18] Nietzsche, *Beyond Good and Evil*, pt 1, sec. 19, 18–19, argued that willing was a process of commanding action that was both 'accompanied by a feeling of the muscles that

Punning on Louis XIV's boast that 'L'état, c'est moi', Nietzsche proposed that *'L'effet c'est moi.'*[19] The will was a metaphor for the feeling of self-command. Successful willing generated an enjoyable feeling of power. Notably, Nietzsche made use of a political analogy. The self was analogous to 'what happens in every well-constructed and happy community', namely that 'the ruling class identifies itself with the successes of the community'.[20] The self was never a simple unity but always a body politic. The appearance of its unity was generated by exclusion, taking a part for the whole. But the rejection of the Kantian noumenal self entailed that Kant's account of the phenomenal self also had to be rejected. The empirical self could not be explained in the causal terms employed by the natural sciences.[21]

Instead, the self and any other categories had to be understood pragmatically: 'The categories are "truths" only in the sense that they are conditions of living.'[22] As such, categories were implicated in Nietzsche's conception of the will to power, the fundamental principle animating reality. Nietzsche thought of all life, including human life, as a struggle not simply for Darwinian survival but for power. 'The struggle for survival is only an *exception*, a temporary restriction . . . the great and small struggle always revolves everywhere around preponderance . . . in accordance with the will to power, which is simply the will to life.'[23]

The notion of the self or subject was only a tool in the service of this will. Social and intellectual change was the result of a characteristically human metaphorising impulse which Nietzsche described as a 'drive [that] continually confuses the conceptual categories . . . by introducing new transferences, metaphors and metonymies'.[24] What mattered was

comes into play through a sort of habit', and internally divided such that 'we are, under the circumstances, both the one who commands and the one who obeys . . . however, we are in the habit of ignoring and deceiving ourselves about this duality by means of the synthetic concept of the 'I'.

[19] Nietzsche, *Beyond Good and Evil*, pt 1, sec. 19, 19. Emphasis in original.
[20] Nietzsche, *Beyond Good and Evil*, pt 1, sec. 19, 19–20.
[21] Nietzsche, *Beyond Good and Evil*, pt 1, sec. 19, 19, denied that the will could be explained as a '*necessity of effect*', in contrast to Kant, who presented the will as an intervention in a causal series (see Chapter 3, above). Emphasis in original.
[22] Friedrich Nietzsche, *The Will to Power: Selections from the Notebooks of the 1880s*, trans. R. Kevin Hill and Michael A. Scarpatti, ed. R. Kevin Hill (London: Penguin Random House, 2017), 515, 299.
[23] Friedrich Nietzsche, *The Gay Science, With a Prelude in German Rhymes and an Appendix of Songs*, ed. Bernard Williams, trans. Josefine Nauckhoff, poems trans. Adrian del Caro (Cambridge: Cambridge University Press, 2008 [2001]), bk 5, sec. 349, 208.
[24] Nietzsche, 'On Truth and Lie', 262.

that categories were efficacious in the contest for domination. Their successful use allowed us to navigate the world understood as an expression of 'abundance, opulence, even absurd squandering'.[25] Classification for its own sake, though, was not something Nietzsche considered fruitful. He was critical of 'philosophers who are basically just schematizers . . . The talent for classifications, for tables of categories, reveals something.'[26]

What it revealed was the substitution of received truths for argument. Nietzsche believed Kant was deceived in thinking that he had '*discovered* a new faculty in man . . . of synthetic judgments *a priori*'. As evidence, Nietzsche cited the way in which 'the young theologians of the College of Tübingen' had used Kant to claim that there was 'above all a faculty of the "super-sensible."'[27] Kant's table of categories had really been manufactured to defend a religiously motivated Idealism. But Nietzsche did not restrict this criticism to Kant. He raised similar objections to Plato. Like Kant's *a priori* categories, Plato's Forms had identified reality with an imaginary transcendental order, all to the detriment of life in the world that we actually inhabit.[28] Here again Nietzsche was notably Hegelian in his criticism.

This criticism prompted Nietzsche's remark that 'philosophizing was always a kind of vampirism'. Nietzsche openly accused Idealism of being like a kind of vampiric 'disease' that started by draining the senses of their vitality and ended with 'only bones and rattling . . . I refer to categories'.[29] Yet Nietzsche's relationship to Idealism was not entirely critical. He specifically praised Hegel for having 'struck through all logical habits and indulgences when he dared to teach that species concepts develop *out of each other*'.[30] Indeed, for Nietzsche, the Hegelian idea of a self-relating series of categories requiring no reference to a transcendental order was what made reality intelligible.[31]

---

[25] Friedrich Nietzsche, *Twilight of the Idols*, in *The Anti-Christ, Ecce Homo, Twilight of the Idols, and Other Writings*, ed. Aaron Ridley and Judith Norman, trans. Judith Norman (Cambridge: Cambridge University Press, 2006 [2005]), 153–229, 199.

[26] Nietzsche, *Gay Science*, bk 5, sec. 348, 207.

[27] Nietzsche, *Beyond Good and Evil*, pt 1, sec. 11, 12–13.

[28] Nietzsche, *Twilight of the Idols*, 226, wrote that 'Plato is a coward in the face of reality, – *consequently*, he escapes into the ideal.' Emphasis in original.

[29] Nietzsche, *Gay Science*, bk 5, sec. 372, 237.

[30] Nietzsche, *Gay Science*, bk. 5, sec. 357, 218. In German, Nietzsche's term for species concepts was 'Artbegriffe': see Friedrich Nietzsche, *Die fröhliche Wissenschaft*, in Friedrich Nietzsche, *Morgenröte Idyllen aus Messina Die fröhliche Wissenschaft Kritische Studienausgabe*, ed. Giorgio Colli and Mazzino Montinari (Munich: Deutscher Taschenbuch Verlag; Berlin and New York: Walter de Gruyter, 1999 [1972]), 343–651, 598.

[31] Nietzsche, *Gay Science*, bk. 5, sec. 357, 218, wrote that 'without Hegel there could be no Darwin'. See also the discussion of Hegel's idea of evolution in Chapter 4, above.

Instead of asking about the 'essence' of a thing in the abstract, Nietzsche argued, we should accept that the first question about the nature of a thing would always be 'what is that to *me*? (to us, to everything that lives, etc.)'[32] This was very similar to Hegel's argument that subject and object were always correlated. Also like Hegel, Nietzsche's argument gave knowledge a social dimension. Knowledge was neither entirely independent of the knower nor purely personal. There was no contradiction in knowledge being both (inter)subjective and possessed of a general validity, but it could never be independent of its context. According to this 'perspectivalist' theory, a full understanding of any kind of knowledge required awareness of its origins, standpoint and uses as well as its truth-value. Nietzsche (and later Foucault) called this approach to knowledge 'genealogy'.[33]

Adorno's *Negative Dialectics* likewise distanced itself from previous philosophies that 'reduced the contents of [full, unreduced] experience to cases of categories'.[34] In *Dialectic of Enlightenment*, however, Horkheimer and Adorno made clear that the problem was not categories in the sense of universals as such: 'Opposition to general concepts is absurd.' The point was rather that the universal was not inherently superior to the particular: 'What many individual things have in common, or what constantly recurs in one individual thing, need not be more stable, eternal, or deep than the particular.' Like Nietzsche, Adorno believed that ancient thought had been prejudiced in favour of the universal. Both Plato and Aristotle had identified the 'scale of categories' with the scale of 'significance', an identification carried forward into modernity.[35]

Negative Dialectics also expressed admiration for Hegel's 'microanalysis of individual categories' in which we see 'each concept pass into its otherness'.[36] In particular, Adorno saw himself as developing Hegel's critique of the concept of identity. 'Identity's dependence on the nonidentical, as Hegel almost achieved it, is the protest against any philosophy of identity.' But as the qualifying adverb 'almost' indicated, Adorno thought that 'Hegel does

---

[32] Nietzsche, *Will to Power*, 556, 323. Emphasis in original.
[33] Friedrich Nietzsche, *On the Genealogy of Morality*, ed. Keith Ansell-Pearson, trans. Carol Diethe, 2nd edn (Cambridge: Cambridge University Press, 2007 [2006]), 87, wrote that 'There is *only* a perspectival seeing, *only* a perspectival "knowing."' Emphasis in original.
[34] Adorno, *Negative Dialectics*, 13, cited 'the science of empirical consciousness' as an example, presumably an allusion to Edmund Husserl's phenomenology.
[35] Max Horkheimer and Theodore W. Adorno, *Dialectic of Enlightenment Philosophical Fragments*, ed. Gunzelin Schmid Noerr, trans. Edmund Jephcott (Stanford: Stanford University Press, 2002), 182.
[36] Adorno, *Negative Dialectics*, 25.

not carry the dialectics of nonidentity to the end'.³⁷ The abstract categories of the *Science of Logic*, Adorno claimed, did not exhibit the non-identity that they should possess according to Hegel's own theory. Whether this was a sound criticism can be disputed, since as we saw in Chapter Four, Hegel in fact treated difference as integral to identity, and had presented the concepts of the *Science of Logic* as only abstractions from reality, not a higher reality.

Nevertheless, Adorno argued that in Hegel, 'The abstract concept necessarily lacks the ability to be nonconceptual.' Adorno criticised Hegel for taking the nothingness or unreality of concepts 'as a merit, as something loftier, as the spirit'.³⁸ In his view, Hegelianism had not avoided the errors of Platonism. Again, whether Adorno was correct is another matter; as we also showed in Chapter 4, Hegel explicitly differentiated his own position from Plato's.³⁹ The larger issue for Adorno, though, was that categories were implicated in the production of social order, something the Platonic rationalist ideal of stasis obscured.

Adorno argued that 'The concept . . . functions in secret as the model of a life that is arranged so that no measure of mechanical progress – the equivalent of the concept – may ever, under any circumstances, do away with poverty.'⁴⁰ Kantianism was its modern version. The noumenal self was blind to the actual conditions of its production, just as the universality of exchange value obscured the diverse forms of economic production: 'the generality of the transcendental subject is that of . . . a whole that coalesces from individual spontaneities and qualities, delimits them in turn by the leveling barter principle, and virtually deletes them'.⁴¹

Adorno's critique of the Kantian self was similar to Nietzsche's. Kant had not acknowledged 'the empirical genesis of what, unanalyzed, was glorified by him as timelessly intelligible'.⁴² But Adorno was also writing after Sigmund Freud, and incorporated a psychoanalytic dimension into his argument. Freud's account of the id was treated by Adorno as a 'metaphysical critique of the subject' that exposed the coercion of the individual in modern society.⁴³ Kant's self-identical ego, the pure 'I', represented not noumenal freedom but a 'compulsory identity' riven by the contradiction of lacking a content. In practice its supposed simplicity resulted in the exclusion of the actual internal diversity found in all human beings.⁴⁴

---

³⁷ Adorno, *Negative Dialectics*, 120.
³⁸ Adorno, *Negative Dialectics*, 121.
³⁹ See Chapter 4, above.
⁴⁰ Adorno, *Negative Dialectics*, 121.
⁴¹ Adorno, *Negative Dialectics*, 178.
⁴² Adorno, *Negative Dialectics*, 272.
⁴³ Adorno, *Negative Dialectics*, 281.
⁴⁴ Adorno, *Negative Dialectics*, 299, wrote that 'Personality is the caricature of freedom.'

This critique of capitalism as socialised madness was later developed at length by Gilles Deleuze and Félix Guattari in *Anti-Oedipus*.[45] But Adorno already believed that in modernity 'Schizophrenia is the truth about the subject, from the viewpoint of the philosophy of history.'[46] After Adorno, Foucault connected categories, madness, and historicity. Foucault's first graduate thesis, published as *Madness and Civilisation*, investigated the conditions of possibility of judgements like insanity or abnormality; the second was a translation of Kant's anthropology with a commentary.[47]

Nietzsche and Adorno had both followed Hegel in criticising Kant for not recognising the historicity of categories; Foucault gave the concept of the 'historical *a priori*' a central role in the constitution of social categories like madness.[48] *The Order of Things* was devoted to the development of categories and classification between the early modern era and modernity. In it, Foucault declared that 'the thought of finitude laid down by the Kantian critique as philosophy's task . . . still forms the immediate space of our reflection'.[49] Unlike Kant, however, Foucault believed we could not avoid the fact that the categories in terms of which we claim knowledge of the world were themselves subject to historicity.

Foucault attempted to clarify the historical *a priori* further in the *Archaeology of Knowledge*. It was distinct from the Kantian *a priori* in that it was 'not a condition of validity for judgements, but a condition of reality for statements'.[50] Foucault's historical *a priori*, unlike Kant's, 'does not elude historicity: it does not constitute, above events, and in an unmoving heaven, an atemporal structure; it is defined as the group of rules that characterize a discursive practice'.[51] At the same time, Foucault did not

---

[45] Gilles Deleuze and Félix Guattari, *Anti-Oedipus Capitalism and Schizophrenia*, trans. Robert Hurley, Mark Seem and Helen R. Lane, 'Preface' by Michel Foucault (Minneapolis: University of Minnesota Press, 2000 [1972]).

[46] Adorno, *Negative Dialectics*, 281.

[47] See Michel Foucault, *Madness and Civilization: A History of Insanity in the Age of Reason*, intro. David Cooper, 2nd edn (Abingdon: Routledge, 2005 [1961]), and Michel Foucault, *Introduction to Kant's Anthropology*, ed. Roberto Nigro, trans. Roberto Nigro and Kate Briggs (Los Angeles: Semiotext(e), 2008).

[48] Foucault, *Order of Things*, xxiii. Edmund Husserl had previously used the term 'historical *a priori*' to describe contrasting conceptions of the viability of transcendental phenomenology. For Husserl's original concept and Foucault's appropriation of it see William Casement, 'Husserl and the Philosophy of History', *History and Theory*, 27 (1988), 229–40, and Thomas R. Flynn, 'Foucault on Experiences and the Historical *a priori*: With Husserl in the Rearview Mirror of History', *Continental Philosophy Review*, 49 (2016), 55–65.

[49] Foucault, *Order of Things*, 419.

[50] Foucault, *Archaeology*, 143.

[51] Foucault, *Archaeology*, 144.

reject the idea that formal *a priori* concepts could have a role to play altogether: the formal *a priori* 'may have in history . . . places of insertion . . . or emergence'.[52] Foucault here resembled Hegel, for whom the dialectic manifested itself in the temporal process but was distinct from it; but unlike Hegel, he tended to be sceptical that there was any overall dialectic at work in history.

Foucault also adopted Nietzsche's pragmatic emphasis on categories in use. Nietzschean genealogy was a major inspiration for Foucault's idea of an 'archaeology of knowledge' that would be a tool of critique and 'diagnosis', not simply analysis.[53] He was particularly interested in the paths by which the ostensibly universal ideal of 'man' had come into being and had been made the subject of the categories of the humanities and social sciences. These categories could now be understood as not simply 'mere empirical concepts of rather broad generality' but rather 'the basis on which man is able to present himself to a possible knowledge'.[54]

The resulting task was to expose the hidden operations of these categories. Foucault's claim was that a particular configuration of European ideas about human identity had been assumed to have a universal status, a configuration that he termed 'humanism'.[55] This configuration had supposedly been setting the terms of inquiry for the humanities and social sciences. Just as Kant had made philosophy responsible for investigating its own assumptions, Foucault wanted a reflexive investigation of the categorial schemes he believed were framing and enabling the production of knowledge.

Knowledge

In an early notebook, Nietzsche wrote that 'All explaining and knowing is really only categorizing.'[56] Knowledge, like the use of categories, was a

---

[52] Foucault, *Archaeology*, 44.
[53] Foucault, *Archaeology*, 227.
[54] Foucault, *Order of Things*, 395.
[55] Foucault used 'humanism' in a very broad sense. Roger Paden, 'Foucault's Anti-Humanism', *Human Studies*, 10:1 (1987), 123–41, 124, argues that Foucault, at least in his early work, treated humanism as meaning any 'theory which attempts to explain social relations and social facts in terms of the unchanging features of the human subject'. But the English word originally derives from a German coinage, 'Humanismus', with a much narrower range of reference. Nineteenth-century advocates of 'Bildung', another word with a complex history that could be translated into English as 'liberal education', used it to describe the ethos of the fifteenth-century 'language teachers, rhetoricians, [and] translators' found in Italian cities such as Florence: see Tony Davies, *Humanism* (London and New York: Routledge, 1997), 4, 9. Foucault's usage arguably subsumed this Renaissance sense of the term, but also included much Christian and progressive thought.
[56] Nietzsche, *Early Notebooks*, 150.

source of power, but also of self-deception. Like Rousseau's discourse on the arts and sciences, Nietzsche treated knowledge as a covert source of pride.[57] 'The arrogance connected with knowledge and sensation [covers] the eyes and senses of men with blinding mists.'[58] Traditionally, knowledge had covertly anthropomorphised the universe, so that the philosopher 'believes that the eyes of the universe are trained on his actions and thoughts like telescopes from all sides'.[59] Kant's argument that there was no contradiction in discerning a rational plan at work both in nature and history was an example of this covert anthropocentrism.

Yet Nietzsche's own approach was still directly descended from Kant's. For example, he described Kant as trying to 'delimit the realm within which this concept [of causality] makes any sense' and remarked that 'to this day we have not yet come to terms with this marking out of the boundaries'.[60] Nietzsche's disagreements with Kant mostly concerned the motivations and status of knowledge, not its conditions. Kant had correctly given knowledge a categorial basis, but had failed to recognise the role of the will to power in motivating its pursuit. But this criticism did not imply a rejection of knowledge; Nietzsche's aim was rather to bring our situation with respect to knowledge into self-awareness. This was a development, not a rejection, of Kant's conception of Enlightenment as emancipation from what Kant had called humanity's 'self-incurred minority'.[61] The difference was that the freedom to choose a Christian confession had become the freedom to choose not to have a Christian confession at all.

Nietzsche also followed Kant in finding a kind of neo-Stoicism ethically appealing. The guiding ideal Nietzsche presented at the end of the essay 'On Truth and Lie' was the man who is 'guided by conceptions and abstractions'.[62] Such a person was not necessarily any happier from living in this way, but as a 'stoic man' was able to learn from experience. This person pursued 'sincerity, truth, [and] freedom from deception'. If he practised any deception of his own it was the adoption of 'a mask dignified by a symmetry of features' in the face of an indifferent universe.[63] The figure

---

[57] See Jean-Jacques Rousseau, 'Discourse Which Won the Prize of the Academy of Dijon on the Year 1750 on this Question Proposed by the Academy: Whether the Restoration of the Sciences and Arts Has Contributed to the Purification of Morals', in *The Discourses and Other Early Political Writings*, ed. Victor Gourevich (Cambridge: Cambridge University Press, 1997), 1–144.
[58] Nietzsche, 'On Truth and Lie', 253–4.
[59] Nietzsche, 'On Truth and Lie', 253.
[60] Nietzsche, *Gay Science*, bk 5, sec. 357.
[61] See Chapter 3, above.
[62] Nietzsche, 'On Truth and Lie', 264.
[63] Nietzsche, 'On Truth and Lie', 264.

of the Übermensch who emerged in Nietzsche's later writings preserved this Stoic ideal of self-mastery, which included an uncompromising commitment to truth. In one of his last works, Nietzsche declared that he was seeking 'A new conscience for truths that have kept silent until now'.[64]

Despite stating that 'Truth is not something that one person might have and another not', Nietzsche has been called 'possibly the single most influential voice in shaping relativistic sensibilities in twentieth century continental philosophy'.[65] In considering whether and in what sense Nietzsche was a relativist, however, we should bear in mind the distinction typically made in contemporary philosophy between strong and weak versions of relativism. The strong version involves a paradox of self-reference. The assertion that all truths are relative must include itself, since it is supposed to have universal extension. But then it follows that there is at least one truth which is not relative, namely, the truth that all truths are relative. This version of relativism is thus contradictory and therefore false. But Nietzsche did not hold that all truths were purely conventional, or identifiable with the subjective standpoints of individuals.

The weak version of relativism is effectively synonymous with perspectivalism, which holds that truth is never independent of 'frameworks of assessment' that are subject to historicity.[66] In this weak sense Nietzsche was a relativist, because he acknowledged different genres of truth. To be German, Nietzsche declared in the *Gay Science*, was to 'doubt with Kant the ultimate validity of the knowledge attained by the natural sciences'.[67] But this did not make science a matter of personal opinion for Nietzsche, any more than it had for Kant. Doubting ultimate validity, and doubting validity altogether, were not at all the same thing. Nietzsche's claims that different kinds of knowledge had different truth conditions, and that not all truths were scientific, were not relativistic in the strong sense of the term. Nietzsche was in fact heavily critical of the subjectivisation of truth. He objected to Christianity, for example, on the grounds that it believed a strong feeling that something was true counted as evidence in its favour.[68]

Kant and Hegel both remarked that their respective theories of categories could be treated as analyses of language.[69] Nietzsche took this tendency further, treating truth as what the later Wittgenstein would

---

[64] Nietzsche, *Anti-Christ*, 'Preface', trans. J. Norman, 3.
[65] Nietzsche, *Anti-Christ*, 'Preface', trans. J. Norman, 52. See Maria Baghramian and Adam J. Carter, 'Relativism', *The Stanford Encyclopedia of Philosophy* (Spring 2022 edition), ed. Edward N. Zalta, sec. 3.
[66] Baghramian and Carter, 'Relativism'.
[67] Nietzsche, *Gay Science*, bk 3, sec. 357.
[68] Nietzsche, *Anti-Christ*, sec. 12, 10.
[69] See Chapters 3 and 4, above.

call a language-game. Truth was a function of language in relation to a particular use.[70] Hence the comparison that Nietzsche drew between truth and playing dice: 'in this dice game of concepts "truth" means using every die as it is marked; counting its dots accurately, establishing correct categories, and never breaching the caste system and the order of the ranks and classes'.[71] This comparison requires careful analysis. It initially appears to strengthen the case for Nietzsche as a strong relativist, because playing dice is typically associated with randomness.

Nietzsche's comparison did not have this connotation of arbitrary outcomes, however. It listed four distinct conditions for truth. The first three were: following established rules ('using every die as it is marked'); making sure we are precise in our assessments ('counting its dots accurately'); and constructing appropriate classifications ('establishing correct categories'). What Nietzsche was actually emphasising was that truth requires rules, accuracy, and the use of relevant concepts. None of this would be thought controversial today by anyone wanting to defend truth. If the issue of relativism is relevant at all, it is thanks to the final clause, 'never breaching the caste system', which seemingly introduces a social dimension to the problem of truth.

Nietzsche's later writings were concerned with how such disruptions to the social hierarchy had occurred, as in the *Genealogy of Morals*. Modernity in his view was the product of just such violations of caste and rank. Rather than reading Nietzsche as asserting literally that something could not be true if it disturbed the social order, we may take him to have been saying that ruling groups in society typically had a vested interest in declaring propositions that threatened their dominance to be false.

Indeed, Nietzsche's own argument was presumably exactly the kind of assertion with the potential to disturb the social order. 'I am not a human being: I am dynamite', Nietzsche exclaimed in his final work.[72] Though Nietzsche never mentioned Marx in print, and his other statements on equality, socialism and democracy show he would not have been sympathetic, this claim to an explosive quality matched Marx's belief that philosophy should have revolutionary practical effects.[73]

---

[70] Wittgenstein, *Philosophical Investigations*, trans. G. E. M. Anscombe, P. M. S. Hacker and Joachim Schulte, 4th edn, rev. P. M. S. Hacker and Joachim Schulte (Oxford: Blackwell Publishing, 2009 [1953]), 15ᵉ, wrote that 'the term "language-game" is used . . . to emphasize the fact that the *speaking* of language is part of an activity, or of a form of life'.

[71] Nietzsche, 'On Truth and Lie', 258.

[72] Friedrich Nietzsche, *Ecce Homo How to Become What you Are*, trans. J. Norman, in *Anti-Christ and Other Writings*, 71–151, 143–4.

[73] Thomas H. Brobjer, *Nietzsche's Philosophical Context: An Intellectual Biography* (Urbana and Chicago: University of Illinois Press, 2008), 70, notes that Nietzsche's library contained several books that mentioned Marx including one in which Marx's name was underlined.

At the theoretical level, however, Nietzsche regarded his view of knowledge as a further transformation in philosophical self-consciousness of the sort that Kant had begun by replacing traditional metaphysics with the reflexive approach of critical philosophy. Nietzsche followed Hegel in highlighting the problematic implications of the concept of identity. All knowledge that depended 'on the presupposition that there are identical things' actually 'came into existence through the . . . belief' . . . that such conditions do obtain in the real world'.[74] It was for this reason that Nietzsche considered identity, like the self or subject, to be a useful fiction.

For Nietzsche, no two things could ever be literally identical. 'Just as it is certain that one leaf is never totally the same as another, so it is certain that the concept "leaf" is formed by arbitrarily discarding these individual differences and by forgetting the distinguishing aspects.'[75] The mistake, common to science and philosophy, was first to treat the universal term as actually existent in nature and then to compound the error by postulating it as the cause of what were assumed to be its instances. The solution was to be self-conscious about the fact that knowledge presupposed a categorial framework.

The argument that any proposition could only be true in terms of an overall framework to which it belonged became prominent in twentieth-century philosophy at large. We noted the ubiquity of the metaphor of the web as a characterisation of knowledge in the previous chapter. Nietzsche's metaphor for truth as 'a construction . . . of spiders' webs' was another instance of this kind of idea.[76] But anyone holding this kind of view faces the problem of what guarantees the integrity of the framework of truth or knowledge itself. By definition, it could have no external support.

As Nietzsche himself put it, truth must be 'delicate enough to be carried along by the waves' (so that it can change shape in response to circumstances) but 'firm enough not to be blown apart by the wind' (so that it has a relative stability to its structure). The truths of scientific knowledge, and indeed of all rational thought, ultimately rested on categorial postulates justifiable only by their internal coherence on the one hand and their theoretical and practical results on the other.

Both Adorno and Foucault likewise stressed the importance of self-awareness about the standpoint from which knowledge claims were being made, but without rejecting truth. Adorno, for instance, explicitly rejected relativism, associating it with 'bourgeois individualism'. It was mistaken

---

[74] Nietzsche, *Human, All Too Human*, ch. 1, sec. 11, 16.
[75] Nietzsche, 'On Truth and Lie', 256.
[76] Nietzsche, 'On Truth and Lie', 259.

to treat the standpoint of the individual consciousness as absolute and to regard all opinions as equally valuable 'as if there were no criterion of their truth'. He insisted that philosophy had a definite 'truth content'.[77]

Like Nietzsche, too, Adorno showed no hostility to science. Adorno's criticism of Enlightenment thought as 'the philosophy which equates truth with the scientific system', a position he attributed to Kant, was not an argument against science but philosophical scientism.[78] Adorno stressed the autonomous nature of scientific thought. He believed, for example, that mathematical physics was an 'increasingly independent language' that was no longer 'retrievable into visuality or any other categories directly commensurable' to ordinary consciousness.[79]

What worried Adorno was the way ordinary consciousness had assimilated modern scientific ideas. Common sense was giving up the old 'anthropocentric sense of life' without adopting a more sceptical outlook. Instead, it had formed a fresh set of scientistic illusions. The old cosmology was being replaced by a crudely nominalistic view of reality as consisting exclusively of individual pieces of observable information. Adorno's labelling of this view as 'positivistic' was arguably unfair, since actual logical empiricists tended to take a holistic view of the truth of scientific facts. Even philosophical believers in atomic facts like the early Wittgenstein treated the world as fundamentally a totality.[80] Nevertheless, Adorno believed that a common-sense view of reality as fundamentally composed of isolated empirical facts was becoming widespread.[81]

Popular culture also misconceived scientific knowledge by identifying it with technology and 'progress in controlling nature'. The conflation of science and technology risked bringing about 'the very calamity it is supposed to protect us from'.[82] *Negative Dialectics* was published in 1966, when the demonstration at the end of the 1939–45 war of the destructive potential of the power to split the atom was still recent and fresh in the imagination.

Adorno was one of several major thinkers in this period, including Martin Heidegger and Hannah Arendt, who suggested a genealogy for the

---

[77] Adorno, *Negative Dialectics*, 36, 197.
[78] Horkheimer and Adorno, *Dialectic of Enlightenment*, 66.
[79] Adorno, *Negative Dialectics*, 67.
[80] Ludwig Wittgenstein, *Tractatus Logico-Philosophicus*, trans. D. F. Pears and B. F. McGuinness, intro. Bertrand Russell (London: Routledge, 2001 [1921]), 1, wrote that 'The world is all that is the case.'
[81] Alex Rosenberg, *The Atheist's Guide to Reality: Enjoying Life Without Illusions* (New York: W. W. Norton, 2011), 20, writes 'the physical facts fix all the facts'.
[82] Adorno, *Negative Dialectics*, 67.

modern quest for the technological mastery of nature.[83] In Adorno's version, since at least the sixteenth century the West had identified scientific knowledge with the technological exploitation of nature for profit. But a purely technologically oriented approach to knowledge 'aims to produce neither concepts nor images, nor the joy of understanding, but method, exploitation of the labor of others, capital'.[84]

Art was a possible counterweight. Here too Adorno resembled Nietzsche, for whom music and the arts in general were sources of joy and inspiration that made life tolerable. For Nietzsche, art was the product of the same metaphorising impulse that was responsible for the creation of categories. Indeed, categorial schemes themselves could be interpreted aesthetically, as expressions of the sensibilities of a particular culture. Art appealed to Adorno precisely because it 'negates the categorial determinations stamped on the empirical world'.[85]

Hence the importance of music, which 'embodies complexes that can only be understood through what is sensuously not present'.[86] Art refuted the purely empirical, instrumental conception of reason that animated capitalism and drove exploitation: 'art is knowledge ... as a result of the implicit critique of the nature-dominating ratio' characteristic of the capitalist technological exploitation of science. Art had the capacity for 'emancipating rationality from what it holds to be its inalienable material in the empirical world'.[87]

Foucault's idea of 'Nonaffirmative painting', which also rested on a critique of the concept of identity, was akin to Adorno's negative dialectics of art. Foucault thought of modern art as potentially 'freeing painting ... from the old equivalence between resemblance and affirmation'.[88] The problem with resemblance was that it 'presupposes a primary reference that prescribes and classes'. In other words, emphasis on resemblance in art 'orders and hierarchizes'. Foucault admired Magritte as an artist who had escaped this use of resemblance, favouring instead 'similitude' which

---

[83] See Martin Heidegger, 'The Question Concerning Technology', in *The Question Concerning Technology and Other Essays*, trans. and intro. William Lovitt (New York and London: Garland Publishing, 1977 [1955]), 3–35, and Hannah Arendt, *The Human Condition*, 2nd edn (Chicago and London: University of Chicago Press, 1998 [1958]).

[84] Max Horkheimer and Theodor Adorno, *Dialectic of Enlightenment*, 2.

[85] Theodore Adorno, *Aesthetic Theory*, trans. and ed. Robert Hullot-Kentor (London and New York: Continuum, 2002 [1970]), 5.

[86] Adorno, *Aesthetic Theory*, 98.

[87] Adorno, *Aesthetic Theory*, 138–9.

[88] Michel Foucault, *This Is Not a Pipe, With Illustrations and Letters by René Magritte*, trans. and ed. James Harkness (Berkeley, Los Angeles and London: University of California Press, 1983 [1973]), 43.

'multiplies different affirmations'.[89] Like Adorno and Nietzsche, Foucault's aesthetic ideals reflected a broader philosophical attitude with practical political ramifications; they all made an analogy with the goal of escaping needless and unjustifiable order and hierarchy in the political realm.

For Foucault, classifications of knowledge were suspect insofar as they could serve repressive forms of power. Although human thought was 'related to very general and universal categories and formal structures', it was the phenomena that evaded these categories which most interested him. For example, Foucault's remark that 'The way people really think is not adequately analyzed by the universal categories of logic' helps with understanding the concept of an episteme articulated in *The Order of Things*.[90] There, Foucault's declared aim was to

> bring to light ... the episteme in which knowledge, envisaged apart from all criteria having reference to its rational value or to its objective forms, grounds its positivity and thereby manifests a history which is not that of its growing perfection.

An 'episteme' was Foucault's term for a particular framework or context in terms of which truth and knowledge were understood, so that, for instance, one could talk about the modern episteme, or the episteme of the sixteenth century, and so on.[91] Epistemes were supposedly peculiar to discontinuous epochs employing quite different standards for truth and knowledge, raising once more the question of relativism.[92]

Foucault's claim that the history of knowledge was not straightforwardly progressive was partly inspired by Jorge Luis Borges's essay on 'The Analytical Language of John Wilkes'. Borges's essay singled out Wilkes from amongst many seventeenth-century writers fascinated by the idea of

---

[89] Foucault, *This Is Not a Pipe*, 46.
[90] Michel Foucault, 'Truth, Power, Self: An Interview with Michel Foucault', in *Technologies of the Self: A Seminar With Michel Foucault*, ed. Luther H. Martin, Huck Gutman and Patrick H. Hutton (Amherst: University of Massachusetts Press, 1988), 9–15, 10.
[91] Foucault, *Order of Things*, xxiv, 33, 268.
[92] Hilary Putnam, *Reason, Truth and History* (Cambridge: Cambridge University Press, 1998 [1981]), 167, treated Foucault as a strong relativist, arguing that 'A relativist need not be concerned to undermine the rationality of all "value" judgments, or to defend Foucault's picture of history as a discontinuous series of "discourses" or "ideologies" which succeed one another for no rational reason.' Our argument is that Foucault came to agree with Putnam that weak relativism or perspectivalism did not undermine the rationality of value judgements, but that even in his early more strongly relativistic phase Foucault never believed that it was impossible to give reasons why one episteme followed another, only that there was no logical or causal necessity internal to such changes that could be invoked to explain them.

universal knowledge. The most famous exemplar was probably Gottfried Leibniz, whose writings on the creation of a *characteristica universalis*, a universal symbolism in which all possible truths could be articulated, partly inspired the twentieth-century logical empiricist programme of a unified science.[93] For Borges, however, Wilkes's search for a classificatory scheme that could reflect the putatively natural divisions of the world was stymied by the fact that there simply is 'no classification of the universe that is not arbitrary and conjectural'.[94]

Borges's essay satirised Wilkes's rationalist ideal by using a fictional *reductio ad absurdum*. Characteristically blending fact and fiction, Borges claimed to have found in the work of Dr Franz Kuhn, who really did exist, a passage from a fictional Chinese encyclopedia, the *Celestial Empire of Benevolent Knowledge*, proposing a classification of animals.[95] In *The Order of Things*, however, Foucault gave no indication that he knew Borges's classification was imaginary.[96] He appeared to treat it literally, using it

---

[93] Gottfried Wilhelm Leibniz, 'Preface to a Universal Characteristic', in *Philosophical Essays*, ed. and trans. Roger Ariew and Daniel Garber (Indianapolis and Cambridge: Hackett Publishing, 1989), 5–10, 6, proposed 'a language or characteristic which embodies, at the same time, both the art of discovery and the art of judgment, that is, a language whose marks or characters perform the same task as arithmetic marks do for numbers and algebraic marks do for magnitudes considered abstractly'.

[94] Jorge Luis Borges, 'The Analytical Language of John Wilkes', in *Other Inquisitions 1937–1952*, trans. Ruth L. C. Simms, intro. James E. Irby (Austin and London: University of Texas Press, 1975 [1964]), 101–5, 104. Borges explains the arbitrariness of classification by saying that 'We do not know what the universe is', citing David Hume, *Dialogues Concerning Natural Religion*, in *Dialogues Concerning Natural Religion and Other Writings*, ed. Dorothy Coleman (Cambridge: Cambridge University Press, 2007), 1–102, pt 5, sec. 12, 45, who had Philo say that theologians had no proof that the world was not 'the first rude essay of some infant deity who afterwards abandoned it, ashamed of his lame performance'. Borges's affinity with the Romantic, fragmentarian position is particularly evident in his remark that 'we must suspect that that there is no universe in the organic, unifying sense inherent in that ambitious word'.

[95] Borges, 'John Wilkes', 103, attributed to Dr Franz Kuhn (1884–1961) a passage from a fictional Chinese encyclopedia, the *Celestial Empire of Benevolent Knowledge*, that classifies animals as '(a) those that belong to the Emperor, (b) embalmed ones, (c) those that are trained, (d) suckling pigs, (e) mermaids, (f) fabulous ones, (g) stray dogs, (h) those that are included in this classification, (i) those that tremble as if they were mad, (j) innumerable ones, (k) those drawn with a very fine camel's hair brush, (l) others, (m) those that have just broken a flower vase, (n) those that resemble flies from a distance'. Compare Michel Foucault, 'Preface', *The Order of Things*, xvi.

[96] Keith Windschuttle, 'Absolutely relative', *National Review*, 49 (15 September 1997), 28, argues Foucault was duped. To be fair, others appear to have been taken in since: see Oxana Timofeeva, 'Animal', *Posthuman Glossary*, ed. Rosi Braidotti and Maria Hlavajova (London and New York: Bloomsbury Academic, 2018), 34–6.

to draw a contrast about the alleged differences between Chinese and Western thought.

Whether or not Foucault was fooled, his remarks were revealing. Foucault argued that in the traditional Western imagination, 'the Chinese culture is the most meticulous, the most rigidly ordered'. Borges's fantastic list was thus disturbing because it suggested there was a culture 'that does not distribute the multiplicity of existing things into any of the categories that make it possible for us to name, speak, and think'.[97]

Foucault's argument was that Kuhn's list was an example of a literally unthinkable classification for those who did not share its assumptions. This suggests that Foucault, unlike Nietzsche or Adorno, entertained a strong relativism, as Jürgen Habermas, for example, has alleged.[98] But even if we take Borges's fictitious Chinese classification seriously, it is not obvious that it is evidence for relativism. Parrochia and Neuville, for instance, have argued that the list is not an instance of a classification unthinkable to Westerners because they lack access to its preliminary criterion.

Rather, it is simply a weak classification displaying problems familiar to anyone educated in a Western context.[99] For example, some of the classes overlap; others are not well-defined, or unstable; and some may generate paradoxes. But these issues do not make the classification itself either unthinkable or unrepresentable. To prove their point, Parrochia and Neuville even created a diagram of Borges's fantastical taxonomy, displaying the various classes it enumerated as intersecting sets represented by ellipses of the plane.[100] Foucault, they concluded, had no grounds for treating Borges's example as evidence for strong relativism.

---

[97] Foucault, *Order of Things*, xx–xxi. Compare Lakoff, *Women, Fire, and Dangerous Things*, 92, who argued that Borges's list did capture the fact that 'people around the world categorise things in ways that both boggle the Western mind and stump Western linguists and anthropologists'. This is doubtless true, but Lakoff's argument is that seemingly unintelligible classifications nonetheless turn out to be intelligible on analysis, which was not the point that Foucault wanted to make.

[98] Jürgen Habermas, *The Philosophical Discourse of Modernity Twelve Lectures*, trans. Frederick Lawrence (Cambridge: Polity Press, 1998 [1985]), 276, writes that Foucault's 'putative objectivity of knowledge is itself put in question ... by the unavoidable *relativism* of an analysis related to the present that can understand itself only as a context-dependent practical enterprise'. Emphasis in original.

[99] Daniel Parrochia and Pierre Neuville, *Towards a General Theory of Classifications* (Basel, Heidelberg, New York, Dordrecht and London: Springer Basel, 2013), 5.

[100] Parrochia and Neuville, *General Theory of Classifications*, 6.

If *The Order of Things* was committed to a strong relativism, however, Foucault softened his position fairly rapidly. *The Archaeology of Knowledge* employed more modest language: 'Archaeology is simply trying . . . to determine . . . to which distinct categories [differences] belong.'[101] This was perspectivalism rather than relativism. Foucault expressed scepticism towards the Hegelian notion of 'spirit', regarding it as unwarranted in favouring a belief in history as a continuous progressive process. Instead, he endorsed the Kantian tradition of identifying conditions of possibility. All discourses, Foucault argued, derived their unity from 'the interplay of the rules that make possible the appearance of objects'.[102]

The similarity between Foucault's unity of discourse and Kant's synthetic unity of apperception is visible here. The latter operated through the interplay of categories to make experience of objects possible in an *a priori* way; the former operated through language to give sense to 'objects that are shaped by measures of discrimination and repression'.[103] Insofar as Foucault wanted to examine the political uses of categorially structured knowledge, the implication was that he thought that truth was not simply a subjective affair, any more than it was for Nietzsche or Adorno.

Politics

Nietzsche linked the argument that there was no independently existing hierarchy of knowledge to a critique of existing political order. We saw this was already an issue for Kant: traditional state claims to authority were partly founded on the literal truth of religious knowledge: 'absolute tutelary government and the careful preservation of religion necessarily go together'.[104] But the Church was 'designed to meet artificial needs', like redemption from sin, which were 'reposing on fictions' that categorial analysis exposed.[105]

Nevertheless Nietzsche found something admirable in principle in the idea of 'an institution possessing a universal goal embracing all mankind, and . . . concerned with mankind's highest interests' in a way that was not 'materialistic'.[106] He was critical of nation-states and nationalism: 'one should . . . proclaim oneself simply a *good European* and actively . . .

---

[101] Foucault, *Archaeology of Knowledge*, 188.
[102] Foucault, *Archaeology of Knowledge*, 36.
[103] Foucault, *Archaeology of Knowledge*, 36.
[104] Nietzsche, *Human, All Too Human*, ch. 8, sec. 472, 171.
[105] Nietzsche, *Human, All Too Human*, ch. 8, sec. 476, 176.
[106] Nietzsche, *Human, All Too Human*, ch. 8, sec. 476, 176.

work for the amalgamation of nations'.[107] Zarathustra's injunction to look 'where the state *ends*' for 'the rainbow and the bridges of the overman' should be interpreted with this remark in mind.[108]

The overman, or Übermensch, is one of Nietzsche's most notorious ideas. It has acquired connotations of racism, partly thanks to the character of the 'blond beast' in the Genealogy of Morals. There, Nietzsche argued that all 'noble races' had been motivated by 'search of spoil and victory'.[109] But first, this 'blond beast' was a figure from the past, not necessarily an ideal for the future. Although Nietzsche thought that a 'hair-raising cheerfulness and joy in all destruction' and 'indifference to and contempt for security, body, life, [and] comfort' had originally formed aristocratic values, their contemporary expression provoked 'deep and icy mistrust'.[110] Second, Nietzsche included the Arabian and Japanese nobilities amongst the cultures exhibiting this aristocratic warrior spirit; peoples who were not blonde, or even European. Third, although, like Machiavelli, Nietzsche cited the Renaissance prince Cesare Borgia, who was not shy of violence, as an example of the 'overman', he praised his own creation of Zarathustra for handling even his adversaries gently.[111]

Nietzsche's historical archetypes for the higher type of individual included non-violent artists as well as violent statesmen. In the Renaissance, he particularly admired Raphael.[112] In modernity, the valuable types of human being included 'the scientific character . . . the genius, the free spirit, the actor, the merchant, the great discoverer', none of whom were notably violent figures.[113] Nietzsche's Übermensch can in fact be placed in the tradition of 'Bildung' associated with earlier German writers like Wilhelm von Humboldt, who espoused a demanding ethic of self-cultivation that came to be synonymous with humanism.

This ideal may now appear elitist and even Eurocentric, but it had education at its core. Nietzsche, a classical philologist, initially sought reform of Germany's schools and universities; his first book was On the Future

---

[107] Nietzsche, *Human, All Too Human*, ch. 8, sec. 475, 175. Emphasis in original.
[108] Nietzsche, *Thus Spoke Zarathustra*, trans. Adrian Del Caro, 36. Emphasis in original.
[109] Nietzsche, *Genealogy of Morality*, 23.
[110] Nietzsche, *Genealogy of Morality*, 23.
[111] Nietzsche, *Ecce Homo*, 101, 130. Niccolò Machiavelli, *The Prince*, ed. Quentin Skinner and Russell Price, 2nd edn (Cambridge: Cambridge University Press, 2019), 23, wrote that he had no 'better precepts to offer to a new ruler than [Cesare Borgia's] actions as a pattern . . . although his efforts were in the end unsuccessful, he should not be blamed, because it resulted from extraordinarily bad luck'.
[112] Nietzsche, *Twilight of the Idols*, 196.
[113] Nietzsche, *Twilight of the Idols*, 219.

of Our Educational Institutions.[114] What Nietzsche arguably wanted was a second Renaissance of European culture, in which the arts and sciences would flourish, and Christian beliefs would be discarded as outmoded and self-serving. Nevertheless, Nietzsche believed, like Hegel, in the value of war. Although war was 'the winter or hibernation time of culture', it also restored and strengthened vitality.[115] He suggested that European decadence required 'the greatest and most terrible wars' to combat it.[116]

War was an opportunity for revitalising displays of heroic individualism. War and art were equally affirmations of human life despite its constant struggles. Nietzsche's discussion of the figure of the tragic artist emphasised heroic fearlessness. Tragic art allowed the 'martial aspects of our soul' to 'celebrate their saturnalia in the face of tragedy'.[117] Yet Nietzsche also cautioned against actively seeking war. He warned of 'the dreadful consequence of the desire for expeditions and adventures, especially when it seizes whole hordes of nations'.[118] Real strength in modernity was not the ability to win a battle, but a capacity for justice.[119]

As with Hegel, Nietzsche knew nothing of twentieth-century extermination camps and atomic destruction, though unlike Hegel he predicted a coming crisis.[120] He also protested against the anti-Semitic intellectual trend in Germany of making the Jews 'scapegoats for every possible public or private misfortune'. While he declared that 'the youthful stock-exchange Jew is the most repulsive invention of the entire human race', in the very next sentence he described the Jews as having 'the most grief-laden history of any people' and as having provided humanity with 'the noblest human being (Christ), the purest sage (Spinoza), the mightiest book and the most efficacious moral code in the world'.[121] The Jews, Nietzsche prophesied, would be part of a coming 'weakening and finally ... abolition of nations' which would be the result of the creation of 'a

---

[114] Friedrich Nietzsche, *On the Future of Our Educational Institutions: Homer and Classical Philology*, trans. and intro. J. M. Kennedy (Edinburgh and London: T. N. Foulis, 1910).
[115] Nietzsche, *Human, All Too Human*, ch. 8, sec. 444, 163.
[116] Nietzsche, *Human, All Too Human*, ch. 8, sec. 477, 176.
[117] Nietzsche, *Twilight of the Idols*, 205.
[118] Nietzsche, 'On the Uses and Disadvantages of History', 74.
[119] Nietzsche, 'On the Uses and Disadvantages of History', 88, wrote that 'no one has a greater claim to our veneration than he who possesses the drive to and strength for justice'.
[120] Nietzsche, *Will to Power*, 7, wrote that 'What I relate is the history of the next two centuries. I describe what is coming, what is inevitable: *the rise of nihilism.*' Emphasis in original.
[121] Nietzsche, *Human, All Too Human*, ch. 8, sec. 475, 175.

mixed race, that of European man'.[122] Such miscegenation was one of National Socialism's worst nightmares.

This remark also provides a context for Nietzsche's critical views on contemporary democracy. Modern democracy, Nietzsche declared, was 'the historical form of the *decay of the state*'.[123] One of its pillars had been religion. Another was the existence of 'two different castes in society: that of the workers and that of the idle'.[124] A leisured aristocracy had historically provided the best chance for the higher type of human being to flourish. Rather like Marx, Nietzsche saw culture as having an economic foundation. Wealth was the precondition for nobility. But where Marx saw nobility as something to be overthrown, Nietzsche exalted it, at least in spiritual form.

In an aphorism headed 'My Utopia', Nietzsche declared that 'In a better ordering of society the heavy work and exigencies of life will be apportioned to him who suffers least as a consequence of them, that is to say to the most insensible.'[125] Even though Nietzsche called Plato an 'old socialist', he shared Plato's vision of a just society in which each person occupied the place for which they were naturally best-suited.[126] Nietzsche's ideal was 'the construction of a pyramidal order according to castes and degrees, the creation of a new world of laws, privileges, subordinations'.[127]

Nietzsche's ideal was not a restoration of the old aristocratic society, though. His upper castes were not religious or ethnic, but drawn from those concerned with 'the production of the supreme cultural values'.[128] Contemporary democracy, which he regarded as effectively synonymous with socialism, was inimical to this ideal. Nietzsche argued socialism's commitment to equality was grounded in a concealed narcissism. It obfuscated the reality that human life was organised around difference, and therefore, by definition, inequality, since the non-identical was also the unequal. Egalitarianism was motivated by a secular version of the ressentiment that characterised Judaeo-Christian morality.[129] A progressive

---

[122] Nietzsche, *Human, All Too Human*, ch. 8, sec. 475, 174.
[123] Nietzsche, *Human, All Too Human*, ch. 8, sec. 472, 173. Emphasis in original.
[124] Nietzsche, *Human, All Too Human*, ch. 8, sec. 439, 162.
[125] Nietzsche, *Human, All Too Human*, ch. 8, sec. 462, 168.
[126] Nietzsche, *Human, All Too Human*, ch. 8, sec. 481, 178 worried that a nationalistic quest for political dominance could injure 'the nobler, tenderer, more spiritual plants and growths' who create the higher culture that served as a justification for life.
[127] Nietzsche, 'On Truth and Lie', 258.
[128] Nietzsche, *Human, All Too Human*, ch. 8, sec. 480, 177.
[129] Nietzsche, *Twilight of the Idols*, 208–9, argued that 'What is common to both [Christianity and socialism] . . . is that somebody is supposedly to blame for your suffering – basically, that sufferers are prescribing themselves the honey of revenge for their suffering.'

politics that favoured equality dragged everyone down to the lowest common denominator. But Nietzsche's view was open to the criticism that natural inequality did not have to be enshrined in legal form; equalities of capacity and status could be distinguished.

Nietzsche's greatest objection to socialism, however, was its irrational optimism regarding sudden radical transformations of society. Appropriating Voltaire, Nietzsche wrote that it was 'the optimistic spirit of the [French] Revolution against which I cry: "Écrasez l'infame!"'.[130] In Nietzschean politics, 'action tends to moderation' because of an awareness of the likely 'uselessness and perilousness of all sudden changes'.[131] If the modern democratic idea of government as 'nothing but an organ of the people' were separated from revolutionary ambitions, then it was actually 'more logical' than the old dual-caste conception.[132] The traditional idea of law based on inherited custom was no longer viable. Any form of positive law that replaced it must be 'impartial' in character.[133] In future, 'the sense of justice must grow greater in everyone, the instinct for violence weaker'.[134] Nietzsche declared this was in keeping with the spirit of an original Greek Enlightenment understood as a 'more natural, rational, and . . . unmythical elucidation of the world'.[135] Albeit in sceptical and pessimistic fashion, then, Nietzsche still professed an attachment to Enlightenment values.

So did Adorno. Admittedly, Adorno declared in *Dialectic of Enlightenment* that 'Enlightenment is totalitarian' because it had 'equated truth in general with classifying thought' in an effort to dominate nature and society in equal measure.[136] But in *Negative Dialectics* Adorno also acknowledged a 'demythologizing' side to the enlightenment (with a small 'e') that was the equivalent of Nietzsche's demand for an 'unmythical' understanding of the world.[137] Adorno's overall philosophy was framed as a contest between ideology and enlightenment.[138] His critique was an attack on former Enlightenment ideals in the name of enlightenment itself. 'The self-reflection of enlightenment', as Adorno put it, 'is not its revocation'

---

[130] Nietzsche, *Human, All Too Human*, ch. 8, sec. 463, 169.
[131] Nietzsche, *Human, All Too Human*, ch. 8, sec. 464, 169.
[132] Nietzsche, *Human, All Too Human*, ch. 8, sec. 450, 165.
[133] Nietzsche, *Human, All Too Human*, ch. 8, sec. 459, 168.
[134] Nietzsche, *Human, All Too Human*, ch. 8, sec. 452, 166.
[135] Nietzsche, *Human, All Too Human*, ch. 8, sec. 475, 175. In this respect at least Nietzsche belongs with Sir Karl Popper as a believer in the idea of an original Greek Enlightenment. See Chapter 1, above.
[136] Horkheimer and Adorno, *Dialectic of Enlightenment*, 4, 10.
[137] Adorno, *Negative Dialectics*, 97.
[138] Adorno, *Negative Dialectics*, 148.

but rather 'an insight into the delusion of the subject that will style itself an absolute'.[139]

Adorno, however, also shared Nietzsche's conservative and quasi-aristocratic outlook on art and culture. Despite his commitment to democracy, his criticisms of the 'culture industry' were often dismissive of popular culture. Adorno reconciled his commitments to great art and to democracy by arguing that the vulgarity of modern society was not inherent in human nature. Its sources were 'the perpetuation of oppression' by the exploitation of culture for capitalist gain and the growth of the 'administrated' order with a logic of its own that abetted it.[140] Negative dialectics was designed to show that arbitrary imposition of a universal could be destructive of individuality not only conceptually but also in practice.

Bureaucracy was a prime instance of this use of 'the general against [the] particular'.[141] National Socialism exemplified the fundamental irrationality and inhumanity of which bureaucratic rationalism was capable by deploying it in the service of extermination. Adorno's remark that 'in the concentration camps it was no longer an individual who died but a specimen' actually recuperated a very old claim.[142] We saw in Chapter 2 that Aristotle argued it was impossible to hate an individual; true hatred must necessarily be of types.[143] We might be angry at individuals, dislike them, even feel contempt for them, but we still recognised them as persons even in doing so. Adorno in effect agreed with Aristotle that hatred, however, excluded individuality, allowing the worst forms of oppression to result.

Adorno's point was that it became legitimate to do anything to people once they were reduced to 'only' being something, whether 'only' a Jew, or 'only' a member of some other group. For Adorno, despite Hitler's defeat, the continuing existence of capitalist and bureaucratic ideas and practices remained threatening to individuality. Formally democratic rules about equality that overlooked individuality could impose oppressive universalisms that were simply the obverse of the alienation caused by mass production.

Foucault, who was sceptical towards the very idea of 'man', expressed this doubt in the form of an attack on 'humanism'. Like Adorno, his criticisms were motivated by a belief that it was a false form of universalism.

---

[139] Adorno, *Negative Dialectics*, 158, 186.
[140] Adorno, *Aesthetic Theory*, 240; Adorno, *The Culture Industry*, 108.
[141] Adorno, *The Culture Industry*, 113.
[142] Adorno, *Negative Dialectics*, 362.
[143] See Chapter 2, n. 133, above.

Foucault understood the term 'humanism' to mean 'the totality of discourse through which Western man is told: "Even though you don't exercise power, you can still be a ruler. Better yet, the more you deny yourself the exercise of power, the more you submit to those in power, then the more this increases your sovereignty."'[144] Contemporary humanism was thus intended to secure the quiescence of the majority.

Yet, like both Nietzsche and Adorno, Foucault still regarded Enlightenment as a path towards emancipation. Kant's question of what 'Enlightenment' meant remained relevant, but since Nietzsche both the problem and the solution had changed yet again.[145] The problem was no longer religious freedom of conscience for the noumenal self, as for Kant, or freedom from religion altogether, as in Nietzsche, but moral self-determination for the embodied subject. Sexuality was particularly important in pursuing freedom from humanist illusions.

As a gay man, Foucault had personal experience of the ways in which power could be used coercively to constrain categories of identity. But that the shift of attention from religion to sexuality still counted as a continuation of Enlightenment is clear from Foucault's remark that 'My role ... is to show people that they are much freer than they feel.'[146] Foucault insisted that nobody was defined socially, nor should be defined, exclusively by their sexual preferences: 'Under no circumstances should the sexual choice of an individual determine the profession he is allowed, or forbidden, to practice.'[147]

Foucault's research on the history of sexuality convinced him that the shifting categories of identity reflected in discourses about sexuality were historically particular. Not only was 'the homosexual' a historical creation, the notion itself was 'finally an inadequate category'.[148] What was true of homosexuality was true of categories of identity more generally. Foucault's specific emancipatory goals included 'the suppression of taboos and the limitations and divisions imposed upon the sexes; the setting

---

[144] Michel Foucault, 'Revolutionary Action: "Until Now"', in *Language, Counter-Memory, Practice: Selected Essays and Interviews*, ed. and intro. Donald F. Bouchard, trans. Donald F. Bouchard and Sherry Simon (New York: Cornell University Press, 1996 [1977]), 218–33, 221.

[145] Michel Foucault, 'What is Enlightenment?', in *The Foucault Reader*, ed. Paul Rabinow (New York: Pantheon Books, 1984), 32–50, 32.

[146] Foucault, *Technologies of the Self*, 10.

[147] Michel Foucault, 'Sexual Choice, Sexual Act', in *Politics, Philosophy, Culture: Interviews and Other Writings 1977–1984*, ed. and intro. Lawrence D. Kritzman, trans. Alan Sheridan et al. (New York: Routledge, 1990 [1988]), 286–303, 290.

[148] Foucault, 'Sexual Choice, Sexual Act', 292.

up of communes; the loosening of inhibitions with regard to drugs; the breaking of all the prohibitions that form and guide the development of a normal individual'.[149]

This agenda, though, was definitely not anarchistic: 'There is no question that a society without restrictions is inconceivable.'[150] What mattered was that any restrictions were 'clear and well defined'.[151] As Foucault put it, 'restrictions have to be within the reach of those affected by them so that they at least have the possibility of altering them'.[152] Despite Foucault's reputation as a radical, his primary political value was the traditional liberal one of freedom. His work on discursive regimes was designed to show that how individuals were categorised and classified determined the kind of treatment they received.

Foucault's understanding of categories and the subject in terms of the historical *a priori*, and his desire to liberate knowledge and art from the category of identity, were connected with his goal of freeing modernity, not from identity as such, but from narrow versions of identity politics. Like Adorno, Foucault's ideal political order avoided reducing individuals to their identity as members of a group. Both also followed Nietzsche in encouraging people to have the strength for self-expression. History was important to them mainly insofar as it promoted this goal.

History

Nietzsche, Adorno and Foucault engaged with historical knowledge primarily to differentiate it from the kind of use of the past they themselves favoured. In 'On the Uses and Disadvantages of History for Life', Nietzsche described history 'as a costly superfluity and luxury' and declared that 'knowledge not attended by action . . . must . . . be seriously hated by us . . . We want to serve history only to the extent that history serves life.'[153] Historical analysis was a potential threat to vitality.[154] Modern historical scholarship's power had been demonstrated by the way it had helped put an end to Christianity as a living religion.[155] It had to be treated with

---

[149] Foucault, 'Revolutionary Action: "Until Now"', 222.
[150] Foucault, 'Sexual Choice, Sexual Act', 295.
[151] Foucault, 'Sexual Choice, Sexual Act', 294.
[152] Foucault, 'Sexual Choice, Sexual Act', 295.
[153] Nietzsche, 'On the Uses and Disadvantages of History for Life', 59.
[154] Nietzsche, 'On the Uses and Disadvantages of History for Life', 83, wrote that 'the forces of life are paralyzed and at last destroyed' by history.
[155] Nietzsche, 'On the Uses and Disadvantages of History for Life', 96–7.

extreme caution. Nietzsche's judgement of the power of historical knowledge was strikingly reminiscent of Marx's remark about the solvent effects of capitalism: 'all that is solid melts into air'.[156] Historical analysis had provoked modernity into a 'madly thoughtless shattering and dismantling of all foundations'.[157]

Indeed, the precise danger that Nietzsche warned against was the adoption of a strong relativism: young people might draw the moral that 'every age is different, it does not matter what you are like'.[158] Nietzsche believed that historians had become specialists so devoted to the study of a particular period that they had lost sight of the differences between one epoch and another. Only cultural confusion resulted from general awareness of historical difference combined with a lack of understanding of the features that gave each age its specific character, or of why one era had passed into another. As result, modernity was in danger of simply being 'overwhelmed and bewildered' by specialised historical study. But what perhaps worried Nietzsche the most about this new 'scientific' approach to history was the belief it could yield generalisations about the forces at work in the past which 'In other sciences ... are the most important thing, inasmuch as they contain the laws'.[159]

Nietzsche opposed this effort to bring history into line with natural science because it involved an unprofitable attempt to identify laws of historical progress. In his own 'historical' narratives, such as the *Genealogy of Morals*, he excluded all interpretations of historical processes as necessarily progressive. In particular, Nietzsche wanted to guard against replacing Christian eschatology with yet another speculative philosophy of history in pseudo-scientific guise. '[W]e are still living in the Middle Ages and history is still disguised theology', he declared.[160] Nietzsche singled out Hegel's philosophy of history, which we saw was acknowledged by Hegel himself as a theodicy, as an example.[161] Hegel had delayed 'the triumph of scientific atheism' in a 'grandiose attempt to persuade us of the divinity of existence'.[162]

Nietzsche also argued that a view of ourselves as standing at the end of something was, paradoxically, likely to foster a pernicious pessimism.

---

[156] Marx and Engels, *The Communist Party Manifesto, with Related Documents*, trans. Samuel Moore, ed. John E. Toews, 2nd edn (Boston: Bedford/St Martin's, 2018 [1999]), 67.
[157] Nietzsche, 'On the Uses and Disadvantages of History for Life', 108.
[158] Nietzsche, 'On the Uses and Disadvantages of History for Life', 98.
[159] Nietzsche, 'On the Uses and Disadvantages of History for Life', 92.
[160] Nietzsche, 'On the Uses and Disadvantages of History for Life', 102.
[161] Nietzsche, 'On the Uses and Disadvantages of History for Life', 96.
[162] Nietzsche, *Gay Science*, trans. J. Nauckhoff, bk 5, sec. 357, 218.

Christian apocalyptic thought had presented the human condition as living in the final days of the world (something that we saw Kant had also wanted to guard against).[163] Reproducing this mentality in a modern secular context could result in a paralysing fatalism.[164] Nietzsche's proposed antidote was what he called a 'suprahistorical' perspective. On this view, 'one giant calls to another across the desert intervals of time and, undisturbed by the excited chattering dwarfs who creep about beneath them, the exalted spirit-dialogue goes on'.[165] By focusing on the works and deeds of the great, we can cultivate the kind of historical consciousness that will inspire us to do great things ourselves.

This emphasis on great men, however, suggests that Nietzsche's rejection of the Hegelian style of philosophy of history was less than fully successful. Likewise, demanding from history a perspective 'which bestows upon existence the character of the eternal and stable' with particular attention to 'art and religion' was in tension with Nietzsche's other declared aims.[166] This essay on history was an early production, and Nietzsche was later critical of this kind of emphasis on the eternal as a variety of the Platonism he was concerned to reject. But even within the confines of this essay, there were difficulties with Nietzsche's notion of the 'suprahistorical' standpoint.

At one point Nietzsche characterised historical knowledge as a standpoint from which contingency was the dominant feature of human reality. He quoted with approval Barthold Niebhur's remark that even the most prominent historical actors are 'unaware ... of the chance nature of the form assumed by the eyes through which they see'.[167] On this view, we were living in a constantly changing world even if we were unaware of it. Perhaps Nietzsche could reconcile the contingent with the eternal by making the latter a productive fiction. Those who think of themselves as timeless, he might say, would be more likely to do great work even if they were self-deceived about their timelessness.

We should note, though, that the 'critical' approach to history that Nietzsche endorsed did not refer to the kind of historical standpoint that treated all events as equally contingent. This kind of scientific approach

---

[163] Nietzsche, 'On the Uses and Disadvantages of History for Life', 101.
[164] Nietzsche's remarks were particularly directed at the German philosopher Eduard von Hartmann. See Anthony K. Jensen, 'The Rogue of All Rogues: Nietzsche's Presentation of Eduard von Hartmann's *Philosophie des Unbewussten* and Hartmann's Response to Nietzsche', *Journal of Nietzsche Studies*, 32 (2006), 41–61.
[165] Nietzsche, 'On the Uses and Disadvantages of History for Life', 111.
[166] Nietzsche, 'On the Uses and Disadvantages of History for Life', 120.
[167] Nietzsche, 'On the Uses and Disadvantages of History for Life', 65.

to historiography, Nietzsche argued, would lead to our no longer taking the past, and ourselves, seriously, because in it we assumed the role of spectators: 'modern man . . . allows his artists in history to go on preparing a world exhibition for him' and so in the end we are no longer even either outraged or smug, but simply mildly curious.[168]

Nietzsche believed that it was precisely the lack of a modern sense of history as the science of contingency that explained the vibrancy of ancient Greek culture.[169] Modern people in contrast had become 'walking encyclopedias', full of information about the 'arts, philosophies, religions, discoveries' of other eras, yet incapable of creativity. Modern Germans in particular had been 'ruined by history'.[170] Pure historical objectivity, Nietzsche declared, would create a race of eunuchs 'incapable of making history themselves'.[171] 'Critical' history for Nietzsche meant, rather, an account of the past concerned with passing explicitly negative judgement: 'every past . . . is worthy to be condemned for that is the nature of human things: human violence and weakness have always played a mighty role in them'.[172]

This mode of historical consciousness demanded a clear-sighted acknowledgement that 'since we are the outcome of earlier generations, we are also the outcome of their aberrations, passions and errors, and indeed of their crimes', and as such 'it is not possible wholly to free oneself from this chain'. At the most, we could 'confront our inherited and hereditary nature with our knowledge, and through a new, stern discipline combat our inborn heritage'.[173] Nietzsche's endorsement of critical history was a moral, evaluative, perspective, albeit one designed to oppose the similarly moral stances of continual outrage towards the past and its obverse, a smugness which imagined that we possess 'the rarest of virtues, justice, to a greater degree than any other age'.[174]

What Nietzsche was really looking for in historical knowledge, therefore, was a reliable capacity for moral judgement regarding the past that would support a will for justice. Nietzsche's ideal historian should 'stand higher than he is to be judged'.[175] This position, however, involved an extra-historical belief in the existence of a naturalistic nobility: 'when

---

[168] Nietzsche, 'On the Uses and Disadvantages of History for Life', 83.
[169] Nietzsche, 'On the Uses and Disadvantages of History for Life', 79.
[170] Nietzsche, 'On the Uses and Disadvantages of History for Life', 81.
[171] Nietzsche, 'On the Uses and Disadvantages of History for Life', 86.
[172] Nietzsche, 'On the Uses and Disadvantages of History for Life', 76.
[173] Nietzsche, 'On the Uses and Disadvantages of History for Life', 76.
[174] Nietzsche, 'On the Uses and Disadvantages of History for Life', 83.
[175] Nietzsche, 'On the Uses and Disadvantages of History for Life', 93.

you put forth your noblest qualities in all their strength ... you divine what is worth knowing and preserving in the past'.[176] True history can only be written by 'the experienced and superior man'. Nietzsche was in effect reviving the classical ideal of history as life's teacher.[177] History (at least as written by this proto-overman of a historian) was to be a source of moral example, so long as one knew which types to admire. But this moralised view of the past was clearly distinct from any analytic conception of historiography as a science of contingency.

Hence Nietzsche's admiration for Thucydides, whom he considered the antithesis of the modern scientific historian.[178] But as we noted above, the choice between Plato and Thucydides was less clear than Nietzsche believed.[179] Nietzsche's defence of Thucydides as sharing the realism of those Sophists who opposed the 'hoax of morals and ideals' associated with Platonism ignored the fact that Thucydides, no less than Plato, privileged the universal over the particular, at least when it came to motivating historiography. The tension in Nietzsche's thought between criticising earlier thinkers for privileging the universal and giving in to the temptation to do likewise was clearly on display in his own declaration that the 'genuine historian' must 'express the universal'.[180]

Nietzsche's genealogical approach thus had an equivocal character. Some of his observations could be described as purely historical, with no contemporary bearing, even if they had a dialectical, Hegelian, character. Nietzsche argued, for instance, that the modern scientific and historical perspectives had developed out of the internal contradictions that Christianity contained. Christian morality had given rise to a 'concept of truthfulness that was understood ever more rigorously', and thus had sown the seeds of its own destruction.[181] But Nietzsche's concern with past events was typically in the service of exposing the roots of the present, the goal informing his notion of genealogy. The past was ultimately of interest as a means to a critique of contemporary morality and politics.

Adorno and Foucault took similar positions. Both emphasised historicity, but treated historical knowledge as ultimately important for

---

[176] Nietzsche, 'On the Uses and Disadvantages of History for Life', 94.
[177] Cicero, *On the Ideal Orator (De Oratore)*, trans. and intro. James M. May and Jakob Wisse (Oxford: Oxford University Press, 2001), bk 2, ch. 9, sec. 36, 133, called history 'the witness of the ages, the illuminator of reality, the life force of memory, the teacher of our lives'.
[178] Nietzsche, *Twilight of the Idols*, 225.
[179] See Chapter 1, above.
[180] Nietzsche, *Untimely Meditations*, 94.
[181] Nietzsche, *Gay Science*, bk 5, sec. 357, 219.

contemporary critique. In *Against Epistemology*, for example, Adorno explicitly invoked Nietzsche's complaint in *Twilight of the Idols* that in the history of Western philosophy, 'becoming' had traditionally been deprecated. 'What is, does not *become*; what becomes, is not' had, according to Nietzsche, been the conventional view.[182] Adorno made this point to highlight the problematic relationship between history and modernity. Like Nietzsche, he argued that modernity was a kind of self-inflicted amnesia in which people 'repress history in themselves and others'.[183] To be modern was to be unconscious of the events that had given rise to one's society, and by extension, to oneself.

Adorno's response, however, was not to stress the importance of historiography, but to revive the speculative philosophy of history. When Adorno undertook an investigation of 'the pivotal categories needed for the construction of a theory of history', he was not concerned with the categories of historical analysis.[184] He was interested, rather, in 'the unity of the historical process'. Adorno still wanted to construct an idea of universal history in the 'speculative' or philosophical manner of Kant and Hegel.[185] Given Adorno's qualified adoption of Hegel's dialectical method, it is perhaps unsurprising that he should have also defended Hegel's approach to history.

While Adorno could not accept that modernity was synonymous with freedom, he agreed with Hegel that 'Modern history begins with the discovery of the individual.'[186] Insofar as Adorno modified Hegel's position, it was to recognise the exploitative class relations that had fractured the prospects for the realisation of individuality. The theme of fragmentation recurred here. Adorno wanted to modify Hegel by borrowing from Walter Benjamin's 'Theses on Philosophy of History' the idea of the historical process as '*discontinuous* in the sense that it represents life perennially disrupted'.[187]

Benjamin's idea, however, presupposed that there was a natural order, only one that is perpetually somehow being broken up.[188] But it was nevertheless this underlying unity that supposedly characterised the historical

---

[182] Nietzsche, *Twilight of the Idols*, 167. Emphasis in original. Quoted in Theodor W. Adorno, *Against Epistemology: A Metacritique: Studies in Husserl and the Phenomenological Antinomies*, trans. Willis Domingo (Cambridge and Malden, MA: Polity Press, 2013 [1970]), 19.
[183] Horkeimer and Adorno, *Dialectic of Enlightenment*, 179.
[184] Adorno, *History and Freedom*, 79.
[185] Adorno, *History and Freedom*, 82.
[186] Adorno, *History and Freedom*, 86.
[187] Adorno, *History and Freedom*, 91. Emphasis in original.
[188] Walter Benjamin, 'On the Concept of History', in *Selected Writings*, 4 vols, ed. Michael W. Jennings (Harvard: Harvard University Press, 1996–2003), iv.389–400, iv.392, wrote of 'the angel of history' whose 'face is turned toward the past. Where a chain of

process for Adorno. It was because history 'clings to the resulting fragments instead of its deceptive surface unity' that 'the philosophical interpretation of history ... acquires a view of the totality that the totality fails to provide *at first sight*'.[189] In this conception, contingency played no positive role. Adorno's understanding of history was dominated by necessity: 'chance is the form taken by freedom under a spell'. Pure chance that did not actually conceal the dialectic at work was the contrary of necessity and was 'stripped of meaning'.[190]

Already in *Dialectic of Enlightenment*, Adorno had worked out with Horkheimer a conception of history in which Homer's *Odyssey* was 'one of the earliest representative documents of bourgeois Western civilization'.[191] For Adorno, the fascism that murdered people in the camps as types was latent in Western thought from its very beginnings. All subsequent history had been working towards this collapse of civilisation. But this was only an inverted version of Hegel's philosophy of history, in which the story of the West was of a movement not towards freedom but disaster.

Foucault, unlike Adorno, did not produce a speculative philosophy of history in the Hegelian tradition. He regarded the discontinuities in the historical process as so pronounced that the ambition of telling a single all-encompassing story of history, whether positive or negative, had to be abandoned. *The Order of Things* had made 'establishing discontinuities' a central goal; its successor, *The Archaeology of Knowledge*, stressed that 'the problem is no longer one of tradition, of tracing a line, but one of division, of limits'.[192] Foucault's later works somewhat downplayed this approach. He claimed that 'In *Les Mots et les choses* I ... tried to ask myself the question: is this discontinuity really a discontinuity? Or, to be precise, what was the transformation needed to pass from one type of knowledge to another type of knowledge?'[193]

But Foucault's argument that 'the whole work of [*The Order of Things*] consisted precisely in setting out from this apparent discontinuity ... and

---

events appears before *us*, he sees one single catastrophe, which keeps piling wreckage upon wreckage and hurls it at his feet ... a storm is blowing from Paradise [that] drives him irresistibly into the future, to which his back is turned, while the pile of debris before him grows toward the sky. What we call progress is *this* storm.' Emphasis in original. Benjamin's angel was an engaged spectator passing judgement on what he regarded as a single process that he himself was involuntarily caught up in. Whatever there is to be said for this perspective on the past, it is not that of analytic historiography.

[189] Adorno, *History and Freedom*, 91. Emphasis in original.
[190] Adorno, *History and Freedom*, 97.
[191] Horkheimer and Adorno, *Dialectic of Enlightenment*, xviii.
[192] Foucault, *Order of Things*, 55; *Archaeology of Knowledge*, 6.
[193] Michel Foucault, 'On Power', in *Politics, Philosophy, Culture*, 96–109, 100.

trying, in a way, to dissolve it' was in tension with some of the things he said at the time.[194] For example, the statements in the *Order of Things* that 'archaeological inquiry has revealed two great discontinuities in the episteme of Western culture' or that 'the coherence that existed, throughout the Classical age, between the theory of representation and the theories of language, of the natural orders, and of wealth and value . . . from the nineteenth century onward, changes entirely' read like unqualified presentations of research findings, not initial statements of problems that will be dissolved.[195]

Nevertheless, Foucault was not primarily concerned with the nature of historical knowledge as an independent form of study any more than Nietzsche and Adorno. Despite his emphasis on discontinuity, historical study was still supposed to serve the 'work of freedom'. We should study the past 'to grasp the points where change is possible and desirable'.[196] The difference between Foucault's 'historical ontology of ourselves' and the view taken by Nietzsche and Adorno was that Foucault was more consistent in his focus on the contingent, the local, and the transient over the necessary, the general and the timeless. As with Nietzsche, however, this remained part of an anti-revolutionary agenda. Foucault argued that we 'must turn away from all projects that claim to be global or radical'. Twentieth-century totalitarianism had demonstrated that 'the claim to escape from the system of contemporary reality so as to produce the overall programs of another society . . . led only to the return of the most dangerous traditions'.[197]

Yet even in Foucault, the impress of the Hegelian tradition remained visible. He was still prepared to talk about the 'singular historical destiny' of Western societies, in which their 'universalizing' tendencies and 'the struggle for freedom' were 'permanent elements'.[198] This was the language of German Idealism, not of analytical historiography. Like Nietzsche, Foucault's treatment of genealogy was equivocal. Alongside a commitment to the 'gray, meticulous, and patiently documentary' approach, which might be called authentically historical, ran the emancipatory goals of Enlightenment mentioned above. These tension between these two tendencies persisted in Foucault because of the

---

[194] Foucault, 'On Power', 100.
[195] Foucault, *Order of Things*, xxiv–xxv.
[196] Foucault, 'What is Enlightenment?', 46.
[197] Foucault, 'What is Enlightenment?', 46.
[198] Foucault, 'What is Enlightenment?', 47–8.

unacknowledged equivocation in his observation that 'from the nineteenth century onward . . . a profound historicity penetrates into the heart of things'.[199]

Ostensibly, Foucault did not conceive of this historicity in terms of transcendental conditions in Kant's sense. Foucault's historical *a priori* was supposed to treat the conditions of knowledge as themselves temporal and material, not timeless and logical. Recognition of this historicist truth had helped to precipitate the final break-up of the idea that there was a 'great narrative common to things and to men'.[200] Interpreting *The Order of Things* is a difficult task because it is not always obvious (as with Hegel's *Phenomenology*) when Foucault is expositing the standpoint of one of his epistemes and when he is writing in his own voice. But at the end of the work, it seems clear that when he wrote of 'the movement of History', he himself believed – at least at that time – that there was such a thing.[201] The transcendental element had quietly re-entered the scene.

Though Foucault declared in the *Archaeology of Knowledge* that 'my aim is most decidedly not to use the categories of cultural totalities (whether world-views, ideal types, the particular spirit of an age) in order to impose on history, despite itself, the forms of structural analysis', from time to time he did just that.[202] As James Schmidt astutely observes, in intellectual matters Foucault was a Frenchman who became German.[203] Though Foucault began from the work of French scholars such as Georges Canguilhem and Gaston Bachelard who had strong interests in the history and philosophy of science, towards the end of his life he described his own writings as belonging to a 'form of reflection' inaugurated by Hegel and passed down 'through Nietzsche and Max Weber, to the Frankfurt School'.[204]

This German influence may explain why Foucault sometimes referred to history as a necessary process. Marc Djaballah remarks that Foucault's standpoint was really 'a form of idealism . . . the focal point of Foucault's studies is . . . a telosless *Geist*'.[205] There is evidence however that Foucault's conception of *Geist* was not always quite as telosless as Djiaballah

---

[199] Foucault, *Order of Things*, xxv.
[200] Foucault, *Order of Things*, 401, 403.
[201] Foucault, *Order of Things*, 404.
[202] Foucault, *Archaeology*, 17.
[203] See James Schmidt, 'Misunderstanding the Question "What is Enlightenment": Venturi, Habermas, Foucault', *Journal of the History of European Ideas*, 37 (2011), 43–52, 49.
[204] Michel Foucault, 'The Art of Telling the Truth', in *Politics, Philosophy, Culture*, 86–95, 95. Also translated as 'Kant on Enlightenment and Revolution'.
[205] Marc Djaballah, *Kant, Foucault, and Forms of Experience* (New York and Abingdon: Routledge, 2008), 14.

suggests. Foucault, that is, did not always follow his own injunction 'to free the history of thought from its subjection to transcendence'.[206] Yet in fairness to Foucault, his actual practice was often indistinguishable from the contextualist approach to intellectual history that became dominant in the Anglophone world after the 1960s.[207]

Foucault's remark that 'if you recognize the right of a piece of empirical research, some fragment of history, to challenge the transcendental dimension, then you have ceded the main point' would probably not have met with any objections from an intellectual historian like Quentin Skinner, for instance.[208] Nor was the idea that 'to speak is to do something' which Foucault made central to his archaeological approach at odds with the contextualist approach.[209] It was, indeed, a continuation of the so-called linguistic turn often attributed to the mid-twentieth century but in reality dating back much further.

Foucault also shared the contexualist goal of identifying the discourses that constituted the intellectual horizon of an era. The description of *The Order of Things* as 'a general attack against history, against historians, against the historical mentality' mischaracterised what he was doing.[210] Foucault did say that 'Knowledge initially implies a certain political conformity in its presentation', so that 'In a history course, you are asked to learn certain things and to ignore others.'[211] But this was not a criticism of either history and historians, or of the historical mentality, but of the teaching of the subject in schools and universities, something which almost inevitably becomes politicised.[212]

---

[206] Foucault, *Archaeology*, 203.

[207] Foucault, *Archaeology*, 204.

[208] Compare, for example, Quentin Skinner, 'Meaning and Understanding in the History of Ideas', in *Visions of Politics*, vol. 1, *Regarding Method* (Cambridge: Cambridge University Press, 2002 [1969]), 57–88, 85, who writes that 'as soon as we see that there is no determinate idea to which various writers contributed, but only a variety of statements made by a variety of different agents with a variety of different intentions, what we are seeing is that there is no history of the idea to be written. There is only a history of its various uses, and of the varying intentions with which it was used.' What Skinner calls a 'determinate idea' here would belong in Foucault's terms to the 'transcendental dimension' that both reject in historiography.

[209] Foucault, *Archaeology*, 230. Compare Skinner, 'Meaning and Understanding', 83: 'there is always a question to be asked about what writers are *doing* as well as what they are saying if our aim is to understand their texts'. Emphasis in original.

[210] George Huppert, 'Divinatio et Eruditio: Thoughts on Foucault', *History and Theory*, 13:3 (1974), 191–207, 192.

[211] Foucault, *Language, Counter-Memory, Practice*, 219.

[212] History textbooks in schools provoke almost universal contestation world-wide. For a case study see David Cannadine, Jenny Keating and Nicola Sheldon, *The Right Kind of History: Teaching the Past in Twentieth-Century England* (London: Palgrave Macmillan, 2011).

Had Foucault been hostile to historical knowledge as such, he would not have wanted to correct the perceived problem that 'Social historians are supposed to describe how people act without thinking, and historians of ideas are supposed to describe how people think without acting.'[213] What Foucault wanted was social history informed by ideas, and intellectual history that took account of social circumstances. These did not necessarily constitute a single narrative. Late in his career he reflected that 'I have written two kinds of books. One, *The Order of Things*, is concerned only with scientific thought: the other, *Discipline and Punish*, is concerned with social principles and institutions.'

This distinction was dictated, at least in part, by the subject matter. In Foucault's view, 'History of science doesn't develop in the same way as social sensibility.' Certainly, scientific thought develops in a social context, but in order to be recognised as scientific discourse, 'thought must obey certain criteria'.[214] Foucault's comments suggest, once more, that his mature position was not strongly relativistic. Scientific thought was not entirely reducible to a function of its historical context, but possessed a dimension that, if not universal, was at least transhistorical.

Conclusion

This chapter has been devoted to that strand of intellectual reaction to Hegel which rejected the idea that categories and selfhood comprised unified and universal concepts. Yet neither Nietzsche, nor Adorno, nor Foucault escaped the orbit of the Kantian and Hegelian categorial approaches altogether. Rather, they shifted towards a more pragmatic emphasis on categories and selfhood as defined by their changing usages and contexts. As such, categories became inextricably linked with historicity. So did knowledge, although the classical hierarchy of knowledge fell away for the same reasons. No single system of the kind that either the classical or the Idealist traditions had produced was now possible. The idea of categories and knowledge as fragmented became a common trope. But the need to separate kinds of knowledge from one another in categorial terms was not in dispute.

This critique of categories and their role in knowledge had significant political implications. What mattered in both respects to Nietzsche, Adorno and Foucault was, again, the uses to which categories were put. The role that categories of knowledge had played in moral and political thought required exposing as both self-interested and naïve. Common

---

[213] Foucault, 'Truth, Power, Self', 14.
[214] Foucault, 'Truth, Power, Self', 14.

sense had taken judgements that were really reflections of unacknowledged desires and prejudices as unmediated accounts of reality. This argument resulted in an assessment of the existing moral and political order that was often deeply negative. Modernity was marred by all sorts of reductive impositions of universal terms that were harmful to a wide range of individuals and groups in society. At the extreme, the abuse of categorial discrimination had been used to legitimate genocide.

Yet this critique still expressed the optimistic hope that if these abuses were pointed out, they could be corrected. In this respect, the fragmentarians all remained sceptical, disillusioned continuators of Enlightenment, even though they disagreed on important issues. Nietzsche's critique of categories led him to quite different political conclusions to either Foucault or Adorno, insofar as he favoured a naturalistic hierarchy of talent as an organising principle for society. Foucault came closer than either Nietzsche or Adorno to endorsing a strong relativistic position in his early work, though in the end he, like Adorno, adopted a Nietzschean perspectivalism which can be described as a weak relativism. Indeed, studying their works suggests that reports of the relativism of postmodern thought have been greatly exaggerated. The arguments that the conditions of truth varied and were subject to historicity were not arguments against truth, but demands for clarifications of its past and future status and usages.

Nonetheless, a sensitivity to historicity did not produce any greater interest in historical knowledge understood as exclusively concerned with the analysis of past events. The interest in the past displayed by Nietzsche, Adorno and Foucault was predominantly oriented towards the critique of the present. The traditional emphasis on what was universal and necessary in historical relationships that we have seen stretched from Plato to Hegel likewise remained in evidence. All three were, to a greater or lesser degree, convinced that contemporary historiography was less valuable than a practical approach to the past. Nietzsche was thoroughly scornful of history whenever he believed it had failed to promote the cultural vitality he deemed desirable; Adorno preferred to embrace an inverted version of Hegelian speculative philosophy of history; and Foucault treated history as at best ancillary to the exposure of the covert and insidious workings of power.

Of the three, Foucault came closest to writing history in the strict disciplinary sense. He certainly did historiography a service similar to Marx, by provoking a tremendous volume of new historical research in reaction. Though Foucault was not the first to be interested in the history of sexuality, he was the single greatest inspiration for what came

FRAGMENTARIANS: THE CATEGORIAL KALEIDOSCOPE

after. Likewise, historical research on the general themes of power, institutions, prisons, medicine, madness and biopolitics gained great impetus thanks to Foucault. But in this respect, as we shall see in the next chapter, he remained an outlier. The other main strand of twentieth-century thought, which wanted to restore, if not a singleness of perspective, then a single dominant perspective, also perpetuated the marginalisation of historiography.

6

Subordinationists: The Quest for a Master Category

We saw that one response to Hegel was to emphasise the impossibility of any kind of unified categorial synthesis. The second response was to stress instead the importance of one standpoint over all others, hence the choice of the term 'subordinationism'. The interest, and the contentious feature, of using this 'subordinationist' label is that it unites philosophers who are normally read as diametrically opposed to one another. In particular, it groups logical empiricism and existential phenomenology together, not of course in terms of style and content, but with respect to an approach that often led to shared positions.[1]

Certainly, the 'subordinationist' view did not necessarily mean a shared preference for a single categorial scheme. Indeed, like the fragmentarians, subordinationists often wanted to reject categorial discourse.[2]

---

[1] These terminological choices accord with dictionary definitions. Richard Creath, 'Logical Empiricism', *The Stanford Encyclopedia of Philosophy* (Winter 2022 edition), ed. Edward N. Zalta and Uri Nodelman, sec. 1, notes that logical empiricism is sometimes also referred to as logical positivism but that the latter designation was typically used by critics and that the members of the Vienna Circle, for example, typically identified themselves as logical empiricists. Labelling Heidegger an existential phenomenologist will be seen by his admirers both as underestimating the extent to which he was sui generis as a philosopher and as disregarding his problematic relationships with those philosophers more usually identified as existentialists or phenomenologists such as Jean-Paul Sartre and Edmund Husserl, but Michael Wheeler, 'Martin Heidegger', *The Stanford Encyclopedia of Philosophy* (Fall 2020 edition), ed. Edward N. Zalta and Uri Nodelman, sec. 1, writes that Heidegger's work is 'perhaps most readily associated with phenomenology and existentialism', even if 'his thinking should be identified as part of such philosophical movements only with extreme care and qualification'.

[2] Alain Badiou, *Theoretical Writings*, ed. and trans. Ray Brassier and Albert Toscano (London and New York: Continuum, 2005 [2004]), 23, notes that both Martin Heidegger and Rudolf Carnap were committed to the end of classical metaphysics, albeit for very different reasons.

But, again like the fragmentarians, this philosophical move ensured they remained implicated with the problem of categories, even if in a negative fashion. Subordinationism also entailed stressing one particular form of knowledge as especially, if not exclusively, important, a position which in turn had implications for ideas about politics and history.

Logical empiricism, represented here chiefly by Otto von Neurath and Rudolf Carnap, and by W. V. O. Quine in the second generation, was initially somewhat divided over the discourse of categories. The concept of a category was associated chiefly with Kant, Hegel typically being dismissed. Neurath wanted to reject the kind of categorial framework associated with Kantian thought altogether as an obstacle to immediate access to the sense data which was supposedly at the base of all sound knowledge.[3]

Yet this foundationalist position proved hard to sustain. Carnap, who had originally been more sympathetic to the Kantian approach, acknowledged even in his mature work that the search for the basic relations that organised our experience could also be conceived in categorial terms.[4] In the end logical empiricism found itself driven back to ideas such as the 'terrain of life', as in Neurath, or that of a web of belief which we have previously noted in Quine, in order to explain the intelligibility of the world.[5]

---

[3] Otto von Neurath, 'Physicalism', in *Philosophical Papers 1913–46, with a Bibliography of Neurath in English*, ed. Robert S. Cohen and Marie Neurath with assistance from Carolyn R. Fawcett, trans. Robert S. Cohen and Marie Neurath (Dordrecht and Boston, MA: D. Reidel Publishing Company, 1983), 52–7, 56–7, wrote that 'The work on unified science replaces all former philosophy. At this point "science without a world-view" confronts "world-views" of all kinds.' Neurath singles out 'everything that was put forward as philosophy by scholastics, Kantians, phenomenologists' as '*meaningless* except that part [which] can be translated into scientific, that is physicalist, statements'. Emphasis in original.

[4] Alan W. Richardson, *Carnap's Construction of the World: The Aufbau and the Emergence of Logical Empiricism* (Cambridge: Cambridge University Press, 1998), 90, argues that Carnap's early work in the first half of the 1920s 'used broadly neo-Kantian epistemological categories'.

[5] Otto von Neurath, *Empirical Sociology: The Scientific Content of History and Political Economy* in *Empiricism and Sociology, with a Selection of Biographical and Autobiographical Sketches*, ed. Marie Neurath and Robert S. Cohen (Dordrecht and Boston, MA: D. Reidel Publishing, 1973), 319–421, 392, wrote that 'The human grouping appears embedded in a terrain of life, influencing it and influenced by it. The totality of customs and their changing, whether in themselves or in their combinations, we may designate as an order of life in the widest sense.' For the metaphor of the web see Chapter 4, above.

Existential phenomenology, of which Heidegger serves as the main example, likewise rejected the use of categorial schemes.[6] Kant's distinction between phenomenal and noumenal reality, for example, presupposed a more fundamental ground, which Heidegger called Being. But as with the original logical empiricist pursuit of pure sense data, Heidegger quickly became dissatisfied with his first efforts to answer what he called the question of the meaning of Being. Heidegger decided that his project of trying to define 'the human being's essential abode from being and toward being' had not broken sufficiently with established terminology, and his later writings made a deliberate 'turn' towards a less technical and more metaphorical style in order to try and address this problem.[7] What did not change was Heidegger's conception of human beings as integral parts of larger order of things. The most urgent philosophical task was to dismantle the existing world-picture enabling the technological exploitation and destruction of the world in favour of recovering this sense of belonging to 'the ground of beings', or Being itself.[8]

United in an attack on categories, the logical empiricists and Heidegger also shared a tendency to emphasise one form of knowledge over all others. For the logical empiricists this was science, though what was meant by a unified science could be broadly conceived to include the social sciences and even, at the limit, the humanities.[9] Overall, though, the primary

[6] Martin Heidegger, 'Enframing', in *The Question Concerning Technology*, 36–49, 36, wrote that 'The essence of Enframing is that setting-upon gathered into itself which entraps the truth of its own coming to presence with Oblivion.' Heidegger in effect took 'enframing' to be a naïve use of a categorial scheme specifically associated with the normalisation of the techno-scientific exploitation of the world.

[7] Martin Heidegger, 'Letter on "Humanism"', in *Pathmarks*, ed. William McNeill (Cambridge: Cambridge University Press, 1998 [1967]), 239–76, 271, wrote that 'the thinking that in *Being and Time* tries to advance thought in a preliminary way into the truth of being characterizes itself as "fundamental Ontology" ... this thinking is already removed from the "ontology" of metaphysics (even that of Kant)'. However, its readers took 'the established terminology in its customary meaning'.

[8] See Martin Heidegger, 'What Are Poets For?', in *Poetry, Language, Thought*, trans. and intro. Albert Hofstatder (New York: Harper Perennial, 2001 [1971]), 87–139, 99; and compare Martin Heidegger, 'The Age of the World-Picture', in *The Question Concerning Technology*, 115–54. As William McNeill notes in *Pathmarks*, 367, n. 1, the German word *der Grund* can mean both 'ground' and 'reason', and 'Heidegger's argument [is] that ground as ratio or λόγος is derivative upon the more primary sense of being (Sein) itself as ground.'

[9] When Neurath sent the Viennese philosopher and historian Heinrich Gomperz his plan for an *Encyclopedia of Unified Science*, Gomperz pointed out that history had not been included. Heinrich Gomperz, *Interpretation: Logical Analysis of a Method of Historical Research* (Library of Unified Science, Monograph Series, no. 8–9. The Hague: W. P. van Stockum en Zoon, 1939) was written in response to Neurath's invitation to Gomperz to fill this gap. See Fons Dewulf, 'The Place of Historiography in the Network of Logical Empiricism', *Intellectual History Review*, 30:2 (2020), 321–45, 333.

emphasis was on our knowledge of the physical, material world. Heidegger altogether rejected this focus on science. He emphasised that the reasons for the modern fascination with science were not themselves scientific.[10] Rather, they were a symptom of a deep-seated tendency in Western thought to treat the world as an object of domination. In the philosophical tradition descended from Descartes, science had been valorised not for its own sake but in response to the unacknowledged promptings of our will to power.[11] For Heidegger, the only potential answer to what he saw as a self-destructive desire for technological mastery was the recovery of our primordial relation to Being.

Whether or not one is sympathetic to Heidegger's critique, logical empiricism can fairly be treated as belonging to a Cartesian tradition in which the pursuit of science was motivated by a desire to enhance our technological capabilities. The logical empiricists were the heirs of what we might call the scientific wing of Enlightenment. They took up the pursuit of universal, encyclopaedic knowledge, which implied the rejection of all traditional authorities in the face of methodological scepticism.[12] As modernists, this inclined the members of the first generation who paid attention to politics, notably Neurath, towards socialism as supposedly the most rational model for government and society.

As logical empiricism migrated to the Anglophone world and gave rise to Anglo-American analytical philosophy in the next generation, it took on a more liberal hue. But in both the first and second generations it displayed a notable inclination towards intellectual intolerance.[13] Even

---

[10] Martin Heidegger, 'Science and Reflection', in *The Question Concerning Technology*, 155–82, 156, asked 'Is there, ruling in science, still something other than a mere wanting to know on the part of man?' and answered his own question by saying 'Something other reigns. But this other conceals itself from us so long as we give ourselves up to ordinary notions about science.'

[11] Martin Heidegger, 'The Word of Nietzsche: "God Is Dead"', in *The Question Concerning Technology*, 53–112, 82–3, wrote that 'The metaphysics of the modern age begins with ... the unconditionally indubitable, the certain and assured [*das Gewisse*], certainty', and argues that for Descartes 'the *ego cogito* [is] that which presences as fixed and constant'. Italics in original.

[12] Otto von Neurath, 'Encylopedia as Model', in *Philosophical Papers*, 145–59, 146, wrote that 'The march of science progresses from encyclopedias to encyclopedias. It is this conception that we call *encyclopedism*.' Emphasis in original. Neurath, 'Foundations of the History of Optics', in *Empiricism and Sociology*, 101–12, 102, claimed that 'Descartes, in his *Method*, demands [the dissection of physical theory] into elementary constituents [using the tools of analysis].'

[13] Martin Heidegger, 'What is Metaphysics', in *Pathmarks*, 82–96, 90, wrote 'The nothing itself nihilates.' Rudolf Carnap, 'The Elimination of Metaphysics Through Logical Analysis', in *Logical Positivism*, ed. A. J. Ayer (New York: The Free Press, 1959), 60–81, 71, wrote in

a notable sympathiser like A. J. Ayer reached for a description of it in dogmatic religious terms.[14] Heidegger's support for National Socialism, rooted in a völkisch nationalism that also contained an intellectualised strain of anti-Semitism, not only betrayed a similar disposition but did real harm into the bargain.[15]

The connection between the themes of categories, knowledge and politics thus continues to hold good, and as with the thinkers we grouped under the label of fragmentarians, the result was again a marginalisation of historical knowledge. Michael Beaney perhaps exaggerates a little in writing of 'the designedly anti-historicist project of early analytical philosophy', but it is true that the main interest of history for a thinker like Neurath was its use as a source of predictive data for social science.[16] As a Marxist, Neurath was interested in the study of past political economy as a weapon in the contemporary class struggle. He engaged in debate with Oswald Spengler in an effort to debunk the ideas of *The Decline of the West*, which crucially concerned not the past, but the future.[17] Heidegger likewise treated historical

---

response that Heidegger was guilty not just of 'gross logical errors' but of writing literally 'meaningless' sentences. Not all philosophers have subsequently agreed. See, for example, Michael Inwood, 'Does the Nothing Noth?', in *German Philosophy Since Kant*, ed. Anthony O'Hear (Cambridge: Cambridge University Press, 1999), 271–90, 274–5, for the argument that Heidegger's sentence did in fact have meaning as part of an effort 'to explain what makes our discourse, including our negative discourse, possible'.

[14] A. J. Ayer, 'Editor's Introduction', in *Logical Positivism*, 3–28, 6, wrote of the 'missionary' nature of the Vienna Circle.

[15] The controversy over Heidegger's involvement with Nazism has been long-standing and centres upon the question of whether racist and fascist ideas were integral to his philosophy. Richard Wolin, *The Politics of Being The Political Thought of Martin Heidegger* (New York and Oxford: Columbia University Press, 1990), 150, answers in the affirmative, writing that 'in the helplessness of Dasein vis-à-vis the mysterious coming to presence of the primordial powers of Being, there survives distinct traces of that masochistic submission of the individual to the collective destiny of the *Volksgemeinschaft* under a totalitarian regime'. Italics in original. For a review of the situation to the early 1990s which includes defences of Heidegger see Richard Wolin, ed., *The Heidegger Controversy: A Critical Reader* (London and Cambridge, MA: MIT Press, 1998 [1993]). The controversy was exacerbated in the twenty-first century by the publication of Heidegger's notebooks containing anti-Semitic passages, discussed below: see Donatella di Cesare, *Heidegger and the Jews: The Black Notebooks* (Cambridge and Medford, MA: Polity Pres, 2018 [2014]). For Heidegger's involvement with National Socialism see Yvonne Sherratt, *Hitler's Philosophers* (New Haven: Yale University Press, 2013), especially ch. 5, 'Hitler's Superman: Martin Heidegger'.

[16] Michael Beaney, *Frege: Making Sense* (London: Gerald Duckworth, 1996), 2.

[17] Oswald Spengler, *The Decline of the West: Form and Actuality*, trans. Charles Francis Atkinson (New York: Alfred A. Knopf, 1928 [1918]), 3, declared that he was undertaking 'the venture of predetermining history, of following the still untravelled stages in the destiny of a Culture'.

knowledge in the strict sense as 'historiology', just another version of the rationalism he condemned in modern thought.[18] His own interest in the history of Western thought understood as the covering up of the question of the meaning of Being was avowedly futural.

Let us stress once more that our argument is not that logical empiricism and existential phenomenology were saying the same things. They understood themselves to be, and are conventionally taken as, opposites to one another for sound reasons. They championed very different forms of knowledge and stood in political terms for entirely different positions. Nevertheless, in a structural sense, their attempts to reject categorial discourse altogether; their tendency to subordinate all forms of knowledge to one particular variety; their inclination towards intellectual intolerance and political dogmatism; and their lack of interest in history, all represent genuinely shared positions that tend to go unremarked. Let us make a start with the topic of categories.

Categories

The explicit use of a vocabulary of categories by the logical empiricists varied significantly. Neurath made almost no mention of categories, except to be critical. For example, when considering natural law, he argued that the concept rested on illicit normative assumptions about the nature of existence and in particular the nature of the good. 'Why should we start such discussion with speculations about the categories "be" and "ought to be?"', he asked rhetorically, finding no good answer to his own question.[19] Neurath's proposed doctrine of physicalism can be understood as a kind of linguistic purification of categorial discourse from philosophy insofar as it was associated with an outmoded metaphysics. Carnap sought a similar kind of linguistic reform, but was more willing to acknowledge a continuing need for at least some categories, particularly in his work on *The Logical Construction of the World*.[20]

This difference was due to Carnap's greater engagement with neo-Kantian thinkers like Ernst Cassirer and Heinrich Rickert. Carnap credited neo-Kantian philosophy of science with the argument that 'the

---

[18] Martin Heidegger, *Being and Time*, trans. John Macquarrie and Edward Robinson (Oxford: Blackwell Publishers, 2001 [1962]), 42, insisted that 'historiology is . . . a deficient mode' of *Dasein*.

[19] Otto von Neurath, 'The Social Sciences and Unified Science', in *Philosophical Papers*, 209–12, 210.

[20] Rudolf Carnap, *The Logical Structure of the World*, in *The Logical Structure of the World and Pseudoproblems in Philosophy*, trans. Rolf A. George (Illinois: Open Court Publishing, 2003 [1928]), v–xxvi and 5–300.

undigested experientially given' was insufficient as a basis of scientific knowledge. In Carnap's version of the project, a unified science rested on descriptions of relations between objects.[21] But this was just the problem of categories in another vocabulary. Carnap recognised this, and said so: 'we can envisage the problem of the basic relations in construction theory as the problem of categories'.[22] But even Neurath, as Michael Friedman has argued, still framed his problems within a Kantian horizon.[23] Although reacting against Kant's doctrines about the nature of space and of mathematics, the logical empiricists were still trying to find a certain basis for our knowledge of nature.

Heidegger, like Neurath, mainly mentioned categories to express dissatisfaction with them. *Being and Time*, for instance, opened by suggesting that the inherited 'presuppositions and prejudices' of 'ancient ontology' have been responsible for the contemporary belief that 'an inquiry into Being is unnecessary'.[24] Amongst these prejudices, Heidegger suggested, were categories themselves as traditionally conceived: '*all ontology, no matter how rich and firmly compacted a system of categories it has at its disposal, remains blind and perverted from its ownmost aim, if it has not first adequately clarified the meaning of Being.*'[25] The reference to 'all ontology' suggests that the categories in question were not only Kantian but also included those of ancient thought. This reading is confirmed by Heidegger's claim that 'the categorial content of the traditional ontology has been carried over' into modern thought, this time citing Hegel as an instance of a modern thinker whose work still encapsulated ancient difficulties.[26]

Originally, however, Heidegger had shown more sympathy for a categorial approach. He had written his habilitationsschrift on 'Duns Scotus' Theory of the Categories and of Meaning'.[27] The argument was that the

---

[21] Carnap, *Logical Construction*, 2, wrote that 'Relation descriptions form the starting-point of the whole constructional system and hence constitute the basis of unified science.'
[22] Carnap, *Logical Construction*, 135.
[23] See Michael Friedman, *Reconsidering Logical Positivism* (Cambridge: Cambridge University Press, 1999). See also Chapter 3, n. 52, above.
[24] Heidegger, *Being and Time*, 22.
[25] Heidegger, *Being and Time*, 31. Emphasis in original.
[26] Heidegger, *Being and Time*, 44.
[27] Martin Heidegger, 'Duns Scotus' Theory of the Categories and of Meaning', trans. Harold Robbins (PhD diss., De Paul University, 1978 [1915]). One of the works Heidegger believed was by Scotus was really by Thomas of Erfurt: see Jack Zupko, 'Thomas of Erfurt', *The Stanford Encyclopedia of Philosophy* (Spring 2019 edition). The confusion apparently arose because Erfurt's *De modis significandi*, probably composed in the first decade of the fourteenth century, was mistakenly included in early editions of Scotus's *Opera Omnia*. But we are interested in Heidegger's use of medieval thought, not the historical accuracy of his reading.

medieval handling of the problem of categories was actually more fertile than modern, Kantian and post-Kantian, efforts. In Scotus, Heidegger found an approach to categories that he thought could rescue the Kantian *a priori* categorial scheme of categories from being what he called 'an inadequate, schematic table'.[28] Heidegger ended this early work by declaring that the ultimate goal of philosophy was 'a theory of categories derived from their fundamental tendencies'.[29] At this time, grasping these fundamental tendencies for Heidegger meant appreciating that they originated in a 'living mind' of which Descartes's cogito or Kant's synthetic unity of apperception were only a partial image.[30]

In *Being and Time* this 'living mind', which Heidegger described in his work on Scotus as a 'hylomorphic duality', became '*Dasein*'. As was the case with the earlier concept, *Dasein*'s mind was not to be grasped as an essence absolutely different in kind from its body. As a way of thinking about the nature of persons, Heidegger suggested that to be an instance of embodied *Dasein* was to be a self-consciously self-determining possibility.[31] We are, as Heidegger put it, 'thrown' into Being and obliged to make sense of the world for ourselves.[32] When Heidegger said that *Dasein* was distinguished by its '"ecstases" of temporality', what he meant was that it was intrinsic to a human being to have relationships to past, present, and future.[33] Of these three temporal orientations, Heidegger's emphasis on possibility tended to privilege the future. This emphasis was reinforced by his argument that *Dasein* was also distinguished by its 'Being-towards-death', Heidegger's term for our orientation towards our own mortality.[34] This orientation was the ultimate source of our concern, or 'Care', as Heidegger called it, for the world.[35] Hence he could say that for *Dasein* having a 'being-in-the-world', or always belonging to a particular environment, was a constitutive feature of its identity that constituted an 'existentiale'.[36]

Since this account of *Dasein* was supposed to avoid the problems of the dualistic distinctions in Descartes and Kant between a material and a mental substance, or a phenomenal and a noumenal reality, there was a clear continuity between Heidegger's work on Scotus, which sought a

---

[28] Heidegger, 'Duns Scotus', 253.
[29] Heidegger, 'Duns Scotus', 256.
[30] Heidegger, 'Duns Scotus', 249.
[31] Heidegger, *Being and Time*, 69.
[32] Heidegger, *Being and Time*, 174.
[33] Heidegger, *Being and Time*, 377.
[34] Heidegger, *Being and Time*, 237, 302.
[35] Heidegger, *Being and Time*, 378, wrote that 'Care is Being-towards-death.'
[36] Heidegger, *Being and Time*, 79.

'solution of the problem of categories' and the project of *Being and Time*.³⁷ *Being and Time* also still stated the question of Being in notably Kantian terms. Heidegger's investigation of what he called the existentialia of *Dasein* was closely akin to a search for *a priori* conditions of possibility, or categories.³⁸ Kant's categories of the understanding were 'an *a priori* logic for the subject matter of that area of Being called Nature'.³⁹ Nature here, however, was understood as the object of scientific understanding. Heidegger in contrast wanted to distinguish between 'sciences which examine entities of such and such a type', which he called 'ontical' and presupposed 'an understanding of Being', and 'ontologies which are prior to the ontical sciences and which provide their foundations'.⁴⁰ Heidegger believed logical empiricism ignored this latter kind of thinking, but that it was fundamental for the question of 'the authentic meaning of Being'.⁴¹ Kant's categories, in other words, had an unacknowledged derivation in something more basic.⁴²

In Heidegger's idea of *Dasein* as self-determining possibility, and even more so in his insistence that it was possible for *Dasein* itself to be authentic or inauthentic in how it went about realising its possibilities, we can see why he has been associated with existentialist thought.⁴³ Authenticity for the individual meant avoiding becoming an instance of what Heidegger called the 'they-self'.⁴⁴ The they-self let itself be defined in terms of 'idle talk'. Though Heidegger claimed that nothing

---

³⁷ Heidegger, 'Duns Scotus', 250, 253.
³⁸ Heidegger, *Being and Time*, 188, argued that 'As *existentialia*, states-of-mind and understanding characterize the primordial disclosedness of Being-in-the-world.' Italics in original.
³⁹ Heidegger, *Being and Time*, 31.
⁴⁰ Heidegger, *Being and Time*, 31.
⁴¹ Heidegger, *Being and Time*, 62, wrote that 'the phenomenology of Dasein has the character of a ἑρμηνεύειν, though which the authentic meaning of Being, and also those basic structures of Being which Dasein itself possesses, are *made known* to Dasein's understanding of Being'. Italics and emphasis in original.
⁴² Robert Brandom, 'Heidegger's Categories in *Being and Time*', Monist, 66:3 (1983), 387–409, 390, writes that for Heidegger, 'Properties . . . are what characterize the present-at-hand in dependently of human practical ends – what would be taken to be true of objects before human beings "attach significances" to them on the neo-Kantian picture Heidegger wishes to invert. Heidegger's problem in the first part of *Being and Time* is to explain how such a category of objective Being could be constructed or abstracted out of the primitive system of appropriatenesses and significances which makes up the world in which we always already find ourselves.'
⁴³ Heidegger, *Being and Time*, 68.
⁴⁴ Heidegger, *Being and Time*, 225, wrote that 'The Self . . . is proximally and for the most part inauthentic, the they-self.'

disparaging was intended by this terminology, it is implausible that in making a distinction between those who live their lives in a world which others have interpreted for them, and those who set their own horizons, he was not also expressing a preference.[45] An unacknowledged elitism had crept into a purportedly philosophical account of the nature of the self. As Richard Rorty put it, 'Heidegger . . . pours Nietzschean wine into Kantian vessels.'[46]

To Heidegger's critics, however, it sometimes looked as if he were attempting to escape from categories altogether. Adorno remarked that in Heidegger, 'The concept of entity at large, ideally without any category, is stripped of all qualifications . . . so it . . . may call itself Being.'[47] Ian Hunter has argued that the attitude Heidegger was gesturing towards was supposed to be 'shaped by the suspension of all categorial conditions of knowledge in order to achieve a state of attunement not to an object of knowledge but to something that will happen'.[48] Hunter's remark draws attention to the way in which Heidegger's philosophy possessed what we could call a quasi-theological character. Heidegger had begun his intellectual career by studying theology before switching to philosophy, and this early exposure to Christian thought left a permanent mark.

Early in Heidegger's philosophical career, he lectured on 'the phenomenology of the religious life', and also contemplated a course on 'The Philosophical Foundations of Medieval Mysticism'.[49] In both *Being and Time* and in his later writings, Heidegger made use of metaphors also prevalent in medieval thinkers with whom he was familiar.[50] These metaphors were also put to sufficiently similar uses to make it unlikely that this resemblance was coincidental, even though Heidegger came to think of Christianity as complicit in obscuring the kind of

---

[45] Heidegger, *Being and Time*, 211.
[46] Richard Rorty, *Contingency, Irony, and Solidarity* (Cambridge: Cambridge University Press, 1993 [1989]), 123.
[47] Adorno, *Negative Dialectics*, 107.
[48] Ian Hunter, 'The Mythos, Ethos, and Pathos of the Humanities', *History of European Ideas* (2014), 40:1, 11–36, 19.
[49] Martin Heidegger, *The Phenomenology of Religious Life*, trans. Matthias Fritsch and Jennifer Anna Gosetti-Ferencei (Bloomington and Indianapolis: Indiana University Press, 2004 [1995]).
[50] S. J. McGrath, *The Early Heidegger and Medieval Philosophy: Phenomenology for the Godforsaken* (Washington DC: Catholic University of America Press, 2006), 85, argues that 'the *Daseinanalytic* finds its clearest medieval resonance . . . in the pious writings of Bonaventure, in the sermons of Bernard of Clairvaux, in Augustine's *Confessions* and Teresa of Avila's *Interior Castle*'. Italics in original.

fundamental understanding he was seeking.⁵¹ In *Being and Time*, for instance, Heidegger used light as a metaphor for authenticity in a manner that ran exactly parallel to Saint Augustine's use of the same metaphor to describe devotion to the religious life.⁵² The later Heidegger continued to employ the metaphor of light when talking of a 'clearing' from within which we could encounter the truth of Being.⁵³ He even wrote about 'the gods', suggesting that his final position was a kind of neo-paganism.⁵⁴

The logical empiricists were convinced that Heidegger's metaphorical language was meaningless. Neurath explicitly accused Heidegger of writing 'literal nonsense'.⁵⁵ To be fair, Heidegger, for his part, thought that logical empiricist philosophy was merely expounding a superficial scientism.⁵⁶ On Friedman's account, the mutual disdain that Heidegger's

---

⁵¹ Heidegger, *Being and Time*, 74, wrote that 'what stands in the way of the basic question of Dasein's Being (or leads it off the track) is an orientation thoroughly coloured by the anthropology of Christianity and the ancient world'. Martin Heidegger, 'Phenomenology and Theology', in *Pathmarks*, 39–62, 51, indicates that Heidegger's mature position was that Christian theology was a genuine science of a practical kind that (as for Hegel) presupposed the deeper truths of his own thought; for example, Heidegger wrote that the Christian notion of sin should be contrasted with guilt as 'an original ontological determination of the existence of Dasein'.

⁵² Benjamin D. Crowe, *Heidegger's Religious Origins Destruction and Authenticity* (Bloomington and Indianapolis: Indiana University Press, 2006), 92–3, notes that 'In Book X of his *Confessions*, Augustine . . . uses metaphors of "light" and "darkness" to describe the situation of humanity apart from God', and that Heidegger employs the same 'Christian metaphors of "darkness" and "light," of "sleep" and "wakefulness," of drunken "numbness" and "sobriety," to intimate the ways of life that are of concern to him' in *Being and Time*.

⁵³ Martin Heidegger, 'On the Essence of Truth', in *Pathmarks*, 136–54, 153–4, argued that 'Truth signifies sheltering that clears [*lichtendes Bergen*] as the fundamental trait of Being . . . Because sheltering that clears belongs to it, Beyng appears originally in the light of concealing withdrawal. The name of this clearing [*Lichtung*] is ἀλήθεια [*aletheia*].' Heidegger's translators use the unusual English spelling of 'Being' as 'Beyng' to reflect an archaic spelling of the verb 'to be' as *Seyn* rather than *Sein* in German. The Greek word *aletheia* is typically translated as 'truth', but in Heidegger is often translated as 'unconcealment'.

⁵⁴ See Martin Travers, 'Trees, Rivers and Gods: Paganism in the Work of Martin Heidegger', *Journal of European Studies*, 48:2 (2018), 133–43.

⁵⁵ See Otto von Neurath, 'Unified Science and Psychology', in *Unified Science: The Vienna Circle Monograph Series Originally Edited by Otto Neurath, Now in an English Edition*, ed. Brian McGuiness, intro. Rainer Hegselmann, trans. Hans Kaal (Dordrecht: D. Reidel Publishing, 1987), 1–23, 4 and 10, n. 4, 277.

⁵⁶ Heidegger, 'Phenomenology and Theology', 56, declared that Carnap's thought exemplified the 'extreme counterpositions' to his own.

existential phenomenology and the logical empiricists displayed for one another marked the beginning of the divide between 'analytical' and 'continental' philosophy.[57] The same attitudes were still visible in some of the leading analytical philosophers of the next generation.

For example, Quine was the most prominent American signatory of a letter opposing the award by Cambridge University of an honorary degree in philosophy to Jacques Derrida.[58] Just as Neurath congratulated himself that 'we have disposed of metaphysics with its senseless formulations', Quine felt able to dismiss Derrida's writings as 'semi-intelligible attacks upon the values of reason, truth, and scholarship'. The extreme hostility that Derrida provoked in Quine has been called 'pathological'.[59] But it can also be seen as the reflex of an inherited tradition, a historical repetition of the initial logical empiricist hostility to Heidegger.

Heidegger, on the one hand, and Neurath and Quine on the other, all failed to recognise that there were deep similarities between the goals of logical empiricism and existential phenomenology. Both philosophies were, in their own way, attempts to eliminate the gap between mental and physical substance, or phenomena and noumena, that had supposedly opened up in early modern and Enlightenment thought. Whereas Heidegger wanted a synthesis of the two, however, Neurath was in favour of a reduction.

Neurath wanted to think of reality as physical without remainder, which proved a difficult position to sustain. Neurath's project of a unified science aimed to abolish 'the difference between the "mental" and the "physical" sciences, or between "philosophy of nature" and of "culture."'[60] In a similar fashion, Carnap treated the self as secondary, or epiphenomenal; since it could not be treated as empirically given, 'it does not belong to the original state of affairs'.[61] Yet Neurath observed that we cannot

---

[57] See Michael Friedman, *A Parting of the Ways: Carnap, Cassirer, and Heidegger* (Illinois: Open Court Publishing Company, 2000).

[58] W. V. Quine et al., letter to *The Times*, 9 May 1992. There was also opposition to Derrida's award within Cambridge itself, which Quine did not instigate, nor was Quine the only signatory of the letter; but he was the most famous.

[59] See David Golumbia, 'Quine, Derrida, and the Question of Philosophy', *Philosophical Forum*, 30:3 (1999), 163–86, 163.

[60] For a contemporary example see Philippe Descola, *Beyond Nature and Culture*, trans. Janet Lloyd (Chicago and London: University of Chicago Press, 2013 [2005]) which suggests that an anthropological theory seeking to take account of 'a new universality that is both open to all the world's components and also respectful of their idiosyncracies' should base itself on the science of chemistry.

[61] Carnap, *Logical Structure of the World*, 260–1.

help wanting 'to form sentences containing the noun soul or mind'. Such sentences were necessary in order to talk about culture at all.[62]

The problem was self-inflicted. As Neurath put it, 'Physicalism does not recognize aspects.'[63] But failing to recognise non-empirical aspects to reality meant that logical empiricism struggled to accommodate the ideas involved in human actions and events. Neurath tried to circumvent this by arguing that Marxism was 'basically physicalistic'.[64] But the fact that concepts such as ideology and class consciousness were fundamental to Marxism made this implausible. We see, once more, how Neurath's dislike of the categorial approach taken by Kant's critical philosophy lay behind his desire for a physicalistic language.

In our discussions of knowledge, Neurath believed, 'we are haunted . . . by the "thing in itself."' Categories that might require the concept of a self, for instance, seemed to Neurath to threaten a return to thinking in terms of a transcendental, noumenal order that would once again open up a gap between empirical and non-empirical reality. The very terms 'appearance' and 'reality' were on what Neurath called, in a jocular allusion to the Catholic index of prohibited books (still then in force), his 'index verborum prohibitorum'.[65] Neurath's physicalism was thus bound up with his project of restricting valid knowledge claims to the domain of science, just as Heidegger's account of *Dasein* was inseparable from the search for a more fundamental knowledge of the meaning of Being.

Knowledge

The logical empiricists rejected Kant's version of a categorial solution to the problem of knowledge as unviable, thanks to developments in both geometry and physics. Moreover, categories seemed to introduce an unwelcome mediating component between subject and object. But we noted that logical empiricism continued to accept the terms of the problem Kant had laid down. The primary goal of philosophy remained how to show how certainty regarding physical and mathematical knowledge was possible, even if the focus shifted from the structure of subjectivity to language.[66]

Carnap, for example, argued that philosophy was henceforth to be restricted to its role as the exact science of the logical syntax of language.[67]

---

[62] Neurath, 'Unified Science and Psychology', 6.
[63] Neurath, 'Unified Science and Psychology', 12.
[64] Neurath, 'Unified Science and Psychology', 11.
[65] Neurath, 'Unified Science and Psychology', 8, 22.
[66] Friedman, *Reconsidering Logical Positivism*, 155.
[67] Friedman, *Reconsidering Logical Positivism*, 179.

Like Neurath, Carnap called metaphysical statements 'pseudo-sentences', and declared that the only meaningful philosophical problems concerned 'the logic of science'.[68] It was these kinds of arguments that gave logical empiricism a reputation for scientism: the non-scientific doctrine that only scientific knowledge is worthwhile. There is, however, another side to the story. A consequence of the logical empiricist rejection of metaphysics was the embrace of a certain kind of pluralism.

Once it became clear that that there was not, as Kant had believed, a single geometry, or a single logic, but that alternative geometries and systems of logic were possible, the question arose of the nature of the relationship between them. Carnap argued that we could not say that one geometry or logical system was inherently better than another, only that it was more useful for this particular problem. Carnap's pluralism thus tended in a pragmatic direction. This pluralistic position, it turned out, could be generalised from formal systems to cover thought at large, and it foreshadowed later-twentieth pragmatism in analytical philosophy. Indeed, 'a shift towards pragmatism' was one of the implications that Quine believed emerged from his own work.[69]

This turn towards pragmatism also brought later analytical philosophy closer to the perspectivalist ideas of the fragmentarians discussed above than has often been realised. If there was no single ideally best system of logic, but all propositions had to be understood as true or false in relation to the specific system to which they belonged, then truth was relative to a 'framework', or 'conceptual scheme' as Quine put it.[70] The common roots of the fragmentarians and the subordinationists in a reaction to Kantian and Hegelian Idealism are visible here. The frameworks or conceptual schemes in terms of which we made sense of the world, as we have emphasised, were effectively understood by both Kant and Hegel as composed of different sets of categories.

The logical empiricists and their analytical successors thus increasingly found that they had taken up positions entailing that propositions could not be said to be true or false, or even intelligible, outside of some categorial framework or other. Even if, in logical empiricism, an explicit discourse of categories somewhat dropped out of the picture in the second half of the twentieth century, their role in giving the world unity and meaning was substantially preserved in the ideas of a 'framework' or a

---

[68] Friedman, *Reconsidering Logical Positivism*, 113.
[69] W. V. Quine, 'Main Trends in Recent Philosophy: Two Dogmas of Empiricism', *Philosophical Review*, 60:1 (1951), 20–43, 20.
[70] Quine, 'Two Dogmas of Empiricism', 43.

'world-version' adopted by some leading analytical philosophers.[71] In the 1970s in particular, the use of such ideas prompted a major debate within analytical philosophy itself.[72] There was an extensive discussion of the problem of relativism that ran parallel to the debates occurring within 'continental' philosophy.[73]

We have emphasised on more than one occasion already that Quine's resort to the idea of a 'web of belief' as a way of grounding the truth of scientific propositions was similar to a perspectivalist position.[74] This 'semantic holism' was taken by Quine in the first instance to apply to the propositions of scientific thought, but just like Carnap's pluralism, it was easily generalisable. The scientific tendencies of logical empiricism were in tension with a contextualism that pointed in another direction entirely. 'There is no court of appeal *outside* the totality of sentences', wrote Neurath.[75] Jacques Derrida's later declaration that *'There is nothing outside of the text'* was not a deliberate echo; nevertheless, the similarity was anything but coincidental.[76]

---

[71] See, for example, Nelson Goodman, *Ways of World-Making* (USA: Hackett Publishing, 1988 [1978]), 93.

[72] Wittgenstein's development from the *Tractatus Logico-Philosophicus* to the *Philosophical Investigations* arguably prefigured this tension within the work of a single philosopher. With some oversimplification, analytical philosophy after 1945 can be understood as internalising a split between 'Tractarian' and 'Investigative' approaches, the former remaining attached to logic and science under the banner of what Lakoff calls an 'objectivist paradigm' (see *Women, Fire, and Dangerous Things*, ch. 11), and the latter endorsing a more interpretative approach. Saul Kripke and David Lewis are identified by Lakoff as amongst the objectivists or realists; Nelson Goodman and Richard Rorty were examples of analytical philosophers who argued for the need to incorporate interpretative concerns.

[73] Donald Davidson, 'On the Very Idea of a Conceptual Scheme', in *Inquiries in Truth and Interpretation*, 2nd edn (Oxford: Clarendon Press, 2001), 183–98, 198, rejected relativism and argued that 'In giving up dependence on the concept of an uninterpreted reality, something outside all schemes and science, we do not relinquish the notion of objective truth – quite the contrary . . . truth of sentences remains relative to language, but that is as objective as can be.' But Nietzsche, Adorno and Foucault would not disagree: the contrast Davidson was describing is equivalent to that between strong and weak relativism, or between relativism and perspectivalism.

[74] See Chapters 4 and 5, above.

[75] Neurath, 'Unified Science and Psychology', 6. Italics in original.

[76] Jacques Derrida, *Of Grammatology*, trans. Gayatri Charkavorty Spivak (Baltimore and London: Johns Hopkins University Press, 1997 [1967]), 158. Emphasis in original. Spivak's translation is misleading if taken as a claim that extra-textual reality was deprecated, when what Derrida meant by 'Il n'y a pas de hors-texte' was that all of reality was intelligible on the analogy of legibility. See Max Deutscher, '"Il n'y a pas de hors-texte" – Once More', *Symposium: Canadian Journal of Continental Philosophy*, 18:2 (2014), 98–124.

In support of this argument, it is worth recalling that Thomas Kuhn's *Structure of Scientific Revolutions*, which became closely associated with post-modern relativism in the social sciences, originally appeared in the library of unified science established by none other than Neurath himself. Kuhn's work also received Carnap's enthusiastic approval.[77] Germanophone logical empiricism contained not only scientism but contextualism and historicism within itself thanks to its reaction to its Idealist inheritance. These inner tensions were passed on, in turn, to Anglophone analytical philosophy.

Insofar as the logical empiricists tried to address the phenomenon of historicity, they typically did so by extending science to include the social sciences. Neurath, for example, argued that traditional disciplines like history and political economy that had been forged in the nineteenth century had come together to create the developing science of sociology. But his conception of sociology was marked by commitments to Marxism and to prediction as the hallmarks of scientificity. Both Marxism and the physical sciences, Neurath wanted to argue, shared a single foundation.

The doctrine of a unified science meant that there was only a 'single empirical science' in which all propositions were about 'spatio-temporal things'.[78] The aim of this doctrine was to eliminate metaphysical and theological elements from historical knowledge. Physicalism, as Neurath put it, was 'always on the surface'. The elimination of depth, so to speak, was designed to rule out any argument that the object of historical knowledge was the psychological life of those concerned.

Neurath associated a psychologistic approach with Wilhelm Dilthey's hermeneutics. Dilthey had indeed made psychic life the primitive datum or object of the human sciences and thus the source of their distinctiveness.[79] But for Neurath this separation of the *Naturwissenschaften* from the *Geisteswissenschaften*, of the natural sciences from the humanities, destroyed the unity of the sciences.[80] The claim that there was a distinct domain of psychic life also opened the more general possibility of a dualistic metaphysics of a Cartesian or Kantian kind in which mental substance, however conceived, had independent reality.

---

[77] Friedrich Stadler, *The Vienna Circle: Studies in the Origins, Development, and Influence of Logical Empiricism* (Cham, Heidelberg, New York, Dordrecht and London: Springer International, 2015), xxiv.
[78] Neurath, 'Empirical Sociology', 325.
[79] Wilhelm Dilthey, *Descriptive Psychology and Historical Understanding*, intro. R. A. Makkreel, trans. R. M. Zaner and K. L. Heiges (The Hague: Martinus Nijhoff, 1977), 27.
[80] Neurath, 'Empirical Sociology', 325.

For Neurath this claim was closely associated with theological argument and religious belief. Mental substance and the noumenal 'I' were secularised versions of the idea of the immortal soul.[81] Those defending such positions were, from Neurath's Marxist perspective, endorsing an ideology held by the ruling class that needed to be swept away. At this point the political dimension of the logical empiricist account of knowledge begins to come into view.[82] There was a connection in Neurath's mind between what he called this old-fashioned 'metaphysical sociology' and the defence of the societal status quo.[83]

Heidegger was no less dismissive of philosophical tradition than the logical empiricists. In Heidegger's case, though, this attitude reflected not a belief in the overwhelming importance of science but rather a conviction that modern thought had overlooked the problem of the meaning of Being. We noted above that Heidegger's distinction between sciences that presupposed 'an understanding of Being' from 'ontologies which are prior . . . and which provide their foundations' was a fundamental one in *Being and Time*.[84]

Heidegger wanted to do more, though, than simply argue that (ontological) philosophy could identify the fundamental assumptions or presuppositions of, for instance, (ontic) science in a way that science could not do for itself. This argument is familiar; we saw that for Aristotle, the investigation of the presuppositions of a given kind of knowledge was not a task for that kind of knowledge itself, but a separate philosophical inquiry. Likewise, Heidegger's claim that the presuppositions of ontic science had actively blinded humanity to the truth of Being was not scientific but rather rooted in a narrative of the history of philosophy.

According to Heidegger, an instrumental attitude that treated the world as composed primarily of things which are 'present-at-hand' or useful to us had become visible as early as Plato.[85] This attitude had culminated in a modern civilisation so exclusively devoted to the scientifically based technological exploitation of the world that it was no longer aware that any other attitude was even possible. Heidegger's claim that the problems

---

[81] Neurath, 'Empirical Sociology', 416, wrote that 'Idealist oriented thinkers endeavour to give a special position to the subject, the "I," "consciousness as such," to individual or social conscience or to some other god-substitute.'
[82] Putnam, *Reason, Truth and History*, 184, wrote that 'Logical Empiricism was fundamentally a sophisticated expression of the broad cultural tendencies to instrumentalism and majoritarianism.'
[83] Neurath, 'Empirical Sociology', 356.
[84] Heidegger, *Being and Time*, 31.
[85] Heidegger, *Being and Time*, 91, 201.

of modernity could be traced back to Greek thought was not original; we have already noted Nietzsche's critique of Platonism as the inspiration for Christianity, for example. But Heidegger developed this narrative in greater depth than any previous philosopher.

In Heidegger's view, the modern sciences, natural or social, were 'ontic' disciplines that missed the most fundamental questions about life. Although *Being and Time* claimed it was not 'passing judgment on the positive work' of disciplines like 'anthropology, psychology, and biology', Heidegger also stated that they 'all fail to give an unequivocal and ontologically adequate answer to the question about the kind of Being which belongs to those entities which we ourselves are'.[86] History, as we shall see later on, was also included in this list. The natural, social and human sciences were all instances of a Cartesian approach to science that treated entities in instrumental fashion while also implicitly presupposing 'an idea of Being whose source has not been unveiled'.[87]

The mathematical projection of nature associated with modern physics was the 'classical example'.[88] It presupposed a view of things in terms of their 'quantitatively determinable' properties which was itself implicitly oriented towards the ways in which they might be useful to us.[89] The importance given to the 'objective' quality of scientific knowledge, understood as its ability to articulate truths about things in terms of variables such as 'motion, force, location, and time', rested on *Dasein*'s choice of its prior, non-scientific, priorities.[90]

Heidegger's argument that scientists are motivated by many considerations that are not themselves scientific was doubtless sound. Any form of thought, insofar as it is exemplified as a practice or takes on institutional form, involves power relations, as Foucault observed. But although science has undeniably been used for the exploitation of the earth's resources, that cannot be what makes science identifiably scientific. The motivations for and uses of science are not the sources of the distinctive structure of science as a form of knowledge. That structure must rest on the ideas around which science is organised, not the uses to which it is put.

Heidegger himself was unsatisfied with *Being and Time* for somewhat different reasons. He came to think that it left the true nature of the source, or ground, or foundation of Being unspecified. In his later writings

---

[86] Heidegger, *Being and Time*, 75.
[87] Heidegger, *Being and Time*, 129.
[88] Heidegger, *Being and Time*, 413.
[89] Heidegger, *Being and Time*, 414.
[90] Heidegger, *Being and Time*, 414.

he took the view that it was easier for 'the openedness of beings' to 'prevail more essentially' when 'beings are . . . only roughly known by science' because 'technical mastery over things bears itself without limit' and 'the openedness of beings gets flattened out'.[91] Science, in other words, was alleged to actively get in the way of our 'attunement' to the world.

Instead, Heidegger increasingly looked for the meaning of Being in other forms, including art. The poetry of Friedrich Hölderlin and the paintings of Vincent van Gogh seemed to Heidegger to capture more of what he was seeking than any of the 'ontic' kinds of propositional knowledge. The metaphor of the 'clearing' noted above also appeared in the context of Heidegger's discussions of the capacity of art to accomplish 'the unconcealment of Being'.[92] The artwork was a means to an encounter with the extraordinary.[93] As in *Being and Time*, however, Heidegger still wanted to contrast the nature of the work of art with our ordinary instrumental attitude to things as present at hand.

For Heidegger, Aristotle's conception of things in terms of substances and their attributes, like Plato's Ideas, had played an important role in forming this attitude. Heidegger argued that our access to the truth found in painting was hindered by treating things as having a substantial element in which predicates inhered as 'natural'.[94] Turning to consider a painting by Van Gogh of a pair of worn shoes, Heidegger claimed that it could avoid this metaphysical problem. The painting was 'the disclosure of what the equipment, the pair of peasant shoes, *is* in truth'.[95] The shoes were not simply things with properties. 'In the shoes vibrates the silent call of the earth.'[96] Van Gogh's painting had succeeded in saying something essential about the 'mode of being' of their wearer that was not captured by the shoes understood simply as things for walking in. It summoned up a whole way of life.

Meyer Schapiro criticised Heidegger for his claim that the shoes Van Gogh painted were those of a peasant woman, when it is more likely that that Van Gogh was painting his own shoes.[97] Certainly, Heidegger's

---

[91] Heidegger, 'The Essence of Truth', 147.
[92] Martin Heidegger, 'The Origin of the Work of Art', trans. Albert Hofstadter, in *Basic Writings from Being and Time (1927) to The Task of Thinking (1964)*, Revised and Expanded Edition, ed. David Farrell Krell (New York: HarperCollins Publishers, 1993 [1977]), 140–213, 200.
[93] Heidegger, 'The Origin of the Work of Art', 179.
[94] Heidegger, 'The Origin of the Work of Art', 149.
[95] Heidegger, 'The Origin of the Work of Art', 160.
[96] Heidegger, 'The Origin of the Work of Art', 159.
[97] Meyer Schapiro, 'The Still Life as a Personal Object – A Note on Heidegger and Van Gogh', in *Selected Papers*, vol. IV, *Theory and Philosophy of Art: Style, Artist, and Society* (New York: George Braziller, 1994), 135–42.

essay was highly revealing of a völkisch sensibility. He invented an entire bucolic biography for the wearer of the shoes, who was full of 'the wordless joy of having once more withstood want' and was 'trembling before the impending childbed'. But Schapiro's criticism was not fatal. He himself argued that Van Gogh's painting showed his shoes as 'inseparable from his body' and as conveying 'a concern with the fatalities of . . . social being'.[98] This, Heidegger could reply, is exactly what he wanted to say about the capacity of art to convey truth. Whose shoes were depicted did not affect this point.

Even if Heidegger were wrong in thinking the pair of shoes van Gogh painted did not actually exist, it would still be open to him to say that the shoes were not being painted simply as objects of a certain colour, shape, size and so on.[99] Reproducing their sensible qualities as accurately as possible would not give us the essence of the shoes, in Heidegger's sense of the term. Nor was Van Gogh trying to do so; he was not a realist painter of a photographic kind. Schapiro was on more solid ground in noting that there was nothing personal in Heidegger's account of the peasant woman, who was really a type rather than an individual, whereas if Van Gogh were painting his own shoes, the meaning of the painting would have been genuinely personal and biographical.[100]

Once again, however, this objection may not be decisive. Heidegger could have responded that his peasant woman would have her own life history, but that the painting disclosed the universal nature of her relationship to her equipment: 'The artwork opens up in its own way the Being of beings.'[101] For Heidegger, indeed, Van Gogh's painting was not supposed to 'make manifest what . . . isolated beings as such are', but to 'make unconcealment as such happen in regard to beings as a whole'.[102]

In art, Heidegger found support for his effort to escape the limitations of propositional thinking he associated with science and metaphysics. Van Gogh's picture had succeeded in showing us something in a way that was not purely 'representational' in the sense of being a copy of an actually existing object. This was presumably what Heidegger means when he says that 'Color shines and wants only to shine. When we analyze it in rational terms by measuring its wavelengths, it is gone.'[103]

---

[98] Schapiro, 'Still Life', 140.
[99] Heidegger, 'The Origin of the Work of Art', 162.
[100] Meyer Schapiro, 'Further Notes on Heidegger and Van Gogh', in *Theory and Philosophy of Art: Style, Artist, and Society*, 143–51, 149.
[101] Heidegger, 'The Origin of the Work of Art', 165.
[102] Heidegger, 'The Origin of the Work of Art', 181.
[103] Heidegger, 'The Origin of the Work of Art', 172.

Yet Heidegger wanted to go beyond the argument that art can express the truth of things in a non-propositional way. He described the world revealed by art as 'the self-opening openness of the broad paths of the simple and essential decisions in the destiny of a historical people', and thus made art a part of his cultural politics.[104] Heidegger treated the artist, and the poet, as demiurges who showed things as they really were, or called things by their true names.

In a fashion reminiscent of the Stoics, Heidegger declared that 'Language, by naming beings for the first time, first . . . nominates beings *to* their Being *from out of* their Being . . . announcement is made of what it is that beings come into the open *as.*'[105] This was in effect a return to the ancient theory of natural kinds in which the name of a thing was a reflection of its essence or true nature. Poetry was given the status of an ur-language, and as a result of this original poetic act, 'truth is thrown toward the coming preservers, that is, toward a historical group of human beings'.[106] The artistic and poetic will to truth was connected in Heidegger's mind with a capacity for existential decisions. Only 'He who truly knows beings knows what he wills to do in the midst of them.'

The will here was not simply the exercise of choice, but 'the sober unclosedness of that existential self-transcendence which exposes itself to the openness of beings as it is set into the work'.[107] This conception of the will notably lacked any safeguard. There was no test that could determine whether somebody truly had knowledge of the Being of beings and had achieved existential self-transcendence. Like the knowledge of the Platonic philosopher ruler, the will of the Heideggerian artist was self-authenticating. The artist-politician deciding the destiny of a people had no reason to brook any opposition from those who disagreed.

Politics

Although Neurath was less concerned with art than Heidegger, he still drew a connection between political order and visuality. The symbolic, if not the aesthetic, realm, seemed to offer a solution to the goal of perfectly transparent communication. 'How to organize human life socially' was 'the great question' for Neurath, and he suggested that a crucial part of the

---

[104] Heidegger, 'The Origin of the Work of Art', 174.
[105] Heidegger, 'The Origin of the Work of Art', 198.
[106] Heidegger, 'The Origin of the Work of Art', 200.
[107] Heidegger, 'The Origin of the Work of Art', 192.

answer consisted in the development of 'a system of rules, a sort of grammar of picture language'.[108] Neurath's development of an 'International System of Typographic Picture Education' to which he gave the acronym of 'isotype' was a visual equivalent of Esperanto, and a forerunner of the universally recognisable icons designed for use in digital interfaces.[109] But his development of a 'series of simple stylized symbols ... designed ... to characterize social facts' was not a purely theoretical creation.[110] It was part of a social engineering project that was integral to Neurath's vision of the good society. The realisation of this vision involved 'a unified, planned, central control of all museums and educational institutions'.[111]

These sorts of remarks saw Neurath accused by contemporaries of 'an overly technical understanding of politics with strong inclinations towards social engineering'.[112] To be fair to Neurath, despite his talk of centralisation, he did recognise that 'the dictatorship of planning is a danger in itself', and he made it explicit that 'a world language does not imply a world dictatorship'.[113] He knew that the search for a single unifying standard could be abused. Compared to some participants in the two short-lived Bavarian Communist regimes established in 1919 in the immediate aftermath of the end of the war, Neurath was a moderate. He was a Marxist, but he was not a violent revolutionary. Though he wanted to see the world adopt socialism, he wanted this process to be peaceful.[114]

Carnap shared Neurath's enthusiasm for 'the construction of an auxiliary language for international communication'.[115] As Friedman has pointed out, the 'language planning' that was supposed to lead to a purified logical language for science was also treated by Carnap as having a political analogue.[116] Although the pursuit of a logical symbolism and an international

---

[108] Otto von Neurath, 'Museums of the Future (1933)', in *Empiricism and Sociology*, 218–23, 222.
[109] Keith Bresnahan, '"An Unused Esperanto": Internationalism and Pictographic Design, 1930–70', *Design and Culture*, 3:1 (2011), 5–24.
[110] Otto von Neurath, 'Visual Education and the Social and Economic Museum in Vienna (1931)', *Empiricism and Sociology*, 215–18, 215.
[111] Neurath, 'Social and Economic Museum', 222.
[112] Hartle, 'Otto Neurath's Visual Politics', 98.
[113] Neurath, 'A New Language (1937)', in *Empiricism and Sociology*, 224–6, 224.
[114] Neurath, 'Marx and Epicurus', in *Empiricism and Sociology*, 283–90, 290, wrote that 'the revolutionary proletariat ... desires happy, peaceful community, it simply wants "happiness", as the Epicureans did'.
[115] Rudolf Carnap, 'Intellectual Autobiography', in *The Philosophy of Rudolf Carnap*, ed. Paul Arthur Schilpp (Illinois: Open Court Publishing, 1997 [1963]), 3–83, 66.
[116] Friedman, *Reconsidering Logical Positivism*, 214, 232.

language for communication were different problems, Carnap nevertheless found them 'somehow psychologically similar'.[117] He recalled having been excited by discovering Esperanto aged fourteen, and actually learned the language. The idea of a planned language was a contribution to 'the humanitarian ideal of improving the understanding between nations'.[118]

The logical empiricists inherited not only the project of defining the conditions of scientific knowledge from the Kantian agenda; they were also heirs to the ideal of a universal peace. They believed, like Kant, that this would be the necessary result of the world becoming ever more rational in its forms of government. But like Neurath, Carnap did not think planning could be reduced to the simple imposition of a solution. 'Planning' for Carnap meant to 'to envisage the general structure of a system', not forcing people to adopt it at gunpoint.[119] The politics of logical empiricism, then, envisaged a benign subordination of society to reason. The project of a 'Unified Science' offered the prospect of the same kind of advances in understanding the laws of individual and social behaviour that had been made in logic, maths, and physics. Once gained, this knowledge would be deployed for peaceful and progressive purposes.

Despite their peaceful intentions, though, the logical empiricists never really confronted the problem of how to deal with those who disagreed with their views. Neurath appears to have thought of himself, at least half-seriously, as surrounded by uneducated people with medieval attitudes. 'When will the Middle Ages be at an end?', he mused to himself.[120] Quine, we might note, would later describe the Middle Ages as a period when 'darkness descended' in the form of the 'mists of myth and mysticism'; that is to say, Catholic Christianity.[121] Quine remarked in a discussion of the concept of 'tolerance' that although he favoured a kind of 'militant atheism', the 'restraints and ideals' of religion could have social value.[122]

In the last resort, however, Quine saw science and religion as in conflict, and thus as raising the political question of what ought to be taught.

---

[117] Carnap, 'Intellectual Autobiography', 70.
[118] Carnap, 'Intellectual Autobiography', 68.
[119] Carnap, 'Intellectual Autobiography', 67.
[120] Otto von Neurath, 'Visual Education: Humanisation Versus Popularisation', in *Empiricism and Sociology*, 227–48, 244, writes: 'When will the Middle Ages be at an end? As soon as all men can participate in a common culture and the canyon between educated and uneducated people has disappeared.'
[121] W. V. Quine, *From Stimulus to Science* (Cambridge, MA: Harvard University Press, 1998 [1995]), 2.
[122] W. V. Quine, 'Toleration', in *Quiddities: An Intermittently Philosophical Dictionary* (Cambridge, MA: Belknap Press, 1987), 206–10, 209. Quine's discussion is indicative of his ahistorical approach to concepts. In its origin, the one thing that toleration could not encompass was atheism. John Locke, *A Letter Concerning Toleration and Other Writings*,

For Quine, modernity was faced with the 'melancholy dilemma between promoting scientific enlightenment and promoting wholesome delusion'.[123] But to regard the beliefs of another as simply 'deluded' tends to rule out the possibility of political dialogue. When the religious and the irreligious are unable even to communicate with one another, violence becomes increasingly likely.

In the context of the 1930s, this kind of attitude played a significant role in the complete breakdown in relations that took place concurrently in Viennese and European society. The logical empiricists did not appreciate the extent to which their rationalistic, modernist views were out of step with the values of many of their fellow citizens: 'The underestimation and dismissal of conservative Vienna ... typified progressive Viennese views during the interwar era.'[124] What was true of Vienna was even truer of Austria as a whole. In the provinces, the majority were conservative and Catholic in their attachments.

From a sociological standpoint, Heidegger's metaphysics represented that part of Germanic society that was still attached to rural, agricultural, traditional life and its associated forms of religious and political order. For Heidegger, who took medieval thought very seriously, an attachment to and continuity with medieval life represented a very positive thing. 'How would a modern Middle Ages have to look?', Heidegger asked himself in his notebooks, in which he inserted vignettes in praise of village life and the countryside while complaining that technology was spoiling everything.[125]

---

ed. Mark Goldie (Indianapolis: Liberty Fund, 2010), 52–3, declared that 'Those are not at all to be tolerated who *deny the Being of a God*. Promises, Covenants, and Oaths, which are the Bonds of Humane Society, can have no hold upon an Atheist. The taking away of God, though but even in thought, dissolves all.' Emphasis in original. Quine showed no awareness of the reversal in meaning by which the concept of toleration had acquired the sense in which he used it.

[123] Quine, *Quiddities*, 209.

[124] Janek Wasserman, *Black Vienna: The Radical Right in the Red City, 1918–1938* (New York: Cornell University Press, 2014), 17.

[125] Martin Heidegger, *Ponderings II–VI: Black Notebooks 1931–1938*, trans. Richard Rojcewicz (Bloomington and Indianapolis: Indiana University Press, 2016 [2014]), 346. Compare Martin Heidegger, *Ponderings VII–XI: Black Notebooks 1938–1939*, trans. Richard Rojcewicz (Bloomington and Indianapolis: Indiana University Press, 2017 [2014]), 226, which recalled 'the church tower of my Swabian homeland ... the sweeping view – daily – from the tower over broad land and its forests, the day and night tone of every bell – the first great gathering of my small world onto the height and essentiality of something abyssally holding sway', with Martin Heidegger, *Ponderings XII–XV: Black Notebooks 1939–1941*, trans. Richard Rojcewicz (Bloomington and Indianapolis: Indiana University Press, 2017 [2014]), 173, which mentioned 'The "farmer," who once walked the fields, and the worker in the foodstuffs industry, who today is well supplied with radios and movies and has to do with "tractors" and "motorcycles."'

The mutual intolerance of faith and reason that Hegel had diagnosed in Enlightenment thought came to a head in 1934 when 'Black Vienna' confronted its Red opponents in the violent clashes that accompanied the installation of the Dollfuss regime.[126] The modernists were not wrong to see their conservative opponents as continuing to entertain some deeply ingrained medieval prejudices. Anti-Semitism, though certainly also informed by spurious post-Darwinian racism, was an authentic survival of Germanic medieval culture.[127] It might seem unsurprising, therefore, that anti-Semitism should have found a place in the political ideas of a thinker like Heidegger who admired medieval thought in other respects.

In fact, though, Heidegger's anti-Semitism was primarily motivated by his philosophical views. He wrote, for instance, that 'The question of the role of world-Judaism is not a racial question, but a metaphysical one.'[128] Inherited medieval Christian hatreds were not much in evidence in his writings, although in his letters he did occasionally express prejudices of a modern, non-religious, racial kind. Yet these attitudes were not strongly held enough to stop him from engaging with philosophers who were ethnically Jewish, such as his mentor Edmund Husserl or Ernst Cassirer, or for that matter from forming an intimate relationship with his then student Hannah Arendt.[129]

Heidegger did nevertheless actively co-operate in the policy of excluding Jews from academic life once Hitler came to power.[130] His decision to join the National Socialist party and take up the rectorship of Heidelberg University in 1933 has been particularly controversial given his lack of any subsequent expression of contrition. Posthumous publication of the so-called 'Black Notebooks' has demonstrated that for at least a year or so, Heidegger was fully committed to Hitler's government.[131] He seems to have persuaded himself that National Socialism represented a movement for spiritual renewal of German education in the tradition of von

---

[126] See Chapter 4, above, especially n. 105.

[127] See, for example, Henry Abramson, 'A Ready Hatred: Depictions of the Jewish Woman in Medieval Antisemitic Art and Caricature', *Proceedings of the American Academy for Jewish Research*, 62 (1996), 1–18.

[128] Heidegger, *Ponderings XII–XV*, 191.

[129] See Di Cesare, *Heidegger and the Jews*, especially pt 3, 'The Question of Being and the Jewish Question', for a discussion of Heidegger's anti-Semitic prejudices prior to 1933.

[130] See Sherratt, *Hitler's Philosophers*, 118–22, for a review of the way in which Heidegger carried out National Socialist racial policy in 1933–4.

[131] Heidegger, *Ponderings II–VI*, 81, contained possibly his most unequivocal endorsement of Hitler: 'The great experience and fortune that the Führer has awakened a new actuality, giving our thinking the correct course and impetus . . . Literary existence is at an end.'

Humboldt and Nietzsche discussed above. By the time he realised that the 'movement' consisted of thugs and opportunists with no interest in universities other than exploiting them for propaganda purposes, the damage was done. After the war, his reputation was permanently sullied by his association with the regime.

If it is going too far to say that 'the politicization of Heidegger exegesis has reached a point that is unparalleled in the history of ideas', the sentiment is nevertheless understandable.[132] Yet anyone expecting Heidegger's notebooks to be overflowing with the kind of hate-filled moronic tirades against 'dirty Jews' typical of National Socialist propaganda will be disappointed. References to 'Judaism' in fact only entered his private notebooks around the start of the Second World War, long after he had become disillusioned with Hitler's regime. Moreover, the references were generally passing ones, and mentions of specific individuals were even rarer.

Indeed, Heidegger's notebooks show him privately distancing himself from National Socialist ideas on 'race' altogether. 'The instituting of racial breeding stems not from "life" itself, but from the overpowering of life by machination', he wrote.[133] 'Machination' here meant the global dominance of technological rationalism which was, in Heidegger's mind, the inevitable culmination of Western metaphysics; National Socialist eugenics, he had decided, was also part of this complex of ideas. Heidegger's anti-Semitic remarks in the notebooks were likewise not racially based, and to that extent, they actually support his public claim never to have been prejudiced on those grounds, although, as we have seen, his behaviour in the years after 1933 arguably contradicts this.[134]

What characterised the notebooks was rather the identification of Judaism with an 'empty rationality and calculative capacity' that made it, in Heidegger's mind, a major contributor to the 'path of devastation' that he saw 'racing over the planet'.[135] Since Heidegger had also assimilated National Socialism to 'rational socialism' or 'the unconditional calculation and computation of the integration of human domains in themselves and with one another' by the early 1940s, Judaism and National Socialism were part of the same overall cultural phenomenon.[136]

---

[132] Peter Sloterdijk, 'Heidegger's Politics Postponing the End of History', in *What Happened in the 20th Century?*, trans. Christopher Turner (Cambridge: Polity Press, 2018 [2016]), 127.
[133] Heidegger, *Ponderings XII–XV*, 44.
[134] Martin Heidegger, '"Only a God Can Save Us": The *Spiegel* Interview (1966)', in Thomas Sheehan, ed., *Heidegger: The Man and the Thinker* (Chicago: Precedent Publishing, 1981), 45–67, 50.
[135] Heidegger, *Ponderings XII–XV*, 206, 212.
[136] Heidegger, *Ponderings XII–XV*, 206, 153.

According to this twisted reasoning, the Jews themselves could thus be said to have been responsible for helping to create the technological civilisation that was now bringing about their destruction. Perverse though this inference was, Heidegger nevertheless drew it, connecting it with the apocalyptic termination of all Western history thus far.[137] It is this view that explains why Heidegger's critics have reacted to his notebooks with horror. It was, at best, a deeply distorted misapprehension of what was actually going on, even if not driven by a personal or racial animus.

Heidegger's incorporation of Judaism into his overall narrative of modernity was nevertheless consistent with his understanding of what politics had become. It 'no longer has anything to do with the πόλις [polis, "city-state"] nor with morals and least of all with "becoming a people."' Modern politics, Heidegger argued, was 'the only appropriate basic form of the forceful gathering of all means of power and ways of violence'.[138] This was, however, just a mirror image of the critique of capitalist society that members of the Frankfurt School such as Adorno were also developing in the same era. Adorno also viewed the modern West as a product of the dominance of an instrumental rationalism with metaphysical roots lying deep in the history of Western thought.

Where Heidegger and Adorno parted company was over the nature of the solution (though even here, there was a common tendency to resort to art). Heidegger regarded socialism as just another version of the problem. He singled out English political thought and practice in particular as 'the paradigm of the final configuration of the modernity which is now proceeding to its end', speculating that this explained why the English had shown no interest in translating his works.[139] Displaying once more the kind of logic that made the Jews the architects of their own downfall, Heidegger decided England was the progenitor of Bolshevik Russia. 'England produced parliamentary (party) democracy and mechanicism – Russia is only the decisive essential consequence, inasmuch as that country first came to terms with the essence of communism and grasped it as "Soviet power + electrification."'[140]

---

[137] Martin Heidegger, *Gesamtausgabe IV Abteilung: Hinweise Und Aufzeichnungen Band 97 Anmerkungen I-V (Schwarze Hefte 1942–1948)*, ed. Peter Trawny (Frankfurt: Vittorio Klostermann GmbH, 2015), 20, writes that 'The high point of historical self-destruction is reached when the essence of Judaism in the metaphysical sense attacks the Jews.' (My translation.)

[138] Heidegger, *Ponderings XII–XV*, 34.

[139] Heidegger, *Ponderings XII–XV*, 90.

[140] Heidegger, *Ponderings XII–XV*, 136.

Insofar as Heidegger did have a solution for the ills of Western civilisation, he followed Nietzsche in envisioning 'a transformation of the human being'.[141] His language on this subject underlined Hegel's point that the languages of faith and Enlightenment easily overlapped. The aim should be that of 'awakening humans'.[142] The early 1930s, precisely the time when his support for Hitler was at its height, was when Heidegger was most optimistic about the possibility. He saw 'A marvelously awakening communal [völklich] will . . . penetrating the great darkness of the world'.[143] By the end of the 1960s, this hope had been replaced by deep pessimism. Heidegger had become convinced, as he notoriously told Der Spiegel in 1966 in an interview widely regarded as a missed opportunity to express public contrition for his early support for Hitler, that 'Only a God Can Save Us'.[144]

Rather than taking literally either Heidegger's early belief in the possibility of a spiritual transformation or his later pessimism, it is better to treat him, like Christopher Rickey has done, as a modern inheritor of the 'theological-political currents of the radical Reformation'.[145] Heidegger's admiration for Martin Luther is well-attested, but it is important to understand the specific form that it took.[146] Rickey argues that it was because Luther emphasised 'a theology of the cross, that arises out of a fundamental humility before God's mystery' rather than attempting 'to explain God from what is visible to human senses' that Heidegger found him attractive.[147]

What drew Heidegger to Luther, in other words, was the mystical, anti-rationalist nature of his attack on medieval Scholasticism. If we can talk about a Heideggerian political 'project', it was to ensure that 'all thinking first be twisted free of those notions of the human being as animal rationale'.[148] Heidegger identified this project with the unique historical mission of the German people. But he never translated it into institutional or policy terms, and doing so would have involved exactly the kind of rational and instrumental means-ends thinking that he

---

[141] Heidegger, *Ponderings II–VI*, 313.
[142] Heidegger, *Ponderings VII–XI*, 16.
[143] Heidegger, *Ponderings II–VI*, 80.
[144] Heidegger, '"Only a God Can Save Us"'.
[145] Christopher Rickey, *Revolutionary Saints: Heidegger, National Socialism, and Antinomian Politics* (Pennsylvania: University of Pennsylvania Press, 2002), 4.
[146] See Crowe, *Heidegger's Religious Origins*.
[147] Rickey, *Revolutionary Saints*, 22.
[148] Heidegger, *Ponderings II–VI*, 364.

condemned. Like the logical empiricists, Heidegger's political hopes ended in despair and disappointment.

History

Heidegger and the logical empiricists also shared an interest in the historical process while giving little attention to the problem of the nature of historical knowledge. The logical empiricist interest in history was primarily motivated by the prospect of treating the past as a source of data from which laws of social behaviour could be derived.[149] This was one reason Marxism appealed to Neurath: economic history was a guide to a possible future. He was not dogmatic about the path that future history had to take, though, and had a reputation for scepticism about Marxism as a source of 'historical prophecies'.[150] But a corollary of Neurath's position was a conviction that bogus theories of historical development should not be allowed take root in wider society. Hence Neurath's critique of Oswald Spengler's *Decline of the West*, which Neurath dedicated 'to the young and the future they shape'.[151]

The first volume of *Decline of the West* appeared in 1918 and matched the mood of a defeated Germany, but not, perhaps, in the way its title might lead one to expect. Far from wartime defeat being proof of Germany's inexorable decline, Spengler told his readers, it was only a symptom of the birth-pangs of a new era that would require Germany to re-enact the world-historical role of the Roman Empire. Spengler asserted that for every civilisation there was 'a series of stages which must be traversed, and traversed moreover in an ordered and obligatory sequence'.[152] He claimed to have discovered a method of analogical reasoning that allowed him to grasp the 'living forms' and 'organic structure' of history in a manner akin to biology. This 'morphology of world history', as Spengler called it, emphasised that 'destiny' lay in organic nature, not mechanical causality.[153]

This revolutionary method, as Spengler presented it, had revealed to him that the modern world was a repetition of the transition from 'the Hellenistic to the Roman age', and Rome, which generated an imperial culture, was most akin to 'Protestant, Prussian' culture. The 'Decline of

---

[149] Putnam, *Reason, Truth and History*, 187, wrote that 'Since [the logical empiricists] did not wish to deny that there is such a thing as historical knowledge ... they were committed to the position that history is a science, and even to the position that what the historian is really trying to do is to subsume individual statements about the past under laws.'
[150] Neurath, 'Memories', in *Empiricism and Sociology*, 3, 54.
[151] Neurath, 'Anti-Spengler'.
[152] Spengler, *Decline of the West*, 1.
[153] Spengler, *Decline of the West*, 42.

the West', then, meant Germany was fated to carry out a final, imperial, phase of Western civilisation. Spengler declared that 'I see in Cecil Rhodes the first man of a new age. He stands for the political style of a far-ranging, Western, Teutonic and especially German future.' Democracy, on the other hand, was simply a cover for capitalist interests that would naturally lead to this future Caesarism. Anti-democrats of all kinds thus found *The Decline of the West* tremendously appealing. The Nietzsche Archives Foundation, run by Elizabeth Förster-Nietzsche, awarded Spengler a cash prize in 1919.[154]

Spengler appealed especially to those Germans who before the war had regarded the Germanic world as the standard-bearer of Western civilisation. This belief in Germanophone cultural superiority was not without justification. There was probably no more creative city anywhere in the world in 1914 than Vienna. Of course, subsequent events essentially inverted Spengler's predictions. Far from the Germanic world recovering its position of cultural and intellectual leadership, Hitler oversaw its destruction, either by killing its artists, scientists and philosophers or by driving them into exile. More generally, Spengler's claim that this new Roman phase would last 'for hundreds or thousands of years' turned out to be almost exactly wrong. Within half a century of the publication of *The Decline of the West*, the dismantling of all the Western empires was far advanced.

In 1918, however, Spengler's book dangled the vision of a glorious revival of Germany's imperial role in the world in front of an eager audience. Hence the importance that Neurath saw, in the aftermath of the collapse of the attempt to establish Communism in Bavaria, of refuting Spengler. Spengler had presented himself as a philosophical opponent, appropriating Kant's rhetoric of the 'Copernican turn' for his theory of the historical process, and even echoing Dilthey's criticism of Kant's failure to develop a set of categories for historical understanding.[155]

---

[154] Oswald Spengler, *Spengler Letters 1913–36*, ed. and trans. Arthur Phelps, intro. A. M. Koktenek (London: George Allen & Unwin, 1966 [1963]), 87. Although Hitler and his supporters courted Spengler for over a decade, beginning in the early 1920s, he was not swayed. Though not an aristocrat himself, Spengler shared the reaction of those German aristocrats who found Hitler lacking in both refinement and intellect. He apparently called the National Socialist party 'the organisation of the unemployed by the work-shy': see Koktenek, 'Introduction' to Spengler, *Letters*, 18.

[155] Spengler, *Decline of the West*, 23, wrote that 'Knowledge, for Kant, is mathematical knowledge. He deals with innate intuition forms and categories of the reason, but he never thinks of the wholly different mechanism by which historical impressions are apprehended.' Compare Dilthey, *Descriptive Psychology and Historical Understanding*, 33, who wrote that 'The formal categories are abstracted from these primary logical functions [of association]' and argues that 'Kant therefore had no need of deducing . . . categories of discursive thinking' of the sort required for historical understanding.

Although Spengler possessed enormous historical erudition, he was no match for Neurath as a thinker. Neurath repeatedly exposed the fact that Spengler's supposedly objective analogical method suffered from the logical flaws of arbitrariness and circularity. Neurath also singled out the problem of historical truth. Spengler had explicitly declared himself a relativist with respect to standards of truth between cultures, but while Neurath was willing to admit, faced with Dilthey's use of the concept, that the concept of a world-view was not meaningless, any defensible version of the idea also had to account for universality. 'The facts that the seasons follow each other, that fire burns and wine makes you drunk, are common to all world-views.'[156] There were some things that were true for everyone, and Spengler's theory had no way of explaining how this could be the case if every civilisation remained sealed within its own unique path of (racial) development.

Neurath was forced to admit nonetheless that Spengler had highlighted an important 'question of principle'. This was that 'we cannot start from a *tabula rasa* as Descartes thought we could' but rather that 'We have to make do with words and concepts that we find when our reflections begin.'[157] Neurath thus recognised that there was a legitimate hermeneutic question about how to allow for self-conscious agents in historical explanation. His own preference was to eliminate 'free will' as a 'pseud-problem'. But Neurath's claim that 'The man who is moved by the earth (gravitational field), by a blow or by a shout, is a physical structure moved in a physical process' indicates the problem he was facing. He could only achieve a reduction to materialism by eliding causation and intelligent action.[158] No one can literally be moved by a shout in the same way as by a blow. A kinetic impact may move the body, but explaining a movement in response to a shout requires reference to agency and meaning and subjectivity, which are not causes of the same kind. But to acknowledge this explicitly would have meant abandoning the project of a unified science.

Neurath nevertheless seems to have admitted the need for such a distinction, at least implicitly, when he wrote that although customs were 'biological facts . . . If we wish to predict what peoples, states or organizations will do we cannot go back to the ultimate physical elements.'[159]

---

[156] Neurath, 'Anti-Spengler', 198, associates 'the field of world-views' with the idea that 'When we progress in our thinking, making new concepts and connections our own, the entire structure of concepts is shifted in its relations and in its centre of gravity, and each concept takes a smaller or greater part in this change.'
[157] Neurath, 'Anti-Spengler', 198. For Neurath on Descartes compare n. 12, above.
[158] Neurath, 'Empirical Sociology', 362.
[159] Neurath, 'Empirical Sociology', 392, 404.

When Neurath criticised Max Weber for treating 'Protestantism like a reality which acts on men', however, he identified a genuine difficulty.[160] Attributing causal power to abstract entities like a religious doctrine can at best only be a shorthand expression for the way in which specific individuals were writing, speaking and acting. Yet Neurath also recognised that the argument that predictions were 'the typical task of historical research' ran up against the fact that historians were 'more interested in the surroundings, the mass' from which their subjects had emerged.[161] The practice of historiography told against the view that the historical study of the past was really about the kind of planning for the future that mostly interested Neurath.

Heidegger's interest in history was likewise explicitly futural, with far more attention being given to the historical process and its likely course of development than to the nature of history as a form of thought. As we observed, Heidegger's narrative of the end of metaphysics embraced the whole of Western history from ancient Greece to the present. But it was crucially directed to what would come next. As he put it a notebook in the early 1930s, 'Thoughtful meditation on the truth of beyng is *primarily* the grounding of *Da-sein* qua the ground of future history.'[162] The whole point of studying history was to understand what the future would hold. The 'Historical truth of historical meditation does not mean that the past is correctly presented as it is in itself, but that the future comes to light in what has been.'[163]

Moreover, just as Neurath was forced to admit a distinction between a sociology oriented towards the future and a history directed towards the past, Heidegger felt the need to distinguish between 'historiology', which referred to history in the academic sense, and his own approach. 'My "historiological" lecture courses and "interpretations,"' he observed, 'are all historical meditations, not historiological considerations of the past', and the point of a 'Historical meditation' in Heidegger's sense was that it 'lets the happening be experienced authentically – i.e., in its *inceptual futurity*'. In other words, Heidegger was self-consciously reading history backwards. It did not matter to him that 'such meditation is always historiologically false'.[164] He was quite happy to accept that his interpretation of Kant, for example, was an 'overinterpretation' from a historical point of view.[165]

---

[160] Neurath, 'Empirical Sociology', 356.
[161] Neurath, 'Empirical Sociology', 408.
[162] Heidegger, *Ponderings II–VI*, 242. Emphasis in original.
[163] Heidegger, *Ponderings II–VI*, 261.
[164] Heidegger, *Ponderings II–VI*, 261.
[165] Heidegger, *Ponderings XII–XV*, 166.

Heidegger's attack on 'historiology' recalled Nietzsche's critique of the enervating effects of historical antiquarianism discussed in Chapter 5. 'Through historiology we have become weak, uncreative, and useless', Heidegger complained.[166] As the 1930s drew to a close, Heidegger's hostility to the idea of history as a science increased markedly, though how accurately his conception matched the reality of the discipline as it existed at that time is questionable. By 'historiology' he sometimes seems to have meant a specifically a 'progressive' interpretation of history which he understood as a secularised form of Christian justification of the present. But it was at just this time that the association of historiography with the legitimation of progressive ideology had begun to be challenged.[167] Heidegger nevertheless condemned historiology as contributing to the development of calculative rationality.

This is why Heidegger declared, for instance, that '"Historicism" becomes the basic form of the unfolding of "nihilism"; for the latter attains its irresistible force only when what was formerly great and essential starts to be flattened down to the level of the masses.'[168] This was another aspect of 'historiology': although it presented itself as progressive, it was symptomatic of the broader cultural collapse Heidegger diagnosed in modernity. Thus he could write that *'technology is the historiology of nature'*.[169] Heidegger and the logical empiricists both assimilated history as a discipline to scientific knowledge, albeit for different reasons. In Heidegger's view, the connection went all the way back to ancient Greece, when 'the ancients distinguished "historiology" not in opposition to the natural sciences (roughly the ἐπιστήμη φυσική) but in opposition to μῦθος ["myth"]'.[170]

'Historiology' in Heidegger's sense of the term can be thought of as academic history made subservient to the pursuit of a cultural agenda in which the representational, instrumental, attitude to the world had prevailed. Here again there was a parallel with Neurath's critique of the idea of history as a science of the mental. The historiological attitude presupposed the idea of the knowing subject that Heidegger believed was characteristic of Cartesianism. 'The historiological animal' could

---

[166] Heidegger, *Ponderings II–VI*, 196.
[167] Herbert Butterfield, *The Whig Interpretation of History* (New York: W. W. Norton & Co., 1965 [1931]), v, wrote that historiography must be aware of the tendency 'to produce a story which is the ratification if not the glorification of the present'.
[168] Heidegger, *Ponderings VII–XI*, 80.
[169] Heidegger, *Ponderings VII–XI*, 90. Emphasis in original.
[170] Heidegger, *Ponderings VII–XI*, 128. Compare *Ponderings VII–XI*, 162: 'Technology and historiology are the same (the metaphysical ground lies in the interpretation of ὄν as νοούμενον ["being as something thought"].'

be understood as 'consummating Descartes's *ego cogito – ergo sum* ["I am thinking – therefore I am"])'.[171] This metaphysical dualism entailed a conception of the subject as defined by the will to exploit the world.

Heidegger read Nietzsche's idea of the will to power accordingly, as the culmination of the Western metaphysical tradition in which even Nietzsche was still deeply implicated despite his diagnosis of the issue. The idea of life as will to power brought out what had been latent in metaphysics at least since Plato first articulated the theory of Forms, or as Heidegger put it, 'since beingness was sealed as representedness (ἰδέα)'.[172] The will to power was the most extreme version of the instrumental attitude towards the world. It extended the attitude that for Descartes was characteristic of the knowing subject to the whole of life. Heidegger's questioning of the history of Being was intended, just like Neurath's Marxist theory of history, to eliminate the dualistic idea of a subject confronted with a world which was understood only as there to be exploited.

Heidegger's rejection of 'historiological categories' was consistent with his rejection of a categorial approach to thinking in general that we noted took place after *Being and Time*.[173] His 'futural philosophy' as he called it, was an attempt to avoid 'the mode of a "systematic" computation of the categories of beingness in a summary representation)'.[174] Just as, in defending the idea of a unified science, Neurath had described Heidegger's metaphysics as senseless, for Heidegger anything but the radical questioning of the truth of Being was simply a 'perversion'.[175]

Other forms of knowledge, including history, were simply to be dismissed; Heidegger's view was the essential view. 'The basic error excluding all modern and contemporary views from history and from a knowledge of history is the view that the happening of history is "development." Precisely what is *never* there in all essential history is development.'[176] Heidegger was, in other words, dealing with what was timeless and universal in history. But as Richard Wolin remarks, 'the inflexible elevation of ontology above the ontic plane virtually closes off the conceptual space wherein real history might be thought'.[177]

---

[171] Heidegger, *Ponderings VII–XI*, 222.
[172] Heidegger, *Ponderings VII–XI*, 329.
[173] Heidegger, *Ponderings VII–XI*, 241, wrote that 'The attempt to distinguish between "categories" and "existentialia" in *Being and Time* does not go far enough.'
[174] Heidegger, *Ponderings XII–XV*, 112.
[175] Heidegger, *Ponderings XII–XV*, 122.
[176] Heidegger, *Ponderings II–VI*, 351. Emphasis in original.
[177] Wolin, *Politics of Being*, 164.

Incidentally, it was probably on these grounds that Heidegger, like Neurath, was 'anti-Spengler', though again for very different reasons. This may seem surprising insofar as Spengler, like Heidegger, was a critic of modernity who tended to favour the traditional, aristocratic, rural order. But Heidegger saw Spengler as, at best, a pale imitation of Nietzsche.[178] The problem with Spengler was that he was another instance of the historiological approach. Heidegger presumably had in mind Spengler's claim to have reduced the interpretation of history to a pseudo-scientific knowledge of the laws governing an iterative process of growth and decline using the biological approach discussed above. This was the kind of 'developmental' theory that Heidegger wanted to criticise.

The truly historical thinker, Heidegger argued, 'seeks . . . the origins of what is necessary' and must have 'A genuine knowledge of the essence' of history in order to bring about the radical transformation of Western culture.[179] But as we have seen, this conception of history was not that of the historian. Heidegger conceived of his 'essential' history as part of his philosophical break with the emphasis on the universal and the necessary aspects of thinking that he argued had dominated the history of Western philosophy.

Heidegger's reading of this history has proved so attractive at least partly because it has some foundation in the facts.[180] We have seen that the theories of Platonic Forms, Aristotelian substances, Kantian categories and Hegelian Spirit all really did involve universalistic claims with wide-ranging implications. But Heidegger's reading of the history

---

[178] Heidegger, *Ponderings VII–XI*, 106, 108.

[179] Heidegger, *Ponderings VII–XI*, 38, 71.

[180] Charles H. Kahn, *The Verb 'Be' In Ancient Greek With A New Introductory Essay* (Indianapolis: Hackett Publishing, 2003 [1973]), 4, argues that 'insofar as the notions expressed by ὄν, εἶναι, and οὐσία in Greek underlie the doctrines of Being, substance, essence, and existence in Latin, in Arabic, and in modern philosophy from Descartes to Heidegger and perhaps to Quine . . . the usage of the Greek verb *be* . . . forms the historical basis for the ontological tradition of the West, as the very term "ontology" suggests'. Kahn goes so far as to say (372) that 'it was not an error [by the Greek philosophers] to suppose that predication, truth, and existence (or reality) belong together in a single family of concepts, the topic for a single body of theory . . . To this extent we justify the tacit assumption of the Greek philosophers (and of many of their successors, from Islamic and medieval times to Hegel and Heidegger) that the key functions of the verb to be represent a unified conceptual system of great importance.' But Kahn, *The Verb 'Be'*, 365, insists that accepting these general arguments does not require accepting Heidegger's specific interpretations. Heidegger's etymology for *aletheia*, for example, is fanciful: 'even in the earliest use, in Homer, there is no trace of "the things themselves" emerging from their hiddenness or showing themselves'.

of Western thought involved the additional argument that this focus on universality had systematically concealed access to the more essential reality he termed Being. It is this argument that has failed to gain acceptance outside of Heideggerian circles.

The tendency to marginalise historical knowledge visible in both Heidegger and logical empiricism continued to be characteristic of analytical philosophy after 1945. This does not mean history was completely ignored, only that it was typically pushed to the sidelines. This was a matter of degree, admittedly. Richard Rorty, one of the later twentieth-century analytical philosophers most sensitive to questions of historicity and the importance of historiography, remarked that Quine believed 'the *Geisteswissenschaften* . . . employ notions which are so unclear that we must simply rub them out when limning the structure of reality'.[181] But Rorty's criticism here was inaccurate. In fact, when Quine distinguished 'aesthetic' and 'alethic' poles in the intellectual sphere, he explicitly included history as one bound of the alethic field, with mathematics delimiting the other.[182]

Though Quine distinguished between 'hard' and 'soft' sciences it thus seems indisputable that he considered history a genuine *Wissenschaft*, to use Rorty's term, capable of truth. But it is still fair to say that Quine never reflected in detail on historical knowledge, and what he did say was problematic. For example, he argued that 'Hypotheses about history, even of the remote past, are part and parcel of science in the inclusive sense, and the arbiter is still prediction', and it is true that historical reasoning consists of chains of inferences such that if something is known to have occurred, then something else must also have occurred beforehand.

So Quine was quite correct that, for example, 'a hypothesis about ancient history implies the findings of some future excavation'. Historical hypotheses involving these sorts of retrospective predictions, or retrodictions as they are sometimes called, are routinely validated in just this way. But Quine also wanted to claim that 'prediction is always the bottom line'.[183] Yet historical understanding cannot be analysed into retrodiction unless the arguments constituting historical narratives are reducible to the material traces from which they are inferred, and this is not obviously the case.

It is also not clear why Quine thought 'Conjectures of history and economics will be revised more willingly than laws of physics, and these more

---

[181] Richard Rorty, *Philosophy and the Mirror of Nature*, 200.
[182] Quine, *Quiddities*, 17. On *aletheia* see nn. 53 and 180, above.
[183] Quine, *Quiddities*, 162.

willingly than laws of mathematics and logic.' It is possible to agree that 'The priority on law', as Quine noted, 'admits of many gradations'. But the historical proposition that, for instance, Hitler's anti-Semitic views were one of the causes of war in 1939 seems as unlikely to be revised as any physical law one could name. Simply because historical propositions do not take a law-like form of the kind found in the natural sciences does not give them a more mutable status.[184]

Some of Quine's remarks on history simply seem inadvertent. His claim that 'Our conceptual firsts are middle-sized, middle-distanced objects, and our introduction to them and to everything comes midway in the cultural evolution of the race' entirely begged the question of how he knew where we were in the cultural evolution of the race.[185] It suggests that Quine's thinking was informed by an implicitly progressive view of the historical process which went undetected.

Overall, although later twentieth-century analytical philosophers generally acknowledged that the elimination of a noumenal or mental order of reality did not mean that we could eliminate 'mentalistic predicates', the implications of this admission for historical understanding (and reflection on historical thinking more generally) were passed over. Yet such predicates were, as Quine and others confessed, both practically and theoretically indispensable.[186] A great deal of attention was given to mentalistic predicates; problems of intentionality, of consciousness, and so on, formed mainstream topics. 'Philosophy of mind' flourished even in mind's absence, as it were. But philosophical analysis of the genre of thinking exclusively devoted to the study of mind at work in the past was generally neglected.

Quine could not help associating 'mentalism' in the last resort with 'a preference for final cause over efficient cause as a mode of explanation' of the sort that had been 'evident in the Middle Ages'.[187] In Quine's reading of the history of science, 'with the rise of physics in the Renaissance . . . matter gained the upper hand over mind. Mind was selflessly doing itself in.' It is unsurprising, given this attitude, that history, which begins from the material remnants of the past activity of human minds, was of no interest.

---

[184] Quine, *Methods of Logic*, xiii.
[185] Quine, *Word and Object*, 4.
[186] Quine, *The Pursuit of Truth*, 72–3, wrote that 'the mentalistic predicates . . . complement natural science in their incommensurable way, and are indispensable both to the social sciences and to our everyday dealings'. Compare Daniel C. Dennett, *The Intentional Stance* (Cambridge, MA: MIT Press, 1988 [1987]), 1: 'It is not just the arts and humanities that need to talk about the mind; the various puritanical attempts to complete the biological and social sciences without ever talking about it have by now amply revealed their futility.'
[187] Quine, *Pursuit of Truth*, 75.

Conclusion

This chapter has argued that there were significant affinities between logical empiricism and existential phenomenology despite their major differences in style and content. Both were attempts to reject the post-Hegelian, neo-Kantian emphasis on categories more or less altogether, yet both remained deeply entangled with it. But this is not the only reason that they should be placed together as representing a single major strand of post-Hegelian thought. Both also set great store by prioritising a single approach to knowledge above all others. In the logical empiricist case this was a conception of science modelled on the natural sciences; for Heidegger it was the philosophical investigation of Being.

This commitment to elevating one perspective above all others by either assimilating everything else to it or marginalising other perspectives also had political implications. For the earlier logical empiricists, it tended to manifest as a commitment to socialist central planning that disregarded the views of more conservative elements of society. Later, as in the case of Quine, it took the form of an intellectually intolerant variety of liberalism, dismissive of religious or philosophical views that did not conform to its own standards. Heidegger in contrast was lead by his quasi-mystical search for the meaning of Being and an insupportable philosophical variety of anti-Semitism into a disastrous misjudgement about the nature of National Socialism. He ended by adopting a pessimism so profound that it amounted to a total rejection of actually existing politics and society.

Finally, logical empiricism and existential phenomenology both tended to marginalise historical knowledge. History, for the logical empiricists, could only be considered as a science if its logic were assimilated to that of the natural and social sciences, which were defined fundamentally by their capacity to predict events. Likewise, for Heidegger, the history that counted was the philosophical history of the future, not historiography as written by historians.

Despite their efforts to reject conventional modes of thought in radical and even revolutionary ways, in this respect both logical empiricism and existential phenomenology were entirely conventional and continuous with very well-established patterns of ideas. What remains is an examination of the third and final thread of the reaction to the post-Hegelian environment, which took the form of an attempt to modify the neo-Kantian position rather than to reject it altogether. This will be the theme of our final chapter.

7
Pluralists: The Search for Categorial Limits

Introduction

The previous two chapters were concerned with the two most common post-Hegelian responses to the question of categories: either emphasising the lack of any unifying categorial scheme whatever, or rejecting categorial mediation in favour of a single dominant form of knowledge on which all others rested, be that natural science or the ineffable ground of Being. Yet there was another, less common, position that we shall call categorial pluralism.[1] This pluralism conceded some of the points made by the other two positions, while not accepting the consequences they drew from them. Nonetheless, the habit of association between categories, knowledge, and politics remained intact in pluralism, not least because of the way it engaged both the other positions.

So, for example, pluralism granted to the fragmentarians that there was no single categorial scheme applicable to all thought and experience across all contexts. Unlike the fragmentarians, though, this did not lead to giving up on the effort to delineate the various kinds of categorial schemes. For the pluralists, these remained identifiably limited in number. Likewise, the pluralists conceded to subordinationism that science was important, as the logical empiricists maintained, and that it was not all-important, as Heidegger insisted. But this did not mean rejecting categorial mediation altogether in considering knowledge, as subordinationism wanted. On the contrary, for pluralism, it was indispensable.

---

[1] 'Pluralism', unlike 'subordinationism' or 'fragmentarianism', is not a neologism, but is appropriately polysemous. For example, *The Stanford Encyclopedia of Philosophy* has a plurality of entries for 'logical pluralism', 'scientific pluralism' and 'value pluralism' (which may encompass both moral and political values). Here it is used as a collective term for thinkers who both deny that there is one standpoint to which all others are subordinate, on the one hand, and that the variety of standpoints is irretrievably fragmented, on the other, proposing instead a determinate arrangement of categories.

In a political context, pluralism typically interpreted mediation as moderation. Pluralists were generally less radical than either fragmentarians or subordinationists. They tended to endorse the state and the rule of law in a broadly liberal manner, with room for variation across the political spectrum depending on the individual.[2] Pluralism was also unusual in being the only position to consistently stress the importance of philosophical attention to the logic of historical analysis. The pluralists shared the fragmentarian indebtedness to Hegelian historicist thought, but also argued that the relative neglect of historical knowledge constituted a lacuna in Kant's critical philosophy that needed to be filled.[3]

Although this pluralist outlook constituted a minority report, it still had prominent representatives in Germany, Britain and France. We will concentrate on Ernst Cassirer, who composed a philosophy of 'symbolic forms'; R. G. Collingwood, who emphasised the importance of presuppositions for all types of knowledge; and Paul Ricoeur, who belonged to the next generation, but shared their interest in the problems involved in interpreting human action.[4] All three owed something to Kant and Hegel. Cassirer endorsed a 'general system' of philosophical Idealism, while emphasising that the concept of the symbol always involved concrete, material expression.[5] Collingwood, in contrast, developed his own position in response to realism at Oxford, another early variant of analytical philosophy, and denied that he was an Idealist; yet he drew on Kant for his account of history.[6] Ricoeur's point of departure in Husserl's

---

[2] For example, Paul Ricoeur, *History and Truth*, trans. Charles A. Kelbley (Evanston, IL: Northwestern University Press, 2007 [1955]), 10, wrote that 'in the phenomenon of authority we find an authentic function of ordering and unification'.

[3] Paul Ricoeur, *Hermeneutics and the Human Sciences: Essays on Language, Action and Interpretation*, ed. and trans. John B. Thompson (Cambridge: Cambridge University Press, 2016 [1981]), 6, wrote that hermeneutics was a 'response to the great lacuna of Kantianism . . . clearly recognised by Cassirer: that in a critical philosophy, there is no link between physics and ethics'.

[4] See Ernst Cassirer, *The Philosophy of Symbolic Forms*, trans. Ralph Manheim, intro. Charles W. Hendel, 3 vols (New Haven and London: Yale University Press, 1980 [1955–7]); R. G. Collingwood, *An Autobiography*, intro. Stephen Toulmin (Oxford: Clarendon Press, 2002 [1939]), especially ch. 5, 'Question and Answer'; Paul Ricoeur, *Time and Narrative*, 3 vols, trans. Kathleen Blamey (née McLaughlin) and David Pellauer (Chicago and London: University of Chicago Press, 1984–8 [1983–5]).

[5] Cassirer, *Symbolic Forms*, i.72.

[6] R. G. Collingwood, *An Essay on Philosophical Method: Revised Edition, with The Metaphysics of F. H. Bradley, The Correspondence with Gilbert Ryle, Method and Metaphysics*, ed. and intro. James Connelly and Guiseppina D'Oro (Oxford: Clarendon Press, 2005 [1933]), 256, wrote in a letter to Gilbert Ryle 'why presume me an Idealist? I have nowhere . . . so described myself . . . I resent . . . the label'.

phenomenology also connected him to Idealism.[7] What these three thinkers shared was not a consistent metaphysical position so much as a wish to find a middle ground between fragmentation and subordination.

Cassirer's starting point resembled that of the logical empiricists, who we saw in Chapter 6 had already been driven towards an account of scientific knowledge as relative to a framework. Cassirer embraced this contextualist view, and generalised it, making all systems of categories into a dynamic developmental series of 'symbolic forms'. These forms, which were always conditional upon language, began with mythical thinking and ended with modern science and rationality. This development had both political and historical corollaries. The modern state had to recognise that a tendency to mythical and magical thinking was a permanent feature of the human mind, while fostering institutions to prevent it from becoming destructive.[8] The form of analysis most appropriate to the problem of political life conceived in these terms was historical.[9]

Both Cassirer and Collingwood were partly inspired to formulate their views by the scientific and mathematical problems thrown up by the advent of modern physics. We saw in Chapter 6 that although Thomas Kuhn's *Structure of Scientific Revolutions* brought the issue to widespread attention in the 1960s, many thinkers in the previous generation, including the logical empiricists, were already convinced that the recognition of the historicity of science had set a new agenda for philosophy.[10]

In Cassirer's view, this agenda included the examination of the historicity of knowledge in general, and of historical knowledge in particular. Cassirer's symbolic forms, like Collingwood's forms of experience, were distinguished by their assumptions or presuppositions, or, in other words,

---

[7] Paul Ricoeur, *Husserl's Ideas I*, ed. and intro. Pol. Vandevelde, trans. Bond Harris and Jacqueline Bouchard Spurlock (Milwaukee: Marquette University Press, 1996 [1950]), 47, wrote that 'The phenomenology which is elaborated in the *Ideas* is incontestably an idealism and even a transcendental idealism.'

[8] Ernst Cassirer, *The Myth of the State* (New Haven: Yale University Press; London: Oxford University Press, 1946), 307, argued that 'Our science, our poetry, our art, and our religion are only the upper layer of a much older stratum that reaches down to a great depth.'

[9] Ernst Cassirer, *An Essay on Man: An Introduction to a Philosophy of Human Culture* (New York: Doubleday & Co., 1953 [1944]), 221, wrote that 'what [the historian] finds at the very beginning of his research is not a world of physical objects but a symbolic universe – a world of symbols'.

[10] Hans-Jörg Rheinberger, *On Historicizing Epistemology: An Essay* (Stanford, CA: Stanford University Press, 2010), 65, writes that 'A tradition of historical epistemology was already established in France in the 1930s.'

by their categories. For both thinkers, these presuppositions were themselves subject to change. The history of thought thus had to allow for the complete transformation of forms of knowledge, or indeed the emergence of entirely new ones. In Ricoeur's terms, the problem of the historicity of knowledge was analogous to the repeated generation of new kinds of texts.[11]

In politics, both Cassirer and Collingwood held that in practice the pursuit of knowledge made a liberal form of government a necessity. Cassirer's *Myth of the State* and Collingwood's *New Leviathan* were both written directly in opposition to mid-twentieth century totalitarianism.[12] Ricoeur, who lived to see out the twentieth century, agreed. His view of the good society remained consistent with their earlier anti-totalitarian concerns, and likewise prioritised individual liberty. Ricoeur followed them in emphasising the need for a liberal legal order within which intellectual life and the arts could flourish.

In *Time and Narrative* and *The Rule of Metaphor*, Ricoeur was centrally concerned with Aristotelian and Kantian categories.[13] Following Husserl's later writings, Ricoeur insisted on including the humanities alongside the natural sciences and mathematics as authentically scientific.[14] Finally, perhaps to a greater extent than either Cassirer or Collingwood, Ricoeur extended the problem of historical knowledge to ethics, theology, and the social responsibility of historiography.

Categories

Cassirer was convinced of the importance of categories, understood as 'general concepts' or 'universals', for the normal functioning of the healthy individual. By the mid-twentieth century it was well known that brain injuries could affect the capacity for abstract thought.[15] Cassirer

---

[11] Ricoeur, *Hermeneutics and the Human Sciences*, 3, defined hermeneutics as 'the theory of the operations of understanding in their relation to the interpretation of texts'.

[12] R. G. Collingwood, *The New Leviathan, or Man, Society, Civilization and Barbarism* (Oxford: Clarendon Press, 1947 [1942]), iii, wrote that his aim was 'to study the new absolutism'.

[13] Paul Ricoeur, *The Rule of Metaphor The Creation of Meaning in Language*, trans. Robert Czerny with Kathleen McLaughlin and John Costello, SJ (London: Routledge, 2003 [1975]).

[14] Edmund Husserl, *The Crisis of the European Sciences and Transcendental Phenomenology: An Introduction to Phenomenological Philosophy*, trans. and intro. David Carr (Evanston, IL: Northwestern University Press, 1978 [1954]), 4, wrote that 'The scientific rigor of all [the concrete humanistic sciences], the convincingness of their theoretical accomplishments, and their enduringly compelling successes are unquestionable.'

[15] Cassirer, *Symbolic Forms*, i.62

used physiological evidence to argue that from a philosophical standpoint, such trauma constituted a reduction in categorial capability. Severe damage to the brain, Cassirer argued, could result in an inability to access the abstract world of symbolic forms, thus precluding any understanding of science, for example. *A priori* categories were integral to these symbolic forms, each of which was a 'specific image-world'.[16] By talking in terms of images, Cassirer did not mean that the symbolic was synonymous with either the visual or the irrational. He was emphasising the connection between thought and language. Linguistic symbolisation made possible the abstractions on which more complex forms of rationality depended.

As Cassirer read Aristotle, the 'categories represent the most universal relations of being, and at the same time the highest classifications of *statement* (γένε or σχήματα της κατηγορίας)'.[17] Cassirer noted the tendency of early modern thinkers to criticise Aristotle for being concerned with words rather than things, a debate we discussed in Chapter 2. Cassirer shared the view that although Aristotle's categorial distinctions had a Greek inflection, this did not justify accepting a strong version of linguistic relativism. Instead, Cassirer defended the view that Aristotle's position implied a 'reciprocal determination of the sensuous by the spiritual and the spiritual by the sensuous'.[18] This was likewise Cassirer's argument. It was a mistake to ask whether words and ideas, on the one hand, or the world, on the other, were prior.

This idea of the reciprocal determination of subject and object (which we saw that Hegel also defended) lead Cassirer to argue that no category could be understood in isolation. Kant had been correct in thinking that the use of any one category implied a schema or synthesis of categories. Where Kant had gone wrong was in arguing that there were only two such schemata, the categories of the understanding and of practical reason, and that they had a permanently fixed structure. Cassirer speculated that in language, the starting point for his own philosophy of symbolic forms, there were three major stages of development.

In its origins, Cassirer hypothesised, human speech had been mimetic, with only a latent distinction between self and world. This claim was presented as an extension of Charles Darwin's theory of the evolutionary basis of the expression of emotion.[19] Yet this first mimetic phase already

---

[16] Cassirer, *Symbolic Forms*, i.113. Samantha Matherne, *Cassirer* (Abingdon and New York: Routledge, 2021), 129, writes that 'in addition to "number", "time", and "space", Cassirer identifies "thing", "property", and "cause" as "basic relations", which condition and remain invariant across all activity of spiritual formation'.

[17] Cassirer, *Symbolic Forms*, i.126. Emphasis in original.

[18] Cassirer, *Symbolic Forms*, i.318.

[19] Cassirer, *Symbolic Forms*, i.180.

contained a latent potential for rationality that achieved partial realisation in the next, analogical, phase. 'Even the uncivilized man . . . has to develop and to use some general forms or categories of thought.'[20]

General or universal categories had only achieved their full development in modern symbolic thought, however. For Cassirer, an increase in symbolic capacity was a movement towards, rather than away from, rationality. The extension of symbols from natural to formal languages, like those of physics and mathematics, constituted tremendous increases in the power of conceptual abstraction. As Cassirer understood the history of modern science, this was the view of mathematicians and physicists themselves; Heinrich Hertz was an exemplary case of this recognition.[21] Here Cassirer approached the position of logical empiricism. The differences were that Cassirer did not dismiss the value of non-scientific categorial schemes, and that he saw the earlier symbolic forms, including our ordinary consciousness, as still having a role to play in social life. Supersession was not abolition.

Collingwood placed less importance on language than Cassirer, but still associated the problem of distinguishing categorial structures with that of differentiating discourses. *An Essay on Philosophical Method* argued that the principle that classes do not overlap, which Collingwood regarded as generally accepted in logic and the exact sciences, was sound for those fields, but did not hold good either in philosophy or for common sense.[22] This, Collingwood argued, was due to the nature of the objects concerned. He gave the example of mathematics, in which a line could be either straight or curved, but 'no line can be both, and there is no third species'.[23]

In philosophy, however, the classes of a genus typically overlapped. Here Collingwood referred to Aristotle's example in the *Nicomachean Ethics* that 'the term "good" is used both in the category of substance and in that of quality and in that of relation'.[24] In Collingwood's interpretation, Aristotle had 'showed that the concept of good overlaps or transcends or diffuses

---

[20] Cassirer, *Myth of the State*, 14.
[21] Cassirer, *Symbolic Forms*, i.75. Compare Heinrich Hertz, *The Principles of Mechanics Presented in a New Form*, intro. H. von Helmholtz, trans. D. E. Jones and J. T. Walley (London and New York: Macmillan and Co., 1899), 1: 'We form for ourselves images or symbols of external objects . . . we can then in a short time develop by means of them, as by means of models, the consequences which in the external world only arise in a comparatively long time, or as the result of our own interposition.'
[22] Collingwood, *Essay on Philosophical Method*, 28.
[23] Collingwood, *Essay on Philosophical Method*, 29.
[24] See Aristotle, *Nicomachean Ethics*, trans. Roger Crisp (Cambridge: Cambridge University Press, 2004 [2000]), bk 1, ch. 6, 1096a, which discussed the various usages of 'good' and declared that 'good is spoken of in as many senses as is being'.

itself across the divisions of the categories'.²⁵ But what was true of 'good' was true of all concepts in philosophy. One and the same action could thus fall under more than one classification at once without invalidating either. We may distinguish acts done from duty and from inclination, but the same act could find a place under both headings without contradiction.

A corollary of Collingwood's argument about overlapping classification was that philosophical concepts possessed a distinct logical structure that could not be assimilated or reduced to the kind of thinking involved in the natural sciences. He agreed with Cassirer that there could not be a single system of categories, or a master system, whether this was identified with science or with some other kind of knowledge. In Collingwood's first major philosophical work, *Speculum Mentis*, the task of creating a 'mirror of the mind' explicitly required recognising such differences: 'the attempt to fit [beauty] into a table of concepts or categories drawn up from the point of view of logical science would be . . . contradictory'.²⁶ The beautiful belonged to the entirely distinctive standpoint of aesthetic experience.

This had been Kant's view, and Collingwood agreed with Cassirer in treating it as broadly sound. The Kantian 'account of understanding' was the 'true' one, at least insofar as it conceived of thought as 'spontaneously originating concepts or categories out of itself with no assistance from the world of fact'.²⁷ But Collingwood, like Cassirer, did not follow Kant in devising a fixed pair of categorial schemes pertaining to freedom and to the understanding. The spontaneity of thought gave it a dynamic quality that always left open the possibility of its 'shifting . . . manifestations' being 'rearranged, subdivided and grouped in [other] ways'.²⁸ As Collingwood later stressed in the *New Leviathan*, any catalogue of the theoretical and practical functions of the mind applied only to its current form, making identity 'entirely matter of history'.²⁹

Collingwood, like Cassirer, thus took a historicist position with respect to categories and selfhood. This, Collingwood argued, required a radical break with Aristotle, insofar as Aristotle's metaphysics had wanted to address Being as such in an ahistorical way.³⁰ Broadly speaking, this argument has

---

²⁵ Collingwood, *Essay on Philosophical Method*, 33.
²⁶ R. G. Collingwood, *Speculum Mentis, or The Map of Knowledge* (Oxford: Clarendon Press, 1946 [1924]), 66.
²⁷ Collingwood, *Speculum Mentis*, 195–6.
²⁸ Collingwood, *Speculum Mentis*, 280.
²⁹ Collingwood, *New Leviathan*, 62, writes 'All this knowledge is about modern European history, the *gesta* of the modern European mind, including my own mind.' Italics in original.
³⁰ R. G. Collingwood, *An Essay on Metaphysics* (Oxford: Clarendon Press, 1948 [1940]), 5, writes that 'Kant observed that logic had undergone no radical changes since it left the hands of Aristotle. The same observation can be made towards the middle of the twentieth about metaphysics.'

been one of the important differences between modernity and earlier periods of thought. We saw that Kant had effectively been attacking Aristotle in declaring that being was not a predicate, and that Hegel had followed him in calling being an empty concept.[31] We then observed that fragmentarians and subordinationists alike believed that philosophy still needed to free itself from the continuing influence of substantialist Aristotelian metaphysics. Where Nietzsche and Foucault, Heidegger and Quine, differed was over how this liberation was to be achieved and what the results should look like.

In Collingwood's case, the fact that Being, supposedly the highest universal, turned out to lack all specific differentiation did not mean rejecting Aristotle entirely (as was also true for Hegel). We saw previously that Aristotle's approach to investigating the differences between kinds of thinking had been to examine their assumptions. For Collingwood, this aspect of Aristotle's philosophical method remained viable. Once the ambition of a science of pure Being had been given up, philosophy became the investigation of presuppositions. Hence Collingwood's call for what he described as a metaphysics without ontology, the chief task of which was the investigation of the emergent forms of knowledge and experience.

Ricoeur likewise held that 'the act of ordering that [Aristotle's] *Categories* represented had remained the perennial signal task of speculative discourse' from the ancient to the modern world.[32] This included the work of Kant and Hegel. More recently, Ricoeur located Husserl within this categorial tradition. According to Ricoeur, Husserl's concept of the task of logic included establishing both the 'formal categories of the object (object, state of affairs, plurality, number, actualities, etc.)' and the 'objectively valid laws ... from which "theories" follow'.[33] Ricoeur also read Husserl as arguing, as Kant had, that there was 'no form of time without elements of experience which flow in it'.[34] The fundamental temporality of experience was a bridge from Husserl's interest in the conceptual assumptions of logic and mathematics to the 'transcendental problem of the world' more broadly.[35] Temporality became synonymous with historicity. Husserl himself came to think that what he called the crisis of the European sciences could only be understood in historical terms, and Ricoeur agreed, as we shall see below.

Ricoeur, who knew Collingwood's work, also shared Collingwood's neo-Hegelian conception of categories as presuppositions.[36] As Ricoeur

---

[31] See Chapters 3 and 4, above.
[32] Ricoeur, *The Rule of Metaphor*, 307.
[33] Ricoeur, *Husserl's Ideas I*, 70.
[34] Ricoeur, *Husserl's Ideas I*, 128.
[35] Ricoeur, *Husserl's Ideas I*, 49.
[36] Ricoeur, *Husserl's Ideas I*, 6.

put it, 'no discourse can claim to be free of presuppositions for the simple reason that the conceptual operation by which a region of thought is thematized brings operative concepts into play, which cannot themselves be thematized at the same time'.[37] But he combined this view with a pluralist position, saying explicitly that 'I should like to plead for a relative pluralism of forms and levels of discourse.'

Ricoeur also distinguished this pluralism from the notion, suggested by Wittgenstein, of a radical heterogeneity of language games'.[38] That is, Ricoeur's pluralism involved arguing that determining the 'highest kinds', to use the Platonic and scholastic term, concerned not the study of substances but rather the categorial conditions of a limited range of specific types of propositions, including philosophical, scientific, historical, artistic and common-sense kinds of utterances. But this did not preclude significant depth and diversity with respect to what could be said in each.

Finally, Ricoeur shared Cassirer's and Collingwood's historicist treatment of categories. Indeed, in *Time and Narrative*, Ricoeur explicitly made time itself a fundamental category, following both Kant and Husserl (and also in response to Heidegger). But whereas 'Kant only recognized those determinations of time that contribute to the objective constitution of the physical world', Ricoeur, as an inheritor of phenomenology, regarded time as necessary for understanding subjective as well as objective reality.[39] Ricoeur's 'schematism of the narrative function', to use his own deliberately neo-Kantian term, thus had clear implications for the division of knowledge. The conception of the unity of science endorsed by logical empiricism had been too narrow, and had resulted in the exclusion of other important kinds of discourse. Cassirer and Collingwood had reached an identical conclusion.[40]

Knowledge

Cassirer, Collingwood and Ricoeur all wanted an account of knowledge that both avoided subordination to a single valid form and resisted a fragmentation resulting in as many instances of knowledge as there were individual knowing subjects. Cassirer's *Philosophy of Symbolic Forms*, for example, was a self-conscious attempt to modify Kant's critical philosophy to incorporate subsequent scientific and philosophical developments

---

[37] Ricoeur, *The Rule of Metaphor*, 307
[38] Ricoeur, *The Rule of Metaphor*, 308.
[39] Ricoeur, *Time and Narrative*, i.244, n. 18.
[40] Ricoeur, *Time and Narrative*, i.111.

while retaining the general position that all of our knowledge was mediated and structured by one or another of a limited number of distinctive types of categorial arrangements. Like Kant, Cassirer was fundamentally concerned with the basis of scientific knowledge while also wanting to find room for moral and religious experience. Unlike Kant, though, Cassirer gave considerable attention to language and myth. He also found room, in his *Essay on Man* (a condensed version of the *Philosophy of Symbolic Forms* written for an English audience after he fled Hitler's Germany), for a distinctive form of historical knowledge.

Cassirer argued that 'objective' knowledge, in the sense of a schematic organisation of the world into a unity containing discrete things with identifiable properties, preceded science.[41] Objectivity was already a latent feature of pre-scientific knowledge. Where Kant had effectively identified our ordinary experience with the objects of scientific investigation, Cassirer argued for an initial, phenomenological, synthesis of experience that preceded science and was logically distinct from it. Following Kant, however, Cassirer held that this initial synthesis, like the schematisms of all the symbolic forms, had a universal nature.

The vocabulary of languages and the content of myths varied widely, but language and myth nonetheless shared a common structure. For example, in all cultures of any duration and complexity, we find language generating a sense of self; giving expression to representations of space and time; and taking initial steps towards number and quantification. Certainly, the world viewed mythically was always dramatic and mutable. Any classification was secondary to a 'collision of [conflicting] powers' in which constant transformation was the rule.[42] But myth was also a condition of a fully objective perspective.

Beauty was equally a human universal. In the *Essay*, Cassirer treated art, along with myth and language, as one of three primitive symbolic forms. He followed Aristotle in treating imitation as 'a fundamental instinct' or 'irreducible fact of human nature', and argued that just as language began in Darwinian fashion in the form of spontaneous efforts to mimic natural sounds, art began from an effort at imitation of things in the world.[43] This was speculative, but what is important for us is that Cassirer treated art as genuine knowledge. '*Rerum videre formas* is a no less important and indispensable task than *rerum cognoscere causas*.'[44]

---

[41] Cassirer, *Essay on Man*, 262.
[42] Cassirer, *Essay on Man*, 103.
[43] Cassirer, *Essay on Man*, 150.
[44] Cassirer, *Essay on Man*, 216.

In referring to art as 'seeing the forms of things', Cassirer was effectively adopting Kant's view that art included a contemplative aspect. This separated it from the experiences of beauty exclusively defined by feeling and emotion that were features of our ordinary experience. But it also highlighted Cassirer's opposition to the logical empiricist notion of the unity of science according to which there was only one valid form of knowledge; like Heidegger, he too thought of art as giving us access to a certain kind of truth.

This pluralism implied no hostility to science on Cassirer's part; quite the opposite. His philosophical starting point had involved modifying Kant's philosophy to account for the transformative impact of the theories of relativity and quantum mechanics on physics. He was very clear that we should regard scientific knowledge as 'the highest and most characteristic attainment of human culture'.[45] The scientific effort to know the causes of things was, nevertheless, subject to historicity, and the more science had developed from the ancient world onwards, the clearer it had become that symbolic abstraction was fundamental to it.

Cassirer presented the history of scientific thought as a process in which things that had been taken to be substantial entities, including numbers themselves, gradually became understood as symbols for relations. The class concepts and general laws of scientific thought were thus not part of nature as such, but theoretical products of a constructive effort to formulate quantitative propositions about it. This process of seeking to understand nature was interminable because nature itself was an inexhaustible source of difference. Yet science was only one of the major symbolic forms necessary for an understanding of human culture, even if its importance could not be overstated. Cassirer never changed his mind regarding his declaration in his early work on Einstein that 'The progress of epistemological analysis' had revealed 'the assumption of the simplicity and oneness of the concepts of reality [as] an illusion.'[46]

Collingwood fully shared Cassirer's aim of identifying the conditions of science while also establishing it as just one amongst several forms of knowledge, although his position on the overall structure of knowledge shifted over time. His early effort at 'the construction of a map of knowledge' in *Speculum Mentis* culminated in the argument that in fact there could be no such map, at least not one that claimed to be anything more than an abstraction.[47] Despite his disavowal of Idealism, the claim that all

---

[45] Cassirer, *Essay on Man*, 261.
[46] Ernst Cassirer, *Substance and Function and Einstein's Theory of Relativity* (USA: Dover Publications, 1953 [1923]), 446.
[47] Collingwood, *Speculum Mentis*, 39, 309.

that really existed was a world of 'absolute mind' provided an example of why his readers were inclined to link him with it.[48] Indeed, the problem of absolute mind was arguably analogous to that of pure Being that we saw diagnosed by Hegel in Chapter 4. That is, absolute mind taken simply as such lacked any internal structure.

In *Speculum Mentis*, Collingwood argued that the only way in which absolute mind could achieve its goal of self-knowledge was 'through the mediation of an external world'. Although this world was only abstract or apparent, there was thus no dispensing with 'the construction of . . . art, religions, sciences . . . historical fact . . . systems of philosophy and so forth'. In his later volumes on metaphysics and philosophical method, in contrast, Collingwood placed less emphasis on the various types of knowledge as forming a progressively more adequate hierarchy insofar as they approached the condition of absolute mind. Whatever Collingwood's exact conception of the relationship between religion, art, science and history, however, the individual studies he devoted to them always presented them as distinctive.

In the case of religion, Collingwood, like Cassirer, made no sharp opposition between religion and rationality, arguing that 'all religion has an intellectual element'.[49] There was a sense, Collingwood told Gilbert Ryle, in which the point of the ontological argument for God's existence that Kant had worked so hard to refute was just to show that 'the term God' had to be 'taken as standing for "that which we are thinking about when we are thinking philosophically."'[50] This sounds reminiscent of Aristotle's conception of metaphysics as the knowledge of the unmoved mover, but in fact Collingwood contrasted ancient Greek philosophical rationalism and Christian faith. While he did not see faith and reason as necessarily opposed, he did argue for the view that faith was 'a higher ideal, knowledge of the infinite object' that went beyond 'syllogistic' and 'argumentative' knowledge.[51]

Collingwood was at least as committed to a religious faith as either Cassirer or Ricoeur. His conviction of the importance of Christianity rested on a view akin to Cassirer's, that religion was a permanent feature of the human condition. Just as Cassirer argued that the advent of science did not mean that mythical thinking had been permanently eliminated, Collingwood believed humanity possessed 'innate and ineradicable

---

[48] See Collingwood, *Speculum Mentis*, 310, and Collingwood, *An Autobiography*, 56–7.
[49] R. G. Collingwood, *Faith and Reason: Essays in the Philosophy of Religion*, ed. and intro. Lionel Rubinoff (Chicago: Quadrangle Books, 1968), 59.
[50] Collingwood, *Essay on Metaphysics*, 257.
[51] Collingwood, *Faith and Reason*, 110, 112.

religious impulses'.⁵² That being the case, it was important that religion should play a positive role, and not find itself in a hostile relation to other forms of experience. Historically, Collingwood declared, religion had 'tried to usurp, in certain respects, the place of science'. He also thought, however, that 'science has retaliated, in more recent times, by trying to usurp the place of religion'.⁵³ Collingwood's overall argument in favour of pluralism was clear; faith and reason both had their proper place and neither should attempt to claim superiority over the other.

Collingwood's treatment of art also resembled Cassirer's. Although art had expressive and emotional components, it could not be reduced to these elements, nor could it be treated as a Platonic *techne* devoted only to making.⁵⁴ Collingwood did hold that there was an important sense for both artist and audience in which art was always an embodied practice, but this did not mean that art was to be identified simply with its material products. The music could not be identified exclusively with the physical sounds, nor the painting with patches of colour on a canvas. Art could be seen on the analogy of a language as conveying an inner emotional experience.⁵⁵ For Collingwood, its claim to truth or knowledge lay in its success in doing so.⁵⁶ Art could be called true insofar as it possessed phenomenological authenticity.

The judge of this authenticity, however, was not the artist in isolation. Art, like everything else, was inflected with historicity. All works of art were subject to the constraints of time and place, and all were aimed, ultimately, at an audience. The artist and the community mutually implied one another; the truth of art was not determined by the artist alone. Using T. S. Eliot's poem *The Wasteland* as an example, Collingwood argued that the artist 'tells his audience, at risk of their displeasure, the secrets of their own hearts'.⁵⁷ Art was thus a serious matter with potential political implications, and Collingwood wanted to distinguish it firmly from amusement or entertainment. Though these too had their place, artistic appreciation required knowledge and judgement that entertainment as such did not.

If there was an important difference from Cassirer, and the Kantian tradition generally, it was Collingwood's insistence that 'Art is not contemplation, it is action.'⁵⁸ At the same time, this claim rested on an

---

[52] Collingwood, *Faith and Reason*, 90
[53] Collingwood, *Faith and Reason*, 89.
[54] R. G. Collingwood, *The Principles of Art* (Oxford: Clarendon Press, 1938), 15.
[55] Collingwood, *Principles of Art*, 274
[56] Collingwood, *Principles of Art*, 287.
[57] Collingwood, *Principles of Art*, 336.
[58] Collingwood, *Principles of Art*, 332.

extended view of action, so that sitting quietly while looking or listening intently still counted as doing something. One potential difficulty with this account was that it suggested a view of art as a kind of moral therapy. Collingwood described it as 'the community's medicine for ... the corruption of consciousness'. It could be objected, perhaps, that the medical metaphor for art collapses art into a *techne* once more.[59] But the overall tendency of Collingwood's theory of art as language was to establish it, like religion and science, as a distinct form of knowledge.

We have already emphasised Collingwood's insistence on the distinctiveness of natural science. Like Cassirer, he denied it was simply an extension of common sense. He was in no doubt that the natural sciences rested on distinct presuppositions.[60] But any account of natural-scientific knowledge had to come to terms with its historicity. Collingwood was aware, like Cassirer, of the 'breach with the Kantian system' that the new physics of relativity and quantum theory involved.[61] While Kant was correct that the philosophy of science should identify the presuppositions of physics, these presuppositions had not remained static. For example, Newtonian physics had assumed a 'principle of continuity' according to which there was always a third term between any two intervals. Quantum theory denied this assumption: 'quantum theory is in principle a mechanical theory based on denying the applicability of the differential calculus [of Leibniz and Newton] *à l'outrance* to the world of nature'.[62]

Logical empiricism, Collingwood believed, had not always accepted the radical nature of this change. There were, however, philosophers who had done so, including A. N. Whitehead and Bertrand Russell. Collingwood read Whitehead as saying that the new physics indicated 'there is no distinction between the events that happen and the bodies to which they happen'. Alternatively, one could say that 'at a given instant, where there are no events, there are no bodies. There is no nature at an instant. Nature is not body as distinct from event.'[63]

It has been argued that the advent of relativistic and quantum-theoretical physics contributed to the decline of philosophical Idealism. Idealism, it is said, involves the claim that 'space and time are not real, but a mere appearance' and that only 'philosophy could deal with a purported reality

---

[59] Collingwood, *Principles of Art*, 336.
[60] Collingwood, *Essay on Metaphysics*, 4, 235.
[61] Collingwood, *Essay on Metaphysics*, 95; Collingwood, *Autobiography*, 65.
[62] Collingwood, *Essay on Metaphysics*, 259.
[63] Collingwood, *Essay on Metaphysics*, 267.

behind appearance'.⁶⁴ Quantum theory has sometimes been taken as an empirical refutation of such views. But even if this is correct, it is worth observing that Collingwood believed Whitehead's account was consistent with his own position, which suggests that, on this issue at least, he was (as he claimed) not an Idealist. Collingwood also used his interpretation of the new quantum-theoretic view to argue that logical empiricism had retained an illegitimate use of the concept of necessary causation in science. In his *Essay on Metaphysics*, for instance, Collingwood argued that the concept of a cause had remained latently anthropomorphic and anthropocentric even in the Kantian era.

Causation had traditionally assumed some relation to human desires and purposes, or at least a divine analogue of them, as we saw in respect of Aristotle's notion of a final cause. Whitehead and Russell were commended for recognising that physics had purged itself of this anthropocentrism.⁶⁵ However, Collingwood also acknowledged the existence of a practical science of nature, or technology, to which the old concept remained relevant. Insofar technology was concerned with enhancing our control of the world, the anthropocentric view still made sense. But it no longer had a place in an objective theoretical account of nature conceived independently of all human concerns.

Ricoeur was somewhat less engaged than either Cassirer or Collingwood with the philosophy of science. His remarks on science occurred largely in the context of discussions of the similarities and differences between the natural and the human sciences. There is no doubt, though, that he considered natural science as distinct from our ordinary experience. In *The Philosophy of the Will*, he wrote that natural science was concerned with 'general laws of objectivity, that is, of number and systematic experiment'.⁶⁶ The point was that the concerns of science did not involve the lived experiences of freedom and selfhood. His study of Husserl had familiarised Ricoeur with the argument that the phenomenological intentionality of consciousness needed to be differentiated from an objective world

---

⁶⁴ Michael Hampe, 'Preface' to A. N. Whitehead, *The Concept of Nature*, vii. However, at least one contemporary philosopher of science with experience as a working physicist has argued that quantum theory is consistent with a metaphysical view of a timeless universe of a quasi-Platonic kind. See Julian Barbour, *The End of Time: The Next Revolution in Physics* (Oxford: Oxford University Press, 1999). In other words, the debate over the soundness of Idealism was not in fact settled by the advent of quantum theory.

⁶⁵ Collingwood, *Essay on Metaphysics*, 69, 340.

⁶⁶ Paul Ricoeur, *Philosophy of the Will*, vol. 1, *Freedom and Nature: The Voluntary and the Involuntary*, intro. and trans. Erazim V. Kohák (Evanston, IL: Northwestern University Press, 1968 [1950]), 220.

of physical things: 'In Husserlian language, the "region" of consciousness is *other* than the "region" of nature. It is perceived *otherwise*, exists *otherwise*, and is *certain in another way*.'[67]

Ricoeur's philosophical efforts were mainly directed at specifying the conditions of that other region. He was indebted to Heidegger's concept of *Dasein*, which we saw was intended as a break with the Cartesian tradition in which a mental substance, the subject of the cogito, confronted an objective world of material substances. As Ricoeur put it, '*Dasein* is not a subject for which there is an object, but is rather a being within being.'[68] Unlike Heidegger, however, Ricoeur did not relegate to a secondary status all forms of knowledge not directly concerned with the investigation of *Dasein*. Nevertheless, he retained an affinity for the Heideggerian concept of 'thrownness' according to which we are mortal beings pitched into a world not of our own making.[69] Ricoeur's account of the will thus emphasised that a great deal of human life was unintelligible as the outcome of choice. All human beings were defined involuntarily by 'a beginning, [and] a nature, that is, the law of a growth' as well as 'an unconscious structure, and finally the form of a personality type'.[70]

For Ricoeur, understanding what Husserl had called the region of consciousness required treating human life as a separate domain of knowledge with its own symbolic structure. The similarity to Cassirer here was not accidental. Ricoeur acknowledged that his own account resembled Cassirer's concept of symbolic forms understood as 'cultural processes that give form to all experience'.[71] Ricoeur likewise regarded all thought, scientific thought included, as symbolic in Cassirer's sense. That is, the use of symbols was an enabling condition of rationality and objectivity.

Ricoeur also resembled both Cassirer and Collingwood in giving a significant role to religion. But both scientific knowledge and ordinary life had forced a transformation of religious claims in modernity:

> the conception of a world composed of three stories – heaven, earth, and hell – and peopled with supernatural powers which descend down here from up there is purely and simply eliminated . . . by modern science and

---

[67] Ricoeur, *Husserl's Ideas I*, 39. Emphasis in original.
[68] Paul Ricoeur, 'The Task of Hermeneutics', in *Hermeneutics and the Human Sciences*, ed. and trans. John B. Thompson (Cambridge: Cambridge University Press, 2016 [1981]), 3–22, 14. Italics in original.
[69] See Chapter 6, above.
[70] Ricoeur, *Philosophy of the Will*, i.434.
[71] Paul Ricoeur, 'The Symbolic Structure of Action', in *Philosophical Anthropology* (Malden, MA, and Cambridge: Polity Press, 2016 [2013]), 176–94, 177.

modern technology as well as by how man represents ethical and political responsibility.⁷²

Religious claims to knowledge of the absolute had been trumped by historicity.⁷³

Ricoeur was a consistent pluralist about knowledge, not wanting any one of the fundamental regions of human experience, whether science, religion or the demands of the lifeworld, to dominate the others. He also made room, like Cassirer and Collingwood, for artistic experience. Notwithstanding, he placed greater importance than either on the concept of narrative, which he argued in *Time and Narrative* was a genuine cultural universal.⁷⁴ Ricoeur described modernity's intellectual horizon as a combination of post-Kantian and post-Hegelian concerns: 'In us, something of Hegel has vanquished something of Kant; but something of Kant has vanquished something of Hegel . . . this exchange and this permutation . . . still structure philosophical discourse today.'⁷⁵

By this rather cryptic remark Ricoeur seems to have meant that Hegel had shown that Kant's account of the will was too abstract to deal with the complexities of moral life, but that Kant was preferable to Hegel in still leaving something for reason to accomplish. In our post-Kantian, post-Hegelian situation, meaning had to be recognised as dependent on narratives constructed by human beings rather than having any externally given source. The pre-theoretical, practical, understanding of action described by Ricoeur's hermeneutic anthropology presupposed the existence of actors with goals and motivations.

These presuppositions were shared, Ricoeur argued, both in fictional narratives of a poetic and literary kind, and by historical knowledge when it achieved the scientific status that both Collingwood and Cassirer attributed to it.⁷⁶ But the fact that some of the symbolic forms that Ricoeur identified had certain presuppositions in common did not license a reduction to a single kind of narrative knowledge. Ricoeur, no less than Cassirer and Collingwood, had a declared preference for what he called an Aristotelian

---

[72] Paul Ricoeur, *Essays on Biblical Interpretation*, ed. and intro. Lewis S. Mudge (Minneapolis: Fortress Press, 1980), 38.
[73] Ricoeur, *Essays on Biblical Interpretation*, 99.
[74] Ricoeur, *Time and Narrative*, i.52.
[75] Ricoeur, *Essays on Biblical Interpretation*, 109–10.
[76] Ricoeur, *Time and Narrative*, i.3, 55, 92.

'methodological pluralism' over what he saw as a Platonic demand for 'a unified scientific method'.[77]

Politics

Cassirer, Collingwood and Ricoeur agreed on the need for pluralistic accounts of the nature of categories and of the different genres of knowledge that these categories structured. When we turn to politics, we find that for all three thinkers the analogue of this categorial and epistemological pluralism was a commitment to a liberal conception of freedom distinguished by the rule of law. There was no specially privileged ruling group just as there was no specially privileged form of knowledge. Yet authority was necessary, and as such needed to be treated with judicious scepticism rather than reflexive hostility. Their ideas were formed by the shared experience of living through mid-century totalitarianism. As a Jew, Cassirer had to flee or face persecution by Hitler's government; Collingwood was too old to fight in the 1939–45 war but lived through the German bombing raids on England; and Ricoeur, who did fight for France, found himself a prisoner of war in Poland.

As Cassirer read Plato, the message of *The Republic* was that 'Philosophy cannot give us a satisfactory theory of man until it has developed a theory of the state.'[78] The challenge for such a theory was to show how 'all the other activities of man' were, on the one hand, 'dependent on the forms of political life', while, on the other, retaining 'a purport and value of their own'.[79] In other words, all the activities that go on under the broad headings of theory and practice presuppose government, but equally cannot be simply subordinated to government without harming their identity. Cultural and intellectual life should be left to develop as autonomously as possible. To tolerate art, religion and the sciences only insofar as they served political interests was destructive, not just of these various symbolic forms, but of freedom.

In contrast with thinkers both inside and outside the liberal tradition who saw law as an impediment to the freedom of the will, Cassirer

---

[77] Ricoeur, *Time and Narrative*, 132. Ricoeur drew this contrast in the context of a discussion of the work of Georg von Wright, but his sympathetic exposition suggests he accepted it as valid.
[78] Cassirer, *Essay on Man*, 87.
[79] Cassirer, *Essay on Man*, 88.

treated government as an enabling condition of freedom. We may call this a Hobbesian position: the only freedom worth having was to be found in a community of laws that acknowledged a common authority. Hobbes had argued in *Leviathan* that without government 'there is no place for Industry' and also 'no Arts' and 'no Letters'.[80] The problem was one of what kind of authority would allow social life to flourish. Legitimacy was a key requirement. The issue for Hobbes, in other words, was 'the *validity* of the social and political order'.[81] The social contract was supposed to answer this problem of how government could be rightful, which Cassirer thought was once again urgent in his own time.

Hobbes notoriously held that any government created by such a contract, however bad, was better than no government: sovereign power could never be as 'hurtfull as the want of it'.[82] For someone in Cassirer's situation, the truth of this statement was no longer self-evident. Although the early modern state as Hobbes knew it was vastly more powerful than anything that preceded it, it was puny compared to the states of the mid-twentieth century. The capacity of sovereign power to be 'hurtfull' had increased so greatly in the interim that Hobbes's claim, even if true in the seventeenth century, had arguably ceased to be sound. Hobbes had known civil war, but he had no experience of a government deciding to simply exterminate a whole class of its subjects.

One could perhaps still represent Cassirer's experience in Hobbesian terms by saying that Hitler's government had embarked on a civil war against the Jews that released them from any obligation to obey. Hobbes had linked sovereignty to protection, and when the sovereign either could not or did not offer security any longer, all justification for submission to its authority was removed.[83] But what Hobbes arguably did not allow for, which Cassirer experienced, was the emergence of a sovereign whose command of industry and technology made it so powerful that all realistic possibility of a persecuted group successfully fighting back had vanished. Death or exodus then became the only options, not just for individual dissidents, but for a whole section of society.

Cassirer wanted to stress that the possibility of such extreme situations could never be discounted. 'In politics we are always living on volcanic

[80] Hobbes, *Leviathan*, ed. Richard Tuck (Cambridge: Cambridge University Press, 2003 [1991]), bk 1, ch. 13, 89.
[81] Cassirer, *Myth of the State*, 174. Emphasis in original.
[82] Hobbes, *Leviathan*, bk 1, ch. 18, 128.
[83] Hobbes, *Leviathan*, bk 2, ch. 21, 153, wrote that 'The Obligation of Subjects to the Soveraign, is understood to last as long, and no longer, than the power lasteth, by which he is able to protect them.'

soil.'[84] One of the main risks of a political eruption was the modern lack of recognition that myth, the sociological and logical starting point of his philosophy of symbolic forms, would always form the basic human orientation to the world. Religion and myth broadly conceived could play a positive role in the state, Cassirer argued, insofar as they fostered what he called 'unity of feeling' and 'awareness of the universality and fundamental identity of life'.[85] But mythical thinking was only incipiently rational. By default, we all live in a world of our own imagination in which we are unable to distinguish what is objective from our own subjective desires. The self-destructive pursuit of illusions was the chief political danger in modernity.

Where myth and religion ceased to encourage sympathy and fellow-feeling and became sectional and dogmatic, they lost any 'objective function'.[86] Cassirer diagnosed National Socialism as a form of mythical thinking prepared to reject all intellectual and ethical restraint in its pursuit of a fantasy of racial purity. It had been further enabled by a kind of fatalism, which he criticised Heidegger in particular for encouraging. For Cassirer, Heidegger's idea of 'thrownness' amounted to finding oneself in a situation one could do nothing about and which simply had to be accepted as given.[87] But Cassirer also understood National Socialism as itself partly a reaction to a hubristic rationalism. This rationalism too rested on magical thinking, in the form of a dream of absolute control over nature by technological means.[88] To that extent, Cassirer was actually in sympathy with Heidegger.

Those whose minds were dominated by this kind magical thinking could only 'act like marionettes in a puppet show', Cassirer argued.[89] In other words, to surrender to political irrationalism was to become a victim of language, unknowingly trapped in patterns of thinking and acting that inherited ways of speaking carried with them. Amongst the conditions of political freedom for Cassirer, then, was learning to use language in a way that respected the logic of symbolic forms. In this modern version of the story of Plato's cave, the choice was between a self-conscious use of language, and allowing language to use us.

Cassirer held that avoiding this kind of political disaster required a recognition that freedom was, as Hobbes had argued, not a natural condition. It required constant active maintenance by the citizens.[90] In

---

[84] Cassirer, *Myth of the State*, 280.
[85] Cassirer, *Myth of the State*, 37.
[86] Cassirer, *Myth of the State*, 45.
[87] Cassirer, *Myth of the State*, 293.
[88] Cassirer, *Myth of the State*, 293.
[89] Cassirer, *Myth of the State*, 286.
[90] Cassirer, *Myth of the State*, 288.

particular, it demanded sensitivity to corruptions of discourse. National Socialism was a symptom of a perversion of language in German culture. Cassirer argued that Oswald Spengler, though not a supporter of Hitler, had abetted him. Spengler had done considerable harm because he 'despised and openly challenged all methods of science'; Cassirer agreed with Neurath that Spengler had substituted a spurious type of analogical reasoning for genuine analysis.[91]

Collingwood, like Cassirer, presented a liberal interpretation of Hobbes that understood authority as vital to liberty. Collingwood's decision to call his response to totalitarianism *The New Leviathan* could hardly have made his affinity with Hobbes clearer. Like Cassirer, who thought that mythical thinking could never be eliminated, Collingwood endorsed the idea of 'primitive survivals' in consciousness.[92] His position here recalled Hegel's theory of sublation, the idea that some part of an earlier phase of development still survived in a modified form in later stages. It provided a partial explanation of how Europe could now find itself so deeply threatened by irrationalism. Also like Cassirer, Collingwood believed that the specific threat of totalitarianism had arisen because Europeans had failed to appreciate that the freedom they had enjoyed was something that needed constant cultivation.

Collingwood placed more weight than Cassirer on the importance of religion in this connection, however. For Collingwood, religion was less a matter of dogma, even in the form of a minimal commitment to monotheism, than a process of achieving self-mastery (though it was not the only route to this end). An important, albeit negative, component of freedom involved liberation from one's own desires.[93] It meant acquiring the capacity to say no to oneself in response to one's own impulses. This was true, Collingwood believed, of most of the world's major religions, a list in which he included Confucianism and Buddhism as well as Christianity and Islam.[94] A decline of religious belief in this sense thus made totalitarianism more likely.

A religious culture could be a positive force for sustaining the scientific mentality and preserving political liberty insofar as religion in Collingwood's sense was opposed to 'escapist fantasies'.[95] Religion and science were compatible with one another as equally forms of self-liberation.

---

[91] Cassirer, *Myth of the State*, 289.
[92] Collingwood, *New Leviathan*, 65.
[93] Collingwood, *New Leviathan*, 91.
[94] Collingwood, *New Leviathan*, 94.
[95] Collingwood, *New Leviathan*, 94.

Religion gave us a better understanding of ourselves, and science gave us a better understanding of the world. But the preservation of both science and religion, which were amongst the chief theoretical and practical functions of the 'complex fact' that constituted the European mind for Collingwood, required the rule of law. Collingwood, like Cassirer, followed Hobbes in thinking that culture and learning rested on the presence of a known law adjudicated by a system of courts in which legal equality prevailed.[96]

Collingwood gave more credit than Hobbes, however, to ancient Rome as a source for the modern European belief that law was integral to civilisation.[97] Hobbes was generally sceptical about the value of ancient political examples, Greek as well as Roman, seeing them as potentially destabilising sources of republican and democratic sentiment, but Collingwood saw Rome as having played a positive role in transmitting the practices associated with the rule of law to a later era.[98] He argued that even those tribes never formally subsumed under Roman rule, such as the Goths and Vandals, who were conventionally viewed as having helped to destroy it, had actually played a major role in preserving Roman legal culture.[99]

Collingwood believed that Rome was an example of a self-conscious recognition, in the form of legal principles, that a community rested on some shared ideas.[100] Likewise, Collingwood's concept of mind as a complex fact implied that the various forms of theory and practice required communities for their instantiation. The idea of a single scientist, for example, could make no sense; nor could there be just one citizen. In legal and institutional terms, Collingwood emphasised the notion of partnership or *societas*.[101] This concept from Roman law was taken up in medieval Europe before being transmitted into modernity in a wide variety of

---

[96] Collingwood, New Leviathan, 327.
[97] Collingwood, New Leviathan, 329.
[98] Hobbes, Leviathan, bk 2, ch. 21, 151, wrote that it is 'by reading of these Greek, and Latine Authors, men from their childhood have gotten a habit (under a false shew of Liberty,) of favouring tumults, and of licentious controlling the actions of their Soveraigns'.
[99] Collingwood, New Leviathan, 330.
[100] Collingwood, New Leviathan, 139.
[101] Collingwood, New Leviathan, 132, wrote that in Roman law '*Societas* is a relation between *personae* (that is, human beings capable of suing and being sued, who must be free men and not slaves, Roman citizens and not foreigners, male and adult, not in the *manus* or *patria potestas* of another but heads of families) whereby they join together of their own free will in joint action.' Italics in original.

spheres, including the economy, education, religion, and most importantly for Collingwood's purposes, politics. The *New Leviathan* was expressly intended to 'bring the central notion [that the ideas of the Roman civilians] express into harmony with the modern European use of words'.[102]

The idea of agreement was central to *societas*. Collingwood defined civilisation itself as a matter of '*living, so far as possible, dialectically*, that is, in constant endeavour to convert every occasion of non-agreement into an occasion of agreement'.[103] Trying to reach agreement did not mean that agreement would necessarily be reached, nor did it exclude the possibility of eruptions of barbaric behaviour like that exhibited by National Socialism. Moreover, not all agreements were universally relevant. The kind of agreement that defined a partnership, for instance, was binding only on the parties concerned and did not extend to anyone not involved in it.[104] The rule of law was, however, a special case of partnership, one that was necessary for equality, and furthermore one that came with obligations. For Collingwood, voting was first and foremost a duty, not a right or a choice.[105]

Ricoeur's political writings, like those of Cassirer and Collingwood, also involved a response to Hobbes. Ricoeur came to see Hobbes as raising a problem for his own phenomenological concerns based on his interpretation of Husserl in which the problem of the other had a central place. In his later work, Husserl had concluded that his reconsideration of the structure of the Cartesian cogito resulted in a concept of the self or ego as necessarily a member of a temporal, historically situated, community of other selves.[106] As Ricoeur put it in *The Course of Recognition*, this created a 'problematic of being among and with' that is 'fundamentally political in nature'.[107]

Hence the relevance of Hobbes: in the state of nature, a legitimate solution to the problem of being with others was simply to kill them whenever they presented a threat to one's own interests. For Ricoeur, Hobbes was thus the figure who 'inaugurates modern political philosophy' by raising 'the possibility of murder'.[108] But as Hobbes himself saw,

---

[102] Collingwood, *New Leviathan*, 256.
[103] Collingwood, *New Leviathan*, 326. Emphasis in original.
[104] Collingwood had in mind the *Digest of Justinian*, trans. and ed. Alan Watson, 4 vols (Philadelphia: University of Pennsylvania Press, 1998 [1985]), bk 17, sec. 2, art. 20 (Ulpianus 31 ad edictum), ii.42: 'For my partner's partner is not my partner.'
[105] Collingwood, *Autobiography*, 153.
[106] Edmund Husserl, *Cartesian Meditations: An Introduction to Phenomenology*, trans. Dorion Cairns (The Hague, Boston and London: Martinus Nijhoff, 1982 [1960]), 139.
[107] Paul Ricoeur, *The Course of Recognition*, trans. David Pellauer (Cambridge, MA: Harvard University Press, 2005), 162.
[108] Ricoeur, *Course of Recognition*, 158–9.

such violence was really no solution at all. Ricoeur thus turned to Hegel, reading the account of the struggle between lord and bondsman in the *Phenomenology of Spirit* as a response to Hobbes.[109]

What was necessary was to explain how recognition could be made mutual, thus avoiding death or domination. The answer, as Ricoeur acknowledged, was the creation of Leviathan, under whose authority the laws of nature are enacted as amongst the rules that govern the civil condition.[110] In his early *Lectures on Ideology and Utopia* Ricoeur had emphasised, following Max Weber, that there was no such thing as a purely rational system of legitimacy. Government required an ideology, in a positive sense, that could provide the grounds for obligation.[111] Ricoeur's position was thus akin to Cassirer's, for whom the 'myth of the state' could either be sustaining or destructive, but was an inescapable feature at any stage of historical development.

While Ricoeur accepted Hobbes's arguments for the necessity of sovereign authority, he found them deficient with respect to the requisite justificatory narrative. Ricoeur argued Hobbes had not included the necessary reference to otherness. If selfhood implied a dependence on others, this was also true of the sovereign.[112] The mutual recognition of the sovereign and its subjects needed institutional expression in the structure of authority, which is why Ricoeur found Hegel's account superior.[113]

Yet although Ricoeur credited him with having been the thinker who 'definitively inscribed the theme of recognition at the heart of political philosophy', even Hegel had not made sufficient allowance in a modern context for 'human plurality'.[114] Ricoeur's later writings were notably sympathetic towards the arguments for diversity that he found in Anglophone liberal thought. In a mature formulation of the problem, he wrote that he aimed 'to join to the hierarchical idea of status or standing, which is a variant of the idea of scale, the horizontal line of the pluralization of the social bond'.[115]

Ricoeur, writing after both Cassirer and Collingwood, also took greater account than either of social and economic rights. The welfare state had

---

[109] Ricoeur, *Course of Recognition*, 152.
[110] Ricoeur, *Course of Recognition*, 165.
[111] Paul Ricoeur, *Lectures on Ideology and Utopia*, ed. George H. Taylor (New York: Columbia University Press, 1986), 13.
[112] Ricoeur, *Course of Recognition*, 171.
[113] Ricoeur, *Course of Recognition*, 172. Paul Ricoeur, *Memory, History, Forgetting*, trans. Kathleen Blamey and David Pellauer (Chicago and London: University of Chicago Press, 2006 [2004]), 272, wrote that 'Hegel is already the thinker of the modern post-revolutionary state, that is, the constitutional state in contrast to the aristocratic one.'
[114] Ricoeur, *Course of Recognition*, 180–1.
[115] Ricoeur, *Memory, History, Forgetting*, 222.

assumed a much larger role after 1945, and Ricoeur adopted the social democratic position that the liberties associated with the rule of law had an economic basis. Rights that people were too poor to exercise had little practical value. Ricoeur explicitly followed Amartya Sen in championing the idea of 'capabilities': the need to help to empower the mass of the population to pursue their goals.[116] Neither Ricoeur nor Sen, of course, held that the capabilities approach was only about money. Ricoeur summarised Sen's position by saying that it was 'the different positive liberties existing in a democratic state, including the freedom to hold regular elections, freedom of the press, and freedom of speech' that ensured good governance and prevented disasters like famines.[117]

Here Ricoeur, like both Cassirer and Collingwood, broke with Hobbes. Though all three accepted Hobbes's argument that the rule of law enforced by a single source of legitimate executive authority was essential in the modern state, Ricoeur insisted that authority must accept peaceful disagreement. This applied in particular to religion, where Hobbes would countenance no public deviation from the teachings of the sovereign. Ricoeur asserted that religious freedom was 'a particular case of the general right to profess opinions without being intimidated by public power'.[118] Hobbes regarded any such freedom as dangerously destabilising; even though Leviathan's legitimacy rested on democratic agreement, the sovereign would be foolish to allow a democratic public sphere.[119]

The starting point for modern Christian theology, in Ricoeur's view, was that absolute knowledge was impossible, and so imposing one's own conception of orthodoxy on others was never warranted. Religion was 'never completed'. The infinite nature of the divine made it impossible to fix within a closed system. As a result, 'the criteriology of the divine is never finished'. But Christianity, reconciled with its own historicity, could be a force for social and political justice. This reconciliation with historicity was also a requirement for avoiding dogmatism in other spheres of thought and activity. Ricoeur thought of himself as defending an Aristotelian pluralism in this respect.[120] Ricoeur, Cassirer and Collingwood all agreed that dogmatism in political, religious and intellectual life must be avoided. Part of their strategy for ensuring this was promoting the recognition that all fields of discourse were fundamentally temporally inflected.

---

[116] Ricoeur, *Course of Recognition*, 143.
[117] Ricoeur, *Course of Recognition*, 144.
[118] Ricoeur, *Essays on Biblical Interpretation*, 102.
[119] Hobbes, *Leviathan*, bk 2, ch. 29, 230, called the 'Liberty of Disputing' an 'infirmity of a Common-wealth'.
[120] Ricoeur, *Hermeneutics and the Human Sciences*, 186.

History

The similarities between Cassirer, Collingwood and Ricoeur extended to their treatment of the problem of history. All of them treated history as a distinctive form of knowledge, the conditions of which demanded serious philosophical attention. But unlike either the fragmentarians or the subordinationists, none of them were interested in devising their own speculative philosophies of the historical process. It might be objected here that Cassirer's philosophy of symbolic forms, for example, was really just another version of the traditional teleological approach to the speculative philosophy of history. Cassirer certainly acknowledged the indebtedness of his own conception of phenomenology to Hegel's arguments about the progressive unfolding of *Geist* in the *Phenomenology of Spirit*. He even went so far as to say that 'The concept of truth conceals an immanent dialectic that drives it inexorably forward, forever extending its limits.'[121]

Cassirer's concept of truth, however, was fully immanent within language, which permitted the creation of the symbolic forms. He had no separate Logic in Hegel's sense, nor did he suggest that the symbolic forms were the self-revelation of Absolute Spirit in world history. Put another way, Cassirer introduced a conditional element into Hegel's teleological account. If thought were to develop, then it would do so in a rational direction. But nothing required that it must; Hegelian dialectical necessity was absent.[122] The advancement of truth required 'conscious intellectual effort'.[123] Cassirer's conviction of the contingency of the historical process explained his refusal to attempt to construct anything resembling a Kantian or Hegelian narrative of world history as having a cosmopolitan purpose or as the realisation of universal freedom.[124]

The only theoretical basis on which Cassirer thought that we could understand the historical process was by employing the symbolic form of historical knowledge. The philosophical analysis of this symbolic form was a very recent development. Though Plato and Aristotle did not ignore the philosophical problems raised by explaining actions and events, and both had ideas about the nature of historical processes, Cassirer thought that the philosophy of historical knowledge in the modern sense was altogether absent from ancient and indeed medieval thought: 'Such an

---

[121] Cassirer, *Philosophy of Symbolic Forms*, iii.282.
[122] Matherne, *Cassirer*, 202, argues that Cassirer rejected 'Hegel's commitment to the necessity of the forward moving progress of culture ... endorsing an account of the contingency of this progress instead'.
[123] Cassirer, *Philosophy of Symbolic Forms*, iii.283.
[124] Cassirer, *Essay on Man*, 260.

analysis did not appear until the eighteenth century.'[125] According to Collingwood, indeed, the philosophy of historical knowledge appeared even later, towards the end of the nineteenth or in the early twentieth.[126]

One obstacle to philosophical reflection, according to Cassirer, was the Greek conviction that ultimate reality or Being was timeless in nature.[127] But Cassirer's argument also implied that the later temporalisation of Being in medieval times had not been historical in the modern sense either. Indeed, the medieval idea that past, present, and future were already known to God, and that they were to that extent independently existing, was positively misleading for the philosophical analysis of historical knowledge. It encouraged a view of historical objectivity as correspondence with an independent order of facts. No such realist view was possible, though. Even if the past were real, it was inherently unobservable, and so the only possible starting point for historical knowledge was in the study of the material traces of the past in the present. These, however, did not announce themselves as such. Historical evidence was a stipulative notion, and historical events of the kind associated with historical knowledge were themselves necessarily symbolic in character.[128]

Using evidence to assemble an explanation of past events required certain other assumptions, such as a common human nature. We must treat the evidence as the product of actions carried out by persons assumed to be beings like ourselves, or we cannot begin to understand it: 'history is fundamentally anthropomorphic'.[129] But this universal assumption was structural. It said nothing about the explanation of any specific series of events. Nor could actual historical explanation be modelled on the natural sciences: 'general epistemology, with its traditional form and limitations, does not provide an adequate methodological basis for the cultural sciences'.[130] Representing events in terms of general physical laws could only result in generic and genetic explanations. While all historical explanations were subject to universal physical constraints (no historical narrative could feature actors being in two places at once, for instance), historical events considered as objects needed to be understood as immaterial meanings: 'Their reality is symbolic, not physical.'[131]

---

[125] Cassirer, *Essay on Man*, 219.
[126] Collingwood, *Autobiography*, 79; Collingwood, *The Idea of History*, 429.
[127] Cassirer, *Essay on Man*, 217.
[128] Cassirer, *Essay on Man*, 222.
[129] Cassirer, *Essay on Man*, 241.
[130] Cassirer, *Philosophy of Symbolic Forms*, i.69.
[131] Cassirer, *Essay on Man*, 233.

Cassirer's theory of historical events as constructed meanings reflected his more general position that all forms of knowledge could only achieve objectivity and rationality via symbolic abstraction. Historical knowledge did not consist of equations and formulae, but it was no less abstract than them. It was entirely evidential and inferential, not experiential. The actual product that resulted was a record of human passions in action. It was also the only way in which a culture could achieve a reliable, stable, collective memory.[132] This reliability, however, was not to be confused with unshakeable fixity; historical knowledge was always open to criticism, and in this sense, Cassirer believed the historical past could change, since the historical past itself could not be absolutely separated from our knowledge of it.

In distinguishing a historical relationship to the past from our ordinary attitude to it, Cassirer argued that the subjective standpoint of the historian was 'intellectual and imaginative, not emotional'.[133] There was a 'pragmatic' conception of history appropriate to the world of action, but it was not to be confused with historiography.[134] This distinction between a practical past which is defined by its utility and a historical past which is the product of theoretical analysis has come to be more widely accepted, thanks, for example, to the work of Hayden White.[135] Cassirer compared the subjectivity of the historian to that of the naturalist. History had to be approached as a kind of 'applied botany which does not deal with plants but with the works of men'.[136]

This certainly meant recognising what was at stake, morally and ethically, for one's subjects, but moral judgement was excluded from historical explanation. Cassirer did not mean that it was wrong to make moral judgements about the past, but that such judgements did not contribute to understanding it. To know that some past action or event was wrong was not the same thing as knowing either what had happened or why.[137] Historical knowledge did not amount to science, Cassirer conceded, if by 'science' one insisted, like Kant, on apodictic certainty.[138] At the same

---

[132] Cassirer, *Essay on Man*, 234.
[133] Cassirer, *Essay on Man*, 242.
[134] Cassirer, *Essay on Man*, 242.
[135] Hayden White, *The Practical Past* (Evanston, IL: Northwestern University Press, 2014).
[136] Cassirer, *Essay on Man*, 243.
[137] Historical knowledge in the analytic sense is morally superfluous to the degree that knowing that slavery is wrong requires no knowledge of the history of slavery. Conversely, the most thorough knowledge of that history has no direct power to convince anyone of the enormity of the injustice involved. It is only if one is interested in the reasons why slavery came about that historical knowledge becomes important.
[138] Cassirer, *Essay on Man*, 256.

time, Cassirer argued that 'the historian is bound by the same strict rules as the scientist'.[139] History was an empirically driven search for truth, though 'truth' and 'empiricism' must be understood in the context of Cassirer's overall theory of symbolic forms.

History and the humanities in general derived their cultural importance from the fact that 'civilization is no harmonious self-enclosed whole, but is filled with the most violent inner tensions'.[140] It was because modern Europe had failed to manage these tensions successfully that National Socialism had been able to gain control of the German polity and plunge Europe into war. How far Cassirer thought that historical knowledge could contribute to preventing such eruptions of irrationalism is unclear. We noted his belief that speculative philosophies of history like Spengler's had played a role in unleashing Germany's darkest instincts.[141] But it seems likely that Cassirer at least regarded historical literacy as the contrary of Spenglerism and as one of the forces making for the maintenance of civilisation. Historical knowledge was presumably one of the means by which Cassirer thought 'the critique of reason becomes the critique of culture' in modernity.[142]

Collingwood, like Cassirer, eschewed the speculative philosophy of history, though his rejection of it was qualified. He did not entirely dismiss the idea that 'large-scale historical changes are due to some kind of dialectic working objectively and shaping the historical process by a necessity that does not depend on the human will'.[143] This was a concession to Kantian and Hegelian approaches. But Collingwood never tried to work out such a theory himself. What interested him in Hegel was the view that 'all history was the history of thought'. He took this to mean that action could not be identified only with bodily motion in its physical or outer aspect, but needed also to be explained in terms of the ideas of the actors concerned.[144] This type of explanation required a distinctive form of knowledge, and Collingwood was rather less reserved than Cassirer in proclaiming history a science.

---

[139] Cassirer, *Essay on Man*, 257.
[140] Ernst Cassirer, *The Logic of the Humanities*, trans. Clarence Smith Howe (New Haven: Yale University Press, 1961), 190.
[141] Cassirer, *Myth of the State*, 291.
[142] Cassirer, *Philosophy of Symbolic Forms*, i.89.
[143] R. G. Collingwood, *The Idea of History: Revised Edition with Lectures 1926–1928*, ed. and intro. Jan van der Dussen (Oxford and New York: Oxford University Press, 1994 [1946]), 56.
[144] Collingwood, *Idea of History*, 115.

For Collingwood, any form of knowledge that showed organisation and system was a science in the broad sense of the term, and history met these criteria. But Collingwood went as far as to say that 'the discovery of a scientific technique in history' was the most 'valuable discovery' that had been made since Kant.[145] This was a bold claim, especially since, as we saw, Collingwood was aware of how quantum theory and relativity had revolutionised both the scientific understanding of the world and science's understanding of its own concepts. If Collingwood found the discovery of scientific history even more important than these developments, it was because he thought it represented a largely new form of human self-knowledge, whereas the early twentieth-century scientific revolutions, epochal though they were, remained modifications of a kind of thinking first established in the early modern era.[146]

The inspiration for Collingwood's own efforts to construct a philosophy of historical knowledge was partly Kantian. His essay on the 'Outlines of a Philosophy of History' was 'arranged under four heads, which, out of compliment to the Kantian critiques, are called Quality, Quantity, Relation, and Modality'.[147] Of these the most important was quality, because it established historical events as objects of thought with no actuality. They were neither empirical things nor logical essences.[148] This view informed Collingwood's argument that one of the corollaries of the discovery of a science of history was the knowledge of human freedom.

The ideality of historical events meant that they could not be understood as caused by physical laws. Our knowledge of the past was itself the construction of an historical intelligence that could not be explained

---

[145] Collingwood, *Idea of History*, 235, writes that 'The most "valuable discovery" that has been made since Kant's time ... has been the discovery of a scientific technique in history.'

[146] Collingwood's account is open to the objection that modern historiography emerged coevally with natural science, if not indeed before it: see, for example, Stephen Toulmin, *Cosmopolis The Hidden Agenda of Modernity* (Chicago: University of Chicago Press, 1992 [1990]), 23, who argued that 'After 1600, the focus of intellectual attention turned away from the humane preoccupations of the late 16th century, and moved in directions more rigorous, or even dogmatic, than those the Renaissance writers pursued.' But unlike Husserl or Heidegger, Collingwood did not trace back the roots of the cultural crisis that modern science had allegedly created to the ancient world. See Collingwood, *Autobiography*, 91–2: 'European man's ability to control the forces of Nature was the fruit of three hundred years' investigation along the lines laid down early in the seventeenth century.'

[147] Collingwood, *Idea of History*, 426.

[148] Collingwood, *Idea of History*, 439.

physicalistically. Likewise, actions and events, both past and present, conformed to physical laws but were not explicable purely in terms of them. Individuals were thus 'free', not because all of their actions were entirely self-conscious or voluntary, but because no purely mechanical or statistical explanation could be given for them.

Collingwood's insistence on differentiating history from the methods of the natural sciences also reflected his experiences as a working historian and archaeologist. He did, however, think of himself as adhering to the scientific method in a Baconian sense, insofar as that meant always asking well-formed questions of the evidence.[149] An archaeological dig was like an experiment in that it was best undertaken as an investigation of a particular question; digging at random did not conform to the canons of historical method.

Collingwood has been credited with helping to secure acceptance for the principle, transformative in its day, that non-written, material forms of evidence could be as valuable as written historical sources.[150] So, when Collingwood wrote that 'The interpretation of sources . . . is the formal element of history, counterbalancing the material element which is the source itself', this view was inspired by the experience of literally unearthing surviving fragments of ancient history.[151]

On the relationship between historical knowledge and moral judgement, Collingwood was also in accord with Cassirer. There was 'a moral energy which it is our duty to devote to the actual problems of life', and to direct this energy at the historical past, which 'we are not in . . . and never can be in' was at best wasted effort and at worst positively confusing.[152] In making moral judgements on the past in the context of historical inquiry, we were making the mistake of acting as if 'the past is still happening'. But the study of history was neither 'a catharsis for our emotions' nor a 'school and training ground for political life' (as history was traditionally regarded in the ancient and Renaissance eras, for example).[153] Collingwood was not claiming that there was no version of the past that was morally relevant to the present. His point was rather that the starting point of a specifically historical kind of knowledge was a past already assumed to be separate from the present.

---

[149] Collingwood, *Autobiography*, 81.
[150] Stephen Leach, 'An Appreciation of R. G. Collingwood as an Archaeologist', *Bulletin of the History of Archaeology* (2009), 19:1, 14–20, 16.
[151] Collingwood, *Idea of History*, 368.
[152] Collingwood, *Idea of History*, 403.
[153] Collingwood, *Idea of History*, 35, 60, 404.

At the same time, insofar as the effects of the past were still reverberating in the present, Collingwood, like Cassirer, thought of history as having an important role in the formation of contemporary political and moral attitudes. Towards the end of his career, as a second disastrous European war loomed, Collingwood became convinced that the pursuit of historical knowledge understood as an exclusively theoretical, contemplative, endeavour was untenable. History also had to make a contribution to practical affairs. Historical knowledge could not provide rules or guidance for action, but it could contribute to the development of educated political judgement by sensitising democratic citizens and politicians alike to the ways in which the present remained entangled with the past.[154] Historians (and philosophers) should actively contest ideas that threatened the liberal order; hence Collingwood's praise for Karl Marx as a 'gloves-off' philosopher.[155]

Ricoeur shared Cassirer's and Collingwood's beliefs in both the autonomy of historical knowledge and its ethical importance. But whereas both Cassirer and Collingwood went back to Kant for their inspiration, Ricoeur took Husserl as his starting point. Since, as we have seen, Ricoeur was also more engaged with theology than either of the other two, he also gave greater attention to history as a process. For Christianity, history was a story of an ultimate salvation or redemption, and Ricoeur was interested in what this could mean in a modern context.

In *History and Truth*, for example, Ricoeur called this the 'philosophico-theological problem of a total or ultimate significance of history'.[156] We saw that Kant and Hegel both wrote theodicies in which the justification of the ways of God to humanity required making sense of history as a narrative with an overall meaning. This question of whether the historical process as a whole had a redemptive purpose became ever sharper during the nineteenth century thanks to advances in historical research into Biblical antiquity in general and into the problem of the life of Jesus in particular.

We observed that Kant was already concerned with the Christian worry that 'The whole value of an example is lost unless it is historical.'[157] Collingwood's early writings show how this worry had been greatly intensified in the interim. If Jesus were a purely mythical figure, it appeared to make no sense to try to imitate him. Insofar as Collingwood resolved this

---

[154] Collingwood, *Autobiography*, 106.
[155] Collingwood, *Autobiography*, 153.
[156] Paul Ricoeur, *History and Truth*, 3.
[157] Collingwood, *Faith and Reason*, 86. Compare Chapter 3, above.

problem in *Philosophy and Religion* he did so by arguing that historical and philosophical knowledge were really identical at base, and that both were identical with theology, because all were ultimately concerned to understand reality as a whole.[158]

Yet Collingwood did not pursue this approach in his later writings, perhaps because of the difficulty entailed in explicating the concept of reality as a whole. While his Christian faith continued to inform his later works such as the *New Leviathan*, he increasingly addressed historical inquiry on its own terms, and separated it from Christian accounts of the past. He came to think that eschatology was 'always an intrusive element in history. The historian's business is to know the past, not to know the future.'[159]

In the end, Ricoeur agreed with Collingwood, even if he remained sensitive to the multiple potential meanings of the concepts of bearing witness and testifying. He did not confuse their theological and judicial meanings with their historical senses. Ricoeur fully shared Cassirer's and Collingwood's arguments for the view that the constructed nature of the historical past distinguished it from the natural past of memory. 'History is writing through and through – from archives to historians' texts', he declared.[160] Ricoeur also insisted that while historiography was an imaginative endeavour that shared the narrative form of literature, it was not a species of fiction.[161] It was grounded in the 'trace', or the persistence in the present of objects, including but not limited to texts, interpreted as evidence for the past. Evidence was thus a stipulative notion: 'Nothing as such is a document, even if every residue of the past is potentially a trace.'[162]

Ricoeur was also strongly committed to the notion that historical propositions had truth-values.[163] While Ricoeur considered the writing of history an inherently interminable project, and was well aware of the

---

[158] Collingwood, *Faith and Reason*, 85.
[159] Collingwood, *Idea of History*, 54.
[160] Ricoeur, *Memory, History, Forgetting*, 234.
[161] Ricoeur, *Memory, History, Forgetting*, 253, criticised Hayden White's theory of historical knowledge for blurring this distinction: 'There is a true category mistake here that engenders a legitimate suspicion regarding the capacity of [White's] rhetorical theory to draw a clear line between historical and fictional narrative.' White, *The Practical Past*, 20, did later recognise that 'I made a mistake by once suggesting that the problem [of true accounts of past events] consisted of the relationship between two substances, "fact" on the one hand, "fiction" on the other.'
[162] Ricoeur, *Memory, History, Forgetting*, 178.
[163] Ricoeur, *Memory, History, Forgetting*, 179, wrote that 'It is this propositional character of the historical fact (in the sense of "fact that . . .") that governs the mode of truth or falsity attached to the fact. The terms "true" and "false" can legitimately be taken at this level in the Popperian sense of "refutable" and "verifiable."'

frequent disagreements amongst historians, these considerations were not arguments against the possibility of historical truth and objectivity. Indeed, the need to perpetually re-write history reflected the existence of an obligation to truthfulness with respect to the past. Ricoeur's account of the ground of this obligation was an original one, couched in terms of what the living owe to the dead. His argument was similar to the claim that inter-generational justice is important with respect to future generations.

Just as we could be said to owe some consideration to those not yet born with respect to the future, we owed something to the people in the past, who had not lost the interest that everyone has while living in having the truth told about them simply because they were no longer present. In historiography, a concern with justice meant an unqualified commitment to the truth. The question of the justice of what had been done in the past was a separate one. A major aim of Ricoeur's last book, *Memory, History, and Forgetting*, which in effect addressed the Nietzschean question of the uses and disadvantages of history for life, was thus to determine the role of historiography in public memory.

Ricoeur treated memory, history, and forgetting as inter-related in the life both of the individual and of society. Memory was an inevitable and indispensable feature of life but could also be a source of abuse, particularly in the case of state manipulation. Any possibility of being at peace with the past required establishing historical truth. Society's living relationship to the past as connected to the future was distinct from the kind of knowledge involved in the historiographical relationship to the past. But the two kinds of relation to the past could in principle interact in a positive way. The public commemoration of events that were no longer in living memory was a feature of civilised life that benefitted from historical knowledge when done properly.

The kind of forgetting that Ricoeur envisaged involved letting go of trauma, but did not entail repression, and was compatible with public commemoration. The public recognition of historical truth was amongst its conditions. Hence the importance Ricoeur placed on the ethical concept of forgiveness, which went beyond legal justice. Just as genuine forgiveness for the individual required full admission of what was done, forgiveness for a community required a full accounting of the record.

Forgiveness, however, was not something any historian as such could grant, and Ricoeur was not naïve about the prospects for success of institutions like the truth and reconciliation commission, initially created to reckon with the past in post-Apartheid South Africa.[164] Denial was even

---

[164] Ricoeur, *Memory, History, Forgetting*, 483.

worse. Historiography could at least help to create the possibility of forgiveness by providing the best available understanding of past events. In this respect, Ricoeur went further than either Cassirer or Collingwood in working out a theory of the public role and social responsibility of historiography.

Conclusion

We have argued that the pattern of association between thought about categories, knowledge, politics and history has once again held good, this time amongst a group of thinkers we have called pluralists. Cassirer, Collingwood, and Ricoeur sought a middle ground between reasserting the dominance of a single categorial structure with a concomitant emphasis on a particular form of knowledge that manifested in the political realm as mandating a single substantive vision of the good life, on the one hand, and arguing, on the other, for an indeterminate variety of categorial frameworks tied ineluctably to the subjectivity of the individual in a way that encouraged epistemological scepticism and refused to treat any authority as legitimate.

The pluralist analysis of categories pointed to the conclusion that there was an irreducible variety of perspectives from which one could claim valid knowledge of the world. At the same time, this variety was limited and specifiable. This had an important political analogue in the form of the need to accommodate different kinds of discourse (but not just any and all discourse whatever) within a formal legal framework. The pluralist standpoint thus tended to be liberal in a broad sense, in that it gave priority to the rule of law and rejected authoritarian and totalitarian forms of politics. On the one hand, it also rejected uncompromising suspicion of authority as self-destructive.

But pluralism also differed from the philosophies of fragmentation and subordination, and indeed from their ancient and modern predecessors, in emphasising the need for a philosophical account of historical knowledge. Human action occurring in the context of a life-world inescapably structured by contingency and imagination needed an appropriate form of analysis if past events were to be understood in their individual complexity. Understanding events as law-governed or as instances of types on the model of the natural sciences was not adequate for the purpose.

This effort at a philosophy of historical knowledge replaced the speculative treatment of the totality of the historical process that could still be found at work in both the philosophies of fragmentation and subordination with a form of discourse about the past that offered the possibility of objective knowledge and for that reason was also vital to the maintenance of a civilised public life in modernity; or so Cassirer, Collingwood and Ricoeur all believed.

Conclusion: The Inescapability of Categoriality

All theories of categories address the problem of how we insensibly make sense of the sensible. It is not least because of Plato's speculations on the question of how we comprehend the visible in terms of the invisible that Whitehead's description of the subsequent history of philosophy as 'footnotes to Plato' contains some truth. But we can now appreciate why any serious discussion of categories must also acknowledge the polysemic nature of the term. The idea of a category, as our studies of Plato, Aristotle, Kant, Hegel and Hegel's successors has established, has meant radically different things at different times. Eternal Ideas; substances and their qualities; *a priori* structures; dialectical concepts; all have been proposed as answers to the question of how the invisible elucidates the visible. Even if we reject all these theories, and deny that categories have any reality beyond linguistic usage, a category may still refer to fundamental concepts; to classes and properties; or to the characteristics predicated of individuals: and this range of meanings is not exhaustive.

So our first, and in some ways most important, finding, is that it is always necessary to establish how the word is being used whenever we encounter it, on pain of finding ourselves at cross-purposes. We may make 'category mistakes' with respect to categories themselves as well as in connection with the kind of knowledge claims that we are dealing with, or concerning the ways in which we are framing people and their properties. A second conclusion, which forms a corollary, is that although it is perfectly possible to deal with the topic of categories in isolation, doing so would miss what has made it so important. Theories of categories have always formed part of a larger complex of ideas.

In particular, we have argued that these theories have persistently been connected with ideas to do with knowledge, politics and history. This is not to claim that these filiations are exhaustive or exclusive; the concept of a category has doubtless been associated with many other patterns of ideas. We are claiming only that it has always at least been linked with these. Our argument was that there has been a persistent habit of association between these themes, even though their meaning and content has changed drastically. We have seen that the concept of a category itself was anything but static; the same has been true of ideas about knowledge, politics and history.

Nevertheless, these themes have remained conjoint despite their constant circumgyrations. To begin with, the concept of a category has been persistently associated with problems to do with selfhood and identity. The self for Plato was identifiable chiefly with its rational part. For Aristotle it was a primary substance. For Kant it was the product of categorial forestructuring; and for Hegel, the 'I' was itself a category. Since Hegel, selfhood has, like everything else, been variously understood. It has been denied altogether by behaviourists, and understood as a specific kind of relation by contextualists of various kinds. Claims to an essential self, to 'really' be this or that kind of a person, are likewise with us still, but this literal substantial interpretation has been rendered deeply problematic by the Hegelian insight that 'Self-consciousness is *in* and *for itself*, when, and by the fact that, it is in and for itself for another self-consciousness; that is, it is only as something recognized.'[1]

The associations of categories, moreover, have not stopped at conceptions of the self. They have typically determined the conditions of knowledge by constituting its objects in one way or another. To know, for Plato, was precisely to know the Forms; for Aristotle, it was to apprehend the nature of substances; for Kant, and for Hegel, it was to experience the world in categorially structured terms, though they disagreed on the detailed nature of that structure. Insofar as there was nevertheless some continuity of content, it was because those categories, knowledge and forms of political order that were generally considered most important typically involved necessity and universality.

Plato was an early and highly influential example. The Ideas or Forms were eternal and essential. The most worthwhile kinds of knowledge approximated these qualities. In the history of Western thought, though it is almost Comtean to say so, metaphysical, religious and scientific propositions have successively been given the lion's share of theoretical attention and practical importance, not necessarily because of their intrinsic importance, but because of the certainty they were held to provide.[2]

---

[1] Georg Wilhelm Friedrich Hegel, *The Phenomenology of Spirit*, trans. M. Inwood (Oxford: Oxford University Press, 2018), §178, 76. Emphasis in original.
[2] Auguste Comte, *The Positive Philosophy of Auguste Comte*, trans. Harriet Martineau, 2 vols (Cambridge: Cambridge University Press, 2009 [1853]), ii.158, proposes the 'law of the three periods', in which theological, metaphysical and positive eras of thought succeed one another.

Certainly, some knowledge may be genuinely universal in extension. If a scientific proposition about a law of nature is true, then it is indeed true everywhere. It is this quality of scientific knowledge that has enabled its efficacious technological application.

Yet universality isn't what it used to be. In the twentieth century it was increasingly accepted that the truth of even the most universal of scientific propositions is not unconditionally true. It is not simply that such knowledge was always in principle vulnerable to change; it also became clear that it was true of things only in their physical aspect, and that scientific approaches could only yield scientific answers. Like all forms of knowledge, science is incontrovertible in its own domain, but there has been a growing realisation that it can only offer evidence, not guidance, once we step outside the point of view it offers us, as we must. The nineteenth-century hope of a literally scientific approach to politics has had to be given up, despite the best efforts of statistical social science to fill the gap.[3] Yet even if we think politics should always take account of scientific knowledge, that is not itself a scientific view.

A third finding of the foregoing inquiry is that the problem of the nature of categories, which may initially seem very abstract and of purely theoretical interest, has had serious practical and political implications. This is only to reiterate a point made by many of the authors we have discussed, though none of them explained it in terms of the pattern of association we have described. Nevertheless, the current study reinforces, for instance, Adorno's view that at the extreme, the application of categories could be a life and death question. As we saw, Adorno can be understood as rediscovering a truth about the nature of hatred already familiar to Aristotle – namely, that it is necessarily of types.[4] Both Aristotle and Adorno offer valuable reminders of the very real implications of how we frame things discursively when talking about other people.

Because of its highly consequential nature, this finding is worth stressing even if it is not novel. It is even more worth stressing because the world does not come with categorial markers on its face. Kant's emphasis on the role of the *a priori* is a reminder that we are not naturally aware that our experience comes to us always already categorially structured in advance. This gives the human condition an ironic tinge. We said that

---

[3] This is not a slur on the value of the natural and social sciences for either the theory or the practice of politics. For a social-scientific study of our contemporary predicament exemplary for both its historical sensitivity and its practical relevance see Peter Turchin, *Ages of Discord: A Structural-demographic Analysis of American History* (Connecticut: Beresta Books, 2016).

[4] See Chapter 2, n. 133, above.

if there is any agreement in this field, it is that it is human nature to use categories.[5] But then it is the unavoidable fate of all human beings to be born unaware of their own nature.

It should not be surprising that actions taken under these conditions have sometimes prompted appeals for forgiveness on grounds of ignorance.[6] But though it was already clear to Plato that there was an invisible world at work, he still treated this as esoteric knowledge. In contemporary modernity, in contrast, the situation has increasingly been recognised outside the academy. In our own time, as Lakoff notes, we must treat a refusal by the lay as well as the learned members of the community to 'find out how our behaviour depends on our conceptual systems' as an abdication of responsibility.[7] This is now part of what it means to 'know thyself'.

In Lakoff's terms, one of these conceptual systems has been just that habit of association which we have been investigating between categories, on the one hand, and knowledge, politics and history, on the other. The dominant tendency was to construct a categorial scheme in which there was some one form of knowledge, be it metaphysics, theology or science, with a universal status that was then reflected in a conception of political order. The story of modernity was one of increasing challenges to this tendency. A knowledge of divine things, or of the fundamental workings of the universe scientifically conceived, no longer necessarily conferred a title to rule. Kant and Hegel are now recognisable both as pivotal and equivocal figures who played crucial roles in bringing about this change.

We said that Kant would have been a Platonist if he could, and that Hegel wanted to salvage as much as possible of Aristotelianism. Both Kant and Hegel nonetheless felt obliged to come to terms with the end of the medieval world-view to which Aristotelianism had been integral, and their recognition of the historicity of all human affairs set an agenda that would play out over the next two centuries. This process, so far as we can tell, is far from complete. The question of the meaning of history, to which doubts about whether there was in fact any such meaning were central, took on a fresh importance once the Christian account of the world as a progress towards salvation no longer commanded general assent. Both

---

[5] Indeed, human nature can be treated as just a sub-category of nature in this regard. George Lakoff and Mark Johnson, *Philosophy in the Flesh: The Embodied Mind and its Challenge to Western Thought* (New York: Basic Books, 1999), 17, write that 'Every living being categorizes. Even the amoeba categorizes the things it encounters into food or nonfood.' The point is that this process is entirely involuntary and unconscious.

[6] Luke 23:34: 'Then said Jesus, Father, forgive them; for they know not what they do' (King James version).

[7] George Lakoff, Women, Fire, and Dangerous Things: What Categories Reveal about the Mind (Chicago: University of Chicago Press, 1990 [1987]), 337.

Kant and Hegel remained optimists, offering reasons to believe that there was a positive meaning to the wars and other miseries that loomed so large in the human past.

The three lines of development that we have considered after Hegel did not always share this optimism. The thinkers we have called fragmentarians stressed the fractured character of modern knowledge, and were typically unwilling to put a limit on the forms of knowing that there are, or even to trust in the very possibility of knowledge as traditionally conceived. This extended to the meaning of history. Nietzsche, for example, rejected Kantian and Hegelian interpretations on the grounds that they were still too entangled with Christian belief, and Foucault followed suit with respect to their secular, humanist, progressive analogues which made universalistic claims that they could not sustain.

Nietzsche, nonetheless, continued to uphold certain aspects of the old Hegelian approach to history, arguing that what was needed was not historical scholarship as such but an inspirational vision of the past focusing on the deeds of the great. Adorno likewise ultimately wanted a redemptive philosophy of history and was even prepared to argue that history was a necessary process. Foucault was more equivocal; although his narratives showed how earlier forms of oppressive power had been overcome, the result, more often than not, was only the creation of more insidious ones. Yet notwithstanding his almost unrivalled fecundity in opening new lines of inquiry in the humanities and social sciences, as well as his attention to detail, Foucault's historical theorising remained marked by a tendency to simply invert Kantian and Hegelian progressivism by emphasising discontinuity instead.

The second, subordinationist approach insisted there was only one way to truly know how things were (be that a Heideggerian revelatory encounter with Being, or the Quinean insistence that only physics can tell us what is real). But on history, the subordinationists were divided. Those in the logical empiricist, and later, the analytical tradition tended to retain optimistic, progressive hopes based on material improvements in science and technology. Phenomenologists, on the other hand, identified these very same developments as sources of looming disaster. Heidegger was not the only major thinker in this style to be convinced that Western civilisation was in crisis by the mid-twentieth century, and not simply because of totalitarianism, which was, in the end, only symptomatic. Edmund Husserl, for example, also diagnosed a 'crisis of European man'.[8] The complaint from

---

[8] See Edmund Husserl, 'Philosophy and the Crisis of European Man', in *Phenomenology and the Crisis of Philosophy*, intro. and trans. Quentin Lauer (New York: Harper & Row, 1965), 149–92.

these quarters since 1945 has typically been that the defeat of totalitarianism did not cure the underlying sickness that had produced it. The West as a whole, it is alleged, has continued to suffer from it.

These first two responses were the dominant ones. There was, however, also a third response, which we have called pluralistic. It was an effort to find a middle ground between the first two positions, but remained a minority view, perhaps because the attraction of either pole typically proved stronger. Against the fragmentarians, pluralists argued it was still possible to identify the main genres of knowledge. Against the subordinationists they insisted that this could not involve treating only one form of knowledge as important, or at least as more important than all others. They tended to accept the fragmentarian view that there was no overall meaning to the historical process, but concluded that history in its totality was thus grounds for neither optimism nor despair. Instead, particular episodes in the past had to be made intelligible in their specificity via the practice of historical research. This emphasis on history as a form of knowledge, that is, as historiography, marked out the pluralists as unusual.

This point leads to a fourth finding: if there was a common feature amongst all the different thinkers and positions we have discussed, ancient and modern, it was the tendency to ignore historical knowledge, broadly conceived as the explanation of individual, contingent past events. The emphasis on the universal in knowledge, whether for or against, and regardless of the type of knowledge concerned, had as its obverse a tendency either to ignore or to marginalise the problem of the conceptual conditions of historical analysis.

This was not the same thing as ignoring historicity or the historical process. Ancient and modern thinkers from Plato onwards were always self-conscious about their own being in time. By historical analysis here we mean the study of human life in the same terms that our historicity requires that we undergo it, as an irremediable flow of ineluctably contingent happenings. Historical knowledge of this kind was traditionally of interest only insofar as it was yet another illustration of the rational universal, or of God's plan, or insofar as it could be subjected to laws of a natural scientific kind.

Since Hegel, in particular, one could say modernity has been locked in an argument with Saint Paul, who declared that 'we look not at the things which are seen, but at the things which are not seen: for the things which are seen are temporal; but the things which are not seen are eternal'.[9] The question of whether and which 'unseen things' can still be understood as

---

[9] 2 Corinthians 4:18 (King James version).

eternal was a central preoccupation of all the different varieties of post-Hegelian thought. Fragmentarians, subordinationists and pluralists were all dealing with the problem of how to come to terms with the historicity of human existence in a variety of contexts, be it the changing nature of moral values or the shifting foundations of scientific knowledge.

The pluralists, we argued, were unusual in claiming that there was a distinctive form of knowledge peculiarly appropriate to understanding our past deserving of much greater philosophical attention than it had hitherto received. They were not naïve enough to believe that were this philosophical lacuna less common, it would translate into immediate practical improvements in social justice. Nor must we conflate subjecting a problem to historical analysis with solving it. We already have plenty of excellent historiography on the theory and practice of race, slavery and imperialism, and on the histories of gender and sexuality, yet inequality and discrimination persist for all that. But historical analysis nonetheless contributes to the ongoing project of Enlightenment understood as the collective human effort at self-knowledge. This was a project to which all three varieties of post-Hegelian thought were, in one way or another, committed (including even Heidegger, from a certain point of view). A sensitivity to the historical dimensions of an issue is implicit in the concept of Enlightenment as a maximal understanding of all aspects of reality.

Of these several findings, the issue of the practical effect of the use of categories is probably of most widespread concern. In particular, our use of categories has fundamental implications for our moral and political judgements. The point is not that these kinds of classifications are inherently a bad thing. They are, as such, inevitable. There is no way to avoid making distinctions between classes of persons in social and political life. Indeed, in many contexts to try to avoid doing so would be foolish. We must sort people for all sorts of purposes. What matters is the details: the particular motivations, intentions and consequences of the lines that are drawn. Where the grounds of the distinctions have rested on dogmatically held convictions or have lacked a basis in reality, the potential for harm has been literally limitless, particularly in the circumstances of the technologically enabled modern state.

Amartya Sen has said that all modern famines are political. We can say likewise that all modern massacres and genocides are categorial.[10] After

---

[10] Amartya Sen, *Identity and Violence: The Illusion of Destiny* (New York: W. W. Norton & Co., 2007 [2006]), 1, writes that 'A sense of identity can be a source not merely of pride and joy, but also of strength and confidence . . . And yet identity can also kill – and kill with abandon.'

all, those being killed are only Tutsis, or Ukrainians. Adorno's remark that the Jews died in the camps as species was exemplary in this respect. Adorno's complaint was not that individuals should not be regarded as instances of types, simply as such. To be an individual is, after all, to instantiate a species. It is impossible not be an instance of a type in various respects.

That is to say, one cannot be Jack or Jill without also being a human being, having a gender, born at a certain time and place, a speaker of a particular language, and so on. Pure individuality, as Hegel was at pains to make clear, is an abstraction. Adorno's point, rather, was that the Jews who were murdered were not *only* types, and were not simply reducible to types. There is nothing wrong in principle with identifying someone as a Jew; but no one is ever only a Jew, nor should being a Jew ever mean that someone can freely be abused. Likewise, no one is ever only their race or gender or sexuality or any other single attribute.

We may all be classified in numberless ways. But to reduce individuals to a group identity has repeatedly invited incivilities with no logical resting point short of complete depersonalisation. It has often been a prelude to attempts at extermination. From an ethical point of view, no doubt, the milder versions of this tendency are merely forms of unfairness. But in the modern world it has involved previously unknown extremes of violence and destruction. Adorno was absolutely correct, in this respect, to argue that the way in which Western thought typically privileged the universal in thinking about categories and classification contained the potential for political disaster.

Popper was also right to think that the way in which Plato connected the Forms with knowledge and authority contained the potential for abuse. This does not mean we must agree that Plato was an enemy of the open society in a modern sense. We live in a world that in many respects lies altogether outside Plato's horizon of experience. But the self-validating quality of the vision of the good enjoyed by the philosopher-ruler that Plato described nevertheless has the potential to encourage an attitude which brooks no dissent.

Anyone believing that their standpoint is the only one from which ultimate reality can be grasped is likely to also consider themselves to have a monopoly of righteousness. Christianity and Islam both owe a considerable amount to Platonism, and the belief on the part of their institutional representatives that they possessed an unusually privileged form of knowledge of the divine has frequently been a license for persecution. Disagreement becomes apostasy or heresy or blasphemy, punishable by death.

CONCLUSION: THE INESCAPABILITY OF CATEGORIALITY   313

Modernity only intensified the problems associated with categories insofar as they relate to identity. A common feature of these problems, once more, was their historicity. For example, twenty-first century issues over race in the West stand in a line of events in the histories of colonialism, imperialism and slavery that goes back to the fifteenth century, if not further. Questions to do with gender and the status of women may plausibly be traced to the ancient world. Attitudes inherited from Aristotelian biology in which the male was the superior active principle and the lesser female was purely passive still shape contemporary discourse. Ideas about sexuality, sometimes in transmuted secular form, remain under the continuing influence of Christian belief. It is only historical investigation that can make all this evident to us (and here one may doubtless be grateful to Foucault).

At the same time, the purpose of such investigations is to understand, not to condemn. Putnam was correct that historiography can't only use value-neutral language. But this equivocates between judgements about the values of past actors, and judgements about the value of those values. We have no choice but to recognise that people in the past often had values of their own that we do not share. History must recognise them where they were present and explain the role they played in events. But this in no way requires historians to pass judgement on them. In this respect the historical standpoint is entirely forensic.[11] Cassirer's suggestion that history is the analogue of the modern, Darwinian, discourse about nature in which evolution is path-dependent but fundamentally undirected remains worthy of consideration. On this view, biological life has no particular goal, it does not need to be thought of as the realisation of a divine idea, and the survival of the fittest has no ethical implications one way or other.[12]

For Cassirer, when we are pursuing the historical study of human life, the relevance of the past for the future is discounted, the question of whether or not there is a plan is redundant, and moral judgement is superfluous. Given the censorial attitude sometimes directed at past philosophers in the contemporary era, Cassirer's point about moral judgement in particular may benefit from some clarification. He was not arguing that condemnation of historical injustices was mistaken; his point, rather, was

---

[11] Hilary Putnam, *Reason, Truth and History* (Cambridge: Cambridge University Press, 1998 [1981]), 200. Analogously, a judicial ruling that a killing was murder treats the judge's personal disapproval as irrelevant to its conditions.

[12] Compare James A. Herrick, *The History and Theory of Rhetoric: An Introduction*, 6th edn (New York: Routledge, 2018), 230.

that it was irrelevant to comprehension. Simply condemning individual thinkers leaves us otherwise ignorant of them.

It is indisputable, for instance, that Aristotle was a supporter of patriarchy and a defender of natural slavery, views that are unacceptable to any modern liberal. But to decide not to read Aristotle in response would render large stretches of past thought incomprehensible. Not just the ancient world, but the medieval and even the modern, simply do not make sense without him. For the same reason, Heidegger's association with National Socialism is unambiguously deplorable, but is not a reason not to study him, if only because, like Aristotle, he has had such an impact on modern intellectual developments.

The point, in other words, is to know only that what was said or done was wrong was not to know what was said or done, or why. Only to condemn past evils and become emotionally outraged by them teaches us nothing about how they began, how they were practised, or what sustained them. One of the most important features of modernity and the associated project of Enlightenment has been a great levelling of hierarchies, both intellectually and politically. All the traditional grounds on which one could conceive of a normative hierarchy of disciplines have been gradually undercut. So have all the grounds on which one could conceive of a natural hierarchy of human beings. But one will not understand the past if one only engages with it in the light of contemporary beliefs.

It might be tempting to think that the emergence of a belief in the equality of the status of different genres of thought, and of a belief in the equality of the status of human beings, were coeval. But in fact, the processes by which these changes occurred have been highly complex, not to mention drawn out over millennia, and although they have sometimes moved in parallel, are not logically interconnected. One could, for example, retain a belief in an intellectual hierarchy of forms of thought while holding a conviction of fundamental human equality, at least in the abstract. Indeed, that was the position towards which Christianity tended, making theology the most important form of knowledge while holding that all human beings were equally marked by original sin.

Christianity generally lent its support to the hierarchy of medieval society, but those social arrangements were never strictly scriptural; they required theologians like Aquinas to legitimate them. Christianity's longevity has partly been a function of this capacity to adapt itself to almost any political order whatever, even when seemingly in tension with its professed principles. But along with the disappearance at gradual and uneven rates of the belief in natural intellectual and human hierarchies, both of which typically assumed a conception of the divine, the corresponding normative conceptions of the good also lost their self-evident character, as did the accompanying beliefs about human nature.

Hence the modern difficulties with articulating a conception of what a human being is in other than biological terms, and with reaching any consensus on the nature of the good life. Perhaps one can exaggerate the novelty of this situation. To give Plato and Aristotle their due, they too recognised that there was no one form of life that was good for everyone. What is now contentious are their claims that people have a nature which definitively fits them for a particular kind of life, and that the contemplative life is absolutely the best. Heidegger's remark that *Dasein* is distinguished by the fact that 'in its very Being, that Being is an *issue* for it' carries weight. No other creature that we know of is a puzzle to itself.[13]

Yet there are difficulties with a view like that of Leo Strauss, who believed that there was such a thing as ancient virtue, that its loss had been a terrible tragedy, and that the only way to redeem modernity was to try and recover it.[14] Strauss's narrative continues to appeal in certain American conservative intellectual circles in particular, but it is really a politicised version of Heidegger's story of the covering up of the insights of the ancient Greeks into Being. It has tended to encourage a reactionary view of politics organised around the nostalgic fantasy that things were better in the past, and that the goal should be to make things great again. The sceptical, historically informed, response is that life for most people has never really been great at any point in the past, and it is only the nature of the difficulties that we face that has changed.

Insofar as the reactionary view treats the alleged lack of an ethical and political consensus in modernity as problematic, it can be said that it is not prima facie obvious that consensus ought to be our goal, as distinct from, for example, learning to agree to disagree as peacefully as possible. Aristotle was very aware that ethical reasoning was not of the same kind as the theoretical reasoning employed in the sciences of mathematics, physics and theology. We must not expect demonstrative certainty in reasoning about political and ethical matters: 'Accepting from a mathematician

---

[13] Martin Heidegger, *Being and Time*, trans. John Macquarrie and Edward Robinson (Oxford: Blackwell Publishers, 2001 [1962]), 32. Emphasis in original. Compare Peterson's remark that while we have seminars about animals, they don't have seminars about us: see the Introduction, n. 8, above.

[14] Leo Strauss, *Natural Right and History* (Chicago: University of Chicago Press, 1965 [1953]), 2, wrote that German thought had imposed 'unqualified relativism' on the West but 'the need for natural right is as evident today as it has been for centuries and even millennia'.

claims that are mere probabilities seems rather like demanding logical proofs from a rhetorician.'[15]

Attempting to recapture a lost ancient virtue is not a viable project for us, as Hegel already recognised. Whatever reality it had was of a piece with a culture that has vanished and which no ersatz effort at revivalism could ever recreate. Fostering a culture in which an analytical perspective on our own past is a more widespread possession – greater historical literacy – at least has the merit of not being an impossible goal. One thing that fragmentarians, subordinationists and pluralists have typically agreed on is that human beings are fundamentally creatures of imagination. This characteristic is at once a precondition of the scientific attitude broadly conceived, insofar as it enables the creation of what Cassirer called symbolic forms of knowledge, and the source of the pathological illusions that concern psychoanalysts. A critical study of and education in history is one possible aid to living a life imagined in rational terms rather than through self-destructive fantasies – if we decide this is important to us.

This ideal remains consistent with the ancient Delphic injunction to self-knowledge. Despite their different conceptions of categories, Plato, Aristotle, Kant and Hegel were at least unanimous that they were indispensable to thinking. No doubt this view can be questioned: Hegel, for instance, has sometimes been read as treating philosophy as pursuing the goal of presuppositionlessness.[16] But (as is so often the case) Hegel can also be read as saying quite the opposite, and seeking to show why such presuppositionlessness is in fact impossible. On this reading, Hegel, like Aristotle, was arguing that all discourses rest on certain fundamental postulates that are not demonstrable by that discourse but that are only useable within it. Unlike Aristotle, Hegel took the view that these postulates or presuppositions were not themselves fixed.

On Hegel's account, the history of knowledge included plenty of what Thomas Kuhn would later call 'normal science', but it was also the story of how changes in the fundamental postulates of one or another genre of knowledge had occurred. When we read past works of philosophy, it is

---

[15] Aristotle, *Nicomachean Ethics*, trans. Roger Crisp (Cambridge: Cambridge University Press, 2004 [2000]), 1094b. Aristotle meant probable reasoning in the political, rhetorical sense; he did not have in mind (and could not have had in mind) the modern mathematical theory of probabilities.

[16] Miles Hentrup, 'Hegel's Logic as Presuppositionless Science', *Idealistic Studies: An Interdisciplinary Journal of Philosophy*, 49:2 (2019), 145–65, argues that Richard Winfield and Stephen Houlgate are amongst those who claim that Hegel wants to find a presuppositionless starting point but that this is a mistake because Hegel thinks reality is always self-mediating.

very obvious to us that they are anything but free from presuppositions. But the fact that we can see this, when past authors themselves could not, suggests that later generations will likewise see our own works as full of prejudices of one sort or another, even though we are now blind to them. Yet at the same time, this is a condition of genuine progress in any area of thought, because a presupposition or prejudice, once detected, can be explicitly searched for in future.

We might also think of this ideal as representing the precipitate of the Renaissance humanist ideal of *l'uomo universale*. This figure was a master of all human knowledge and accomplishments: Leonardo da Vinci was supposedly an exemplary case, both deeply learned and at the same time an ingenious inventor and a great artist. It is impossible now to emulate Leonardo's comprehensive mastery of art, science, and practice (whether or not he was really so omnicompetent.) Modern specialisation has made enormous gains in knowledge, but advances have come from delving ever more deeply into an ever-narrower subject matter.

To avoid becoming victims of our own success, the solution is not to give up the depth but to allow for some breadth alongside it. The modern *l'uomo* (or *donna*) *universale* cannot know everything, but it remains possible to be someone who, in addition to being aware of the nature of their own discourse, has some understanding of the other kinds of knowing that figure in their society's public sphere. Awareness of positionality, to be meaningful, cannot be only sociological. It must include the knowledge not only that one has a point of view, but of the *kind* of a point of view it is.

The argument that genre needs to be taken into account was fundamental to the metaphor of perspectivalism. As developed by fragmentarian thought, this involved a self-conscious revision to the idea of what it meant to be Enlightened. The fragmentarians stressed that our individual point of view also always has a framework; Nietzsche's criticisms of Christianity were aimed at the confusion of the moral perspective with the logic of self-interest. We saw, also, that the fragmentarians typically distinguished their arguments for perspectivalism from a strong relativism that resulted in contradiction and thus offered no grounds for weighing the merits of different frameworks. But in contemporary popular culture this distinction has typically been missed, and 'post-modernism' has become a synonym for a form of relativism that few, if any, of the thinkers typically gathered under that label actually held.

Yet even if we disregard the charge of relativism, the metaphor of perspective still prioritises the role of the observing subject. As Kant noted in the first *Critique*, when the subject moves around an object they are looking at, there is not normally any fundamental discontinuity in their perceptions.[17] We realise we have a different view of the house as we see it now from the front and now from the back, but we know we are seeing the same thing. But this metaphor does not capture the difference between one *type* of viewpoint and another. It only distinguishes perspectives with respect to space and time. It does not draw attention to the existence of whatever other categorial conditions govern our experience. Indeed, insofar as there are as many perspectives in this sense as there are knowing subjects, Kant's account may inadvertently offer support for the relativistic position. I (or we) see things one way from where I am standing, and you (or they) see them another way from over there, and that is apparently all there is to be said.

Kant's example thus omitted precisely the consideration of the *kind* of view the different parties were taking. Kant's system as a whole, admittedly, did link different kinds of knowing to different faculties. Though the example of seeing different sides of a house did not make it as plain as we might like, Kant knew very well that whether or not different parties were understanding things in the same sort of way was a consideration distinct from their respective spatio-temporal locations. Moreover, the number of 'highest kinds' of knowledge in the Kantian sense was fairly small. Kant's system distinguished philosophical, political, aesthetic, mathematical and scientific kinds of viewpoints, for example; but there were certainly not infinitely many such kinds, and the conditions of each were exhaustively specifiable.

The fragmentarians were not alone in resorting to metaphor to convey their position. The subordinationist desire to give priority to one form of knowledge over all others did likewise. This was certainly the case with Heidegger, whose later writings exploited the metaphors of medieval Christian mysticism. Like the metaphor of perspective, however, discourses of revelation fail to capture a key fact about categoriality, namely that even the clearest and most distinct ideas, the most objective and truest of thoughts, nevertheless remain ideas and thoughts of a certain *kind*. Heidegger's metaphor of the 'ground' overlooks that there is always a fact of the matter about the specific type of ground that we are on. None of this means that we are doomed to seeing through a glass darkly, but it does imply that there are conditions to even the most apparently transparent mystical vision.[18]

---

[17] Immanuel Kant, *Critique of Pure Reason*, trans. and ed. Paul Guyer and Allen M. Wood (Cambridge: Cambridge University Press, 1998), 305–6. See also Chapter 3, above.

[18] 1 Corinthians 13:12: 'For now we see through a glass, darkly; but then face to face: now I know in part; but then shall I know even as also I am known.' (King James version.)

The analytic variety of subordinationism did not eschew metaphor either. When Quine wanted to argue against the existence of universals, he wrote that an 'overpopulated universe ... offends the aesthetic sense of us who have a taste for desert landscapes'.[19] Quine's commitment to physicalism committed him to regarding categories of any extra-linguistic nature as at best useful fictions. Quinean philosophy 'repudiated the infinite universe of universals as a dream world' and insisted on being guided exclusively by science when it came to the nature of reality. It was only acceptable to 'impute infinitude' to a 'universe of particulars' if physicists had established it as an 'objective fact' that the universe really is infinite.[20] But as P. F. Strawson put it, 'With a Roman ruthlessness [Quine] makes a solitude in which he can quantify peacefully over lumps of rock.' Quine's position, Strawson remarked, was motivated by a quite unphilosophical 'aesthetic puritanism'.[21]

The need to accommodate mathematical objects meant that in the last resort the nominalism Quine was endorsing could not be reduced to physicalism. Nominalism could at least restrict the kinds of infinities it could accept, however, and so Quine wrote that anyone adopting this position could 'allay his puritanic conscience with the reflection that he has not quite taken to eating lotus with the platonists'.[22] Even if we treat this identification of nominalism with Puritanism as humorously self-aware, however, both Quine's metaphors and his concessions to mathematics suggest that his desire to make science the sole index of reality was philosophically problematic as well as unscientific. It was motivated by a commitment to a tradition of philosophical realism that has typically struggled to accommodate the meaningful and artefactual phenomena of the human world. As Lakoff puts it, in an allusion to Plato's *Sophist*, 'you can carve nature at any joints you like, you can't carve out a government'.[23]

Our contemporary situation remains the product, to a significant extent, of the tension between the demands of subjectivity and objectivity represented by fragmentarians and subordinationists respectively. There

---

[19] W. V. O. Quine, 'On What There Is', *Review of Metaphysics*, 2:5 (1948), 23.
[20] W. V. O. Quine, *From a Logical Point of View: 9 Logico-Philosophical Essays*, 2nd edition (New York: Harper Torchbooks, 1963 [1953]), 128–9.
[21] P. F. Strawson, 'A Logician's Landscape', *Philosophy*, 30 (1955), 229–237, 229.
[22] Quine, *From a Logical Point of View*, 129. Though a neat correspondence between nominalism and Puritanism as historical movements would be convenient for the sake of this example, the reality is more complex. Nominalism long preceded Puritanism, and Puritanical theological commitments by no means always led their holders to endorse nominalistic metaphysical views.
[23] Lakoff, *Women, Fire, and Dangerous Things*, 243–4.

is thus scope for a metaphor that avoids these polar oppositions. Here the idea of the spectrum may be helpful. It is in the Kantian tradition of the example of viewing the house; retains the physicalist basis Quine sought; and can incorporate the kinds of qualitative shifts in kinds of subjective perception emphasised by perspectivalism. Think, for example, of seeing something under normal light, and under ultraviolet (UV) light, where the object appears to us to glow in a way that only happens when it is exposed to light of that wavelength.

What we see in both cases is real. The object as seen under normal light, and as seen under UV light, is still entirely itself; but it now discloses a quality or property that does not become visible unless and until we take up another relation to it by using a different kind of light to reveal it. If we only look at the object under normal light, we may take it for granted that that is all there is to see, being unaware that the object can have other qualities at all. But the view under UV light is not a *replacement* for the normal view; it is not 'truer' than the view we normally see. It is objectively an aspect of the thing, but is only disclosed under certain conditions.

Furthermore, the views under both kinds of light are equally dependent on the terms of the subject-object relation, and neither view is better in any absolute sense. Whether the view of the object under natural light or under UV (or infra-red, or X-rays) is preferable is not a question that can be answered independently of the reasons for wanting to see something that way in the first place. Nevertheless, once we have seen something in another way, our understanding is permanently modified, at least to the extent that we now know that another kind of view is possible.

At the same time, the spectrum is finite and definable. There are only so many bands within it, and we can say with precision where the divisions between them fall. The number of possible *kinds* of view we can take is not limitless. Lastly, the fact that most of the spectrum is normally *invisible* to us serves to remind us of the way in which thinking readily leaves the sensible world altogether behind, as it inevitably does even in daily life, never mind in more formal, theoretical situations.

The metaphor of the spectrum corresponds to the pluralist case for a limited variety of types of thinking. Each position on the spectrum offers a different kind of light, where the light is a figure for a distinctive set of presuppositions. Within each position there may also be many further subdivisions. Each shows us something that is true and real, but none shows us all that there is to see. As Lakoff puts it, we are not rejecting objective reality but the idea that there is one uniquely privileged form of access to it.[24]

---

[24] Lakoff, *Women, Fire, and Dangerous Things*, 259.

CONCLUSION: THE INESCAPABILITY OF CATEGORIALITY 321

On the other hand, no band on the spectrum relies for the view it offers on any of the others; each has its own relative completeness and independence. And yet, at the same time, they imply one another in each forming part of a continuum which displays definite transitions that are ultimately only definable in terms of one another. Nor is recognition of the utility of a given band on the spectrum at the expense of any of the others. Each of the divisions in the spectrum allows us to know something that could not be known without it. None can show us everything, and certainly not everything at once.

The principle of opportunity cost also applies. There is so much to see at any given point on the spectrum that we may never find a reason to move outside it. Indeed, understanding what we are seeing becomes more demanding as we continue to look ever more closely. There is no reason not to think of the pursuit of knowledge as an endless, infinite task. We shall never be done with science or history or philosophy. This should not be adjudged a Sisyphean situation but one that permanently guarantees us the excitement that comes with fresh discovery. At least, we must imagine Sisyphus happy.[25]

In our modern situation, all that most of us can do is to concentrate on our work at our own narrow frequency. There are few Leonardos who can traverse more than one of the different bands in the spectrum of knowledge and even fewer (if any) who can roam through all of them, certainly not with equal facility. But it remains open to everyone to appreciate that other parts of the spectrum exist, and to supply an informed audience for the things that go on outside their own areas of competence. Indeed, by doing so, we may hope to acquire the kind of good amateur judgement that for Aristotle was the mark of the educated.[26]

---

[25] Albert Camus, 'The Myth of Sisyphus', in *The Myth of Sisyphus and Other Essays*, trans. Justin O'Brien (New York: Vintage Books, 1991 [1955]), 4–87, 78, wrote that 'One must imagine Sisyphus happy.' But Camus, 'The Myth of Sisyphus', 4, also prioritised ethics over epistemology in philosophy, saying that 'There is but one truly serious philosophical problem, and that is suicide. Judging whether life is or is not worth living amounts to answering the fundamental question of philosophy. All the rest – whether or not the world has three dimensions, whether the mind has nine or twelve categories – comes afterwards.' Camus was effectively reformulating Nietzsche's objection to categories as Kantian skeletons rattling in the closet: see Chapter 5, n. 29. Henry Miller, *Tropic of Cancer* (New York: Grove Press, 1994 [1934]), 55, went further, effectively providing a profane distillation of subordinationism by having the narrator say: 'Fuck your two ways of looking at things. Fuck your pluralistic universe.'

[26] Aristotle, *Nicomachean Ethics*, trans. Roger Crisp (Cambridge: Cambridge University Press, 2004 [2000]), 1094b.

The metaphor of the spectrum also accommodates the political analogue stressed by pluralism, which seeks to value both diversity and limits. It entails that there are outer bounds, yet is capable of incorporating at least some of the radical political critique mounted by the philosophers of fragmentation. The arguments of critical theory, post-colonialism and feminism about the dangers of imposing categories on others still have their origins in arguments about the logic of identity that go back to Hegel.

Hopefully, we understand these and other contemporary conceptions of categories better when we appreciate what they owe to earlier philosophical discussions of the subject. We have also sought to demonstrate how the constantly changing philosophical answers to the question of the nature of categories have nevertheless been persistently bound up with a further set of fundamental questions. These questions concern what a human being is; what we know and the kinds of things that we know; our sense of our own being in time; and probably most importantly for those not normally interested in philosophical questions about categories, our beliefs about personal identity and political order.[27] Only by grasping this history can we comprehend why contemporary category discourse has become so ubiquitous.

It would be going too far to say that history as a form of knowledge has become the modern replacement for metaphysics, because history is not philosophy, nor ever will be; but it is one of the larger pyres burning in the Kantian hell of self-knowledge.[28] Expecting its' fire to keep us warm will only lead to disappointment, but it nonetheless helps to illuminate the cave and rescues us from groping entirely in the dark. Since we are ending with an old Platonic metaphor, let us give a mathematician the last word: 'The humanities are the best language we have for understanding as much as we can about what it is to be human.'[29] It seems that to be human is to be fated to historicity under the sign of *homo distinguens*; and that is at least some kind of answer to the puzzle of *Dasein*.

---

[27] Lakoff and Johnson, *Philosophy in the Flesh*, 9, write that 'Living a human life is a philosophical endeavour.' But this conflates the fact that life is categorially mediated with life as the subject of self-conscious theoretical analysis. Certainly, 'We go around armed with a host of presuppositions about what is real, what counts as knowledge, how the mind works, who we are, and how we should act.' Plato's point, however, was that this did not make anyone a philosopher simply as such. Nor does it now.

[28] Hayden White, *The Practical Past* (Evanston, IL: Northwestern University Press, 2014), 33, writes that 'historical discourse [has] quietly slipped into the place formerly occupied by religion and metaphysics and become a kind of degree zero of factuality . . . limiting itself to establishing what really happened in discrete domains of the past and resisting any impulse to draw lessons for the present'.

[29] Marcus Du Sautoy, *What We Cannot Know Explorations at the Edge of Knowledge* (London: 4th Estate, 2016), 419.

Index of Subjects

Absolute, 12n, 24, 87, 122–3, 135–6, 149, 152, 155–6, 158–60, 171, 186–7, 281, 286, 294–5
action, 34, 41, 46–7, 72, 80–2, 92–4, 96, 99, 101, 109, 118, 122, 143, 145, 244, 262, 271, 276, 282, 289, 295, 297–8, 300–1, 304, 308
aesthetics, 54, 109, 113, 126–7, 193, 208–9, 252, 267, 276, 318–19
aether, 84, 102
agreement *see* consensus
alchemy, 165
alienation, 175–6, 217
anarchism, 219
anthropology, 3, 46, 115, 127–9, 139, 144, 169, 286
antinomies, 122–3, 131, 138
apocalypse, 13n, 65, 138, 181, 221, 258, 302
appearance, 24, 34, 48, 113, 115, 118, 137, 144, 152, 159, 163, 283
apperception, 115, 152, 212, 239
aristocracy, 21, 70, 130, 173, 195, 205, 213, 215, 222, 261n, 266
assumptions *see* presuppositions
astrology, 49
astronomy, 14, 37, 83, 138
astrophysics, 110
atheism, 220, 254
atomism, 38, 169
authenticity, 240, 263, 282
authority, 8, 62, 86, 89, 108–9, 129, 132, 134, 136–7, 140, 172–3, 195, 212, 235, 287–8, 290, 293–4, 304, 312

beauty, 19, 37, 41, 49, 107, 113, 125–6, 133, 280
Being, 3–4, 27, 37–8, 42, 52, 88, 114, 125, 138, 152, 155–8, 161n, 234–5, 237–42, 244–5, 248–52, 263, 265–7, 269, 276–7, 281, 285, 296, 309, 315
biology, 17, 69, 83, 85, 103, 116, 125, 141, 167–9, 260, 266, 297, 313
biopolitics, 231
body, 118, 126, 140, 144, 146, 154, 158, 169, 174, 196–7, 213, 218, 237, 239, 251, 262, 282, 298

capitalism, 175, 201, 208, 217, 220, 261
caste *see* aristocracy
categorical imperative, 23, 117, 127, 128n, 133
categories
  Aristotle's list of ten, 68, 71–2, 74–5, 148
  as *a priori* conditions, 25, 74, 111–13, 116–17, 124, 129, 131, 140, 144–5, 148, 152, 163, 194, 198, 201–2, 212, 227, 239–40, 266, 274, 276, 299, 305–7
  as dynamic, 24–5, 150–1, 160, 183, 186, 198, 305–6
  as Forms, 6–7, 33, 72, 151, 305–6
  as fundamental or basic concepts, 21, 33–7, 41, 47, 51, 65, 102, 112, 148n, 156, 219, 229, 233, 237–41, 245, 261n, 265, 270, 273, 275–7, 305
  as invisible, 3, 73, 102, 147, 159, 305, 308, 320

categories (*Cont.*)
  as predicates, 5, 37, 40n, 75, 111, 123, 125, 157, 169, 195, 240n, 277, 305
  pattern of association of, 7–10, 13, 15,18, 25, 29, 33, 66, 146, 174, 185–6, 196, 236, 269–70, 305–8, 322
category mistakes, 4, 46, 142, 302n, 305
causality, 57, 96, 112–3, 115–18, 121–4, 126–7, 144, 167, 197, 203, 206, 262–3, 284
cave (Platonic story of), 34, 42, 63, 81, 123, 159, 289, 322
certainty, 23, 70, 93–4, 97, 103, 109–10, 139, 146, 164, 238, 244, 297, 306, 315
change, 35, 37, 42, 48, 54, 56, 61, 64, 69, 72, 82–3, 94, 118, 197, 216, 221, 226, 229, 273, 297, 307, 314
chemistry, 149, 169, 243n
chi, 16
citizenship, 90–2, 94, 132, 170
civilisation, 4, 292, 298, 303–4, 309
classes
  conceptual, 3, 40–1, 101, 114, 151, 208, 275, 280, 311
  social, 28, 35, 44–5, 55, 61–2, 89, 91, 175–6, 178, 187, 197, 205, 215, 224, 236, 244, 248, 288
classification, 2, 44, 80, 92, 195, 198, 201, 205, 208, 210, 216, 274, 279, 311–12
colonialism, 89, 175, 177, 313
common sense, 20, 43, 75, 82, 93, 158–9, 161, 163, 207, 229–30, 278
community, 2, 43, 51, 53, 55, 61, 81, 92, 134–5, 138, 153, 173, 175, 197, 259, 283, 291, 303
conduct *see* action
consciousness, 24, 122, 156, 162–3, 262, 268, 283–4, 290–1, 306
consensus, 135–6, 146, 292, 315
constitution, 35–6, 48, 51, 58, 60–2, 71, 91–2, 99, 130–1
contemplation, 21, 35, 46, 81, 87, 102, 280, 282, 301, 315
context(s), 6, 27, 72, 115, 142, 183, 185, 199–200, 207, 209, 228–9, 247, 270, 272

contingency, 49, 58n, 63, 70, 82, 92, 95–7, 99–102, 117, 146, 167, 184, 186, 221–3, 225–6, 295, 304, 310
contract, 18n, 90n, 132, 137, 175–6, 288
cosmology 7n, 14, 15, 16, 17, 20, 39, 52, 57, 82, 84, 109, 207
critical theory, 3, 26, 163, 322
cultural studies, 3
culture, 62, 143–4, 153–4, 174, 187–8, 194, 207–8, 211, 213–15, 217, 222, 226, 243–4, 256, 260, 262, 266, 279–80, 287, 290–1, 297–8, 316–17

Dasein, 239–40, 244, 249, 263–7, 269, 285, 315
death, 84, 109, 143, 158, 179, 239, 288, 293, 307, 312
debate/deliberations, 52, 92–5, 101, 135
decisions, 53
definition, 38, 41, 53, 65, 86, 114
democracy, 21, 27, 36, 45, 50–2, 61–2, 89, 99–100, 173, 205, 215, 217, 258, 261, 294, 301
demonstration, 9, 42, 68–9, 82–3, 85–6, 90, 93, 97, 102, 125, 315–16
dialectic, 8, 46, 47–8, 52, 65, 79, 90, 93, 156, 158, 161, 166, 175, 178, 181, 186, 200, 202, 217, 223–4, 292, 295, 298
dictatorship, 51, 253
difference/diversity, 56, 91, 128, 169, 174, 176, 200, 215, 220, 280, 293, 322
discourse *see* speech
divided line, 42–3, 46–7, 81, 160
divinity *see* God (Index of Proper Nouns)
dualism, 37, 265
duty, 45, 94, 108–9, 117, 127, 133–4, 137–8, 276, 288, 292–3, 300, 303

education, 46, 50n, 70, 86, 127, 140, 148, 253, 256–7, 316, 321
elementalism, 38, 84, 121, 166
embodiment *see* body
emotion, 196, 274, 280, 282, 297
empiricism, 3, 9, 72, 77, 82, 107, 109, 111–12, 115–17, 119, 121, 123–5, 127, 129, 133–4, 138–45, 162, 164, 168, 194, 196–7, 200, 202, 208, 228, 243–4, 247, 284, 298–9

enthusiasm *see* fanaticism
episteme (in Aristotle), 79n, 80–2, 84–5, 86n, 87
episteme (in Foucault), 209, 226–7
epistemology, 6, 146, 160, 186, 189, 280, 287, 296, 304
equality, 18n, 45, 55–6, 61–2, 88–90, 131, 177, 181, 205, 215–17, 291–2, 311, 314
eschatology *see* apocalypse
ethics, 19, 63, 79, 98, 103, 170, 273
ethnicity, 2, 128
eugenics, 45, 257
events, 64, 94–5, 98–9, 139, 146, 184, 188, 244, 283, 295–7, 300, 303
evidence, 22, 100, 296, 300, 302
evolution, 46, 116, 167–8, 268
executive, 35
experience, 4, 6, 18, 22–3, 28, 36–7, 40, 42, 72, 80, 107, 110–18, 121–4, 127, 129, 137–8, 144–5, 151, 158–60, 163–4, 194, 199, 203, 212, 233, 263, 270, 272, 276–7, 279–80, 282, 284–6, 306–7, 318
experiment, 82, 284, 300

family, 103, 150, 154, 172–4, 176, 179–80
fanaticism, 127n, 135
fascism, 225, 236n
feminism, 3, 17, 322
Forms (Platonic), 4, 8, 19, 20–1, 22, 25, 33–43, 49, 56, 63–5, 68, 72–4, 102, 108, 122, 147–8, 151, 250, 265–6, 306, 312
fragmentarians, 10, 25, 28, 189, 193–233, 236, 270–2, 277, 295, 304, 309–11, 316–19
freedom/free will, 51, 61–2, 90, 94, 108n, 109, 115, 117, 119, 122–3, 125, 130–1, 137, 143, 145–6, 150, 153, 171–3, 178, 181–2, 187, 200, 219, 224–6, 262, 276, 284, 287, 289–90, 294, 299
future, 53, 64, 70, 92, 94, 101, 183, 236–7, 239, 260, 263, 265, 269, 296, 303

Geist, 24, 149, 154–5, 170, 174, 183, 185, 187, 200, 212, 227, 266, 295

gender, 2, 18, 46, 128, 154, 176
genealogy, 199, 202, 223, 226
general will, 132, 137
genocide, 195, 230, 311
geography, 141
geometry, 36, 47, 83, 85, 93, 110, 114, 121, 244–5
global *see* universal
gods *see* paganism
Good, 19, 34, 41–3, 49, 52, 56, 65, 80, 86, 107, 109, 119, 275–6, 312, 315
government, 16, 20, 21, 23, 33–4, 37, 46–8, 51–2, 56, 60–1, 65, 70, 133–5, 140, 145, 150, 170, 174, 216, 235, 254, 287–8, 319

happiness, 126–7, 130, 253n
hatred, 92, 217, 256, 307
hermeneutics, 262, 271n, 286
hierarchy, 13, 15, 19, 21, 23–4, 33–4, 42, 52, 55–6, 65, 68–70, 80, 84–5, 87–9, 94, 96, 102, 109, 112n, 119, 129–31, 147, 160–1, 186, 208, 212, 215, 229–30, 281, 293, 314
historical *a priori*, 201, 218, 227
historicism, 182–3, 186, 236, 247, 264, 271, 276
historicity, 9, 24, 27–8, 56, 76, 102, 115, 118–19, 149, 156, 188–9, 195, 201, 204, 223, 227, 229, 247, 267, 272–3, 280, 282–3, 286, 294, 308, 313, 322
history, 3, 5, 8, 9, 22, 26, 28, 57, 70, 138, 156, 158, 169, 202, 209n, 224, 236–7, 252, 259–60, 262, 310
  as apocalyptic, 57, 138, 143
  as cyclical, 20, 33, 35, 57, 61–2, 64, 99, 109, 142
  as decline, 35, 57, 60, 260, 266
  as discontinuous, 225
  as exemplary, 60, 64, 222–3
  as historiography, 35–6, 58, 63–4, 71, 95, 97, 99–100, 109, 118, 128–9, 139, 141, 145–6, 183–4, 195, 219, 222, 224, 226, 228–30, 247, 260, 262–4, 266–9, 273, 279, 281, 286, 295–304, 310, 316, 321–2
  as historiology, 27, 237, 263–5

history (*Cont.*)
  as necessary, 65, 131, 138, 142, 185, 227, 260, 265–6, 295, 298, 309
  as progressive, 143, 150, 181, 188, 203, 212, 220–1, 254, 264, 268, 295, 309
  as salvational, 12, 13n, 65, 109, 116, 137–8, 141, 143, 150, 301, 308
  logic of, 23, 142, 146, 182, 261, 269, 271, 310
  speculative philosophy of, 24–5, 60, 138, 178, 180–4, 195, 201, 221, 224–5, 230, 295, 298, 304
homo distinguens, 2, 322
homosexuality, 218
homo sapiens, 2
humanism, 202, 217–18, 309
humanities/human sciences, 141, 169, 202, 234, 273, 284, 298, 309, 322
humanity, 35, 49, 69, 71, 128, 135, 138, 141, 154, 203, 214, 248, 281, 308, 301
human nature, 21, 49, 55, 73, 94, 115, 127–8, 187, 217, 279, 296, 315

I *see* self
Idealism, 87, 194, 198, 226, 229, 245, 247, 271–2, 280, 283–4
Ideas *see* Forms (Platonic)
identity, 1, 26, 39, 94, 154, 169–70, 175, 180, 195, 199–200, 206, 208, 218–19, 306, 312–13, 322
ideology, 216, 244, 248, 264, 293
imagination, 28, 115, 126, 137, 211, 289, 304, 316
imperialism, 4, 179, 260–1, 311, 313
implicit bias, 2
individuality, 1, 51, 64, 127, 153, 158, 169, 172, 206, 214, 217, 251
individual(s), 21, 26, 44–5, 47, 55, 73, 150, 169, 181, 195, 224, 303, 312
inequality *see* equality
injustice *see* justice
institutions, 23, 48, 51, 272
interpretation, 9, 134, 141, 263, 300
inter-subjectivity, 154, 174–5, 199
intuition, 35, 86, 121

judgment, 2, 35, 46–8, 65, 80–1, 103, 111, 114, 124–5, 130, 201, 321
judiciary, 35
justice, 2, 19, 35, 37–8, 40–2, 46, 52–5, 60, 214, 216, 222, 294, 303, 311
  as fairness, 53

kairos, 35, 47, 49, 81, 86
kinds, 13, 47, 73, 278, 318, 320
knowledge, 3, 8, 9, 10, 18, 20–2, 27, 33–4, 44, 46–9, 61, 65, 68, 70, 79, 81, 84, 86–7, 95, 102, 107–8, 113–14, 120, 123, 127, 130, 139, 147, 156, 160–2, 164–5, 170, 183, 186, 188, 194, 199, 202–4, 206, 208–9, 225, 228–9, 233, 235, 237, 241, 244–5, 261n, 265, 267, 270, 272–3, 278–81, 283, 285–7, 297–8, 305–10, 312, 316–18, 321
  archaeology of, 212, 225, 228
  as esoteric, 42
  as hell, 145, 322
  as practical, 21, 35, 43–4, 47–8, 69, 80–1, 85, 90, 96, 110, 151, 206
  as theoretical, 21, 35, 47–8, 69, 81, 85, 110, 151, 206

language, 24, 68, 76–8, 120, 151, 155, 157, 162, 193, 195, 204, 207, 209, 212, 237–8, 242, 244, 252–4, 272, 274–5, 278–9, 282–3, 289, 295, 305, 312
law
  moral or natural, 109, 120, 125, 127, 131, 237, 293
  physical or social, 112, 116–17, 119, 123–6, 139, 152, 164, 196, 220, 254, 260, 266–8, 277, 280, 284–5, 296, 299–300, 307, 310
  positive or civil, 28, 47–8, 54n, 58, 70–1, 89, 92, 94, 103, 130, 132–4, 140, 173, 177n, 179, 188, 215–16, 271, 287–8, 291–2, 294, 304
liberalism, 143, 175, 187, 219, 269, 273, 287, 293, 304, 314
liberty *see* freedom
life, 39, 162, 197–8, 200, 215, 224
lifeworld *see* world

limits, 10, 22–3, 62, 71, 82, 87, 89, 91, 107, 111, 119, 122–3, 132, 137, 145, 170, 180, 196, 200, 203, 218, 225, 250, 267, 270, 278, 295–6, 304, 309, 311, 320, 322
linguistic turn, 120, 228
logic, 3, 25, 34, 43, 67, 75–6, 78–9, 93, 98, 101, 103, 120–2, 157–8, 161, 169, 209, 245, 253, 268, 275, 277
logical empiricism, 10, 26–8, 110, 151, 207, 232, 234–5, 237–8, 240, 242–5, 247–8, 254, 260, 264, 267, 269–70, 272, 275, 278, 280, 284, 309

materialism, 43, 157
mathematics, 3, 8, 14, 16, 19, 34, 42–3, 47–9, 54, 61, 65, 69, 84, 86, 114, 116, 121–2, 161, 165, 238, 244, 249, 254, 267–8, 273, 275, 277, 284, 315, 318–19
matter, 13, 48, 82, 87, 112, 116–17, 121, 157, 168
meaning, 1, 4, 8, 19, 27, 29, 43, 75, 94, 111, 139, 184–6, 225, 234, 237–40, 242, 244–5, 248, 250, 262, 269, 286, 296–7, 301, 305, 308–10, 319
medieval era, 9, 11, 13, 67, 75–6, 121, 123, 174, 181, 220, 241, 254–6, 259, 268, 291, 295, 308, 314, 318
memory, 28, 223n, 297, 302–3
metaphor, 5, 47, 162, 174, 193, 197, 206, 208, 234, 241–2, 283, 317–20, 322
metaphysics, 6, 22, 33, 78, 82–3, 86–88, 107–8, 119–20, 122–4, 136, 139, 145, 159–60, 162, 176, 196, 200, 206, 238, 243, 245, 247, 251, 255, 257, 265, 277, 281, 306, 308, 322
mind, 24, 38, 57n, 87, 116–17, 157, 166, 169, 239, 244, 247, 268, 276, 281, 285, 291
modernity, 5, 9, 12, 15, 26, 76, 91, 94, 103, 108, 147, 154, 172, 177, 181, 184–6, 188–9, 193, 199, 201, 205, 208, 217, 219–20, 224, 230, 238, 243, 248, 255, 258, 264, 266, 277, 285, 288, 291, 299, 304, 308, 311–12, 314–15
monarchy, 51, 70, 88, 174, 177

morality, 23, 38, 64, 108–9, 114–15, 121, 127, 131, 133, 139–40, 145–6, 170, 173, 215, 222–3, 229, 258, 279, 283, 286, 297, 300–1, 311
motion/movement, 14, 37n, 39n, 41, 49, 60, 82–3, 83n, 84n, 99n, 108n, 124, 131, 151, 249, 298
music, 47, 54–5, 178n, 208, 282
mysticism, 42–3, 47, 87, 241, 254, 259, 269, 318
myth, 45, 59, 63, 65, 88, 188, 216, 264, 272, 279, 289, 293, 301

narrative, 58, 64–5, 95, 119, 146, 184, 188, 220, 227, 229, 248, 258, 263, 267, 278, 286, 293, 295–6, 301–2, 315
nation/nationalism, 154, 212–14, 236
natural history, 141
natural philosophy, 43, 85, 98, 110, 121, 149, 161, 164, 166–7
nature, 23, 25, 27, 44, 46, 49, 57, 62, 72, 95–6, 117, 125, 139, 146, 163–4, 207, 240, 284
necessity, 95, 97, 99, 113, 117–18, 124, 127, 142, 145–7, 163, 182, 184–6, 226, 306
nihilism, 187n, 214n, 264
nobility *see* aristocracy
nominalism, 6n, 14, 74–6, 207, 319
normativity, 34, 41, 46, 52, 73
nothing, 37n, 157–8, 160n, 200
noumena, 23, 37, 109, 115, 117–18, 123, 137, 143–6, 148, 153, 159, 173, 196–7, 200, 234–5, 268
nous, 80–1, 86–8

objectivity, 26, 28, 107–8, 115, 126, 129, 145, 149, 159, 161, 170, 185, 187, 209, 222, 246n, 249, 262, 277–9, 284–5, 289, 296–8, 303–4, 318–20
obligation *see* duty
oligarchy, 61, 89, 99
One *see* whole
ontological argument, 108n, 125, 281
ontology, 75–6, 226, 238, 240, 248–9, 265, 266n, 277
organicism, 174
others, 1, 23, 44, 126–7, 130–2, 153–4, 175, 181, 208, 224, 241, 292–4, 306–7, 322

paganism, 12, 27, 55, 60, 63, 69, 82–4, 86, 88, 143, 188, 242
paradigm shift, 183
particular(s), 1, 4, 8, 47, 59, 70, 80, 92, 95, 97, 101, 124, 184, 199, 223
patriarchy, 17, 314
pattern, 9, 66, 160
perpetual peace, 143
perspectivalism, 194, 199, 204, 209n, 211, 230, 245, 304, 317–18, 320
perspective, 193, 269, 318
pessimism, 216, 220, 259, 269
phenomenology, 151, 199n, 201n, 232, 234, 237, 243, 269, 278–9, 284, 309
philosopher-rulers, 20, 21, 23, 35, 42–50, 52, 55, 60, 70, 86, 89, 130, 252, 312
philosophy, 3, 7, 34, 61, 67, 79, 84, 86–7, 102, 119–20, 123, 140–1, 145, 149, 160, 162–3, 167, 172, 177, 182, 187, 193, 198, 204–7, 237, 244, 272, 276, 278, 302, 309, 316–17, 318–19, 321–2
  as footnotes to Plato, 36, 305
  history of, 11, 17, 19, 22, 67, 73, 77, 119, 146, 150–1, 186, 224, 243, 248, 266
  medieval, 8, 97, 166
  of nature *see* natural philosophy
phronesis, 80–1
physicalism, 237, 244
physics, 23, 69, 83, 85, 110, 164–5, 168–9, 207, 244, 254, 267–8, 275, 280, 283, 315
place *see* space
Platonism, 11, 12, 109, 122, 136, 145, 158–9, 186, 200, 221, 249, 278, 287, 308, 319
pluralists, 10, 28–9, 56, 91, 189, 245, 270–304, 310–11, 316, 320, 322
poetry, 22, 71, 97, 184, 250, 252
polis, 52, 58, 91, 172, 258
political science, 3, 81n, 87, 92
politicians, 50, 82, 89n, 93, 252, 301
politics, 18, 21, 23, 33, 35, 46, 48, 51–2, 54, 61, 68, 70, 79, 81–2, 87–9, 92, 94, 96–7, 100, 102–3, 108, 115, 117, 129–30, 146, 170, 183, 186, 194, 216, 219, 223, 229, 235, 237, 252–3, 260, 269–70, 288–9, 301, 304, 307, 311–12, 314–15, 318, 322

poor, 61, 89, 91–2, 176, 294
positionality, 317
positivism, 207
possibility, 95, 113
post-colonialism, 3, 25, 322
post-humanism, 3
post-modernism, 3, 25, 317
power, 16, 18n, 91n, 123, 125, 130, 197, 203, 209, 218, 220, 230–1, 249, 258, 279, 294, 309
practice, 48, 65, 70n, 82, 114, 249, 282, 287, 291, 317
pragmatism, 151, 202, 245
prana, 16
prediction, 135, 181–2, 186, 247, 261, 263, 267
presentism, 183
presuppositions, 3, 14, 24, 76, 85, 103, 143, 149, 158, 162–3, 206, 248, 271–3, 277–8, 283, 296, 316–17
progress, 139, 317
progressivism, 2, 4, 26, 136, 195, 202n, 215, 254–5, 264, 309
proof *see* demonstration
property, 56, 90–1, 132, 144, 170, 172–3, 178
psychoanalysis, 3, 185, 200
psychology, 3, 149, 156, 169

race, 128, 175, 215, 257, 262, 289, 311, 313
racism, 18, 178, 213, 236n, 256
reality, 2, 6, 9, 14n, 19, 21–4, 34, 36–8, 42, 87, 108, 113, 120, 144, 154, 158–60, 163–4, 196, 198, 200, 230, 243–5, 280, 283, 296, 302, 309, 311, 320
reason/rationalism, 12, 19, 22, 27, 39, 41, 43, 47, 69–70, 73, 80, 83–4, 86, 92, 94, 96, 108, 114, 116, 118, 120–23, 125, 130, 133, 135–6, 139–40, 145, 153–7, 160, 162, 167, 173–4, 186, 188, 200, 206, 208, 217, 243, 255–8, 264, 272, 275, 281, 285–6, 289, 295, 297–8
recognition, 153, 175, 179, 293, 306
reflexivity, 87, 100, 145, 160, 187, 189, 206, 216

INDEX OF SUBJECTS

reincarnation, 84
relation(s), 3, 66, 111, 113, 157, 169, 233, 238, 249, 275
relativism, 25–6, 38, 78, 142, 194, 204, 206, 209, 211–12, 220, 229–30, 246–7, 262, 274, 317–18
religion, 3, 4, 19, 25, 27, 43, 69, 82, 88, 108, 119, 133–4, 140, 145–6, 155–6, 171–2, 189, 196, 198, 215, 221, 241–2, 248, 254–5, 263, 269, 279, 281–2, 285–7, 289–91, 294, 306
republicanism, 137, 179
responsibility, 91, 273, 286, 304, 308
revolution, 183, 194, 205, 216, 226, 253
rhetoric, 3, 53, 55, 70, 79n, 93, 103, 135–6
rich, 62, 89, 92
rights, 293–4
romanticism, 10, 27, 188, 193, 210n
rules *see* law

scepticism, 25–6, 131, 145, 193–6, 202, 207, 212, 216, 218, 230, 235, 260, 287, 291, 304, 315
science, 3, 4, 8, 23, 27–8, 38, 43, 71, 76, 79, 82–3, 85, 87–8, 95, 97, 98, 103, 108, 110, 114–15, 119–21, 123–4, 127–8, 136, 139, 141, 145, 149, 156, 161, 163–4, 171–2, 177, 182, 188, 194, 196, 203–4, 206–8, 220, 227, 229, 234–5, 238, 240, 243, 247–9, 251–4, 262, 264, 267–70, 272–3, 275, 277–84, 286–7, 290–1, 296–300, 304, 306–8, 317–19, 321
scientism, 207, 242, 245
secularisation, 189
secularism, 27
self, 14n, 19, 22–6, 41, 109, 115–17, 143–4, 146, 149, 152–4, 156, 158–60, 170, 173, 194, 196–7, 200, 206, 229, 243–5, 248, 276, 279, 284, 306
sense data, 26, 42, 139
sexism, 18
sexuality, 2, 218, 230
sin, 212, 242n, 314

singulars *see* particular(s)
slaves, 88–90, 175n, 177–8, 291n, 297n, 311, 313–14
socialism, 27, 55, 205, 215, 235, 253, 258, 269
social science, 64–5, 98, 169, 202, 234, 236, 247, 249, 263, 307, 309
societas, 291–2
society, 3, 6, 35, 44, 54, 61, 70, 102, 117, 153, 195, 205, 217, 219, 224, 230, 235, 253, 255, 261, 269, 273, 288
sociology, 3, 59, 247
sophia, 80–1, 86–8
soul, 23–4, 39n, 41, 43n, 49, 52, 54, 61, 79, 83–4, 115, 166–7, 196, 244, 248
sovereignty, 130, 132, 137, 218, 288, 293–4
space, 3, 19, 113–15, 118, 121, 123, 164, 238, 279, 283, 318
species, 3, 69, 167–8, 312
speech, 21, 53, 70, 92, 94, 103, 111, 136, 154, 218, 228, 278, 316
state, 54n, 56, 89–91, 109, 130n, 131–2, 134–5, 143, 146, 150, 171–6, 177n, 178–81, 194, 212–13, 215, 258, 262, 271–2, 287–8, 293–4, 303, 311
subject, 24, 115, 131, 137, 147, 149, 152, 195, 199–200, 206, 217, 219, 244, 262, 274, 278
subjectivism, 204, 212, 319
subjectivity, 24, 38, 108, 121n, 147, 152, 158–9, 166–7, 170, 172–4, 177, 186–8, 244, 262, 297, 304, 319
subordinationists, 10, 28, 189, 232–72, 295, 304, 309–11, 316, 318–19
substance, 13, 14, 21, 23, 25, 40n, 41n, 56n, 67–9, 72–3, 78–9, 87, 92, 102, 112–3, 116–18, 128–9, 132, 151–2, 157, 166, 189, 196, 239, 247, 250, 266, 275, 285, 305–6
symbol, 2n, 127, 141, 174, 193, 210, 252–3, 271–2, 274–5, 279–80, 285, 289, 295–8, 316
system, 22, 79, 119, 148–9, 156, 189, 229, 238, 245, 276

techne, 44, 46–8, 79n, 80–1, 90, 92, 96, 282–3
technology, 207, 235, 248, 255, 257–8, 264, 284, 288, 307, 311
teleology, 39, 41, 46, 73, 90, 94, 96, 99, 109, 116, 126–7, 129, 166, 168, 181–2, 207, 227, 295
theodicy, 23, 25, 138, 143, 150, 181, 186, 220, 301
theology, 13n, 109, 125, 129, 136–7, 140, 143, 159, 166, 171, 185, 220, 241, 242n, 247–8, 259, 273, 294, 301–2, 308, 314–15
theory, 7, 48, 65, 82, 266n, 273n, 287, 291
time, 3, 5, 9, 19, 34, 56, 64, 84, 113–15, 118, 121, 123, 137–8, 161, 164, 182, 201, 221, 226, 277–9, 283, 310, 318
toleration, 235, 237, 254n, 256, 269
totalitarianism, 26, 50, 170–2, 182, 195, 216, 226, 273, 287, 290–1, 304, 310
truth, 19, 23, 25, 34, 38, 53, 72–3, 79, 82, 93n, 101, 107, 141, 163, 171, 187, 197–8, 203–7, 209, 212, 216, 243, 245, 252, 262–3, 267, 280, 282, 295, 298, 302–3, 320
tyranny, 62, 99

Übermensch, 204, 213
uncertainty *see* certainty
unity, 52, 56, 61, 91
universal(s), 1, 3, 4, 5, 9, 14n, 15, 23, 25, 28–9, 34, 36, 63–4, 68, 71, 75–8, 80, 92, 95, 97–8, 101–2, 109, 111, 117–18, 124–5, 135, 138–9, 142, 145–7, 158, 163, 173, 184, 195, 199, 202, 204, 206, 210, 212, 217, 223, 226, 230, 236, 251, 253, 262, 266–7, 273–5, 279, 289, 296, 306–7, 310, 312, 319
unmoved mover, 12, 83, 86–8, 156n, 281

value, 34, 38, 45–6, 50, 53, 60, 68, 81, 85, 92, 97, 103, 115, 121, 140, 145, 177, 187, 195, 200, 207, 209, 213–16, 219, 226, 230, 243, 254–5, 270n, 275, 287, 294, 299, 307n, 311, 313, 322
virtue, 9, 16n, 19, 49, 79, 81, 86, 107, 127, 134, 222, 315–16

war, 98, 129, 179–80, 214, 288, 301
web of belief, 66, 162, 196, 206, 233, 246
whole, 3, 11, 19, 24, 42, 47, 56, 81, 96, 122, 124–5, 135, 144, 148, 152, 154, 161n, 163, 173–5, 183n, 184n, 193, 194, 197, 200, 207, 250–1, 298, 301–2
will, 12, 25, 173, 196, 235, 252, 259, 265, 285–6, 298
will to power, 197, 203, 235, 265
wisdom, 8, 69n, 79–81, 87–90, 92–3, 96–7, 103, 174, 185n
women, 17, 45, 49–50, 56, 61, 88–90, 128, 132, 154n, 176–7, 313
world, 1, 2n, 4, 7, 12–13, 15, 19–21, 25–8, 37–9, 41–4, 48–9, 56, 58, 60, 68n, 73n, 75, 76n, 78–9, 83, 84n, 90, 94–5, 102, 108–10, 113n, 115, 117–18, 122–5, 134n, 136, 138, 140, 143–4, 150–1, 154, 155n, 159–61, 170, 172–4, 175n, 181n, 185, 188–9, 193–4, 198, 201, 206–8, 210, 216, 221, 233–5, 239, 241, 243n, 245, 248, 250, 252, 259, 264–5, 272n, 274, 275n, 276–9, 281, 283–6, 289, 291, 299, 304, 306–8, 319–20, 321n
world view/*Weltanschauung*, 115, 142, 144, 153–4, 227, 233n, 234, 245, 262

Index of Proper Names

Adorno, Theodore, 10, 26, 194–5, 199–201, 206–9, 211–12, 216–18, 223–6, 229–30, 241, 258, 307, 309, 312
Afghanistan, 187
Africa, 177–8, 184
Alcibiades, 97
Antigone, 177, 187
Aquinas, Saint Thomas, 13, 314
Arabia, 213
Arendt, Hannah, 95, 207, 256
Aristeides, 100
Aristotelianism, 11, 17, 22, 73, 75, 97, 103, 108, 113, 121, 166, 181, 277, 286–7, 294, 308, 313
Aristotle, 4, 5, 6, 7, 9, 12, 15, 17, 18, 20–2, 24–5, 29, 33, 36, 38–40, 53, 55–6, 58, 66, 67–104, 107, 111–2, 116–18, 120–1, 129–30, 135, 142–3, 146–8, 150–1, 154, 157, 160, 166–7, 172, 176, 178, 184, 199, 248, 250, 274–6, 279, 284, 295, 305–7, 314–16, 321
Asia, 181, 186
Aspasia, 17
Athens, 22, 36, 46, 50–2, 57–9, 61, 64–5, 90, 98–100, 102–3
Atlantis, 57
Augustine, Saint, 11, 134, 242
Austria, 255
Ayer, Alfred Jules, 236

Bachelard, Gaston, 227
Bacon, Sir Francis, 300
Bader, Ralf, 117

Bavaria, 253, 261
Beaney, Michael, 7n, 236
Beauvoir, Simone de, 176
Benjamin, Walter, 224
Berlin, Isaiah, 8
Bible, 4n, 12, 141–2, 144, 155, 166n, 301
Bonaparte, Napoleon, 181, 185
Borges, Jorge Luis, 209–11
Borgia, Cesare, 213
Bosworth, Stephen, 174
Boule, 100
Brahmins, 16
Brentano, Franz, 74
Britain, 271
Buck-Morss, Susan, 177–8
Buddhism, 290
Burnyeat, Miles, 44

Caesar, Julius, 185
Callicles, 50
Cambridge University, 243
Canghuilem, Georges, 227
Carlson, David Gray, 160
Carnap, Rudolf, 233, 237–8, 243–5, 247, 253–4
Cassirer, Ernst, 10, 28, 63, 237, 256, 271–6, 278–301, 304, 316
China, 15, 77–8, 187, 210–11
Christianity, 11, 43, 56–7, 65, 76–7, 84n, 97, 103, 109, 120, 133–4, 136–7, 141–2, 155–6, 166, 181, 186–7, 189, 202n, 203–4, 214, 219–21, 223, 241, 242n, 249, 254, 256, 264, 281, 290, 294, 301–2, 308–9, 312–14, 317

Cicero, 136
Collingwood, Robin George, 10, 28, 271–3, 275–8, 280–7, 290–6, 298–301, 304
Communism, 27, 135, 137, 176, 181, 253, 258, 261
Comte, Auguste, 306
Confucianism, 29
Confucius, 16
Copernicus, Nicolaus, 107–8, 111, 136, 261
Cornford, Francis Macdonald, 36, 41
Crete, 58, 60
Critias, 58–9

Danto, Arthur, 101, 183
Darwin, Charles, 46, 116, 167–8, 197, 198n, 256, 274, 279
Da Vinci, Leonardo, 317
Deleuze, Gilles, 201
Derrida, Jacques, 157, 243, 246
Descartes, René, 8, 14, 22, 103, 116, 144, 152, 196, 235, 239, 247, 262, 264–5, 285, 292
Dilthey, Wilhelm, 163, 247, 261
Diotima, 17
Djaballah, Marc, 227
Dollfuss, Engelbert, 256
Duns Scotus, John, 75

Egypt, 56, 58, 61
Einstein, Albert, 280
Elea, 51
Eliot, Thomas Stearns, 282
England, 43, 258, 287
Enlightenment, 25–7, 38n, 103, 133, 155, 171, 195, 203, 207, 216, 218, 226, 230, 236, 243, 255–6, 259, 311, 314, 317
Epicureanism, 127
Eritreans, 98
Euclid, 114
Europe, 179, 181–2, 185, 202, 212, 214, 255, 277, 290–1, 298, 301, 309

Fanon, Frantz, 177
Förster-Nietzsche, Elizabeth, 261

Foucault, Michel, 26, 60, 150, 186, 189, 194–6, 199, 201–2, 206, 208–11, 217–19, 223, 225–31, 249, 277, 309, 313
France, 271, 287
Frankfurt School, 227, 258
Frege, Gottlob, 121–2
Freud, Sigmund, 200
French revolution, 130, 170, 172, 177, 180–1, 216
Freudianism, 185
Friedman, Michael, 238, 242, 253
Fukuyama, Francis, 187
Furtado, Francisco, 77

Galilei, Galileo, 136, 171
Germany, 27, 180, 187, 213, 222, 259, 261, 271, 298
Gerson, Lloyd P., 73
Geuss, Raymond, 63–4
Glaucon, 44
God, 12, 21, 23, 43, 56, 83, 86–8, 95, 97, 108–9, 114n, 115, 118–19, 122–3, 125, 129, 155, 157, 159–60, 162, 167, 171, 181, 185, 259, 294–6, 310, 312, 314
Goths, 291
Greece, 71, 76, 90, 99–100, 119, 130, 153, 172, 181, 187, 193, 216, 222, 263–4, 274, 281, 291
Guattari, Félix, 201
Guyer, Paul, 111

Habermas, Jürgen, 136, 163, 211
Hacker, Peter, 75, 79
Haiti, 177
Hegel, Georg Wilhelm Friedrich, 6, 7, 9, 12, 17, 23–6, 28–9, 37, 79, 84, 87, 119, 139, 148–89, 193–6, 198–202, 204, 206, 213, 220, 223–7, 230, 232–3, 256, 259, 269, 271, 274, 277, 286, 290–1, 293, 295, 298, 305–6, 308–9, 312, 316, 322
Heidegger, Martin, 10, 26–7, 52, 119, 138, 144, 207, 234–5, 238–43, 248–52, 255–60, 263–7, 269–70, 277–8, 280, 285, 289, 309, 311, 314–15, 318, 322

INDEX OF PROPER NAMES   333

Heidelberg University, 256
Heraclitus, 160
Herodotus, 20, 58, 63, 98
Hertz, Heinrich, 275
Hinduism, 16
Hippias, 59
Hitler, Adolf, 180, 217, 256–7, 259, 261, 268, 279, 287, 290
Hobbes, Thomas, 91, 103, 131–2, "288–94
Hölderlin, Friedrich, 250
Homer, 69, 88, 225, 266n
Houlgate, Stephen, 167–8
Humboldt, Wilhelm von, 213, 256–7
Hume, David, 23, 110, 119, 124, 145
Hunter, Ian, 241
Husserl, Edmund, 201n, 256, 271, 277, 284–5, 292, 301, 309

India, 15
Inwood, Michael, 165, 179, 184
Iraq, 187
Islam, 290, 312

Japan, 213
Jesuits, 77
Jesus Christ, 65, 133, 155, 214, 301
Jews, 214, 217, 236, 256–8, 287–8, 312
John, Saint, 11

Kant, Immanuel, 5–7, 9, 17, 22, 23, 25, 28–9, 37, 43, 60, 79, 104, 107–49, 151, 155, 157, 159–62, 167, 171, 173, 176, 179, 181, 183, 186, 193, 196, 203–4, 206–7, 221, 224, 227, 233, 238–9, 244, 247, 254, 261, 263, 270–1, 274, 276–80, 286, 295, 297, 301, 305–9, 316–17, 320
Kepler, Johannes, 138
Kreines, James, 181
Kripke, Saul, 246n
Kuhn, Franz, 210–11
Kuhn, Thomas, 183, 247, 272, 316

Lakoff, George, 6, 18, 308, 319–20
League of Nations, 143
Leibniz, Gottfried Wilhelm, 210, 283
Lewis, David, 246n

Li, Chih-tsao, 77
Locke, John, 139
Louis XIV, King of France, 197
Luther, Martin, 259
Lyceum, 99

Machiavelli, Niccolò, 47, 213
Magritte, René, 208
Maroneia, 101
Marx, Karl, 25, 60, 137, 139, 150, 175, 178, 181, 183, 186–7, 205, 215, 220, 230, 301
Marxism, 27, 185, 244, 247, 260
Mauthner, Fritz, 76
Mediterranean, 90
Meier, Christian, 63
Menn, Stephen, 86
Mill, John Stuart, 89, 179
Minerva, 88
Monoson, Sara, 51
More, Henry, 43

National Socialism, 27, 215, 217, 236, 256–7, 261n, 269, 289, 292, 298, 314
Neurath, Otto von, 10, 27, 233, 235–8, 242–4, 246–7, 252, 254, 261–6, 290
Neuville, Pierre, 211
Newton, Sir Isaac, 124, 165–6, 283
Newtonianism, 23, 43, 110, 138, 145, 163, 283
Niebuhr, Barthold, 63, 184, 221
Nietzsche, Friedrich, 10, 17, 25–6, 63–4, 146, 186, 193–209, 211–24, 226–7, 229–30, 249, 257, 259, 261, 264, 266, 277, 303, 309, 317

Orient *see* Asia
Oxford University, 271

Parmenides, 37–8, 40
Parrochia, Daniel, 211
Paul, Saint, 310
Peloponnesian war, 98
Pericles, 50
Perry, Michael, 165
Pinkard, Terry, 186

Plato, 4, 6, 9, 17, 19, 20–2, 24–5, 29, 33–66, 68–9, 76, 80–2, 84, 86–9, 91, 93, 96, 98, 102–4, 113–14, 118, 120, 122, 127, 129–30, 135, 137, 142, 146–8, 151, 160, 162, 170, 172, 174, 181, 198–9, 215, 223, 230, 248, 250, 265, 287, 295, 305–6, 308, 310, 312, 315–16
Plotinus, 33, 42
Poland, 287
Popper, Sir Karl, 38, 50, 76, 170–2, 174, 179–80, 182–3, 312
Porphyry, 75, 77
Protestantism, 103, 155n, 171, 260, 263
Prussia, 129–30, 171, 260
Puritanism, 319
Pythagoras, 16

Quine, Willard Van Orman, 10, 76, 163, 233, 243, 245, 254, 267, 277, 309, 319–20

Radcliffe Richards, Janet, 46, 167
Raffaello Sanzio da Urbino aka Raphael, 20, 213
Rawls, John, 53, 90n
Renaissance, 214, 268, 300, 317
Rhodes, Cecil, 261
Rhodes, Peter John, 99
Rickert, Heinrich, 237
Rickey, Christopher, 259
Ricoeur, Paul, 10, 28, 271, 273, 277–8, 281, 284–5, 292–5, 301–2, 304
Robespierre, Maximilien, 185
Roman Catholicism, 11, 103, 155n, 244, 254–5
Rome, 181, 184–5, 187, 260, 291
Rorty, Richard, 241, 267
Rousseau, Jean-Jacques, 131–2, 144, 203
Russell, Bertrand, 165, 283
Russia, 187, 258
Ryle, Gilbert, 33, 40, 44, 46, 271, 281

Salamis, 100–1
Sardis, 98
Schapiro, Meyer, 250–1
Schofield, Malcolm, 45

Scholasticism, 8n, 13, 14n, 71, 77, 112, 189, 233n, 259, 278
Scotus, Duns, 238–9
Second World War, 28, 287
Sen, Amartya, 294, 311
Sisyphus, 321
Skinner, Quentin, 228
Smith, Robin, 84
Socrates, 17, 38, 40, 43–5, 49–50, 53, 56–7, 72–3, 84, 91, 118
Solon, 58, 99
Sophists, 53, 59, 93, 135, 223
Sorabji, Richard, 76
South Africa, 303
Sparshott, Francis Edward, 52–3
Sparta, 58–60, 64, 91
Spengler, Oswald, 28, 236, 260–2, 266, 290, 298
Spinoza, Benedict, 214
Stoicism, 127–8, 188, 203–4, 252
Strauss, Leo, 315
Strawson, Peter Frederick, 319

Taylor, Charles, 171–3, 175, 188
Thrasymachus, 38
Thucydides, 8, 20, 59, 63–4, 98, 223
Tocqueville, Alexis de, 182
Troy, 88
Tübingen, 198

Ulysses, 88
United Nations, 143

Vandals, 291
Van Gogh, Vincent, 250–1
Vienna, 255–6, 261
Vlastos, Gregory, 36–7, 41
Voltaire, François-Marie Arouet de, 216

Wardy, Robert, 77–8
Weber, Max, 188, 227, 263, 293
West, 4, 6, 16, 17, 27, 37, 211, 225–6, 235, 237, 257–61, 263, 265–7, 309–10, 312–13
White, Hayden, 297
Whitehead, Alfred North, 33, 36–7, 283–4, 305
Wilkes, John, 209–10

William of Ockham, 74–5
Wittgenstein, Ludwig, 18, 120, 157, 183, 204, 246n, 278
Wolin, Richard, 265

Yunus, Harvey, 55

Zarathustra, 213
Zeus, 88

EU representative:
Easy Access System Europe
Mustamäe tee 50, 10621 Tallinn, Estonia
Gpsr.requests@easproject.com

www.ingramcontent.com/pod-product-compliance
Lightning Source LLC
Chambersburg PA
CBHW050201240426
43671CB00013B/2212